The Linguistic Turn
in Contemporary Japanese
Literary Studies

Michigan Monograph Series in Japanese Studies
Number 68

Center for Japanese Studies
The University of Michigan

The Linguistic Turn
in Contemporary Japanese
Literary Studies:
Politics, Language, Textuality

Edited by Michael K. Bourdaghs

Center for Japanese Studies
The University of Michigan
Ann Arbor, 2010

Open access edition funded by the National Endowment for the Humanities/ Andrew W. Mellon Foundation Humanities Open Book Program.

Copyright © 2010 by The Regents of the University of Michigan

Published by the Center for Japanese Studies,
The University of Michigan
1007 E. Huron St.
Ann Arbor, MI 48104-1690

Library of Congress Cataloging in Publication Data

The linguistic turn in contemporary Japanese literary studies : politics, language, textuality / edited by Michael K. Bourdaghs.
   p. cm. — (Michigan monograph series in Japanese studies ; no. 68)
Includes index.
ISBN 978-1-929280-60-5 (cloth : alk. paper) — ISBN 978-1-929280-61-2 (pbk. : alk. paper)
   1. Japanese literature—Showa period, 1926–1989—History and criticism—Theory, etc.   2. Japanese literature—Heisei period, 1989——History and criticism—Theory, etc.   3. Linguistics in literature.   I. Bourdaghs, Michael K. II. Title.   III. Series.

PL726.65.L56 2010
895.6'09382—dc22

                                                                2010002115

This book was set in Palatino Macron.

This publication meets the ANSI/NISO Standards for Permanence of Paper for Publications and Documents in Libraries and Archives (Z39.48–1992).

Printed and bound by CPI Group (UK) Ltd, Croydon, CR0 4YY

ISBN 978-1-929280-60-5 (hardcover)
ISBN 978-1-929280-61-2 (paper)
ISBN 978-0-472-12748-1 (ebook)
ISBN 978-0-472-90143-2 (open access)

In Memory of Mitani Kuniaki

(1941–2007)

Contents

Introduction: Overthrowing the Emperor in Japanese Literary Studies

Michael K. Bourdaghs

By the mid-1980s, the world of literary studies in Japan had been hearing rumbles of revolt for some time. For more than a decade, a new generation of scholars and journalist-critics (*hyōronka*) had been chipping away at many of the foundational assumptions that governed the study of literature, especially modern Japanese literature. Academics who preferred the old ways, however, could still dismiss the upstarts as mere journalists interested more in keeping up with fashionable trends in theory than in serious scholarship, or, better yet, they could simply ignore them.

But in 1985 the rebels showed up at the main gate to the palace, battering ram in hand. A group of younger scholars—most notably Komori Yōichi (b. 1953) and Ishihara Chiaki (b. 1955)—launched a radical rereading of Natsume Sōseki's 1914 novel *Kokoro* (The Heart), a work that had long been central to the canon of modern Japanese literature. This marked the onset of what came to be known as the "*Kokoro* ronsō" (*Kokoro* debate), a multipronged dispute that would occupy center stage in the discipline for several years to come.

Where did the challengers come from? As scholars, both Komori and Ishihara were trained in institutions that in some ways were peripheral to the institution of literary studies in Japan, a position that likely predisposed them toward innovations in approach.[1] While it would be overly simplistic

---

1. Komori was a student at Hokkaido University, a prestigious national university yet one without the long tradition in literature studies that marked more central institutions such as Tokyo University or Kyoto University. Ishihara was trained at Seijō University, a private university in Tokyo. As Atsuko Sakaki notes, it is symptomatic that while the radical new readings were published in fairly obscure journals the response by establishment critics tended to be published in the most widely respected journals in the field. See her *Recontextualizing Texts: Narrative Performance in Modern Japanese Fiction* (Cambridge: Asia Center, Harvard University, 1999), 29–53.

to suggest some sort of institutional determinism as an explanation for their work, clearly institutional positioning played a role in the debate.

But what really separated the two sides in the debate were fundamental differences in theoretical and methodological grounding, especially in their basic stances regarding the nature of communication, the structure of linguistic and semiotic processes, and the relationship between politics and language. As a result, the debate provides a convenient entryway into a discussion of the theoretical issues and historical events that link the essays presented in this volume.

The new readings of *Kokoro* were deliberately provocative. Ishihara accused previous scholars of misreading the novel, of mistakenly lionizing the character known as Sensei. Whereas Sensei had long been celebrated for his ethicality in the face of modern alienation and egotism, in fact—according to Ishihara—his ethic was implicitly murderous, an infantile narcissism that aimed primarily to destroy the Other in order to preserve its fantasy notion of the self.[2] Komori in his readings went even farther and directly accused establishment scholars of murdering the text, of stabbing it in the heart.[3]

Response to these accusations was swift in coming. In particular, Miyoshi Yukio (1926–90), professor emeritus at Tokyo University—the heart of the scholarly establishment—became the central voice in defending the established readings and methodologies. Space constraints do not allow me to rehearse in any detail the course of the debate over *Kokoro*, and other scholars have provided useful accounts, including Atsuko Sakaki and Oshino Takeshi.[4] I will merely summarize a few of the positions that marked the new readings of the novel by Komori and Ishihara, as well as the responses made by their critics, especially those that are relevant to a reconsideration of the "linguistic turn" in recent Japanese literary criticism.

Whereas standard readings had always stressed the second half of the novel, the section titled "Sensei and His Testament," the new readings tended to focus on the first half, the two sections narrated by the nameless student, who refers to himself using a polite form of the first-person pronoun in Japa-

---

2. Ishihara Chiaki, "Manazashi toshite no tasha: *Kokoro*," originally published in *Tōkō Kokubungaku* in March, 1985 and reprinted in Ishihara Chiaki, *Hanten suru Sōseki* (Tokyo: Seidosha, 1997), 155–80.

3. Komori Yōichi, "'Kokoro' wo seisei suru haato," originally published in *Seijō Kokubungaku* in March 1985 and revised and reprinted in Komori Yōichi, *Buntai toshite no monogatari* (Tokyo: Chikuma Shobō, 1988), 293–317.

4. See Sakaki, *Recontextualizing Texts*, 29–53; and Oshino Takeshi, "*Kokoro* ronsō no yukue," in *Sōryoku tōron: Sōseki no* Kokoro, edited by Komori Yōichi, Nakamura Miharu, and Miyagawa Takeo, 12–27 (Tokyo: Kanrin Shobō, 1994). The latter volume contains a number of useful essays that take up the *Kokoro* ronsō.

nese: Watakushi. The revisionist readings stressed Watakushi's ethicality over that of Sensei, and—perhaps the real source of outrage on the part of the establishment—they speculated on the possibility of an erotic relationship between Watakushi and Shizu, Sensei's wife, after Sensei's suicide. Miyoshi Yukio titles one of his response pieces "Was Sensei a Cuckold?" a rhetorical question that hints at the sense of outrage the new readings provoked.

In terms of methodology, Komori's radical new readings were also marked by an insistence on calling *Kokoro* a "text" (*tekisuto* in katakana) as opposed to a "work" (*sakuhin*). As Oshino notes, this methodological conflict was at the core of the debate. In using the term *text*, Komori meant in part to stress the openness of *Kokoro* to its outside both in terms of its insistence on intertextuality and in terms of its narrative incompletion, the open-endedness of its story that seemed to require active intervention by the reader. By insisting that literary value lay not so much in the text itself as in the relationship between the text and its reader, Komori's stance challenged not only the position of *Kokoro* as an anchor securing the national canon, but also that of Sōseki as its author, who was no longer positioned as the guarantor of value standing behind the text. This novel about the death of father figures—including, notably, the Meiji Emperor—was transformed in the *Kokoro* ronsō into a topos for debating the death of the author in Japanese literary studies.

Komori's insistence on calling *Kokoro* a text was specifically a challenge to the widely used methodology of *sakuhinron* (studies of a single work), an approach closely identified with the figure of Miyoshi Yukio. Komori's attack on orthodox *sakuhinron* was in some ways ironic because Miyoshi himself had been perceived as a Young Turk in the 1960s and 1970s when he first advocated for the (then) new methodology. Miyoshi's earlier advocacy of *sakuhinron* had involved him in, among other things, a fierce debate in 1976–77 with Tanizawa Eiichi (b. 1929) over methodology and its place in literary studies.[5] By the time of the *Kokoro* debate, however, *sakuhinron* had won wide acceptance as one of the standard methodologies in the field and hence presented a prime target for a rebellious generation of younger scholars.

In some ways similar to American New Criticism, *sakuhinron* stressed the primacy of the individual literary work and its internal structures and hence challenged methodologies, such as literary history, that had previously held sway. The relationship between *sakuhinron* and another dominant methodology, *sakkaron* (author studies), is more complex and became a question debated in the *Kokoro* ronsō. *Sakuhinron* shifted scholarly focus

5. On Miyoshi's debate with Tanizawa, see Irmela Hijiya-Kirschnereit, *Was heisst: Japanische Literatur verstehen?* (Frankfurt am Main: Suhrkamp, 1990), 188–210.

from author to individual works, but, as Miyoshi himself argued, it ultimately aimed to return its readings of individual texts back to some sort of authorial intent.[6] The problem, as Reiko Abe Austead notes (paraphrasing Maeda Ai), is that "*sakuhinron* as an alternative for *sakkaron* does not touch the heart of the problem, which actually lies in the choice of method rather than in the subject of discussion."[7] Moreover, as Tanizawa Eiichi argued, Miyoshi's stress on *sakuhinron* as a quasi-scientific methodology concealed its grounding in an implicit worship of the author as a semi-mystical, transcendent "prophet," a stance that mystified the actual historical position of the literary work and its author.[8] The rejection of *sakuhinron* by Komori and Ishihara was in part an attempt to demystify the position that earlier methodologies had assigned to the author as the final guarantor of meaning of literary texts.

Nonetheless, in their attempt to replace *sakuhinron* with new theories and methodologies, the younger scholars who launched the *Kokoro* ronsō were in large measure repeating the tactics by which the old guard (Miyoshi et al.) had established its position a generation earlier when its members had used the seemingly abstract and obscure methodology of *sakuhinron* to critique the existing field of literary studies in Japan. As Pierre Bourdieu notes, "permanent revolution" is characteristic of the field of cultural production in which newcomers, in order to "occupy a distinct, distinctive position," must "assert their difference, get it known and recognized," a process they carry out "by endeavoring to impose new modes of thought and expression, out of key with the prevailing modes of thought and with the doxa, and therefore bound to disconcert the orthodoxy by their 'obscurity' and 'pointlessness.'"[9]

As the *Kokoro* ronsō progressed, the revisionists would in some ways back down, distancing themselves from positions they had taken earlier in the dispute.[10] Yet it was clear that, at least in part due to the debate itself, they had emerged as the leading force in the field of Japanese literature studies. "One of the difficulties of orthodox defense against heretical transformation of the field," to quote Bourdieu again, "is the fact that polemics imply a form

6. See Miyoshi Yukio, "Watoson wa hainshinsha ka: *Kokoro* saisetsu," *Bungaku* 56:5 (May 1988): 7–21.

7. Reiko Abe Austead, *Rereading Sōseki: Three Early Twentieth-Century Japanese Novels* (Wiesbaden: Harrassowitz, 1998), 18.

8. Tanizawa Eiichi, "Bungaku kenkyū ni taikei mo hōhōron mo arienai," *Bungaku* 45:1 (January 1977): 108–13. This passage appears on page 113.

9. Pierre Bourdieu, *The Field of Cultural Production*, translated by Randal Johnson (New York: Columbia University Press, 1993), 52, 58.

10. See, for example, Komori Yōichi, "'Watakushi' to iu 'tasha'sei: *Kokoro* wo meguru ōtokuritikku," *Bungaku* 3:4 (Autumn 1992): 13–27.

of recognition; adversaries whom one would prefer to destroy by ignoring them cannot be combated without consecrating them."[11] Ishihara and Komori went on to become editors of the influential journal *Sōseki kenkyū*, and Komori was already a faculty member at Tokyo University, taking up institutionally a position similar in prestige to that held earlier by Miyoshi. In many ways, the rebels were now the establishment.

The *Kokoro* ronsō helped establish a new set of critical methodologies, many of them adapted from linguistics and semiotics, as the new methodological standard for literary studies in Japan. By the time the *Kokoro* ronsō had reached its (ultimately inconclusive) conclusion, literary scholars and critics in Japan were more likely to read "texts" than "works." It became, then, one of the culminating moments in what might be called the "linguistic turn" in Japanese literary studies. As in the American academy, the rise of "theory" in literary studies in Japan was often propelled by the adaptation of concepts and methodologies originally developed in the realm of linguistics, be it in the structuralism of Saussure, the dialogism of Vološinov and Bakhtin, the theories of linguistic subjectivity derived from the work of Benveniste, or the analyses of codes, message, and poetic function carried out by Jakobson and the Prague School.

Moreover, while Komori's and Ishihara's linguistics-informed readings of *Kokoro* enraged many establishment scholars, they were attacked by younger scholars for not going far enough. These objections, too, were often grounded in concepts derived directly or indirectly from linguistics and the philosophy of language. Kōno Kensuke, for example, noted that behind Komori's critique of modernity and capitalism (and of the debased form of language that Komori thought they had introduced) lay the utopian fantasy of a prelapsarian community, one marked by perfect communication, for which the mother-infant relationship served as the model. This view, grounded in Jakobson's notion of the circuit of communication, ignores the noise, the discommunication, that is an inherent part of any process of communication and that alone renders possible some sort of encounter with the Other, the self-proclaimed goal of Komori's ethical stance. Instead of an encounter with Otherness, Komori's implicit communication model results in what Briankle G. Chang calls the "transcendence of difference" that inadvertently results in the "unquestioned valorization of identity over difference, of the selfsame over alterity."[12] Komori has mounted an impressive

---

11. Bourdieu, *The Field of Cultural Production*, 42.
12. Briankle G. Chang, *Deconstructing Communication: Representation, Subject, and Economies of Exchange* (Minneapolis: University of Minnesota Press, 1996), xi.

critique of the utopian fantasies that reigned in previous literary studies, Kōno concludes, only to replace them with another potentially solipsistic utopian fantasy.[13]

Oshino argues likewise and proposes replacing the symmetrical model of communication that Komori implicitly relies on with an asymmetrical model, such as Wittgenstein proposed in his philosophy of language games, in which no presumption is made of a preexisting shared linguistic code between sender and receiver.[14] Suga Hidemi, in turn, argued that Komori had mistakenly equated narrative (*monogatari*) with prose fiction (*shōsetsu*) and ordinary spoken language with the specific deconstructive force of writing (*écriture*). This confusion risked co-opting whatever might be radical in *Kokoro* into the conventional genre of the psychological novel in which words are taken as expressions that are ultimately anchored in certain ideal character types rather than as openings for exploration of the constant unraveling of meaning and identity.[15] Suga's critique in some ways paralleled recent developments in linguistics, where such figures as S. Y. Kuroda had begun to explore the specific linguistic properties of fictional narratives. These scholars were fascinated by the realization that certain sentences—those written in *style indirect libre*, for example—which would be considered ungrammatical and/or impossible if spoken in ordinary conversation, were nonetheless considered quite proper when they appeared within the context of a novel or short story.[16] When one adapted concepts from linguistics for use in literary criticism, one had to keep in mind that the language of fiction did not necessarily follow the rules for language usage in general.

On top of this, the linguistic turn in Japan was complicated because of the uncomfortable co-presence of competing disciplinary forms of linguistics. In addition to departments of Western-style linguistics (*gengogaku*), Japanese universities typically also included departments of "national language studies" (*kokugogaku*) where scholars studied the Japanese language using what are believed to be a largely homegrown set of tools and methodologies. *Kokugogaku* traces its lineage back to premodern scholars of the Japanese language that worked outside the traditions of Western linguistics such as Fujitani Nariakira (1738–79) and Suzuki Akira (1764–1837). But the

---

13. Kōno Kensuke, "Komori Yōichi-shi no nicho wo megutte: Yūtopia no kanata e," *Bai* 5 (December 1988): 92–99.

14. Oshino, "*Kokoro* ronsō no yukue," 21–24.

15. Suga Hidemi, "Shōmetsu suru shōkei moji: *Kokoro* wo yomu," *Shinchō* 86:6 (June 1989): 194–205.

16. S. Y. Kuroda, "Where Epistemology, Style, and Grammar Meet: A Case Study from Japanese," in *A Festschrift for Morris Halle*, edited by Stephen R. Anderson and Paul Kiparsky, 377–91 (New York: Holt, Rinehart and Winston, 1973).

modern discipline of *kokugogaku* was established in the 1890s with the work of Ueda Kazutoshi (1867–1937), who established the department at Tokyo Imperial University at the same time as his faculty colleague Haga Yaichi (1867–1927) was establishing the first modern department of "national literature studies" (*kokubungaku*).

This co-presence of competing forms of linguistics meant that the linguistic turn in Japanese literary studies involved turns in more than one direction. This provided some unusually complicated vectors of development. For example, while many of the literary critics and scholars involved in the linguistic turn invoked various forms of structuralism derived directly or indirectly from the work of Saussure, in fact the implicit theory of language underlying the work of many scholars in orthodox *kokubungaku* lineages was derived from a post-Saussurean critique of structuralism. Establishment scholars often explicitly or implicitly turned to the theories of *kokugogaku* scholar Tokieda Motoki (1900–1967) whose work provided one of the first sustained critiques of Saussure's central notions of *langue* and *parole*. In the 1930s and 1940s, Tokieda developed a brilliant critique of Saussure's model of language, proposing in its place what Tokieda called "language process theory," which rejected the entire notion of *langue* as an abstract structure of rules governing language usage. Linguistic expressions were always utterances spoken in a specific place and time, by a specific someone, addressing a specific someone else, Tokieda argued. Only by taking up language from the situation of concrete utterances and the intersubjective relationships they brought into being could one hope to begin to understand its true nature. The essay by John Whitman in chapter five of this volume takes up the work of Tokieda, especially examining its legacy for postwar linguistics in Japan.

In other words, in the linguistic turn in Japanese literary criticism, one sometimes encountered the odd situation in which one form of linguistics (Saussurean structuralism) was perceived as a new methodology that critiqued another form of linguistics (*kokugogaku*), a form that—at least in its Tokieda-derived lineage—had begun as a critique of that first form of linguistics.[17] On the other hand, critics advocating the new methodologies were often criticized for merely borrowing foreign-originated (*gaizaiteki*) theories and methodologies and applying them blindly to a Japanese reality that was supposedly ill suited to them. Ishihara Chiaki, for example, in a 1987 article written at the height of the *Kokoro* ronsō, directly challenges accusations that he employs too many *katakana* (i.e., foreign-originated) words

---

17. To complicate matters further, many of the critics and scholars associated with the linguistic turn also expressed a sympathetic interest in Tokieda's linguistic theories. Whitman's chapter, for example, discusses how Kamei Hideo and Karatani Kōjin view Tokieda.

in his articles.[18] Whitman argues in his chapter that in fact the reaction that Tokieda's *kokugogaku* provoked on the part of many linguists was evidence of a turf war over which discipline was going to control the linguistic capital that accompanied the power to produce authorized translations of concepts from Western linguistic theory. Scholars trained in Western linguistics were offended that someone from the *kokugogaku* lineage would presume to possess the competency to critique the basic concepts of Western traditions. Beneath this outrage lay another paradox as well: if Tokieda's native *kokugogaku* was produced in response to Saussure's theories, what precisely was "Japanese" about it?

As we have seen, the scholars and critics involved in the linguistic turn were often accused of blindly borrowing foreign theories and forcibly applying them to a Japanese reality that was intrinsically foreign to them. In some ways, this was a replay of the debates that nearly a century earlier had led to the dual structure of linguistics/*kokugogaku* in Japanese academia in the first place. It is a debate, too, that has seen its counterpart in many other non-Western countries when scholars have confronted the claims of universal validity made on behalf of Western forms of knowledge.

But a glance at the actual examples of criticism from the 1970s and 1980s translated in part one of this volume, four essays written in the midst of the linguistic turn, serves as a persuasive rebuttal to this charge of overly facile borrowing. For example, in chapter one the criticism of Noguchi Takehiko, one of the most influential scholars of literary and intellectual history in contemporary Japan, clearly takes hints from Jakobson and Saussure as he explores the semiotic codes and poetic functions at work in Japanese literary works. But Noguchi consistently uses the frameworks of semiotics as a kind of sounding board against which he can discover not only aspects that Western semiotics would expect but also aspects of Japanese literary texts that cannot easily be identified with existing Western terms, poetic tropes, for example, that cannot be classified according to such conventional categories as metaphor, metonymy or synecdoche. Likewise, in the essay translated here (chapter one), Noguchi uses ideas from semiotics and structuralist narratology to trace the development of a new form of literary criticism in the Japan of the 1850s, a development that likely could not be perceived without the framework of narratology. In reading through a commentary on *The Tale of Genji* by one Hagiwara Hiromichi (1815–63),

18. Ishihara Chiaki, "Seido toshite no 'kenkyū buntai," *Kindai Nihon bungaku* 37 (October 1987): 114–18.

Noguchi uncovers a remarkable attempt to theorize the poetic functions of language and their role in constructing the threads of fictional narrative, functions that Noguchi notes foreshadow Jakobson's ideas about the paradigmatic and syntagmatic aspects of speech. In other words, Noguchi uses his remarkable fluency in Western-originated forms of linguistic and literary theory to render visible for the first time elements of literary and linguistic practices specific to Japan. In this way, Noguchi works to reveal the limits both of existing forms of literary theory in Japan *and* of supposedly universal Western theories.

Likewise, the other essays from the linguistic turn translated here demonstrate that the word *borrowing* hardly describes the relationship between Western-originated linguistic theories and the new generation of scholars that appeared in 1970s and 1980s Japan. In chapter two, "The Embodied Self," an essay taken from his 1977 book *Koga no shūgōsei: Ōoka Shōhei ron* (The Collectivity of the Individual: On Ōoka Shōhei), Kamei Hideo situates Ōoka Shōhei's war literature from the late 1940s and early 1950s in a revised version of modern Japanese literary history, one focused not on the rise of the "modern self" (*kindai jiga*), a shibboleth of conventional literary history in Japan, but on the deployment of intersubjectivity and intertextuality as keys to self-understanding. Along the way, Kamei uses linguistic theories of expression, in particular theories that insist on the dialogic nature of language, to mount an explicit challenge to the author-oriented methodologies (*sakkaron*) that dominated modern literature studies in the 1960s and early 1970s.[19]

Hirata Yumi in a 1984 essay translated in chapter three uses tools from structuralist linguistics and narratology, especially theories of the relationship between linguistic expression and subjectivity, to analyze the shifting structure of narrative discourse (in particular, the gradual splitting off of fictional "narrator" from "author") in late Edo and early Meiji fiction. In turn, Mitani Kuniaki, a highly respected scholar of classical Japanese, provides in chapter four a rebuttal to the work of both Kamei and Hirata, arguing that the rise of the narrator characteristic of modern Japanese fiction in fact represented the loss of a variety of possibilities that were inherent in the linguistic expressions of classical literature, in particular markers of perspective that fit only loosely the categories of linguistic aspect or tense and express

19. The chapter provides a kind of first draft of issues Kamei would explore at greater length in his major study, *Kansei no henkaku* (1983), available in English translation as *Transformations of Sensibility: The Phenomenology of Meiji Literature*, translation edited by Michael Bourdaghs (Ann Arbor: Center for Japanese Studies, University of Michigan, 2002).

a multiplicity of possible subjective relationships to temporality. For Mitani, the key to understanding the modern novel lies in its unification of the text around the past-tense marker auxiliary verb –*ta*, one that signals the presence of a single author whose perspective dominates the entire text.

These scholars are not mere imitators or borrowers—any more, that is, than are all scholars and critics. One of the great motivating factors that has led us to organize the present volume is the desire to bring their remarkable work to a wider audience.

———

To introduce a theme that links the essays contained in part two, let me return to the *Kokoro* ronsō. In a later reflection on the debate, Komori Yōichi would trace the origins of his radical rereading of the novel back to his own experiences in high school. Komori was a leader in the student protest movement in Japan, a movement that successfully shut down many university and high school campuses for extended periods, including the high school Komori attended, where classes were suspended for more than a year. After classes resumed, on his first day back in school, his lessons began with *Kokoro*, long one of the centerpieces of the pedagogical canon used in secondary education, especially in ethics and *kokugo* ("national language," meaning Japanese language) classes. Komori began to wonder about what happened after the events narrated in the novel. What, for example, happened to Watakushi and Shizu after Sensei's suicide? When he raised these questions with his teacher, he was rebuffed; those topics were not directly written about in the novel and hence did not "belong" to the range of legitimate topics of discussion about it.[20]

The anecdote is telling for several reasons. For starters, it situates the origins of the *Kokoro* ronsō specifically in the collapse of the student protest movement and the fall of the New Left after 1970 in Japan. Moreover, it reveals that the debate was as much about politics and ideology as it was about linguistic methodology and literary hermeneutics. The crucial issues under dispute in the *Kokoro* ronsō, in fact, revolved largely around the ideological issues of ownership. Who did the novel belong to, the author, its original readers in early Taishō, or the contemporary critic? And what contents could properly be said to belong to it? Could, for example, apparent gaps within the text legitimately be filled in and, if so, by whom? Ultimately, the *Kokoro* ronsō represented a struggle over ownership of Sōseki and his works: which

———

20. Komori Yōichi, transcription of symposium opening remarks, in *Sōryoku tōron: Sōseki no Kokoro*, edited by Komori Yōichi, Nakamura Miharu, and Miyagawa Takeo, 9-11 (Tokyo: Kanrin Shobō, 1994), 10.

school of interpretation was going to win the right to legitimacy for its readings of the novel?

In one of his earliest salvos in the debate, Miyoshi Yukio surveyed notable events that occurred in 1985 in the field of modern literature studies in Japan, one of them being, of course, the publication Komori's revisionist reading of *Kokoro*. Leading up to the discussion of Komori, Miyoshi describes an essay by Tanaka Minoru (who would later be an active participant in the *Kokoro* ronsō) that provided a new rereading of Mori Ōgai's 1890 story "Maihime." Miyoshi disagrees with Tanaka's reading, and concludes:

> This sort of nearly arbitrary "reading" of a modern literary work has all of a sudden begun to spring up everywhere lately. It is an inescapable byproduct of the boom in such methodologies as structuralism, cultural semiotics, and theories of the body.[21]

Miyoshi then moves into a discussion of Komori's new thesis on *Kokoro*, complaining that it and other new interpretations of canonical texts (interpretations that Miyoshi insists on calling *sakuhinron*) try too hard to create new readings—or misreadings—by concentrating excessively on only one specific aspect of the text at hand, an approach that Miyoshi thinks can only lead into an unproductive vicious cycle.

Miyoshi then moves on to discuss a new edition of the collected works of the novelist Ibuse Masuji (1898–1993), for which the author had substantially revised works that had already attained canonical status. Miyoshi defends Ibuse's right to engage in this sort of self-revisionism.

> As something written by the author, a work is clearly owned by the author (*sakuhin wa akiraka ni sakka ni yotte shoyū sareru*). At the same time, however, through the medium of industrial capitalism in the form of publishing houses, as something *sold to* an indeterminate number of readers, a work also in part is something that belongs to readers (*sakuhin wa nakaba dokusha no shoyū ni zoku suru*).

Readers are free to choose between the old and new versions of the work, Miyoshi argues. "This is not a problem relating to evaluation, nor is it a problem relating to copyright," he writes. For researchers in modern Japanese literature, it only becomes a problem in that it "presents an aporia that

---

21. Miyoshi Yukio, "Kokubungaku: kindai gendai," in *Kokugo nenkan: Shōwa 61-nen ban,* edited by Kokuritsu Kokugo Kenkyūjo (Tokyo: Kokuritsu Kokugo Kenkyūjo, 1986), 44–45.

cannot be solved by the methods of classical bibliographical methods (*koten bunkengaku*)." What is the real text (*honbun*)? [22]

In this passage, Miyoshi clearly deals with literary texts in terms of property. Authors have certain rights of ownership over literary works, as do readers. But there seem to be no rights of ownership granted to literary scholars; they must simply respect—perhaps even police—the property rights of the other two parties in the exchange.[23] Miyoshi portrays literature as a closed economy, an equal exchange of value between producer and consumer in which each can claim certain legitimate ownership rights and in which interference by a third party can only be something arbitrary and illegitimate, a form of theft. Such scholars, with their forced interpretations, resemble Sensei's uncle, who cheated Sensei out of his proper inheritance. They deprive readers of the value that the author intended to bequeath to them. Or, as Miyoshi maintained a decade earlier, in the essay that set off the 1976 *ronsō* over methodology, literary scholarship (*kenkyū*) must be distinguished from literary criticism (*hihyō*) on grounds of propriety and ownership. "Whereas criticism always possesses the freedom to pursue creation (*sōzō e no jiyū o shoyū suru*)," he wrote, "scholarship is always blocked from the road followed by the object of its study, literature." The work of a literary scholar can be considered a literary work only if it stops being literary scholarship and crosses the boundary to become a literary work (*sakuhin*) itself because literature is the "object" (*taishō* and *kyakutai*) of literary studies, not its "subject" (*shutai*).[24]

As veterans of the Japanese New Left and its critiques of modern capitalist alienation, Komori and Ishihara in their readings explicitly work

22. Ibid., 45. Emphasis in the original.
23. We see a similar stance in Miyoshi's critique of the playwright Hata Kōhei's stage adaptation of *Kokoro* in which Watakushi and Shizu end up together after Sensei's death. Miyoshi criticizes the reading of the novel that Hata uses to justify his revisionist play. But, Miyoshi notes, he is not denying Hata's freedom as an author to create a new fictional work using the characters and situations from *Kokoro*, writing, "I repeat, I have no intention of disputing Hata in his drama creating a new *possible* narrative based on *Kokoro*. Rather, it is when it is brought back to being a problem of a reading of Sōseki's *Kokoro* that I raise my objection." As an author (*sakka*), Hata has free rights of ownership over his play, but as a critic he must respect certain preexisting norms of ownership. Miyoshi Yukio, "'Sensei' wa kokyu ka," *Kaie* 5:11 (November 1986): 190–91, emphasis in original.
24. Miyoshi Yukio, "Bungaku no hiroba," *Bungaku* 44:11 (November 1976): 52–53. In the article Miyoshi critiques recent scholars who rely on theories of expression (*hyōgen*), arguing that the path to independence for modern literature studies in Japan from its reliance on classical literature studies is to develop a methodology that uses empirical evidence in a logical manner to prove or disprove hypotheses.

through different models of readership and ownership.[25] Komori argues that, in Miyoshi's charge that the new readings have rendered Sensei a cuckold, the very notion of "cuckoldry" depends on the modern patriarchal view of women as pieces of property exchanged between men, a view that Komori's reading aimed to undermine.[26] (Miyoshi somewhat sarcastically responded to their accusation, "I accept the charge that, in my daily life, I am caught up within the framework of a capitalist system.")[27] Komori insists that while Watakushi and Shizu may have had a sexual relationship after Sensei's death, and may even have produced a child as a result, they would never marry since that would co-opt the radical ethicality of their relationship back into bourgeois norms of patriarchy and property.

For Miyoshi, literary scholarship is a kind of science, concerned with proving and disproving hypotheses. But for Ishihara and Komori literary scholarship is a mode of ideology critique. It might be helpful to reconsider the economic model that underlies their work in terms of Marcel Mauss's theory of the gift and especially Jacques Derrida's critical rewriting of that theory.[28] A social formation organized around and by the gift takes a spiraling, open-ended form, and in it the role of a third party is crucial. Gift exchanges between two parties have a tendency to decay into simple bartering, a closed-circle economy in which goods of equal value are exchanged. A third party guarantees, to borrow Lewis Hyde's somewhat problematic but still useful formulation, that the gift keeps moving along an unending chain, that it never comes back in the same form to the original donor, and that its value remains arbitrary and incalculable. Such an approach shifts our focus from the sociological search for value to an ethical probing of relationality. The gift establishes an erotics of sociality with others in which one constantly gives oneself away with no guarantee of anything like equal value in return. A gift that stops moving, that is not

---

25. While the Japanese New Left was highly critical of the orthodox Left represented by, for example, the Japan Communist Party and the Japan Socialist Party, it nonetheless shared with the old Left a critical stance toward capitalism and its effects on modern society. This critique at times arose from Marxist and anarchist philosophical roots and at other times from sometimes utopian versions of folklore studies, which stressed the communal solidarity of premodern Japanese folk culture.

26. Komori Yōichi, "Kokoro no yukue," *Seijō kokubungaku* 3 (March 1987): 55–61.

27. Miyoshi, "Watoson wa hainshinsha ka," 13.

28. Marcel Mauss, *The Gift: The Form and Reason for Exchange in Archaic Societies,* translated by W. D. Halls (New York: Routledge, 1990); Jacques Derrida, *Given Time I: Counterfeit Money,* translated by Peggy Kamuf (Chicago: University of Chicago Press, 1992). I have explored these issues at greater length in my "Property and Sociological Knowledge: Natsume Sōseki and the Gift of Narrative," *Japan Forum* 20:1 (March 2008), 79-101.

continuously passed on through an endless string of third parties, is instead transformed into capital or other form of stable property, and it loses its quality of being a gift.[29]

The notion of an open-ended, spiraling, and constantly moving social formation, one in which giving and movement are stressed over owning and stability, is the implicit model underlying the new readings of *Kokoro* proposed by Komori and Ishihara. As Atsuko Sakaki has argued, each attempted a performative intervention in the field of modern literature studies. Whatever surplus values are produced through the intervention of the critic, moreover, must not accumulate in any one location in the social formation—be it the location of the author or of the critic—but rather must be continuously redistributed throughout the community of singular readers.[30] Komori's and Ishihara's readings stressed not only the ethicality of relating to Otherness but also the ways in which the novel violated hegemonic norms of property, propriety, and patriarchy. As such, they deliberately challenged existing interpretations that attempted to locate a stable value in the text, a value that could then be traced back to a legitimate owner, the author. To push their readings farther in the directions suggested by Kōno, Oshino, and Suga, this ethical stance implied a rejection of a simple communicative model of transmission between sender and receiver and instead insisted that all linguistic exchanges are mediated by one or more third parties— akin to Ludwig Wittgenstein's work on language games—and the semantic value of any utterance is never stabilized into identity.

This reformulation of the problem of ethicality can be traced back, in part, to the politics of New Left activism, the breeding ground from which many of the scholars of the linguistic turn emerged. The essays collected in part two of this volume explore in particular the politics of the linguistic turn. The linguistic and poetic theories that Yoshimoto Takaaki developed in the

29. Lewis Hyde, *The Gift: Imagination and the Erotic Life of Property* (New York: Vintage, 1979), esp. 11–24. Hyde's formulation is problematic because he remains fully under the spell of literature and conceives the social order of the gift in terms of a closed-circle, static economy, precisely the mode of structuralist sociology that Derrida is at pains to reject. This leads Hyde to assert problematically that the disembodied rationality of the social sciences (especially ethnography) can provide a full understanding of the gift (see esp. 74–92) despite his assertions elsewhere that the gift can only be understood through the body (through the "heart" and "feelings"). This is to say, his stress on eros in discussing the politics of economics gives way to a stress on logos when he turns to the politics of knowledge. The model of erotics that I am using here is adapted in part from William Haver, *The Body of This Death: Historicity and Sociality in the Time of AIDS* (Stanford: Stanford University Press, 1996).
30. Here I am adapting ideas from José Gil, *Metamorphoses of the Body*, translated by Stephen Muecke (Minneapolis: University of Minnesota Press, 1998), esp. 45–52.

1960s were crucial to this: in many ways, the linguistic turn was a response to the theory of "expression" that Yoshimoto had unfolded in a series of influential works. As Richi Sakakibara argues in chapter seven, Yoshimoto's work involved an attempt to develop a new form of political critique that rejected orthodox Marxism, which also meant rejecting the Stalinist version of linguistics that had been so influential in Japan since the early 1950s.

In chapter six, Kamei Hideo carries forward this exploration of the connection between the Japanese New Left and philosophies of language in a new essay. He analyzes the model of communication used by student radicals in 1960s Japan, one that rejected linguistic rules because they were perceived to be one component of the corrupt "everydayness" of modern society that the students vowed to overthrow. This led, not surprisingly, to breakdowns in communication when the students attempted to negotiate their demands and also to unexpected complicity between the language of the student movement and that of advertisement copywriting in the increasingly consumerist Japan of the period. Kamei traces how philosophers of language in 1970s Japan reacted to this situation as they tried to mount a new philosophy of language that saw in Saussure's notion of *langue* a site of ideological reproduction that had to be overthrown before a new society—and a new mode of communication—could arise.

Hence, the linguistic turn sought in language the means for radical political practice. Yet the rise of "theory" in Japanese literary scholarship has also been frequently criticized for both its conservatism and its co-optation by the market. The linguistic turn introduced a new concern with linguistic and literary form, a form whose materiality was often linked to the materiality central to historical materialism. But, as Norma Field writes in chapter 8, "Designating form as itself material—part of a broad tendency over the past quarter century to reclassify as material anything deemed consonant with revolutionary aspirations—assuredly revitalizes both the reclassified entity and the category of the material itself but necessarily at a cost." Field explores this cost as she traces the debate between Kamei and Mitani in an attempt to link "politics" as understood by the "Old Left," especially the proletarian literature movement of the 1920s and 1930s, and the new theoretical tools developed in the 1970s and 1980s.

The essays contained in part three are marked by a shared interest in the literature of the Meiji period (1868–1912). It is hardly surprising that the scholars and critics involved in the linguistic turn often focused on Meiji works. For starters, these works had been largely ignored or denigrated by previous scholars (with some notable exceptions), making them ripe for rediscovery and reevaluation by the rising generation. Moreover, the legacy of writer-activists from the people's rights movement of the 1870s and 1880s, which met with brutal suppression at the hands of the Meiji state, held obvious appeal for young scholars who had so recently lived through the fall of the New Left.

Most important for our purposes here, works from the Meiji period were characterized by remarkably diverse linguistic experiments. In the 1880s and 1890s, Japanese novelists and poets toyed with multiple new forms of written expression in their attempt to produce novel sorts of literary effects: third-person omniscient narration, interior monologue, and so on. Some of the experimental forms were fleeting; others eventually coalesced into *genbun itchi* (the unification of spoken and written languages), the writing style that finally gained hegemony around 1905 and is still the predominant form used in Japanese fiction today. These experiments in literary language were bound to attract the attention of a generation of scholars that was already captivated by the mechanics and politics of linguistic expression. As a result, one of the richest harvests of the linguistic turn was a still ongoing rediscovery of the literature of early Meiji, a fact well evidenced by the newly translated essays from the 1970s and 1980s that we have included in part one of this volume, all but one of which focus on that period.

The essays collected in part three, in turn, represent some of the latest developments in this continuing reevaluation. Each turns to some aspect of Meiji literature and builds on the work of scholars from the linguistic turn, especially the way in which they subjected the basic categories of literary studies—"literary value," "canon," "aesthetics"—to a rigorous interrogation, one that aimed to historicize and thereby relativize those categories. In chapter nine, Kōno Kensuke (who was, as we have seen, a participant in the *Kokoro* debates) explores the literary prize contests sponsored by commercial publishers in the years around 1900, especially the role they played in establishing new ideas about authorship and literature. Kōno demonstrates how prize contests lured aspiring writers with promises of fame and fortune even as they participated in the creation of a new discourse of literature that claimed it was immune to market forces.

Likewise, in chapter ten Guohe Zheng explores how the concept of literature held by Western scholars, along with their problematic assumptions about the Japanese language, have led to the exclusion of the political novel—perhaps the dominant genre of Japanese fiction in the 1880s—from the canon of modern Japanese literature. This exclusion has relied on an ideology of the aesthetic to produce the image of a supposedly apolitical modern Japanese literature, erasing the otherwise clearly evident traces of the entanglement of Japan's modern literature with the history of Japanese imperial expansion. Joseph Essertier in chapter eleven revisits the various proposals made for the reform of literary language in the 1880s, using a sociolinguistic approach derived from Bourdieu to unpack the implicit social hierarchies that were at stake in various assertions made during the period about what constituted "tasteful" or "vulgar" language. Finally, Leslie Winston in chapter twelve revisits the problem of subjectivity and narrative, one of the driving concerns of the linguistic turn, but introduces a gender-specific perspective that has too often been missing from Japanese literary scholarship. In exploring how two female writers from mid-Meiji produced the "voice of sex" in their narratives, Winston demonstrates that their strategies of linguistic expression were aimed at performing into being new forms of agency, forms that amounted to interventions in the field of gender politics.

———

Most of the new essays contained in this volume were originally presented at Sensibilities of Transformation: The Linguistic Turn and Contemporary Japanese Literary Criticism, an international conference held at the University of California, Los Angeles, on April 19–20, 2002. I would like to express my gratitude to the UCLA Center for Japanese Studies and its director, Fred Notehelfer, for the support they provided as the main sponsors of the conference. I am also grateful to the Center for Interdisciplinary Research on Asia and the Department of Asian Languages and Cultures at UCLA for additional support. Lauren Na, Jennifer Cullen, and Hisayo Suzuki provided invaluable support in organizing the conference events. All of the paper presenters were invited to contribute to this volume, but for a variety of reasons several papers are not included here, and I would like to acknowledge and thank those presenters for their contributions to the conference: Charles Shiro Inouye, Susie Jie Kim, Jennifer M. Lee, Mirana May Szeto, Atsuko Ueda, and Tomiko Yoda. I would also like to thank those who served as panel chairs or discussants at the conference: Christopher Bolton, Shoichi Iwasaki, Kinsui Satoshi, Namhee Lee, Rachel C. Lee, Seiji Lippit, Richi Sakakibara, David Schaberg, and Mariko Tamanoi. Finally, I would like to express my gratitude to the Japan Foundation for a 2000–2001 Research Fellowship that supported my own work on Natsume Sōseki, which I have drawn on in writing this introduction.

PART ONE

Pieces of the Linguistic Turn: Translations

Flowers with a Very Human Name: One *Kokugaku* Scholar Pursues the Truth about the Mysterious Death of Yūgao

Noguchi Takehiko

Translated by Suzette A. Duncan

1

The sequence of events described in the "Yūgao" chapter of *The Tale of Genji* is well known. In the summer of his seventeenth year, Hikaru Genji by chance meets and falls in love with a young woman of unknown birth, known ever since as Yūgao (Evening Faces). Then, on the fifteenth night of the eighth (autumnal) month, Genji heads toward the wretched quarters on Gojō, the location of Yūgao's humble cottage. Intending to spend one more night together hidden from the public gaze, he takes her "to a nearby villa" (*Genji*, 68).[1] The incident in question occurs on the sixteenth at midnight. A mysterious apparition appears in their sleeping quarters, and Yūgao dies of fright.

Who possibly could be the culprit that sent Yūgao to her death?

The iron rule of any murder investigation is that the person who discovers the crime must be the first suspect. However, Genji has absolutely no motive for murdering Yūgao. Genji's retainer, Koremitsu, has an alibi: he had already returned home that night. Moreover, Genji testifies that he observed the presence of the form of "an exceedingly beautiful woman" (*Genji*, 71) in the room. What about Yūgao's maid, Ukon, who was asleep in the adjacent room at the time of the crime? Given her customary devotion to her mistress, she, too, is above suspicion.

For these reasons, numerous commentaries on *The Tale of Genji* have deduced that the criminal is one of the female characters who happened not to

---

1. Quotations from *The Tale of Genji* are taken from Edward Seidensticker's 1976 translation, Murasaki Shikibu, *The Tale of Genji* (New York: Knopf, 1987). They are cited parenthetically as *Genji*.

be at the scene of the crime, a noblewoman who in this chapter of the story is completely offstage. In *Sairyūshō* it is written, "one has to think it is the lady."[2] *Mansui ichiro* also concludes it is "the lady."[3] The various commentaries consistently identify the woman that appeared above Genji's pillow as the disembodied spirit (astral projection) of the Rokujō lady, with whom Genji was also having a relationship at the time of his affair with Yūgao. Certainly, the circumstantial evidence points this way. We can verify this by going back over the sequence of events in the "Evening Faces" chapter.

The author begins the story of Genji's visit to the house on Gojō as follows: "On his way to court to pay one of his calls at Rokujō, Genji stopped to inquire after his old nurse, Koremitsu's mother, at her house in Gojō" (*Genji*, 57). What does "to pay one of his calls" mean? According to the common sense shared by readers of *Genji*, this refers to Genji's clandestine visits to the mansion of the Rokujō lady. Of course, that is correct. The Rokujō lady is a proud woman who was once the wife of Tōgū, a crown prince. Since his death she has withdrawn from the world, remaining closeted indoors. "Yūgao," building on the "Hahagiki" (The Broom Tree) and "Utsusemi" (The Shell of the Locust) chapters that precede it, describes Genji's love escapades with middle-rank women, a series of affairs that arises from the discussion comparing the merits of women from various ranks in the famous rainy night scene. However, in the midst of these affairs Genji also risks approaching this older woman of dark passions. The prideful Rokujō lady does not intend to be easily won over by Genji. But after Genji has forced his attentions on her, Lady Rokujō, who continues to harbor reservations, senses the gradual cooling of Genji's passion. This is the situation at the beginning of the "Yūgao" chapter.

The relationship between Genji and the Rokujō lady began at some point in time before the events narrated in "Yūgao." Strangely, however, the author does not write about the beginning of their love in any of the earlier chapters. In other words, even at its first mention in the text, the relationship between Genji and Lady Rokujō is presented as if it were a matter already known to readers. This question continues to be a point of debate among *Genji* scholars. Some even hypothesize that there is a lost chapter. To fill in the blank, in jest the nativist scholar Motoori Norinaga (1730–1801) wrote the chapter "Arm for a Pillow" (Tamakura) describing the beginning of their love.

Throughout the chapter "Yūgao," the Rokujō lady is an offstage presence. Readers are informed only that the woman Genji visits is a widow of

2. *Sairyūshō* is a *Genji* commentary by Sanjōnishi Sanetaka (1455–1537) compiled between 1510 and 1520.
3. *Mansui ichiro* is a *Genji* commentary by Noto Eikan, dates unknown.

rank who lives on Rokujō, that there is a difference in age between them, that she is proud, and that her passion was fired by the younger Genji. At this stage, the lady is still not identified by rank. Readers only come to know that the previously mentioned woman is the Rokujō lady through the development of the story in the chapters that follow.

In spite of this, the author takes extreme care in shaping the personality of this still anonymous woman. First, the author casually brushes against the psychology of Genji as he unconsciously compares the lady's "strangely cold and withdrawn " (*Genji*, 61) manner with that of the still unseen Yūgao. Second, she writes that the lady "is subject to fits of despondency" (63) after surrendering to Genji once and that she grieves on the nights that the youthful Genji does not visit her. Third, on the very night that Yūgao and Genji spend together at an unnamed villa, in his heart Genji thinks that on the same night the lady is probably longing for him. He compares her to Yūgao, the woman now in his arms, thinking, "here was the girl beside him, so simple and undemanding; and the other was so impossibly forceful in her demands. How he wished for some measure of his freedom" (70).

In a word, Lady Rokujō is a woman of deep passion who is almost pathologically proud. In the various commentaries on *The Tale of Genji*, her character and psychology are considered sufficient evidence of a motive for murder. But the most damning evidence comes from the words hurled at Genji by the "exceedingly beautiful woman" he witnessed just before the crime: "You do not even think of visiting me, when you are so much on my mind. Instead you go running off with someone who has nothing to recommend her, and raise a great stir over her. It is cruel, intolerable" (*Genji*, 71).

I have not mastered the colloquial language of the Heian period, but these words of rage sound like the language of one who has lost all sense of modesty or control. Various commentaries have declared that these words could only have come from the mouth of the Rokujō lady. The circumstantial evidence seems perfectly compelling after all. And almost unanimously the commentaries have convicted the spirit of Lady Rokujō in the murder of Yūgao.

However, one commentator of *The Tale of Genji* dared to resist the general trend and insist on the innocence of the Rokujō lady. This is the *kokugaku* (nativism) scholar Hagiwara Hiromichi (1815–63), who wrote *Commentary on the Tale of Genji* (*Genji monogatari hyōshaku*) in the Kaie era (1848–53) near the end of the Edo period. The fourth scroll of that work is devoted to his commentary on "Yūgao": "Various commentaries mistakenly attribute this to the grudge of the Rokujō lady. The true circumstances are made clear in my additional commentary. We ought to think of her only as an extremely mysterious and attractive woman. This [murder] seems instead the work of a spirit that haunts the villa."[4] In this way he dismisses the suspicions directed at the Rokujō lady by various commentaries as being a false charge. Who is the real criminal? Demons or monsters that haunt the unnamed villa where the murder took place. The grounds for this argument appear in detail in *Additional Commentary on the Tale of Genji (Genji monogatari yoshaku)*, a separate volume of the same work. If we summarize the main points of his argument, they are as follows.

1. In various earlier theories "it was the subsequent 'Aoi' (Heart-vine) chapter that led commentators to attribute this to the hateful feelings of the Rokujō lady."

2. Certainly the "Yūgao" chapter mentions the Rokujō lady from the beginning. However, it only mentions "movement to and from the home of an aristocratic lady of the Rokujō area" without "yet expressing what kind of person she is."

3. "Because this Yūgao affair occurred suddenly, it seems unlikely that the Rokujō lady could know about it, meaning that there is no way that she could hold a grudge."

4. Therefore, "it can only be regarded as the work of spirits that haunt that desolate villa."

5. At the same time, however, "The Rokujō lady casts a lingering light (*nihoi*) over the scene." The author describes the Rokujō lady's character at length and has the murderous spirit speak words of rage reminiscent of her because "the spirit that haunts the old mansion manifests itself in a likeness of the Rokujō lady."[5]

The first point that Hiromichi opposes is grounded in an inference based on the "Aoi" chapter of *Genji* in which the Rokujō lady, humiliated when her carriage is pushed aside by the one carrying Genji's wife Aoi at the Kamo festival, becomes a spirit and kills her. In these events (and only these events) the Rokujō lady is completely guilty. Although the culprit herself may not have been consciously aware of it, the spirit that departed from her body returned soaked in the smoke of poppies from Buddhist prayers, providing clear physical evidence of her guilt. But, Hiromichi insists, one cannot immediately jump to the conclusion that the assailant in this death

4. Hagiwara Hiromichi, *Genji monogatari hyōshaku*, reprinted in *Genji monogatari kochūshaku taisei*, 11 vols. (Tokyo: Nihon Tosho Sentaa, 1978), 4:288.
5. Hagiwara Hiromichi, *Genji monogatari yoshaku*, reprinted in *Genji monogatari kochūshaku taisei*, 11 vols. (Tokyo: Nihon Tosho Sentaa, 1978), 4:709–10.

was also responsible for the mysterious death of Yūgao. Such an assumption amounts to nothing more than a self-fulfilling prophecy, an investigation driven by foregone conclusions. In the Yūgao case, the Rokujō lady is innocent. Hiromichi draws on Genji's own words as the grounds for his argument, saying, "if the version offered by the earlier commentators was correct, then Genji would never have said she was an exceedingly beautiful woman, but would have described her simply as the noble woman who lived in the Rokujō area."[6]

For the moment, I will set aside Hiromichi's point that the murderous spirit took on the appearance of the Rokujō lady. What sets this *kokugaku* scholar's commentary apart from earlier commentaries is that his interpretation reads the work entirely through the psychology of the protagonist, Hikaru Genji. In describing how "situations unfold in relation to Genji's mind," Hiromichi sees deeply into "the talent of the author."[7] In exactly the same way, we, too, are startled by the critical genius of Hagiwara Hiromichi and his illuminating interpretation of *The Tale of Genji*.

Yamaguchi Takeshi was astonished when he rediscovered Hiromichi's commentary, and it was Yamaguchi's *Regarding the Apparition That Appears in "Yūgao"* (*Yūgao no maki ni arawaretaru mononoke ni tsuite*, 1925) that introduced the significance of Hiromichi's work to modern readers. Yamaguchi Takeshi's essay provides a worthy example of an all too rare genre of scholarly essay. Allow me to quote the profile of Hiromichi that appears in Yamaguchi's essay.

> Who was Hiromichi? Not a disciple to any particular teacher, he produced his *Commentary on the Tale of Genji* after many years of independent research. In critiquing that work he takes up one by one the previous interpretations and comments on them in all aspects. His commentary only extends to the "Festival of the Cherry Blossoms" chapter, but among *Genji* commentaries it is a work of unprecedented excellence. He also wrote fiction. When Bakin stopped writing after completing the fourth volume of his *yomihon*, *Kaikan kyōki kyōkaku den* (Tales of Chivalrous Protectors of the Powerless), it was in fact Hiromichi who, at the publisher's request, authored a fifth volume under the penname "The Master of Sannen."[8] We need to keep this fiction-writing experience in mind when we consider how he reached an appreciation of *Genji*

6. Ibid., 4:710.
7. Ibid.
8. The first volume written by Bakin was published in 1832. The volume that Hiromichi penned was published in 1849. The work was based on Chinese tales about survivors of the Southern dynasty.

as a unified work, as a unified novel and how, dissatisfied with the existing interpretations of *Genji*, he came to write his own commentary. Previously Motoori Norinaga had looked at *The Tale of Genji* as a work of art, as a novel, and had elucidated its artistic theory. Hiromichi acknowledged this farsightedness and carried on in its wake. This is the reason why, although Hiromichi had no direct master, he referred to Norinaga as his teacher.[9]

This concise portrait sufficiently tells of the epochal position of Hiromichi's *Genji* in the history of commentaries. Hiromichi stood at the point of intersection between Norinaga's *kokugaku* and Bakin's fiction. Furthermore, Hiromichi combined these two streams into a single coherent approach. His *Commentary on the Tale of Genji*, which was born at this intersection, not only revolutionized the existing commentaries, but it opened the way for what we now call "criticism."

The following essay is not an attempt to reread "Yūgao" according to Hiromichi's commentary. Nor is it an attempt to position Hiromichi in the history of *Genji* commentaries. Instead, while taking as my object Hiromichi's *Commentary on the Tale of Genji*, I will attempt to excavate from this unfinished work the outline of its theory of the novel and the critical vocabulary through which it speaks to us, and at the same time go beyond these to uncover the operations of the conceptual apparatus that builds on them and seems to approach a full-blown theory of the language of fiction.

2

Writing literary criticism in some respects resembles conducting an orchestra. To the unskilled eye the words and phrases in a literary text are just strings of written characters. Like a conductor who transforms a musical score into music, the critic must bring to life this assemblage of written signs by transforming them into *words*. Through his work the critic explicates how certain words should be understood, just as the conductor interprets a musical composition. And just like a conductor who picks up on a forgotten phrase—a delicate figure played by a single oboe, for example, hidden away above the fifth line in a complexly layered score—and thereby renews our enjoyment of the composition as a whole, the superior critic brings new life to a work, shines light on words that were buried, and cleaves open a new perspective on the work.

9. Yamaguchi Takeshi, *Yūgao no maki ni arawaretaru mononoke ni tsuite*, reprinted in *Yamaguchi Takeshi chosakushū*, 6 vols. (Tokyo: Chūō Kōron, 1972), 2:450.

When we read "Yūgao" with Hagiwara Hiromichi's annotations, we cut through the sedimented commentaries that have clouded the text and feel as though, with the flash of his conductor's baton, we can at last hear clearly the true music. At twilight on a summer night, Genji journeys through the unfamiliar outskirts of the capital in his carriage; by chance, he rests his eye on the strange white flowers coiled around the eaves of a shabby cottage. When Genji asks the name of these flowers, his attendant responds that they are known as *yūgao*, evening faces: "The white flowers far off yonder are known as 'evening faces' . . . a very human sort of name—and what a shabby place they have picked to bloom in" (*Genji*, 58). How does Hiromichi interpret this passage? Commenting on how the text rhetorically describes the flowers as if they "had a rather self-satisfied look about them" (57), smiling with raised eyebrows, Hiromichi writes, "they are probably called *yūgao* above all to make them seem like a person. A very interesting effect." With regard to the above-mentioned reply of the attendant, he writes, "Connecting it to 'face' makes it seem like a person. Calling it 'self-satisfied' then should be appreciated as an *engo* [conventional association: a standard trope of classical Japanese poetics]."[10] These words—"self-satisfied," "smiling," and "eyebrows"—are all *engo* that combine with the name Yūgao to make this flower into a person; in other words, he argues, they represent a personification of the flower.

Hiromichi lets us hear the music of *Genji* because it is thanks to his commentary, alive with a remarkable sensitivity to language, that we readers at last are able to hear the main melodic theme of this chapter, what ought to be called the leitmotif of "Yūgao": the harmonizing of "person" and "flower." Yūgao is not at all *like* a flower. Going beyond the boundaries of simile to approach metaphor proper, she *is* a flower; the woman is treated as the incarnation of the flower and vice versa. Already in this scene she stands still in the shade of the flowers waiting for her fateful meeting with Genji. Of course, this name Yūgao was given to her by later generations (it was already in currency by the end of the Heian period), and she is not called by that name in the book itself. In *The Tale of Genji* female characters usually do not have personal names and are instead referred to by rank or social position. In many cases, flower metaphors became substitute names for them. Traces of how this person Yūgao became identified with the flower *yūgao* in the author's consciousness are too numerous to list exhaustively here. People call the location of their first meeting "the Yūgao house." Was this because it was the house where *yūgao* flowers were blooming or because it was the house

10. Hagiwara, *Genji monogatari hyōshaku*, 4:254.

where the person Yūgao lived? Furthermore, when it is recollected that her relationship with Genji was a "strangely fleeting association," we note that this fleeting interval overlaps by association with the short lifespan of the *yūgao* blossom. And, of course, the evening of Yūgao's death coincides with the seasonal time when *yūgao* blossoms wither.

Hiromichi's interpretation calls our attention to the main melodic theme that governs these words. The name Yūgao is by no means a simple pronoun, a proper noun or sign that simply indicates a specific person. It is the linguistic objectification of a woman who is endowed with the essence of a short-lived flower. What Hiromichi's commentary sheds light on is the most important aspect of the text: the power of this word to summon up mental images through association.

Of course, Hiromichi's revered predecessor Norinaga in his *Genji* commentary, *Tama no ogushi*, also provided novel explanations of words in the text. But from my perspective Norinaga seems insensitive to the aspects to which Hiromichi was so keenly attuned. For example, in "Chūshaku no bu," the sixth section of his commentary, Norinaga makes no reference to the previously quoted section at all but comments on the phrase in the work describing the *yūgao* as "an unfortunate flower, even to its branches," explaining that "A *yūgao*'s branches are vines that grow lushly" (by the way, Hiromichi reproduces this remark in his *Commentary*).[11] Characteristically, Norinaga's focus is not on the personifying adjective *unfortunate* but rather on the objective reality described in the phrase. Of course, this one instance cannot provide an adequate survey of Norinaga's approach, but what we have here is something like the tip of the iceberg. Norinaga's main concern in his commentary was to restore the proper meaning words had in classical language and to recover the ways in which meaning was determined in specific historical contexts.

There is no denying the important role that is played by Norinaga's *Tama no ogushi* in the history of *Genji* commentaries. We cannot overemphasize the significance of Norinaga's rejection of the previously dominant Confucian- or Buddhist-inspired commentaries and his insistence on what we might call the "autonomy" of literature. However, in Norinaga's nativism, the emotionalism that is based on the famous *mono no aware* theory was merely just another "ism" in the end.[12] Boiled down to its essence, it prescribed the

---

11. Motoori Norinaga, *Tama no ogushi*, reprinted in *Motoori Norinaga zenshū*, 23 vols. (Tokyo: Chikuma Shobo, 1969–93), 4:374.

12. *Mono no aware* (sensitivity to the sadness of things) was a central aesthetic category in Norinaga's thought through which he attempted to explicate not only *Genji* but also the nature of Japanese culture as a whole.

following normative definition: literature is a discourse that expresses human emotions. Therefore, while it might acknowledge the existence of distinct genres, as a matter of theoretical principle it recognizes no distinction between poetry and tales. Of course, even at the stage of the early *Shibun yōryō* (1783), which was a prototype for *Tama no ogushi*, Norinaga writes, "All *monogatari* [tales, narratives] create events that do not really exist."[13] In other words, he recognized the fictionality of *monogatari*. Norinaga here is by no account repeating a self-evident assertion. He is in fact proposing a sharp antithesis to the conventional Confucian view of literature, which held that *monogatari* and other forms of fiction were nonliterary *precisely because of that fictionality*: they were regarded as a second-rate form of writing. However, here again the logic of emotionalism raises its head. Norinaga writes, "Especially in this *monogatari* [*Genji*], the characters are frequently made to say things that the teller wants them to say."[14] In other words, the *monogatari* is regarded as a nonpareil proxy device for the expression of the author's own emotions. Norinaga is not concerned with the hows and whys of the constructed nature of fiction. In the introductory *Shibun yōryō*, he writes that he "will write in detail about literary style separately," but in the subsequent *Tama no ogushi* he never carries this out.[15]

Instead Norinaga emphasizes chiefly the need to learn the feeling of *mono no aware* from *Genji* and above all to use it as a guide in following the way of poetry. Norinaga says, "If one regularly reads this *monogatari*, one's mind becomes of the world of the people in the story. When one reads the poems in it, one is naturally moved by the elegant passions of the past. The passions of the people of that world are lofty, so that even when they see the same moon or flowers as others, they feel an incomparable depth of *aware*."[16] This is the same view Norinaga expounded in *Isonoue no sasamegoto* (1783) and his other treatises on poetry. For Norinaga, *waka* poetry was above all a discourse of emotional expression endowed with *shirabe* (tune) and *aya* (rhetorical flourish). *Shirabe* refers, of course, to the set form of thirty-one syllables divided into five lines. *Aya* refers to the rhetorical embellishment that beautifully ornaments the words. And in order to express more beautifully these emotions the vocabulary for poems was limited to the special poetic diction that used ancient refined language (*gago*). When Norinaga emphasizes that this artificial limitation amounted to a kind of aesthetic fabrication, clearly this idea of an artificial or fabricated language shares common

13. Motoori Norinaga, *Shibun yōryō*, reprinted in *Motoori Norinaga zenshū*, 23 vols. (Tokyo: Chikuma Shobo, 1969–93), 4:83.
14. Ibid.
15. Ibid.
16. Motoori, *Tama no ogushi*, 4:242.

ground with the idea of the fictionality of *monogatari* that we looked at previously. The author of *monogatari* and the poetic master both fabricate "the mind of the people in the monogatari."

This is naturally reflected in Norinaga's theory of language. If we look at his commentaries on *waka* poetry, such as *Shinkokinshū Minōnoke zuto* (1794) and *Kokinshū tōkagami* (1793), we find much evidence that Norinaga thought it was possible, if one followed a certain procedural order, to reconstruct a one-to-one relationship between a given *waka* poem and the equivalent emotional expression that would have been used in the ordinary colloquial language (*zokugo*) of the period in which it was composed. Furthermore, these are not simple emotional outbursts. What makes them poems is that, in addition to having both *shirabe* and *aya*, they are woven from the refined words (*gago*) of poetic diction. The relationship between refined and ordinary language, *gago* and *zokugo*, can be expressed by the following formula: "positive versus negative aesthetic valuation between words of semantic equivalence." So what does this all mean? Put in terms of Roman Jakobson's linguistic theory, Norinaga's interest pertained mainly to language's indicative functions (whereby language indicates its referential objects) and its emotive functions (whereby language expresses the feelings of the speaking subject). And finally, for precision's sake, we should also note his interest in the poetic functions (language that calls attention to itself) of language, when, that is, the language in question was the refined language of poetic diction.

Norinaga's characteristic attitude toward language permeates his *Tama no ogushi* as well. Of course, scholars of subsequent generations received a considerable scholarly boost from Norinaga's work. His chronological table for the events depicted in *Genji* would undergo a few corrections, but it remains today the basic foundation for *Genji* studies, and it is hard to imagine that modern *Genji* scholarship as we know it could have taken place in the absence of his rigorous historical investigations into the classical language. However, even as we acknowledge these contributions, we are not relieved of the task of pointing out Norinaga's own idiosyncrasies.

3

In theorizing the essence of *monogatari*, Hiromichi basically follows in the footsteps of the explanation given in *Tama no ogushi*. It seems that for Hiromichi the theories of Norinaga on the fictionality of *monogatari* were completely self-evident premises, so he felt little need to revise or further develop them. Hiromichi was satisfied merely to express respect for this, his master's theory.

The new facets opened up in his *Commentary on the Tale of Genji* involved not a theory of the essential nature of fiction but rather a theory of the *construction* of fiction, a sphere not touched on by his predecessor Norinaga. More precisely, in the late Edo period, through the work of this nativist scholar, the Japanese theory of the novel acquired its first understanding of fictional structure. In order to see what kind of steps he followed and how this theory took shape, we must return to the scene of the *yūgao* flowers. Let us begin with the words of the attendant that were cited earlier: "[Flowers with] a very human sort of name—and what a shabby place they have picked to bloom in" (*Genji*, 58). Hiromichi's attention is directed at the adjective *shabby* (*ayashi*, meaning "mysterious, unusual, strange, incorrect") in this quotation. In the passage below, we find Hiromichi engaging in a critique, in a critical evaluation of this passage.

> This chapter mainly hangs on the case of the apparition that appears later. Early in the chapter it is written, "what sort of women might they be?" [57], and there appears "the shabby place [fence]" (*ayashiki kakine*) and then "leaning precariously" (*ayashiu uchiyorobohi*) [58]. The word *ayashi* is used as the primary word in this story line. Therefore, in this work I have underlined this word when it appears. One should pay close attention to this.[17]

The word *ayashi*, which Hiromichi calls "the primary word" (*ganmoku no go*) and to which he draws the reader's attention by means of underlining, appears overall in about twenty places in the chapter "Yūgao." Why is this to be regarded as the *primary word*? It is because he regards it as a key word that foreshadows the climax of the chapter, prefiguring in advance the strange apparition that will appear then. Even at the lyrical beginning of the love story woven together by the mental image of delicate white flowers, the word *ayashi* is casually inserted, thereby suggesting the story line that is about to develop and sending out flashes of a darker wavelength. *Ayashi* in the phrase "*ayashiki kakine*" refers to a fence that is "humble" or "poor." In the phrase "*ito ayashiu mono ni osoharetaru hito*," it refers to the "strange" apparition. We are able to interpret the word as meaning "mysterious" when, after Yūgao's death, Genji recollects that his longing was "*ayashiu kokoro ni kakarite*." Genji's conduct at this time is described as being, "*hitobito ayashigarite*," or as seeming "suspicious" to people.

In this way, the adjective *ayashi* is used with a variety of meanings, each determined by the context provided in the discourse of the *monogatari*.

---

17. Hagiwara, *Genji monogatari hyōshaku*, 4:254.

In compliance with the author's idea (*Meinung*), this word's significance (*Bedeutung*) presents a different sense (*Sinn*) with each appearance. However, this word has a single common originary, even sensuous, kernel of meaning from which all the other semantic contents derive. The kernel of meaning common to such notions as strangeness, mysteriousness, and suspiciousness is obvious. Why is the humble fence for Genji an "*ayashi kakine*?" It is because for Genji, born a crown prince, that fence, the likes of which he has never seen before, is highly unusual. *Ayashi* signifies the emotional reaction of a person to an unusual object.

As one would expect, Hiromichi, with his sharp instincts, espied this manifestation of the notion of "extraordinariness" in the emotional atmosphere that flows through the "Yūgao" chapter and understood that it provided the tonality of the *monogatari*. The previously mentioned melodic theme of the *yūgao* flowers unfolds within this tonality. Hiromichi traces the outcroppings of the primary word *ayashi*, calling this a "string of words" (*gomyaku*). If the tale's discourse is expressed as D and these outcroppings are expressed as a_i, Hiromichi's string of words can be expressed in the formula $D(a_1 + a_2 + a_3 + \dots a_n)$. Whether he speaks of the "primary word" or a "string of words," Hiromichi clearly directs his attention at words themselves. Each individual *ayashi* certainly describes the circumstances of the people or phenomena that are indicated in the text. However, Hiromichi reads the text as if the author were demanding that one see these depicted things *through* the filter of words. Hiromichi does not use special terminology beyond the examples just noted. However, if we were to express it in today's language, his linguistic sense points exactly to what we would call language's poetic function.

Moreover, Hiromichi provides a critique of the line uttered by Yūgao when Genji, hiding his station, visits her dressed in threadbare hunting clothes and she thinks it *ayashi*, "as if he were apparition from an old story" (*Genji*, 65).

> Here an "apparition" is spoken of for the first time. This introduces a thread that extends all the way to the scene of the apparition at the unnamed villa, like a cord stringing together jewels. It ought not to be carelessly overlooked. Therefore, the places where this foreshadowing of the plot appears draw attention to the coming apparition. We must note the diligence of the author, who wrote subtly and extremely well, making seem natural the unlikely pursuit of a suitor who remained entirely unknown, whose very face remained unseen. She made all of these things seem mysterious

(ayashi) as part of her plan in leading up to the subsequent appearance of the apparition.[18]

The terms *foreshadowing* (*fukusen*) and *plan* (*kekkō*), which Hiromichi uses in his criticism, originally come from Ming period literary and drama criticism in China by such figures as Jin Shengtan (1608–61). A stance of reading novels as novels never took root within Japanese nativism due to the circumstances mentioned above. It was rather the so-called Confucian literati of mid-Edo who provided significantly more skillful readings of novels, a skill they honed in reading such Chinese novels as *The Water Margin*. They remained Confucian even though they demonstrated flexibility and did not treat Confucianism as a rigid ideology.

It is of great interest that in *Kujakurō hikki* (Notes from My Study, 1768), one such Confucianist, Seita Tansō (1715–85), writes, "[S]o far as I have seen, among our country's allegorical writings, *The Tale of Genji* is certainly the best." Moreover, he picks the "Yūgao" chapter in particular as being the highlight of the work. Tansō writes, "[I]n the 'Yūgao' chapter Genji is a middle captain (*chūjō*). This middle captain's rank is deeply significant." The youthfulness of Genji, emphasized by this rank of middle captain, is evidence of the author's skillful construction: "When he is first appointed middle captain, already it hints at the apparition of the Kawara villa." In other words, it becomes a definite foreshadowing of the plot.[19]

The terminology that Hiromichi uses in his *Commentary* originates from this current of novel-oriented literary criticism. Whether he is discussing "foreshadowing" or "plan," it is Hiromichi's aim to remind readers that what "ought not to be carelessly overlooked" are the elements that compose the structure of the *monogatari* or fictional narrative.[20] Nakamura Yukihiko describes Tansō's critique of "Yūgao" as being "a kind of theory of structure, one that includes consideration of formal techniques of structure and gives weight to suggestiveness."[21] Mizuno Minoru argues that Hiromichi is "concerned with the formal rules necessary to literature."[22] These assertions

---

18. Ibid., 4:273.
19. Seita Tansō "Kujakurō hikki," reprinted in *Nihon koten bungaku taikei*, 100 vols. (Tokyo: Iwanami Shoten, 1957–69), 96:317–18.
20. Hagiwara, *Genji monogatari hyōshaku*, 4:273.
21. Nakamura Yukihiko, "Kakuretaru hihyōka: Seita Tansō no hihyōteki gyōseki," in *Kinsei Bungei Shichō Kō* (Tokyo: Iwanami Shoten, 1975), 248.
22. Mizuno Minoru, "Bakin makkansaku no zokuhen wo megutte," in *Edo shosetsu ronsō* (Tokyo: Chuo Kōron Sha, 1974), 243.

are quite correct. I would like to argue, however, that Hiromichi went a step beyond merely applying the terminology of criticism from Chinese novels to *Genji* in order to discover its formal structural principles.

In *Kujakurō hikki*, this is how Tansō discusses the scene of the mysterious apparition in "Yūgao": "In a large old palace, the sixteen- or seventeen-year-old youth is with a beautiful girl of similar age. The beautiful girl is killed by an apparition at night when it is still the fourth hour [around 10:00 P.M. as measured by modern clocks], and he cannot know where the apparition lurks in wait now. At that time, how he waits for the night to end—how very terrifying!"[23] This is evidence of a fine appreciation of the passage as befits a work of discerning criticism. In turn, what Hiromichi provides in his reading of this scene of Genji's mounting terror is a close analysis of the flow of sentences. He unlocks the secret of how the author's sentences combine to produce that sense of fright. Hiromichi translates and reconstructs this into his own critical vocabulary.

The first moment in the "gradual unfolding of the thread leading up to the apparition" comes when Genji appears in the girl's eyes as something like an apparition, creating a negative association for the word. However, Hiromichi does not concern himself with the word *apparition* (*henge*) beyond this. The problem here, unlike the case of *ayashi*, does not lie at the level of a string of words that can be unpacked by tracing through the outcroppings of that specific word. What comes to the eye of Genji when he goes with Yūgao to the unnamed villa is a desolate sight: "Genji looked up at the rotting gate and the ferns that trailed thickly down over it" (*Genji*, 68). According to Hiromichi, this is "the second moment in the thread leading up to the apparition." The third comes when, due to the appearance of the old palace, which has fallen into ruin, Yūgao "seems frightened, and bewildered" (69). In this way, Hiromichi picks out fifteen distinct moments (*suji*) in the thread, from the moment when the "exceedingly beautiful woman" appears by their pillow, through the scene of Genji's horror, which was discussed in the passage previously quoted from *Kujakurō hikki*. These are what Hiromichi calls "places where foreshadowing of the plot appear."

But what precisely does *foreshadowing* mean? In the explanatory remarks on usage that follow his opening summary, Hiromichi clearly defines this terminology.

> The character *sen* in the word *foreshadowing* (*fukusen*) means "thread" (*itosuji*). Starting from far away, threads are woven together, over and under, combining into a pattern, so that when

---

23. Seita, "Kujakurō hikki," 96:318.

you reach the end, if you pull on one of the ends, all of the seams move. This is the same kind of thing as what is called the plan (*kekkō*) The plan is the pattern prepared in advance.[24]

This kind of foreshadowing is not visible at the level of individual words. It is something that emerges at the level of sentences—or chains of sentences—within the assemblages of characters' psychological states, mental phenomena, and scenic descriptions. Hiromichi used the term *nihoi* ("lingering light" or "scent") to name this effect. In the "Yūgao" chapter, we can see how, as the time of day at the unnamed villa advances, first from afternoon to evening and then from evening to nighttime, hints of the mysterious (*ayashi*) subtly build until finally they come to dominate the entire scene. Hiromichi's foreshadowing of the plot can be expressed in the formula $A(x_1 - x_2 - x_3 - \dots X)$, where Genji (character A) begins with a premonition touched off by the atmosphere of the place, one that develops into a series that reaches its endpoint, X, with the strange apparition. In fact, because the author's technique produces an exquisite crescendo, this might be better expressed as $A(x_1 < x_2 < x_3 \dots X)$.

In Hiromichi's view, the "syntax" or "grammar" that the author uses does not stop with "foreshadowing" and "plan." For example, the author does not depict the scene on the night of fifteenth day of the eighth month when Genji and Yūgao are supposed to have consummated their relationship. Instead, she writes, "the details are tiresome and I shall not go into them" (*Genji*, 65). This is an instance of ellipsis: $A(x) - (\ ) - A(z)$. Also, the author does not write exclusively about Genji and Yūgao. In order to provide variety to the plot line, she inserts into the main line of the narrative various incidents, including the sequel to the story of the Lady of the Locust Shell, and the Rokujō lady or, rather, the love affair with the woman who lives in the Rokujō area. These are narrative pauses: $A(X - Y - X^1 - Y^1 \dots)$. As its title suggests, Hiromichi's *Commentary* (*Hyōshaku*) clearly distinguishes between *hyō* (criticism) and *shaku* (explanation). *Shaku*, which can also be read *toku*, signifies primarily the paradigmatic explication of words, while *hyō* as a rule centers on the analysis of narrative "syntax" and through it attempts to produce an original "critique" or interpretation of the work.

As noted above, the terminology by means of which Hiromichi describes the novelistic "grammar" he extracts from *The Tale of Genji* is not necessarily of his own creation. The terminological categories that Hiromichi enumerates—I will forgo a comprehensive description of each—are principle and auxiliary (*shukyaku*), opposition (*hantai*), correspondence (*shōō*),

24. Hagiwara, *Genji monogatari hyōshaku*, 4:64.

foreshadowing (*fukusen*), and ellipsis (*shōhitsu*). These almost completely overlap with the "Seven Rules for Fiction" that Kyokutei Bakin (1767–1848) compiled more than a decade earlier in the ninth volume of his *yomihon*, *Story of Eight Virtuous Heroes* (*Satomi hakkenden*, 1814–32). However, Bakin's rules are, at least in part, a kind of behind the scenes discussion of his own work, an attempt to borrow for it the authority of Chinese novels. To put this in the language of the Russian formalists, this was an instance of purposely baring the technique. For example, this is how Bakin describes foreshadowing: "What is called 'foreshadowing' means to sketch in faintly, several episodes in advance, something that will necessarily occur later."[25] Is this close to Hiromichi's definition? Hardly. The problem is the degree of abstraction of the concept that each is taking up. Bakin writes about the technique in his own work, bragging from his position as author about his own technique, whereas Hiromichi is moving toward something quite different: a general theory of the structure of the novel.

As he pursues his commentary on *The Tale of Genji*, what Hiromichi is groping for—or rather what he is well on the way to discovering—is the secret of what makes *Genji* a timeless work of art. To push this farther, he is pursuing the workings of language that render this tale *Genji* into a *monogatari*: the linguistic functioning that makes it into a fictional narrative. He is on the verge of entering into the realm of a universal theory of the language of fiction. As Hiromichi himself writes in the introductory summary to his commentary, it is not that from the start the author Murasaki Shikibu knew the rules for Chinese novels and applied them to her work but rather that what later generations would provisionally come to name as "rules" were already alive and functioning in *The Tale of Genji*. At the time, Hiromichi did not have anything at hand other than the terminology that had crossed over from the continent with which to express the ideas he had in mind. But while he used that language, he is actually trying to tell us something that exceeds it.

4

The true criminal in the strange murder of Yūgao is not the Rokujō lady. Hiromichi's apologia seems almost completely isolated, an opinion shared by few in the tradition of *Genji* commentaries through the Edo period. It is,

25. Kyokutei Bakin, *Nansō satomi hakkenden*, reprinted in *Nansō satomi hakkenden kōhon*, 4 vols. (Tokyo: Waseda Daigaku Shuppanbu, 1993–95), 1:332.

however, by no means simply a deliberate or pedantic attempt to flout common wisdom. Above all his view is supported by the words, and the linguistic functioning of those words, that weave together this fictional narrative.

Hiromichi's *hyō* (criticism) and *shaku* (explanation) exist in a relationship like that between the two sides of a medallion. On the one hand lies a delicate sensitivity aimed at each individual word, as we saw, for example, in the case of *ayashi*. Hiromichi, through the working of his intellect, traces back through the linguistic senses of the word *ayashi*, distinguishing between the overtones of connotation that mark each individual appearance of the word, and thereby catching the full wavelength of meaning that emits from it. On the other hand, what is analyzed at the level of *hyō* is the variety of formulas through which the syntactic substitution of individual words as variables functions to render concrete the narrative discourse of the *monogatari*.

Just as with the wheels of a cart, if one of these two approaches is missing the critic will not get far. In *Tama no ogushi*, Norinaga writes, "This *monogatari* shows *aware*, especially in how it expresses the extent to which people doubtlessly feel things."[26] What Norinaga considered the main point was generally the process of emotional identification with the characters in the work. In contrast, what was central to Hiromichi's criticism was clarifying exactly what kind of linguistic mechanism conveyed this sense of *aware*, as well as how words functioned—above and beyond their role as mediums for semantic communication—to solicit distinct and fleeting mental images with each concrete usage. *Shaku* is charged with explicating the meaning and emotional elements that words take on within the context of each individual appearance of those words in the narrative discourse. *Hyō* then takes these up as its significant units and analyzes how the characters and incidents of the narrative are woven from them into something like three-dimensional geometric figures. Put in terms of contemporary critical vocabulary, it is the relationship between the paradigmatic/semantic function and the syntagmatic function of poetic language.

The *Commentary* is not a superficial appreciation of a *monogatari*: it is a rigorous and sophisticated meta–reading, a radical rereading (*yomiokoshi*). In the interweaving of the paradigmatic and syntagmatic functions of language, the characters, things, scenery, and events of the *monogatari* flicker past in the form of mental images summoned up by language, fleeting images that take on depth and shadows. The visage of "the exceedingly beautiful woman" who killed Yūgao next to Genji's pillow is diffracted through the prism of Hiromichi's critical method, and, like a ray of light revealed to

---

26. Motoori, *Tama no ogushi*, 4:203.

be a compound of multiple wavelengths, the linguistic elements of the passage are each broken down into their own constituent elements.

In fact, it seems to me that Hiromichi's statement on this is somewhat lacking, especially in its concluding sentence: "Various commentaries mistakenly attribute this to the grudge of Rokujō lady. . . . We ought to think of her only as an extremely mysterious and attractive woman. This seems instead the work of a spirit that haunts the villa."[27] Yamaguchi Takeshi puts his finger right on the contradiction that mars Hiromichi's commentary here: "While he treats the entire 'Yūgao' chapter in terms of its psychological descriptions, so that he deals with even the apparition in terms of its status as a mental phenomenon, the minute he encounters something that cannot easily be explained in these terms he jumps to the conclusion that it must be the work of some nonhuman supernatural agent."[28]

The traditional commentaries that Hiromichi challenged were characterized above all by a kind of *literalism* (*junkyoshugi*). The *Genji* commentaries, which began appearing late in the Heian period, arose due to the circumstance that readers were no longer able to understand the vocabulary in the work without supplemental knowledge. This was why these commentaries focused on explaining ancient court practices and providing authoritative definitions of archaic terms. These commentaries consistently strive to return all questions to the authority of linguistic facts, manners, and customs of the court, historical sources, literary transmissions, and so on. They operate within a conceptual circuit that always attempts to link textual questions to some sort of empirical historical background. In this sense, there is no contradiction in the way in which many of the commentaries on the one hand offer the Kawara villa once owned by Minamoto Tōru and mentioned in the legend of Tōru's ghost threatening the Emperor Uda as the authoritative identity of the "unnamed villa" in the chapter, while on the other hand they identify the Rokujō lady as the culprit in the murder.[29] The logic of the literalism that specifies Kawara as the correct identity of the villa left tantalizingly unnamed in *Genji* does not necessarily lead one to conclude that the strange woman who appears is a ghost that haunts the unnamed villa. The ghost of Minamoto Tōru, after all, would not be a woman. Instead, the commentators stick to the actual context of the work and, through an act of retroactive inference from the subsequent "Aoi" chapter, they reach the conclusion that the ghost is the Rokujō lady. She was guilty of the second

27. Hagiwara, *Genji monogatari hyōshaku*, 4:288.
28. Yamaguchi, *Yūgao no maki ni arawaretaru mononoke ni tsuite*, 2:456.
29. The legend is included in *Gōdanshō*, a late Heian anthology of *setsuwa* narratives.

murder, and therefore, they conclude, she must be the assailant in the first as well.

Hiromichi, in contrast, attempts to unravel the problem secondhand, like the reader of a detective novel, basing his conclusions on the presumed reliability of Genji's testimony. In other words, he reexamines the woman at the scene of the crime through the psychological filter of Genji as the perspectival character. The scene is viewed through his perceptions of it and through the surface provided by the words of the author, which give concrete shape to that filter. The woman's face floats on this surface. Genji sees this woman at three distinct moments. The first time, it goes without saying, is the most famous encounter. The second time, by the light of the lantern he made the night watchman bring, "he had a fleeting glimpse" of the face of a woman he thought he saw in a dream, but then "it faded away like an apparition" (*Genji*, 72). The third time is once again in a dream. Genji, who wishes to see Yūgao even if only in a dream, instead sees "the woman who had appeared that fatal night" (85).

In the latter two instances, the author clearly emphasizes that what appears is the woman's face. Notwithstanding the clear impression he receives of seeing a face, Genji never recognizes her as the Rokujō lady. Moreover, this woman freely moves between dreams and reality. This, at any rate, seems to be the path that Hiromichi's line of thought follows. Therefore, Hiromichi positively concludes, citing Genji's thought near the end of the chapter, that "he had attracted the attention of the evil spirit haunting the neglected villa" (*Genji*, 83), that the "author intends" this as a "female apparition," one that must be seen as "resolving the case of the apparition depicted earlier," and "we should understand the various commentaries that identify this as the spirit of the Rokujō lady to be mistaken."[30]

If we look at it this way, Yamaguchi Takeshi's criticism, cited above, begins to seem like an anachronistic projection of modern psychologism onto Hiromichi's commentary. The Bakumatsu era during which Hiromichi lived was an age marked by a mentality in which various odd ghosts and spirits, residents of the dark, still stirred; it was prior to the dawn of civilization and enlightenment when such things would be driven into the realm of the unconscious. Hiromichi, concluding that these strange apparitions were all summoned up by Genji's mind, praises the author's talents.

> The explanations current in China, which say that phantoms arise
> out of people, seem to underlie this. The skillful touches of the

---

30. Hagiwara, *Genji monogatari hyōshaku*, 4:327.

author's writing brush, suggesting such things but leaving them
finally unresolved, repeatedly provide ample evidence of the author's rich skill.[31]

Phantoms may be born out of people, yet this does not necessarily mean that
the "female apparition" was an illusion originating in Genji's psychology.
Hiromichi deduces that it was a ghost haunting the unnamed villa that suddenly appeared, one that lay in wait as part of the shadowy realm of night
that existed in counterpoint to the glory of the Heian court but that here
took advantage of Yūgao's frail character, as well as of Genji's unease and his
pangs of conscience over the Rokujō lady.

Therefore, what Hiromichi praises at length is the "skillful touches
of the author's writing brush, suggesting such things but leaving them finally unresolved." That is to say, what he praises is her use of ambiguity.
Hiromichi locates the author's skill in a style of writing that does not permit
one finally to pin down people, places, or objects with any authority. In response to the fourteenth-century *Kakaishō* commentary, which identifies the
unnamed villa as the Kawara villa and provides the supposed historical origins of the Yūgao scene, Hiromichi writes, "This is an example of 'literalist'
commentaries, but when the name of the villa is deliberately hidden and it
is merely called the 'such-and-such villa' (*nanigashi no in*), we should understand this merely as being an unspecified villa somewhere close to Yūgao's
residence. It seems to be a separate residence for Genji."[32] According to his
commentary, the site where Yūgao meets her sad destiny is deliberately left
unspecified; it exists in a realm that is discontinuous with extratextual reality. But within the fictional world constructed in the work, this desolate
scene with its ghastly atmosphere appears as a perfectly autonomous space.
All forms of literalism remain trapped in the closed circuit of language's indicative functions. But Hiromichi escapes this. He alone is able to grasp the
autonomous, for-itself image produced through the narrative, the virtual
image that emerges only by means of a different semantic function, one that
is filtered through the poetic functions of language. We see this in his reading of the unnamed villa and even more so in his explication of the truth
of the female apparition. In the introduction to his annotation of "Yūgao,"
Hiromichi writes that "because all made-up tales are by definition things
that are created, apparitions which take astonishing forms" are numerous
in them.[33] And in general, he notes, such mysterious apparitions are in the

31. Hagiwara, *Genji monogatari yoshaku*, 4:710.
32. Hagiwara, *Genji monogatari hyōshaku*, 4:282.
33. Ibid., 4:249.

end usually resolved and order restored by calling on the power of the spirit of Kannon or some similar entity. But the author of *Genji*, Hiromichi writes with admiration, makes the female apparition appear "in one passage in a remarkable scene," and she "never resorts to this sort of forced device."[34] Yamaguchi Takeshi quite correctly says that this represents the surprise that Hiromichi felt upon discovering something that was not in Edo novels, which were characterized by "plots that were contrived and dramatized to the point of absurdity."[35]

A critic from the mid–nineteenth century in the Edo period attempts an original interpretation of a narrative from roughly 850 years before his time and comes to admire the newness of its writing techniques, a newness that seems fresher than the fiction written in his own day. And now, as we reconsider his work, it is our turn to admire the freshness of the critical gaze that Hiromichi turned on *Genji*, the freshness of his methodology, whereby he explicated the narrative discourse of a fictional *monogatari* solely through the functioning of the language in which it was composed. The problem of theorizing poetic language, especially that of fictional narratives, which Hiromichi began to uncover before illness halted his work prematurely, is continuous with contemporary criticism and the issues that it faces more than a century after Hiromichi's work. Next to the remarkable complexity and breadth of the problems his *Commentary on the Tale of Genji* attempted to resolve through the terminology that was available to him, the representative works of what we call criticism in this modern period cannot but pale in comparison.

NOTE

This essay was originally published in *Kaie* 4 (October 1978): 246–59.

34. Ibid.
35. Yamaguchi, *Yūgao no maki ni arawaretaru mononoke ni tsuite*, 2:451.

The Embodied Self

Kamei Hideo

Translated by Jennifer M. Lee

Although the topic is quite removed from a discussion of Ōoka Shōhei's *The Battle for Leyte* (*Reite senki*, 1967–70), in order to rethink the issues at stake in it from the ground up I would like first to return to the work of Tsubouchi Shōyō (1859–1935). As is well known, in *The Essence of the Novel* (*Shōsetsu shinzui*, 1885–86) Shōyō defines the novel as follows: "The main business of the novel is human nature (*ninjō*). Social conditions and behaviour rank second. By 'human nature,' I mean man's sensual passions, what Buddhism calls the one hundred and eight appetites of the flesh."[1] He adds:

> A novelist is like a psychologist. His characters must be psychologically convincing. Should he contrive to create by his own invention characters at odds with human nature, or worse, with the principles of psychology, those characters would be figments of his imagination rather than human beings, and not even a skillful plot or a curious story could turn what he wrote into a novel. (*Essence*, 24)

To begin with, I would like to address the reasons why Shōyō introduced psychology in the *Essence of the Novel*, as well as the methodology of psychology he employed.

It is likely that Shōyō read the abridged translation by Inoue Tetsujirō (1855–1944) of Alexander Bain's *The Senses and the Intellect* (1855) in a university psychology class. Although I know very little about Alexander Bain (1818–1903), Inoue identified the defining characteristics of his work as

---

1. Tsubouchi Shōyō, *The Essence of the Novel*, translated by Nanette Twine, Occasional Papers, no. 11 (Brisbane: Department of Japanese, University of Queensland, 1981), 23. Further quotations from this translation are cited parenthetically as *Essence*. All the footnotes are by the translator.

follows: "In the original text, Bain approaches psychology from a physiological perspective. This represents his outstanding achievement in the field of psychology." That is, in order to elucidate the processes whereby objective external reality elicited the formation of mental concepts inside a person, Bain began from a neurological explanation of the sense organs. From our present-day perspective, his was nothing more than a commonplace form of empirical associative psychology, one that traced the acquisition of concepts through the accumulation of experiences of sensibility, their possible associations, the internal affective experiences that arose in response to the sensual experience of external images, and the expansion of the emotional realm through acts of memory and anticipation. Traces of idealism continued to cling to it, but psychology, which had distanced itself from philosophical idealism and adopted the methods of the natural sciences, was at the time almost the sole true science of the human being. Shōyō's understanding of psychology was based on this. Inoue Tetsujirō constructed a genealogy of psychology as a natural science, linking Alexander Bain to John Stuart Mill and Herbert Spencer. In his theory of the novel, Shōyō regarded the physio-psychological domain that constituted the object of observation of this science as being the essential nature of human beings. His theory of the novel advocated the need to express "human nature" (*ninjō*) in a way that affirmed this nature just as it was; it rejected works that manipulated characters like marionettes in order to fit them into preexisting concepts.

Still, Shōyō did not call for observing people in the manner of a psychologist, a sound position on his part. He certainly understood the necessity of basing characters on observation. But since he did not make a short-circuited equation of observation with description, and of description with novelistic expression, he did not assert that psychological observation would by itself lead to the depiction of lifelike characters, writing, "The characters and events of the novel, unlike those of an ordinary biography or history, are entirely figments of an author's imagination. They are pure invention" (*Essence*, 48). As such, the aim of novelistic "style" (*bun*, meaning *ji no bun*, passages of narrative description rather than spoken dialogue) was not to reproduce faithfully the object of observation since "Language is spirit and style is form" (59-60). Furthermore, "Style serves both as a vehicle and an adornment for thought" (50). For these reasons, to presume the theory of realism as it was subsequently espoused in naturalism and, taking *The Temper of Students in Our Times* (*Tōsei shosei katagi*, 1885–86) as a "realistic" novel in that sense and then criticizing its failure to achieve consistent realism, is to completely misread what Shōyō meant in his theory.

That being the case, how can people's nature be discovered and how can this be given expression? Shōyō thought this could be realized through the dialogue that characters exchange with one another. The word *language* (*kotoba*) in "Language is spirit" meant the spoken dialogue of the characters in a story. Emotions "expressed with complete frankness in speech" (*Essence*, 60) ought to be depicted without embellishment. In short, this is what Shōyō meant by the "depiction of human nature." In the preface to *The Newly Polished Mirror of Marriage* (*Imotose kagami*, 1886), too, he asserted that "Spoken dialogue is natural language. The novel is based on nature. If one aims to depict the reality of nature, one must use natural language. . . . By depicting the language just as it is, one renders visible the wonderful workings of nature."[2]

Sometimes, though, unexpected things happen. It is not difficult for us today, of course, to locate fundamental shortcomings in Shōyō's understanding of language. Nonetheless, he faithfully put that theory into practice. For example, the unsophisticated speech of women of Tsukiji, located in the lower-town (*shitamachi*) section of Tokyo, was reproduced unaltered in *The Newly Polished Mirror of Marriage* even as Shōyō appended comments such as "the reader is cautioned that from time to time this woman uses crude language" (*MBZ*, 16:165). "Depiction of human emotion" meant to express emotions using "natural language." But the problem still remained as to how to convey inner feelings that were not verbally articulated to others. Shōyō devised a surprisingly honest solution to this problem. At first, he depicted a maidservant, Okagi, muttering a soliloquy out loud to herself. But he subsequently experimented with expressing Oyuki's interior monologue after giving it the following setup: "Let's take out our magic mirror and reflect her innermost thoughts" (16:216). Techniques that are now familiar to us as matters of simple common sense, such as internal confession or stream of consciousness, were only realized in the history of the modern Japanese novel after having gone through this kind of roundabout procedure. Moreover, this achievement led to another change in mode of expression. A character's interior confession now also attempted to depict the external surrounding environment as it appeared to that character. It was at this point that a mode of expression was born in which the external world was unified with the internal necessity of the character in question so that a description of the external world was capable of revealing the interior state of fictional characters. Shōyō put this technique into practice in *The Wife* (*Saikun*, 1889).

---

2. *Tsubouchi Shōyō shū*, edited by Inagaki Tatsurō, in *Meiji bungaku zenshū*, 99 vols. (Tokyo: Chikuma Shobō, 1965–83), 16:164. Subsequent passages quoted from this series are identified parenthetically as *MBZ*.

Recently a certain journal published a special issue on the *genbun itchi* (unification of written and spoken language) writing style, but all the articles in it failed to grasp the essence of the problem. A novelist first establishes the perspectival character, a character that is under the sway of the immanent necessities of the fictional world. The novelist then gives expression to the external environment only insofar as it seems necessary to the senses and emotions of that character. The writing style born out of this is what we now call *genbun itchi*. The conventional schema, which maintains that Shōyō continued to use the older literary *bungotai* style and that it was only with Futabatei Shimei (1864–1909) that true *genbun itchi* was created, in fact completely misses the point. Defining *genbun itchi* as a writing style based on spoken language is insufficient. The defining quality of this style is that it is mediated by internal confessions that appear only with the rejection of spoken dialogue exchanged between the characters in the story, that is, by the internal consciousness of a character who has no interlocutor with whom to speak. Incidentally, modern literary standards for nature description were also created from these same circumstances. Taking the hint from psychology, sense perception and sensibility are regarded as constituting the essence of human nature, and a tendency arises to depict the external world as it is contemplated by the eye and ear. We have become accustomed to considering expressions that depict nature in this way as accurate and reliable descriptions. If we fail to see this, we will never satisfactorily resolve the problem of literary "naturalism," which has been a topic of such debate lately.

Try comparing part 1 of Futabatei's *Ukigumo* to *The Temper of Students in Our Times*, part 2 to *The Newly Polished Mirror of Marriage*, and part 3 to *The Wife*. It soon becomes clear that Futabatei was in fact following in the tracks of Shōyō's experiments. However, Futabatei was ahead of Shōyō on one point. To illustrate this, I highlight a line from a collection of Futabatei's notes, *Piles of Fallen Leaves: A Second Basketful* (*Ochiba no hakiyose*, 1889): "Any given thing exists in itself. And simultaneously it also exists for itself. A thing that exists only in itself is an 'object' and cannot be a 'subject.' A thing that exists simultaneously in itself and for itself is both 'object' and 'subject'" (*MBZ*, 17:42).

Futabatei probably became acquainted with this Hegelian epistemology through his studies of Vissarion Belinsky. Rereading *Ukigumo* through this epistemology, one can see that he clearly distinguished between the emotional expressions of Osei and Bunzō in part 3. In other words, Osei was unable to go beyond the "thing in itself" aspect of her emotions. Bunzō, too, was like that at one time until:

His outer calm contrasted sharply with the activity within him. Jolted into awareness by the cruel treatment he had received, he suddenly saw things in an entirely new light. The veil of passion which had been distorting his reason was torn away and his mind grew clear. With his dormant intellect finally awakened, he was able to evaluate the world around him sensibly and objectively. In some intangible way, Bunzō was reborn, although not completely, of course. And when he reviewed the events of the past few days with the benefit of this new insight, he was amazed at how foolish he had been.[3]

Subsequently Bunzō is able to objectify his own emotions in both their in-itself and for-itself aspects. At the same time, Bunzō comes to see clearly Osei's unhappiness, condemned as she is to fluctuate continuously as the passive object of environment and circumstance. The author's viewpoint on the work's characters is now carried over without alteration to take the form of Bunzō's self-understanding and his critical consciousness toward Osei and Honda Noboru. To put it differently, a protagonist who was immanent to the fictional world of the work yet capable of taking up the author's viewpoint on that world here made its first appearance in the history of Japanese fiction.

Futabatei, too, seems to have encountered Alexander Bain's work. In *Piles of Fallen Leaves: A Third Basketful* (composed late in 1890), we find the following observation.

If a person wants to study psychology, he first must discuss what consciousness is. . . . According to Bain, "consciousness" has two meanings. In a broad sense, it means awareness of sensation [*reidan jichi*, a Buddhist term] in contrast to a state of unconsciousness. In the narrow sense, the term means in particular the active form of self-reflection. . . . If this is so, we can provisionally define *consciousness* as the mental function by which the mind becomes aware of its own functioning. To clarify and explain in more detail this self-awareness of its own functioning, assume for a moment that something exists in the external world. That external thing acts as a stimulus to the five senses. The operations of the five senses then produce an image in the brain. A person is not "consciously" aware of the processes in the body that produce

3. Marleigh Grayer Ryan, *Japan's First Modern Novel: Ukigumo of Futabatei Shimei* (New York: Columbia University Press, 1967), 333. Subsequent quotations from this translation are cited parenthetically as *Ukigumo*.

this image, but is aware that the images thus produced appear "consciously." This is what we mean by consciousness. Seen in this way, consciousness and the production of mental images are two distinct functions of the mind. (*MBZ*, 17:186–87)

Shōyō regarded the physio-psychological domain that is the object of psychology as constituting the essence of human nature, but he had no interest in how psychology came to be established as a form of knowledge. Futabatei was exposed to Bain and came to believe that psychology consisted precisely of the consciousness of physio-psychological processes (the mental phenomenon produced by images in the brain when the five senses receive stimuli from an external object). If there existed no consciousness that was aware of its own processes in this way, then humans would be unable to posit as an object of knowledge their own human nature. The human being can only cognize as its own essential nature those physio-psychological processes that human beings become consciously aware of. This consciousness and the processes of which it is conscious taken together are called the "mind" (*kokoro*). The mind knows its own desires, and at the same time it must accept these desires as constituting its own essential nature.

The mind is aware of its own act of seeking. The object of sensibility that it seeks is also, of course, present. A literary work that focuses primarily on this sort of mental state by its very essence has to adopt the form of a first-person narrative. We typically regard the mode of expression in such works as belonging to a person who has awakened into self-consciousness just as we have created the convention of taking such works to be the reflections of the interiority of the author's own self. The protagonist in *Chance Encounters with Beautiful Women* (*Kajin no kigū*, 1885–97) in many aspects closely resembles the author, Tōkai Sanshi (1852–1922), and so it has been labeled Japan's earliest autobiographical work. However, hardly anyone reads it as an I-novel (*shishōsetsu*). The nature of its mode of expression does not allow it to be read as such. In comparison, the personal circumstances of the author Futabatei and his protagonist Bunzō in *Ukigumo* are quite different, yet Bunzō is often read as if he were a stand-in for Futabatei. This mode of reading did not simply arise out of preexisting studies into authorial biography; rather, it was the protagonist's mode of self-expression that prompted readers to turn their interest to the author's life. In that sense, it seems clear that while Futabatei was writing *Ukigumo*—and in particular part 3—he was putting into practice his understanding of psychology, which, as we have seen, was suggested to him by Bain's work.

Just when Futabatei succeeded in creating the mode of expression for portraying the mental world, one that depicted the dawning self-consciousness so typical of what we call "modern literature," at precisely that moment he abandoned writing *Ukigumo*. Shōyō, too, gave up writing fiction soon after he had successfully developed his technique of using inner monologue as a means of giving expression to the external environment in a way that meshed precisely with the protagonist's interior. Why? It is not simply that their experiments were ahead of their time. In fact, the reasons why they abandoned novel writing are located within the very successes they had achieved.

To repeat, the mind is aware of its own desires, and the object of sensibility that it desires exists before the eyes. However, that is not a complete picture of the mind. The mind also produces objects of a spiritual nature that transcend sensibility; moreover, it is entangled in institutional and political processes that can never become direct objects of cognition or sensibility. It is inconceivable that the latter aspect of mental functioning was absent in the case of Futabatei. But because his interest was limited to those aspects of the mind that were believed to constitute the essence of human nature, he was able to take up as the object of expression only the emotional confusion evoked by the real object of sensibility. To understand why Bunzō was fired from his job, one would have to probe the institutional and political situation at the government office where he worked. Yet Bunzō seeks the cause solely in the emotional situation that exists between him and his boss. He can only find crude explanations such as "I must have been fired because I wouldn't play up to the boss. The boss is a bastard" (*Ukigumo*, 226). This plebian narrowness of Bunzō's mind (and of his sphere of concern) originates in part, of course, in the author's one-dimensional understanding of the mind, but it was also a matter of necessity that the mode of expression of that mind would be limited to the sphere of personal negotiations between members of the family. When Shōyō, too, turns his perspective away from the standpoint of grasping the interior and toward expression of the external environment, the world that his method could give expression to was inevitably limited to the domestic sphere of the family. Limiting the fictional world to the emotional conflicts elicited in the process of negotiating with concrete others who are immediately at hand was the only method either author possessed for actualizing what they understood to be the workings of the mind.

Moreover, this viewpoint that limited itself to the domestic space of the family could see only the following sort of wretched condition: "Underneath lay a loathsome, greedy, self-indulgent, immoral, cruel mass. . . . They thought only of themselves. They spoke only in self-interest and acted to satisfy their greed. They deceived each other and were deceived" (*Ukigumo*, 350). This is the reality of family that is exposed in all its ugliness. But we must note that this is, in fact, the human condition bestowed by Futabatei on Bunzō and his narrow-mindedness. Ultimately, what is wretched here is Bunzō's own mentality. Must we accept this miserable state of mind as constituting the essence of human nature, its "naturalness"? In the end, it seems that Futabatei had no interest in confronting the question of whether this actually constituted human reality. As a result *Ukigumo* was abandoned unfinished. In Shōyō's abandonment of novel writing, too, it seems likely that similar circumstances were at work.

But what we are dealing with here is something more than a simple abandonment of fiction. From the *Temper of Students in Our Times* through the opening sections in *The Newly Polished Mirror of Marriage*, and in parts 1 and 2 of *Ukigumo*, we find an attempt—albeit a brief one—to create a literary style that clearly worked to solicit increased sympathetic identification on the part of the reader's gaze. For example, in the opening of *The Newly Polished Mirror of Marriage*, Otsuji is introduced as follows.

> She is around sixteen or seventeen years old. Her skin color is re-
> markably white. Her eyes are extremely pure. . . . It looks as if she
> has just put on makeup. Her hair is in the popular *tenjin* style. Al-
> though the bound hair is thick, it looks light. Two or three strands
> of loose hair have ever so pitiably wandered astray (*aware hotsure*)
> around her eyebrows and enhance her elegance. One flaw is that
> her teeth are not straight. (*MBZ*, 16:165)

In general, the mode of expression here is quite commonplace, but the ex-pression of "ever so pitiably wandered astray" clearly strains credulity. Of course, it is not an expression that is born out of a desire to portray the depicted object faithfully and accurately. That being the case, we should understand it as an expression that manifests the author's own claim on the depicted object. But, as is clear from the light and playful tone, the author does not narrate this claim out of some powerful personal motivation. *How about we throw in yet another attractive attribute for this already charming lady?* The passage is written out of this sort of idea, as if the narrator was indulg-ing in lighthearted gossip with the reader. In this way, the reader seems to join in the game of deriving fanciful figures for depicting the object in an in-teresting manner, the game of tossing off harmless commentaries and criti-cisms. This kind of expression can be found in abundance in the first half of *Ukigumo*. It is produced under the premise that writer and reader occupy a single, shared place or, rather, that such a shared place must be produced.

However, once the focus shifts to depicting characters' internal monologues, this attempt to produce a sphere of mutual interest shared with the reader disappears. Once passages of description come to be measured by a new standard, which rejects both the excessive and the underdeveloped, such expressions and the idea behind them are rejected and expunged from the work as superfluous. What was the end result of the rejection of this mode of expression and of its replacement by a mode based on identification with the interiority of a specific character in the work? It was the narrow-mindedness of a person who could only depict the wretched reality of other people that was manifested when they were grasped through that person's interiority, that is, only as they appear as items of interest to that single person's mind. Once the literary style that tried to live out a sense of shared interest with the reader was discarded, the cause that would eventually lead to the abandonment of fiction writing was in place.

As may be clear already, what I want to argue here is that while we may have followed the path that Shōyō and Futabatei so painstakingly pioneered the fundamental problem that they confronted remains unsolved. Far from it: the writers associated with naturalism tried to leap over in one fell swoop the procedures that Shōyō and Futabatei had followed so painstakingly, and as a result those writers fell completely under the sway of the concept of the "naturalness" of human nature, a concept they dull-wittedly transformed into a vulgar theory of instinct. Facing the phenomenological aspect of nature, one that was created by human hands, they depicted this as if it were unadulterated nature itself so that this theory of depiction inadvertently rendered the self-limitations of their perception into something even more fixed. Moreover, even the workings of the author's sensibility as it perceives the object were subjected to the norms of naturalism. These writers had no interest, of course, in the problem that led Shōyō and Futabatei to abandon fiction writing.

Many of them were at some point influenced by Christianity. Taking this point into account, it seems they ought to have been familiar with the manner in which human minds seek a spiritual object that transcends sensible perception. However, we must note that almost invariably they ended up moving away from Christianity after some sort of awakening to sensuality (sensual pleasures), as they frequently narrate in their autobiographical writings; it was thus that they reached the state of full-blown naturalism. It was as if the very act of accepting as "natural" a desire for the opposite sex, as if this transformation in and of itself was the truly "natural" course for human nature to follow. A few still pursued the idea of a conflict between spirit and flesh, but they were incapable of developing this into a depiction of the grand conflict between the spiritual and bestial qualities that coexist in a single individual. Rather, they all fell into the same outcome: worshipping at the altar of "divine" flesh. To put it bluntly, this was nothing more than a convenient pretext to justify running off to a new woman. Yes, it is true that even in their "narrow-mindedness" they did at times confront the question of art and its relation to action. But because of their narrow-mindedness they lacked from the start a driving interest in historical processes of an institutional and political nature; the only form of action they could countenance was to use the naturalistic view of humanity to topple the false idols that were the conceptual norms of everyday life and common sense.

Ironically, this form of "action" was adopted by critics as a methodological principle. While critics after naturalism faded did outgrow the more vulgar theories that explained human nature through instinctual determinism, their approach, which used the supposed naturalness of human sensibility and emotions as a standard against which to judge and dismiss the intellectual content of a work, was an identical twin to the "action" espoused earlier by the naturalists.

In this sense, it is obvious that behind the critics who rely on this criterion of naturalness there stands the figure of Shiga Naoya. This is because Shiga, recognizing the often violent power of mental and physical desire, remained to the end utterly faithful to his emotions and therefore became the writer who most successfully achieved a sense of absolute reality in the expression of sensibility. He rejected the gloomy view of instinct that characterized the naturalists and thereby reached a solution to the problem of the "naturalness" of human nature that had confronted writers since Shōyō; he was less a writer of naturalism than of naturalness-ism. He believed that remaining candid and faithful to one's emotions was precisely the way to elucidate emotion; just as it was also the way to grasp the value of the object of sensibility and to see through the true identity of others. Shiga did not attempt to write critical essays, nor did he place any faith in literary critics, yet there is no other writer who evidenced more clearly the fundamental attitude that critics ought to have taken up, nor any who put into practice more fully the normative realism that was characteristic of the expression of sensibility. No matter how much later critics vented their dissatisfaction over the self-centered nature of the I-novel, as long as their fundamental attitude remained unchanged it was impossible for them to uproot the normative authority Shiga enjoyed as the most complete realization of the ideals that characterized modern literature in Japan. What's more, in the end the critics themselves were forced to limit their own practice to a kind of empiricism that sought in the author's real life models for the objects of sensibility that composed the protagonist's mental state. This method of criticism was a priori powerless in the face of the literary work, yet, because everyone has a certain degree of understanding with regard to everyday life, it was possible for these critics to whitewash their powerlessness through criticism that feigned a "knowing" attitude. Moreover, by contrasting the work with the empirical facts they had uncovered regarding the author's real life, they were able to make various statements regarding it even if such statements were grounded in such uninspiring notions as "authorial license" or an "authorial blind spot." The generation of literary critics who attempted to create and produce postwar literature, of course, attempted to overcome this method, but the period in which they raised their doubts about postwar literature was also a period that saw a revival of this form of literary criticism. Once again empirical studies into the real lives of authors flourished, as did the critics who relied on them.

Be that as it may, as Futabatei had already pointed out, one's emotional self as it "exists in itself" must be lived out straightforwardly and sincerely. Yet in addition to that it must also exist as an object "for itself." First of all, one must honestly and openly bring one's emotions into view. But if one then thoroughly probes the situation that has compelled one to have the emotions thus objectified one realizes that the cause of them does not lie solely with the object of sensibility that lies before one's eyes; one becomes able to perceive the society and its modes that caused the object to take this phenomenal shape, a shape that determined the emotional response one could have toward it. At this point, one begins to see how society should be changed and to grasp the form of revolutionary process that seems necessary and inevitable to one's self. It was with this idea in mind that Nakano Shigeharu (1902–79) approached proletarian literature. But the proletarian literature movement as a whole could not bring this brilliant idea to life. Instead, it presumed that sociopolitical knowledge had first to be established and only then could a class-conscious, revolutionary worldview be bestowed on the workers' emotional selves with regard to the evil capitalists and the agents who controlled them. This mode of expression of emotion was nothing but an inadvertent recycling of the naturalism that had produced Shiga-like norms, so it could give rise only to expressions of haughty and narrow-minded emotions of aggression and bald-faced self-justification for the words and deeds that arose from such emotions. It was unable to carry out Nakano Shigeharu's method, one of breaking through narrow-mindedness and opening up onto the realm of the social and political by negating the very emotions one had expressed affirmatively. As a result, it was unable to develop into a movement that lived out the internal necessity of the individual author.

In order to cover this flaw and incorporate the desired class and revolutionary feelings into literary works, the writers themselves became party members. But this resulted only in the death of everyday sensibility as evidenced in the following passage from *Life of a Party Activist* (*Tō seikatsusha*; 1933) by Kobayashi Takiji (1903–33): "My mundane life as an individual existed no longer. Now even the seasons existed for me only as one aspect of party life. Things such as flower viewing, blue skies, and rain could not be thought of as independent things."[4] In *The Cannery Boat* (*Kanikōsen*; 1929), Kobayashi distinguished himself as a great author by successfully giving expression to the violent passions that derived from the (self-)knowledge arising out of the fishermen's bodily existence. But he regarded this passion as something "naturally" produced by class. He attempted to develop it into a mode of expression that would serve as the rigid norm for revolutionary emotion. Ultimately he had no choice but to transform himself into a normative model for the revolutionary human being, which in turn resulted in the death of sensibility. His belief that emotion constitutes the natural in human nature was problematic from the start.

As the proletarian literature movement collapsed, once again a school of critics emerged that called for the restoration of human nature. What they meant by human nature was a group of concepts selectively chosen in order to affirm emotion and desire as the essence of human existence, in which, of course, a tendency toward normative standardization already existed. If, in spite of this, one is deceived by the external appearance of their being human nature, and if one is dragged along unself-reflectively by this already sketched-in tendency, the only possible result is the rise of a new set of institutional and political norms. This explains the appearance of the Japan Romantic School (Nippon Romanha), which succeeded in overlaying this "natural" external appearance of emotions with an additional set of norms, norms of an ethnic and national character. What awaited the people who supported this and attempted to adopt these norms, needless to say, was the death of the human being. This same process has been repeated many times. Even now there are many writers and critics who are blithely convinced that emotions are the most natural part of human nature. It behooves us to listen with skepticism to their statements whether they are linked to the political Left or Right or even when they are politically neutral.

4. Kobayashi Takiji, *Tō seikatsusha* (Tokyo: Shinkō Shuppansha, 1946), 220.

As the reader may be aware by now, I am not trying to write a conventional author study (*sakkaron*) in the ordinary sense of the term. Instead, I am tracing the work of Ōoka Shōhei (1909–88) in order to reconsider fundamentally, just as he did, the theoretical problems I have been discussing.

Of course, Ōoka did not begin writing fiction for the purpose of launching a comprehensive critique of the history of the modern Japanese novel. For example, the first chapter, "Tsukamaru made," of his *Taken Captive: A Japanese POW's Story* (*Furyoki*, 1952), begins as follows.[5]

> On January 25, 1945, I was captured by American forces in the mountains of southern Mindoro in the Philippines. The island of Mindoro, situated to the southwest of Luzon, is about half the size of our Shikoku. It had no military facilities to speak of, and the forces deployed there comprised but two companies of infantry nominally occupying and patrolling six strategic points along the coastline.[6]

This is a startling opening—at least in terms of its disturbing subject matter—yet the narrative voice in fact adopts a calm, matter-of-fact reportage (documentary) style. "Tsukamaru made" was written at a time when it was still common for soldiers to feel shame and guilt about having been captured; therefore, Ōoka was particularly concerned neither to fall into self-denigration nor to overcompensate by becoming aggressively defensive about his past. Nor, of course, could he adopt a hyperbolic tone. In this way his self-discipline gives rise to an impression of objectivity. Writers of I-novels, through sustained practice, had already developed a way of writing that adopted a stance of detached observation toward the self; this work was written out of a resolve to grasp the real situation in an even more prosaic fashion, in other words, to cognize it as lucidly as possible.

The intended recipients of this report were all those who until August 15, 1945, were trapped under the conditions of war whether at the front or behind the lines, in other words, a large number of fellow Japanese. The content of the report consists of a detailed account of how a middle-aged

5. In April and May of 1946, Ōoka wrote "Furyoki," which was later retitled "Tsukamaru made." A collection of thirteen reminiscences, it was published in book form in 1952 under the title *Furyoki*.
6. Ōoka Shōhei, *Taken Captive: A Japanese POW's Story*, translated by Wayne P. Lammers (New York: Wiley, 1996), 1. Further quotations from this translation are cited parenthetically as *TC*.

recruit became a prisoner of war (POW). Just as those behind the front lines faced the daily threat of aerial bombardment, those sent to relatively quiet or inactive battle zones experienced war in their own way. In each battle zone, of course, fierce combat and aerial bombing produced many casualties. It might appear that those who survived and who, as they scrambled blindly seeking cover, were taken captive by the Americans had a comparatively easy and comfortable life. But those POWs, under constant surveillance, hardly enjoyed a life of ease. They were subjected to enforced idleness, which they had no choice but to live out, just as others elsewhere had no choice but to live out the particular conditions of war that they encountered. Presenting the POWs in this way rendered them into persons as qualified to talk about their war experiences as anyone else.

But what Ōoka introduces first is the situation on Mindoro Island, where his garrison was stationed, as well as the general reaction to the war among "we soldiers." Among the members of the garrison, the first one singled out as an object for individualized description is the squad leader. At the same time, the narrating "I" clearly takes up the position of the protagonist. From this point on, a tone reminiscent of the I-novel comes to dominate.

I do not know to what degree Ōoka himself was conscious of this, but in his works the protagonist's self-understanding tends to grow clearer in tandem with his understanding of some objectified "Other." It is a form of literature diametrically opposite to that which is characterized by interior monologues. Here, the "I" understands the commander in the following terms.

> He had been cast in the mold of the sensitive commander—the kind who accepted the dictates of the war as his highest calling, yet felt a deep sense of personal responsibility when it came to passing those dictates on to his subordinates. As a rule, men like him find it difficult to justify what they ask of their subordinates with anything other than their own deaths. (*TC*, 5)

Naturally, due to the difference in rank, interaction on friendly terms with this commander was not permitted. But rather than saying that the protagonist reached this conclusion by observing his commander's everyday behavior, it seems more accurate to say he reached it through a kind of dialogue carried out wordlessly through everyday behavior and mutual observation. Ōoka's gazing eye bore a form of visual intentionality that pursued as its object the internal self of the Other. This is the defining characteristic of Ōoka's literature, one that clearly distinguishes it from the mode of expression of most modern literature, which attempts to peer into the mind of the Other by way of the self's own interior.

The gazing eye that is produced through this kind of visual intentionality not only observes, contemplates, and absorbs the visible but also intuitively understands even processes that are not readily visible. The following passage illustrates this.

> The young lieutenant had gained his rank by way of the reserve officer training corps. He was only twenty-seven, but he had a taciturn, mournful air that made him look no less than thirty. Never once did he speak of what he had seen or experienced at Nomonhan, but I daresay it showed in the expression of his eyes, of his face. Sometimes I even thought I could smell the stench of his dead comrades still clinging to his person. (*TC*, 4)

Battlefield experiences involuntarily forced on this young commander leave him in a situation where only his own death can make up for what has happened to those around him. The gazing eye of the "I" who intuits this harbors an emotional response of pity toward the commander. In later years, Ōoka would say that he did not especially sympathize with those who died under the conditions he had endured. This surprising statement is perhaps best understood as Ōoka's shame speaking, as it tries to drown out the traces of his own meek and gentle personality. Be that as it may, in this work he interpreted this young and melancholic commander's difficult position thus: "He had been cast in the mold of the sensitive commander—the kind who accepted the dictates of the war as his highest calling, yet felt a deep sense of personal responsibility when it came to passing those dictates on to his subordinates." Likewise, in *The Battle for Leyte* he evidences great sympathy as he retraces the actions of midlevel commanding officers.

This "I" who fixed his gaze on the commander also reveals his own interior self.

> I identified closely with this young CO [commanding officer] and was privately very fond of him. Though in a considerably different sense from him, I, too, lived in the face of my own certain death. . . . I held nothing but contempt for the General Staff who had dragged our country into such a hopeless fight. Yet, since I had not had the courage to take any action toward preventing that fight, I did not feel I could claim any right, at so late a stage, to protest the fate to which they had consigned me. This reasoning, which placed a single powerless citizen on an equal footing

with the massive organization by which an entire nation exercises
its violent power, seemed almost comical to me; and yet, had I
not taken such a view, I could not have kept from laughing at the
absurdity of the predicament in which I found myself, traveling
rapidly toward a meaningless death. . . . Eventually I realized
it was not the nature of the impending death that troubled me;
it was simply living with my own certain extinction so close at
hand. (Adapted from *TC*, 5–6)

This is an almost frighteningly clear resolve and, as the last sentence of the quote discloses, it also demonstrates one way to come to an
understanding of one's life. Moreover, this resolve cannot be simply
dismissed as an abstract concept. The proposition that freedom is nothing
but a necessity that has been recognized and accepted was often a subject of
debate when the Marxist movement was thriving. However, *necessity* in this
case means that of historical processes, and, setting aside the question of
whether this necessity can actually be recognized, is there not another kind
of necessity that we must encounter more personally? In other words, when
we acknowledge the inevitability of our own death, does this recognition
of necessity lead to another kind of freedom? Marxism could provide no
satisfactory answer for such a personal question. Here one can benefit from
the thought of Lev Shestov (1866–1938). Although Kobayashi Hideo (1902–83)
took up Shestov while pursuing a different motive, he used him to discuss
true human freedom in his interpretation of the following poem by Yoshida
Shōin (1830–59).

The summoning voice
I wait for it
Nothing else to wait for
In this world of living

Here the summoning voice is that of the executioner, who will summon the
prisoner to his death. The poem is set, of course, in wartime.

Ōoka Shōhei's resolve belongs to the same lineage as this poem; he was
painfully aware that the summoning voice was sending him to his death.
The political processes that became visible when he consciously recognized
the relation to historical necessity of his inevitable death now appeared
ridiculous. But since he had never attempted to stop these processes in the
past, he was not entitled to protest being sent to his death now. He resolves
that he must die this meaningless death. To expand on the implications
of this, it means that as long as the political realm exists in this world the
potential for unnatural death will always threaten the people who live

within it. This is because human beings are fated to carry the burden of the political. In this sense, dying under the sway of the political is always for the person in question a disastrous accident.

What "I" observed in the young commander's countenance and behavior was the tragic spiritual wound of the catastrophe at Nomonhan, as well as a foreshadowing of the catastrophe still to come. For "I" there is nothing more pitiful than to see the commander smile his "victim's smile." The reason is that this smile not only reveals his status as a victim of fierce fighting in the past but also that he remains a victim in the present moment. His present self, placed in the unhappy position of having to force his powerless subordinates into battle, attempts to tough it out by smiling a victim's smile. Even from the perspective of this officer, who takes the demands of war as if they were a categorical imperative, the combat and death awaiting "I" and his comrades have no great moral value; nor does their sacrifice possess any great strategic value. Even from the perspective of this young officer, who believes in the war, the deaths of the soldiers who bring to his lips the victim's smile were meaningless. What was the point of it all?

One reaches an understanding of some other person; this then becomes the medium through which one comes suddenly to perceive one's own self and its situation. This was Ōoka's characteristic mode of self-awareness, and it appears in passages such as the following from "Tsukamaru made."

> The time came to move out. As I started to fall in after the others, the sergeant turned toward me, though avoiding my eyes, and said, "Ōoka, you think maybe you should stay?" His words made me realize how much of a hindrance I was likely to become to the others, as well as how my present condition must have looked to the eyes of a professional soldier. I replied, "Yes, Sir," and lowered my rifle from my shoulder. (TC, 9)

It also gives birth to the following passage from *Fires on the Plain* (*Nobi*; 1952):[7] "When I said good-by, I noticed that one of the soldiers with whom I exchanged glances had a twisted look on his face. I wondered if the twisted look that I felt on my own face was catching, like a yawn."[8]

---

7. *Nobi* appeared in serialized form in *Buntai* (only the first half, up to the chapter entitled "Salt") in the December 1949 and July 1950 issues, after which time the journal folded. After the author revised it, particularly the opening section, it was serialized in *Tenbō* from January to August 1951. In February 1952, it was published in book form, and in the same year Ōoka was awarded the Yokomitsu Literature Prize.

8. Shōhei Ōoka, *Fires on the Plain*, translated by Ivan Morris (Rutledge, Vt.: Charles Tuttle, 1957), 12.

Some might say that this represents an excess of self-consciousness, but in fact Ōoka's reflective self-understanding manifests a kind of innocent simplicity. Those who are possessed of an overly sensitive self-consciousness are characterized by excessive self-conceit and are easily wounded by even trivial matters. Compared to the cowardly self-justifications and emotional criticism of others that such persons tend to spout, Ōoka's self-reflection seems extraordinarily evenhanded, highly tolerant, and candid. Perhaps this is why his acquaintances are left with the impression that he gives in too easily ("Tsukamaru made"). Of course, the majority of these people are not aware that his self-consciousness is mediated through the mirror of their own behavior and words. In the face of his seemingly naive and simple attitude, they were apt to assume an overbearing and high-handed manner, only too ready to impose their own feelings. In the beginning he tolerates this, exhibiting an objective impartiality, yet all the while he is endeavoring to achieve as full a conscious awareness as possible of the totality of relationships linking the "I" and the Other. Pursuing this to the very limits of his ability to tolerate, he fosters an uncompromising critique. This is my understanding of Ōoka's realism, of his attempt to reach conscious awareness of reality. It was only because he saw through the true character of politics and the military that he was able and willing to resign himself to his fate. Looking at the young commander's victim's smile, Ōoka came to understand the reality of the sacrifice that would be borne together by the commander and the soldiers in his unit.

The story continues.

> Yet, once we had lost our only route of escape and my brothers in arms began dying one after the other, a peculiar transformation came over me; I suddenly believed in the possibility of my survival. Clearly, the deepening shadows of death that surrounded me had triggered an inborn determination to survive. (*TC*, 6)

He then describes Shigeno, the son of a fisheries company executive.

> His father sat on the board of directors of a large fisheries firm, but [Shigeno] dreamed of going to the front to fight as a common solider instead of becoming an agent of the capitalist's greed. . . . Finding the manner in which our forces were conducting the war utterly witless, he declared it would be a pure and simple waste to die on such a battlefield.
>
> His words came as a revelation to me. Suddenly I could see the patent self-deception in proudly insisting to myself that I had

chosen this path of death at my own volition. To die helplessly
in these faraway mountains as the victim of some foolishly conceived war plan was indeed a "pure and simple waste" and nothing more. (6)

It is not clear whether the sudden change in his feelings arose first as a
"reaction of the flesh" that prompted a flash of self-understanding or as a rev-
elation provoked by Shigeno's words; in any event, it is clear that he was not
driven to it out of some natural instinct for self-preservation. Ōoka writes,
"Comrades were dying one after another," but this was not from combat
but rather because most of them were afflicted with malaria. Looking back
on this, "I" comes to the surprising realization that he is still healthy. His
physical body still has no shadow of death hovering about and therefore is
not threatened by the notion of imminent death. It is important to note that
this feeling arose in him before he was infected with malaria.

The 99 percent certainty of death was abruptly swept aside in
my mind. I found myself imagining instead a medley of ways by
which I might actually ensure my survival, and I determined to
pursue them. At the very least I would exercise all due care in everything I did. It seemed senseless to do otherwise. (TC, 6)

His body lives on, refusing to accept this death, death from malaria and
therefore, at least in external appearance, a natural death and yet in reality
a death in battle (political death or, again, fated death). This resisting body
comes to represent to him a new kind of possibility. To resign oneself to
death is to accept a vision of the future as being cut off from all worldly
human relations, but his body rejects such a vision.

Moreover, his comrades' "meaningless" real deaths seem somehow
at odds with the concept of death as he had resolved to accept it. Because
his own death was simply an abstract concept, he was free to attach any
meaning to it, just as he was free to negate it in the abstract. But the deaths
taking place before his eyes lack any meaning whatsoever. Here, confronted
with the reality of death, Shigeno finds his core beliefs shaken, and "I,"
too, is forced to question the meaning of death anew. The precondition that
brings him back to this point is his discovery of the existence of the body, in
particular the body as life harboring future possibilities.

It is not my intention to claim that Ōoka Shōhei had already at this
stage reached a clear awareness of the body as a potential form of (self-)
knowledge. Clearly, though, he had grasped the fact that to exist means to
live in the body and that to be alive in the flesh means to exist in the form of

a life harboring future possibilities. Ōoka was attempting to remain faithful and true to this most fundamental self-understanding of human existence.

To reiterate, Ōoka's self (*jiga*) is one that has become conscious of itself through the mediation of the Other. Moreover, superimposed on this is a self-understanding bound up with the bodily existence of the self. If this is true, is it not then the case that everyone is leading life in the same way? Indeed, it is true. But prior to this, writers had concluded arbitrarily that the interior constituted the self. The belief that the self consists only of one's mentality, which one peers at as if through a window, became a kind of unshakable idée fixe. A second presumption, one supplementary to the first belief, also led to this view: the belief that human beings are simply a part of nature. Taking this consciousness as their implicit premise, many people mistakenly believed that they had adequately accounted for the significance of the body in human existence. What emerged was an attempt to understand psychology from the perspective of the presumed "naturalness" of human existence, what I touched on in the beginning of this chapter.

Indeed, human beings are a part of nature. But we must realize that within nature they occupy the position of the most fully "humanized" nature. If one pays close heed to this, one can no longer claim that the body is the most natural part of the human, nor that human mentality is the interiority that arises when the body is rendered human. Our perceptions and sensibilities clearly manifest in their active operations the fact that they are already fully humanized faculties. When Shōyō and like-minded writers attempted to describe the naturalness of humanity (*ningen no shizensei*), they ultimately ended up talking about the humanness of humanity (*ningen no ningensei*) and vice versa. What does this mean? In short, that with their faculties of observation—that is, with their own humanized nature—the only human "naturalness" they were able to observe was that which manifested itself in an already humanized form. Perceptions and sensibilities that seem natural are in fact simply well harmonized with the observer's faculties. Of course, perceptions and sensibilities are undoubtedly an important part of the self. But we need to go beyond them. Only when perceptions and sensibilities are understood as being fully humanized, active faculties are we able for the first time to properly understand that the body is in fact a form of the self that includes among its functions a kind of embodied (self-) knowledge. Only then can we overcome the "narrow-minded" version of the self-as-interiority that has hitherto predominated. In the moment of crisis in "Tsukamaru made," the scene in which his fellow soldiers are dying one after another, Ōoka Shōhei provided a first glimpse of this possibility.

———

In fact, Ōoka Shōhei would face an even greater crisis, to wit, as the American military advanced, his ill equipped squadron fell into full-scale retreat, and he was left behind in a debilitated state, suffering from malaria with barely "enough strength to walk to the latrine" (TC, 9). And that was not all. As we have seen, for Ōoka, personal experience of self (in terms of self-awareness) was something accumulated only when the self is with others. For him to be thrown into a battlefield alone like this meant being thrown into a space where experience and consciousness lost all certainty. It meant trying to sustain the self through the self's own powers, lost in a situation in which there was no external witness present. It is this crisis that causes the turn to a more strained form of description at this point in "Tsukamaru made."

Another distinct characteristic that stands out in this work is Ōoka's attempt to render conscious the specifically retrospective nature of "Tsukamaru made." The typical modern Japanese novel is grounded in interior monologues by the fictional characters, so it gave birth as a matter of necessity to the I-novel, a form characterized by an absence of the Other in the most fundamental sense. A common characteristic of the I-novel was that the author re-created a past moment of his own interior through recollection. But because authors tended rather blindly to attribute to their past selves insights that they had only acquired after the fact, their protagonists inevitably appeared as the possessors of selves deformed by an excessive degree of self-consciousness. The authors themselves remained largely unaware that they were arbitrarily adding wrinkles of complexity to their remembered self-portraits. As a result, they were able to create only absurd characters, figures possessed of apparent omniscience with regard to their own selves yet nonetheless prone to repeatedly committing foolish blunders. Categorizing "Tsukamaru made" as a work of recollection literature (kaisō bungaku) means that it shared common characteristics with the I-novel. With its contents, too, only that which is essential and necessary to the "I" are narrated. This likewise demonstrates that it does not stand outside of the common characteristics that define the conventional modern Japanese novel. But, unlike other writers, Ōoka clearly realized that this was a literature of recollection (sōki no bungaku), and precisely for that reason he labored to reproduce as faithfully as possible the experiences that remained in his memory. This is what gave birth to the new and distinct characteristic that distinguishes this work.

The events narrated in this work represent the most accurate expression possible of the experiences of that past time. But the choice of events to be narrated and their relative importance are determined in the present moment according to the interests of the author's past-oriented visual intentionality.

It might be helpful to retrace the events depicted in the order in which they objectively occurred at the time: the incidents already discussed, the period subsequently spent wandering around with unendurable thirst, the meeting with an American GI, the suicide attempt, the time he falls unconscious, his being captured by American soldiers, and so on.

Among this string of incidents, the experience of failing to shoot the American GI is singled out for extended description. From the string of events as they objectively occurred, it is difficult to discover any necessity for making this experience in particular into the thematic center. "I" has collapsed at the edge of a forest, next to a grassy field.

> The GI was a tall youth of about twenty, his cheeks red beneath the deep-set steel helmet covering his head. Standing erect and holding his rifle at an angle before him, he advanced toward me with the gentle stride of someone on a pleasure outing in the mountains. . . . My breath caught in my throat. I, too, was a soldier. . . . No matter how drained I might be in strength, I had seen him first, and he was standing at full height completely in the open: I could not miss. My right hand moved instinctively to release the safety on my rifle.
>
> When the GI had traversed approximately half the distance between us, a sudden burst of machine-gun fire broke out at the stronghold.
>
> His head spun around. . . . His stride quickly gained speed, and soon he had exited my field of vision.
>
> I heaved a sigh of relief. "Well, well," I said with a wry smile. "A mother somewhere in America should be thanking me right now." (TC, 17)

Considered in terms of the incident's objective appearance, this is all that happened. If Ōoka had been a writer who wanted to emphasize the human condition as it exists under extreme circumstances, he would have placed the weight of his narrative on such events as the threat of attack by American military bombardment, the squad leaders' selfishness in abandoning diseased or wounded soldiers, or the physical or psychological bitterness of wandering in the mountains that eventually drove the protagonist to attempt suicide. Likewise, if he had been a person who wallowed in self-introspection, in depicting this incident so trivial it hardly deserves the name "incident," he would likely have added a note of self-ridicule, something along the following lines: *Although I released the safety of my rifle, my fingers stiffened out of nervousness, and I did not shoot because the American*

GI was oblivious to the danger. I also began to think of the fellow American soldiers who were no doubt somewhere near at hand, and weakness and terror gripped me. The type of person, one who blithely confuses a past experience with the interpretations of it that arose subsequently, would probably append some sort of explanation for his actions. For example, perhaps he did not shoot the young soldier because the minute he realized the other was a twenty year old he was paralyzed by paternal solicitude.

However, Ōoka chose not to write this in the conventional manner (or at least in what I take to be the conventional manner). It was out of a different motive that he grasped this scene, using an unconventional technique. In "Tsukamaru made" he states, "Since then I have often reflected on this encounter, and the decision that preceded it," and continues, "I am surprised, first of all, by my own humanity" (*TC*, 17–18). Of course, he did not bring this up to emphasize his own humanism. If he wanted to convey humanism, he could have done so by nonchalantly inserting appropriate hints in the depiction of the scene in question, topping it all off with something like, *in the end, I could not bring myself to shoot the young American GI who stood so exposed before me.* What Ōoka does narrate, instead, is a detailed examination of the scene as it remained in his memory. He refuses to add an explanatory reason, refraining from saying, for example, *my love for my fellow man kept me from shooting.* Instead, he concludes that it was a "personal reason" that stopped him: "Though not from love for all humanity, might I have held my fire out of love for the young soldier as an individual?" (20). This "personal reason" seems similar to saying, "I secretly loved this young officer"; in both cases, he is attracted to the youthfulness of the Other. Moreover, after he explains that he could not shoot for this personal reason, he cautions himself that this is apt to lapse into manufactured self-glorification. This is, after all, a battlefield, and the person who is completely exposed before him is an enemy soldier. Out of surprise, he cannot but question his own reaction; under those conditions, what could it possibly mean that he felt an attraction to the youthfulness of the soldier, an emotional reaction that prevented him from shooting? When Ōoka transforms this questioning into his central theme, he has already left behind the perspective that naively believes in the naturalness (i.e., the normativity) of human emotions.

I believe this phrase is the key: "Since then I have often reflected on this encounter, and the decision that preceded it" (*TC*, 17). Judging from his debilitated condition at the time, the elaborate self-reflection that follows could not have occurred in the immediate aftermath, as the American GI walked away. The frequently repeated acts of self-reflection began later, after he became a POW. There is a similar phrase in the chapter "Rainy

Tacloban," too, one that acts as a prelude to the narration of a crucial self-reflection (the reason for which will be discussed below):

> At night I lay alone within my own little mosquito net, but I seldom found myself bored with this nocturnal solitude. Since being called up for service, I had spent countless hours in forced idleness, after lights out or when standing watch, and I had grown quite accustomed to passing such solitary hours in contemplation and thought. In all my life, I had never been so contemplative as in the military.
>
> Now I found myself returning repeatedly to the question of what had really kept me from shooting that young GI in the mountain meadow. No matter how many times I replayed the scene in my head, I could not determine whether my actions through the entire encounter remained consistent with my decision beforehand to refrain from shooting. In fact, in spite of the consensus that will is the most basic element of human consciousness, each new effort at introspection seemed only to obscure further the shades of my intentions. (62)

Each of his fellow prisoners naturally has his own "precapture" story. Among them are some who are eager to relate their personal experiences, and, while he may not have believed their stories entirely, the fact that Ōoka went out of his way to lend them his ear is well demonstrated by the contents of the first chapter of *Taken Captive*. In particular, when it comes to the precapture stories of his fellow prisoners from Mindoro, he actively seeks them out. His self-reflection occurs in solitude, and perhaps he is not able to talk about it with his fellow prisoners; nonetheless, it is clearly in an environment in which he is living out a common interest shared with his fellow prisoners that he begins to engage in repeated acts of self-reflection.

Prior to his capture, Ōoka experienced his own solitary wandering, which he described in "Tsukamaru made." But his self-introspection and the testimony of his fellow soldiers about their experiences, a testimony that serves as a kind of critique, take place simultaneously. This tendency to simultaneously carry out introspection and seek the critical perspective of others is also apparent in the fact that Ōoka wrote *Fires on the Plain* and *Taken Captive* simultaneously. And it goes without saying that he achieved a synthesis of the two tendencies in *The Battle for Leyte*. I plan to discuss at greater length elsewhere the problematic of introspection and the possibilities for external critique that the presence of the others provides.[9] Note here that

---

9. These issues are addressed in chapters 5 and 6 of *Koga no shugōsei: Ōoka Shōhei ron*, the volume from which this chapter is taken.

from Ōoka's perspective, as he simultaneously pursues both introspection and external critique, the various stories he hears about experiences his fellow soldiers had before capture all can be testified to by only a single witness, the person who tells the story. In the stories of his fellow POWs' experiences, he frequently finds points of dubious veracity. What he gained from prisoner camp life is the understanding that—and this serves to summarize *Taken Captive* as well—human existence is characterized by the struggle to become in reality what we wish we were. Therefore, in order to relieve the boredom of their lives as prisoners they tell their stories. But the essential nature of these stories is not a desire to convey the truth accurately; rather, the stories are shaped by a need that arises in the moment of their telling: a concern for how they will be perceived by the listener. Many of the prisoners, in an effort to become more like their ideal self-images, narrate their precapture experiences in a manner they hope will produce in their listeners an image of bravery or, again, tragic suffering. In the majority of their stories, the person telling the story is the only witness to the events described. Even if those speakers have no intention of distorting their experiences, they still tend to stress only those incidents that are well suited to the tone of story they want to tell. Listening to their stories, Ōoka must have become increasingly aware of the decisive impact of the manner or technique through which a past experience was conveyed. It was precisely by pursuing this problematic, it seems, that he came to discover an effective means of giving life to the narratives of those who had personal experiences of war. By sharing a common interest with them, Ōoka was able to obtain their cooperation.

Immediately after the American GI moved away, "I smugly congratulated myself for the 'good deed' of having spared him" (*TC*, 21). Sparing him, he reflects then, was the result of the determination he had made while lying collapsed in the grass, the resolve that he would not shoot if an American solider were to appear before him. This is Ōoka's earliest act of self-interpretation. In "Rainy Tacloban," too, we find a similar reference to a "sudden resurgence of my boyhood humanism" to which he had at first attributed this reaction (64). Whether or not he actually spoke them aloud at that moment, he uses the word *humanism* (*jinruiai*) to describe the resolve made in advance while he uses the word *spare* (*tasuketa*) to explain after the fact his act of not shooting. It would be in no way unusual if he had ended up accepting this explanation or had persisted in accepting it during his stay at the POW hospital. What is important to note here is the level at which this explanation arises. It represents the inadvertent mixing of subsequent reflections into what a teller intends as a depiction of the event itself.

Yet Ōoka returns to this scene repeatedly. This is because the real reason for his not shooting can only be found in those several seconds when the American GI was fully exposed before "I." The only possible way to return to that past scene is to objectify and thereby pursue the image of it that remains in present-day memory. In this, sense perception is of absolute importance. Only the sense perceptions of that past moment can reveal the real reasons for his not shooting. That is to say, only his eyes and ears know the real reason. This is because his eyes and ears produced whatever it was that kept him from shooting. His eyes see the American GI's rosy cheeks, as well as a kind of harshness and melancholic expression around his eyes. His ears hear his voice: "Though the words he shouted escaped me, his voice was a clear tenor, matching his youthful countenance, and when he finished speaking he pinched the corners of his mouth in the manner of a child. Then, lowering his head, he turned his gaze farther down the other side of the canyon as though surveying the path his buddies would take" (*TC*, 20). At the moment he sees and hears these things, he feels a movement: "The movement of my heart upon seeing the GI's extreme youth resembled feelings I had experienced from time to time, since becoming a father, at the sight of young children or of nearly grown children who still carried an air of adolescent innocence" (20).

He writes, "My first reaction when I saw the GI standing tall and fully exposed was one of apprehension. . . . I recall how astonished I was at his lack of caution" (*TC*, 19). For whom did he feel this apprehension? It is clear from the way in which the expression is constructed that it was not for "I" alone. For the GI, "I" is a dangerous enemy that lies in ambush. This is how "I" grasps the situation, and he even places himself in the position of the GI and feels apprehension over his obliviousness to the danger at hand. Of course, if the GI was not a dangerous enemy to the "I" there would from the start be no need for such fear. In this light, we can say that the apprehension felt here is for both of their sakes. His gaze simultaneously comprehends both the position of the GI in relation to "I" and the position of "I" in relation to the GI. And from this grasp of the situation, he realizes the danger to both that lies within it. As the GI approaches closer, the sense of apprehension intensifies. The GI would shoot if he discovered "I" as his enemy, but even before that could happen the "I" would have to carry out his role as an enemy. But at the last possible moment "I" stops and finds himself moved by the GI's youth. "I" feels a sense of affection toward the youthfulness of the GI. What this means is that even in this moment "I" places himself in the position of the GI and thereby feels the way the GI cherishes his own youthfulness. Even in this extremely dangerous and tension-filled situation, the gaze of "I" lives out through visual intentionality the position of the Other, and even in the present moment of the narration it continues to live out the emotional traces of that moment that remain in the remembered image of it. It is in this sense that I earlier stated that the eye and the ear were what really stopped him from shooting and therefore they alone knew the truth about it.

One conclusion that Ōoka arrived at seems, at least from the perspective of common sense, quite odd: that an "omnipresence of paternal affection" prohibited "I" from shooting the young American GI that appeared before his eyes. In truth, in his memories from the time of the incident there is not the slightest feeling of "paternal affection," but in spite of this "I" states, "I am drawn to the hypothesis that my feelings as a father forbade me to shoot, even though I cannot remember consciously feeling anything of the kind at the time. Both the image of youthfulness preserved in my memory and the nature of the thought that came to mind immediately after the soldier disappeared seem to bear this hypothesis out" (TC, 20–21). According to common sense, emotions or feelings, for better or worse, are for the person who has them the clearest and most trustworthy form of inner experience. For that reason, even in cases in which external conditions are gradually forgotten, this form of internal experience should remain within memory. Or at least it remains in memory longer than any other form. Precisely due to this fact, when we try to explain the ultimate cause of our own actions to someone (including cases in which we try to explain them to ourselves), it is only natural that we probe our psyches for internal corroboration. While this may be the case, don't we need to distinguish between the emotions the person in question originally experienced at some past moment and any emotions that he subsequently hypothesizes as having been logically necessary at that time even though they lack internal corroboration?

In asking this question, I am treating common sense almost as if it were a form of psychoanalysis. But I don't believe that Ōoka's self-analysis includes any substitutions of this sort, whether made purposefully or unconsciously. My understanding is that what Ōoka called paternal affection referred precisely to the workings of the eye that I described earlier. Even if Ōoka's explanation seems somewhat forced, most likely this is due to the apprehension and fear that arises in this "I" from the contradictions and antagonisms that arise as his eye visually intends the standpoints of both the Other and the self. Or, in cases in which these two positions exist in a more harmonious relationship, it would arise from the sense of symbiosis felt with the Other. The emotions that we experience include within them the standpoints of others that we have visually intended; hence, they can be said to be something produced jointly by ourselves and others. And yet the experience of emotion can only be understood individually. Because of this limitation, the tendency has arisen to grasp emotions solely as the inner experience of isolated individuals and to understand them only in terms of their individualized aspects. Ōoka, too, was dragged along by this tendency to a certain degree. But when he tries to discover psychologistically his (remembered) emotion, in the end it remains elusive. Even then he is not able to abandon the notion of trying to explain emotions as if they were purely psychological entities, and so he is forced into the absurdity of theorizing the existence of hypothetical emotions.

Still, something like paternal affection is clearly at work in this scene. Of course, it did not exist in the form of a psychological reality at the time of the incident. But it certainly is present within the image of the incident extracted through the process of self-analysis. Ōoka modifies *paternal affection* with the adjective *omnipresent*. The eye, it goes without saying, is an individualized faculty, yet at the same time it is capable of functioning in an omnipresent mode by stepping away from its individuated position and, having grasped the totality of the situation in which it finds itself, taking up the position of the Other. When he discovered the existence of this visual intentionality of the eye within the mental image, Ōoka demolished the understanding of perception and sensibility that had held sway since Shōyō. Moreover, as he further pursued his inquiries he came to understand that when one seeks out the psychological reasons behind a given action in the end the supposed unity and coherence of individual psychology vanishes. With this realization, Ōoka completely dismantled the concept of the interior self that had dominated modern Japanese literature.

Even before this, of course, the problems of the absence of interior motivation, of psychological derangement, and of the dissolution of the self had been discussed in premonitionary form among writers. However, this did not necessarily undermine their existing sense of identity as human beings. It only meant that the abstract concept of the interior self that held sway in modern literature had started to unravel at an abstract, conceptual level. Because this concept was prone to falling into chaos the minute it was exposed to prolonged consideration, it summoned up any number of literary experiments characterized by chaotic forms of expression, yet it was never able to call into question the self-identity of the author. Or again we might put it this way: the author's sense of self-identity was never undermined, yet because he was unable to raise the question of why his self was maintained as his self across time and because he lacked any cognitive method of creating new forms of self-understanding he was increasingly trapped by the confusion internal to this concept. Literature of this kind, in terms of literary history, is typically called contemporary literature (*gendai bungaku*). In this sense, Ōoka as a writer evidences a brilliant critique of contemporary literature, too. Confronted with the reality of the lack of any consistency or unity in human psychology, he was able to overcome this crisis without lapsing into mental confusion or resorting to deliberately chaotic forms of expression. This was because he was able to grasp the mode of existence of an embodied self, one that was open to the Other via its visual intentionality, what he called the working of a paternal affection. Only a self that exists in this manner possesses a basis for constructing a true human identity.

———

It seems, however, that paternal affection as an explanation was not entirely satisfactory, even for Ōoka himself. In "Rainy Tacloban" he had introduced another concept: "the voice of God" (*TC*, 62). To speak of the order in which these ideas were conceived, first the concept of the voice of God came to mind, but he rejected it. It was then that he reached paternal affection as his explanation, but it is clear from *Fires on the Plain* that Ōoka had not completely abandoned this problem of the voice of God. Human beings could not exist without searching for a spiritual object, one that exceeded the limits of sensible perception. Because Ōoka was unable to leave this important issue unresolved, I, too, cannot afford to ignore it.

In "Rainy Tacloban" he discusses one further instance of "my present thinking about the encounter" (*TC*, 65). The word *present* in this case refers to moment in which "Rainy Tacloban" is being written, that is, after "Tsukamaru made" had been published. Ōoka shows here that he understands that the causes that led to the scene in which two soldiers meet on a lonely Philippine mountain are fundamentally related to political processes, processes that decisively control both the American GI and "I." He concludes with the words, "The man I faced at that moment was not my enemy. The enemy existed, and still exists, in another quarter" (65). *The Battle for Leyte* represents Ōoka's subsequent pursuit of this insight.

NOTE

This essay was originally published as chapter 3 of Kamei Hideo, *Koga no shūgōsei: Ōoka Shōhei ron* (The Collectivity of the Individual: On Ōoka Shōhei) (Tokyo: Kōdansha, 1977).

CHAPTER	The Narrative Apparatus of Modern
3	Literature: The Shifting "Standpoint"
	of Early Meiji Writers

Hirata Yumi

Translated by Tess M. Orth

1

If we look at the evolution of Japanese literature from the early modern to the modern novel, we can view it as a process centered on the establishment, development, and diversification of the narrator (*jojutsusha*) as the subject of expression. As I will attempt to verify, this process can be understood using the following hypothetical formula.

(Author = Storyteller) $\Rightarrow$ (Author $\cong$ Narrator 1) $\Rightarrow$ (Author $\neq$ Narrator 2)

Novels of the latter part of the early modern period may be split into two extremes: the *yomihon*, as part of the genealogy of "narrative literature"; and its opposite, the *kokkeibon/ninjōbon*, as a form of "drama." In either case, however, the narrator is not yet distinct from the author and exists only as a speaker outside the story world.

The transformation from the narrator of the early modern novel, in which the storyteller (*katarite*) is inseparable from the author, to that of the modern novel begins with the differentiation of a narrator who records his circumstances from within the world of the text from the author who controls the story world from outside the text. Beginning with *Tōsei shosei katagi* (The Character of Present-Day Students, 1885–86), this transformation is visible in many novels referred to as "Meiji *gesaku*," novels that appeared from the late Meiji 10s to the early Meiji 20s.[1] In many cases, a narrator within the story world will claim to be the author and provide commentary and criticism

---

1. Tsubouchi Shōyō (1859–1935), *Tōsei shosei katagi*, in *Meiji bungaku zenshū* (hereafter *MBZ*), 99 vols. (Tokyo: Chikuma Shobō, 1965–83), 16:59–163. All notes are the translator's except where noted.

on events and characters as though he were a distinct person (Narrator 1 in the hypothetical formula). The other characters cannot see this narrator, nor does the narrator converse with them. To the reader, however, the narrator's existence is clear. This narrator even frequently speaks directly to the reader. Insofar as this type of narrator takes the form of a distinct person acting as the alter ego of the author, readers cannot project themselves onto this narrator, making it impossible for them to place themselves within the world lived by the characters in the work or to enjoy a pseudo-personal experience within the textual world.

Subsequently, hypothetical Narrator 1 loses the ability to make such comments and gives way to Narrator 2. Narrator 2 does not exist in the story world as the author's alter ego and is nothing more than a device that serves the function of narrative perspective. At this stage, it becomes possible for the narrative perspective to overlap with that of the characters so that the narration is conducted through the perceptions of those characters. It thereby allows readers to identify their own perspectives with that of the narrative device, enabling them to take up the perceptions and experiences of the characters in the work as if they were their own. In addition, the author can now portray a character objectively by assuming a perspective separate from him (the character). The author can even reveal—via unconscious levels of consciousness rather than direct commentary by the narrator—the psychological state of the character, a state of which the character might not be aware.

Looking at modern literature in terms of this separation of author from narrator, as well as of the change in the nature of the narrator itself, we can no doubt say that Futabatei Shimei (1864–1909) was in the vanguard. However, we can also identify this transformation in novels by Shōyō or Saganoya Omuro (1863–1947), which are often lumped together as mere predecessors to Futabatei's *Ukigumo* (Drifting Clouds, 1887–89). We also see this process of transformation in novels by members of groups such as the Ken'yūsha, led by Ozaki Kōyō (1867–1903), as well as by other known and unknown writers. The formation of modern literature should be considered in its entirety, including these types of works.

But this transformation of the narrator should not be grasped as an evolutionary process. A writer, well versed in the functions of perspective as a narrative device, holds in his or her grasp a wide variety of possible narrators from which to choose. A writer can also utilize as a narrator a storyteller such as that of *setsuwa* literature or again is free to construct multiple narrators within the same novel. For example, the author may use an omnipotent narrator like the storyteller found in *yomihon* to give the reader an unimpeded perspective on the textual world or may use a limited narrator like that of a detective in a mystery novel to conceal actual events from the reader's eyes. An author can also choose to disrupt the flow of time in the text by using a narrator who frequently intervenes to make comments about the characters and events in the work or, on the other hand, may use an inorganic narrator who does nothing more than record events. It is safe to say that the great variety of literary texts since the beginning of the modern period has been made possible by the increased variety of narrative devices available.

2

No clear boundary exists between author and narrator in early modern novels whether in the text or in the consciousness of author and reader. The narrator/author often appears within the textual world, inserting various comments addressed directly to the reader.

In design and literary style, we see that *yomihon* inherited the tradition of "narrative literature" so that in it the author is the source of the story. In other words, the author functions as a storyteller who speaks directly to the reader. This storyteller/author can manipulate the characters as he or she wishes and adopts a stance of omniscience with regard to their fates. Yamaguchi Takeshi (1884–1932) discussed *yomihon* authors who used the Chinese novel as a model and freely manipulated the threads of cause and effect. Yamaguchi argues that the author in them "did not assume the stance of one who holds up a clear, brilliant mirror to Nature, but adopted the pose as Old Man Creator of the small world appearing on the pages of his work."[2]

The storyteller engages the reader, acting as god of the textual world and holding all the characters in the palm of his or her hand. The words exchanged between characters are conveyed to the reader only after passing through the storyteller. As a result, stylistically their language is far removed from colloquial speech and is shaped through the same elegant style used in passages of narrative discourse attributed to the narrator's voice (*ji no bun*). Hence, it is not the characters' voices that the reader hears but the storyteller's. In other words, their speech is formally subordinated to the storyteller's so that it forms something like an indirect quotation woven into the passages of narrative description.

In this kind of text the storyteller is free to silence the voices of the characters and can digress from the story line at will. He or she can insert

---

2. Yamaguchi Takeshi, "Yomihon ni tsuite" (Regarding *Yomihon*, 1927), in *Yamaguchi Takeshi chosakushū*, 6 vols. (Tokyo: Chūō Kōronsha, 1972), 2:159. [Hirata note]

commentary, moral instruction, and even unrelated idle talk. In *Nansō Satomi hakkenden* (Biographies of Eight Dogs, 1814–41), after telling the story of Keno, who enacts revenge, and of Shūsuke and Kobungo, who come to his assistance, the author inserts remarks arising from a separate dimension, one completely outside the story world: "Everyday events occur in a fleeting moment, but when I write about them I use adjectives. I use emphasis," and so on. After going to great lengths with this type of metatextual intervention, the author returns to the story line, simply saying, "But to return to the subject, meanwhile, Nitayama Shingo . . ."[3]

In addition to such unconstrained deviations from the story world, we also find set phrases such as "Let's set aside this idle talk" or "Let's set that aside," by means of which the author arbitrarily returns to the story world. At these points, the existence of an author who controls the textual world is clearly visible. In other words, in *yomihon* it is the author who directly engages the reader. The author as storyteller (= narrator) relegates the other characters in the work to stand in his or her shadow. It is only through the mediation of this storyteller that the reader is able to peek into the story world.

Kokkeibon and *ninjōbon* are located at the opposite pole. In *yomihon*, the speaking subject position is occupied by the author's voice as it occurs in passages of narrative description. In contrast, in *kokkeibon* and *ninjōbon* the dialogue exchanged between characters is key. Passages of narrative description in *kokkeibon* and *ninjōbon* typically follow passages of spoken dialogue and consist of simple stage directions that describe the actions and circumstances of the speaker, transcribed in a smaller font in the so-called *togaki* style. These stage directions provide only objective descriptions of the situations of the characters while the narrator does not appear. The author aims at faithful reproduction of the dialogue between the characters and of the conditions that give rise to it. Such texts do not utilize a narrator who utters subjective commentary or didactic speech, as are found in *yomihon*.

| Tō: | Oh, the robe—thank you, thank you. Ahh, you came at just the right time. He whispers something to the maid. She dashes off back to the inn. |
| Chō: | Tō-san, I'm so sorry to have to put you to all this trouble. She fidgets anxiously. From within the bathhouse Sakuragawa peers through the grated window.[4] |

3. Takizawa Bakin (1767–1848), *Nansō Satomi hakkenden* (Tokyo: Kawade Shobō, 1971), 235–44.
4. Tamenaga Shunsui (1790–1843), *Shunshoku umegoyomi* (Colors of Spring: The Plum Calendar), 1832–33. The translation is adapted from that of Alan S. Woodhull in his "Romantic Edo Fiction: A Study of the Ninjōbon and Complete Translation of 'Shunshoku Umegoyomi,'" PhD diss., Stanford University, 1978, 290.

From within the bath. Thump, thump, thump. "Cool it off. Cool it off, huh? It's too hot!"
"Don't make it any cooler! It'll be nothing but cold water!"

Manager: "There's more hot water now. Get the rinse buckets ready."

Boy: "Yes, sir." He leaves with a bucket.

An old man, clearly a busybody, was in the dressing room. Pushing aside with his foot a pail that someone was using to soak a towel, "Look here, you youngsters, get that drain board good and clean. It's dangerous for old people."[5]

These texts are formed strictly from dialogue, the actions and circumstances that accompany dialogue, and physical elements such as the sounds that exist in the textual world. Psychological aspects—interventions by the narrator, for example, describing characters' feelings—are given little weight.[6]

In short, the reader is confronted directly by the story world in which the characters live. As a general rule, the author does not make interjections or otherwise appear within that world. Thus, when this principle is broken the author must clearly indicate that his or her remark is of a dimension separate from the textual world. These breaks are typically marked by the smaller font used in the two-line *togaki* style or by explicit stage directions such as "note from the author," "prologue," or other bracketed forms of expression.

Tome: "Graybeard. Hey!" Here, because he is mimicking the Confucianist who appeared in the previous volume, Tome is telling an inside joke not understood by outsiders.[7]

Tanjirō: "I won't have you being seduced by Tō-san!"

Yonehachi: "You needn't worry—I'm not like you!" Saying this, she regretfully makes her departure.

5. Shikitei Sanba (1776–1822), *Ukiyoburo* (Bath of the Floating World), 1809–13. The translation is adapted from that of Robert W. Leutner in his *Shikitei Sanba and the Comic Tradition in Edo Fiction* (Cambridge: Harvard University Press, 1985), 162.
6. They are even given little weight in *ninjōbon*. See, for example, *Shunshoku Umegoyomi*, book 4, where the characters' inner thoughts are expressed by such means as indirect speech but the narration has been placed completely above the characters' exchanges. The author intends that those inner thoughts be observed through the characters' behavior and speech. [Hirata note]
7. Shikitei Sanba (1776–1822) and Ryōtei Rijō (1777–1841), *Ukiyodoko: Ryūhatsu shinwa* (Barbershop of the Floating World), 1813–14 (Tokyo: Tenbōsha, 1974), 284.

> The author would like to remark that lover's quarrels are not likely to be solved so simply. . . . What will come of it all?[8]

Old woman: "If so, for sure it's the 5th."

Hane: "Aa."

> Note from the author: Saying "aa" like this, is a woman's response. Of course, this is limited to Edo speech, as will be clear in the following.[9]

In *kokkeibon* and *ninjōbon*, the greater part of the textual world is occupied by the characters themselves while the narrator is nothing more than an observer and transcriber. Any commentary and interruptions made by the author, beyond recording the story world, appear in the margins or are attached as explanatory notes marked as coming from outside the textual world.[10] With regard to the author's perspective vis-à-vis the text, neither *yomihon* nor *ninjōbon* situates its narrators within the story world. The reader never goes beyond receiving the story world in the form of hearsay from the storyteller or taking up the position of an "eavesdropping third party" like a spectator at a theatrical performance.

3

In modern literature, where the separation between author and narrator is relatively distinct, the narrator serves to cover the author's tracks and emerges as a means by which the reader is manipulated. In *yomihon*, where the narrator equals the author, the reader is made aware of everything thanks to the presence of a storyteller who has full knowledge of the textual world. But when the author begins to deliberately manipulate the narrator the reader is deprived of this privileged knowledge of the textual world. In other words, construction of the narrator as a being that possesses only a partial knowledge of events and facts in turn restricts the reader to a position from which he or she can perceive only that portion.

8. Tamenaga Shunsui, *Shunshoku umegoyomi*, translated in Woodhull, "Romantic Edo Fiction," 311–12.

9. Shikitei Sanba, *Ukiyoburo*, translation adapted from Leutner, *Shikitei Sanba and the Comic Tradition in Edo Fiction*, 162.

10. In the middle section of book 4 of *Ukiyoburo*, we find metatextual comments in the margins, including such things as directions to the reader on pronunciation and an advertisement for medicine mentioned in the body of the text. [Hirata note]

In Ishibashi Shian's *Hana Nusubito* (The Flower Thief, 1889), a girl appears who is deep in thought, but the narrator says nothing of the melancholic contents of her ruminations.

> She suffers from many troubles, like a plum blossom buried under snow. I feel as though I want to brush them away, but perhaps the reasons for her sadness are profound and numerous. Even to the author, who is utterly innocent in these matters, she does not speak freely. How frustrating![11]

Here the narrator is not an omniscient, omnipotent, and godlike author who controls the textual world but instead is subordinate to the story world and has restrictions placed on his or her knowledge. A narrator like this, who also restricts the reader's knowledge and teases in order to draw out the reader's interest, is often seen in novels of this period.

With the appearance of such narrators, there was an increasingly clear separation between the author who controls the text and the narrator who is controlled by the text. Kōyō, in his early work *Fūryū kyōningyō* (Elegant Doll of the Capital, 1888–89) begins part 4 of the work as follows.

> [A] Kōyō says: "In the opening line of the preceding issue, describing the summer scenery, I wrote 'Facing east, seated on the printed cotton cushion at the larch desk. . .' But someone wrote to a certain newspaper: 'Wasn't a printed cotton cushion too warm to be suitable for summer?' I am grateful for this kind suggestion and so have immediately altered it to a leather cushion."
>
> Chapter Four: Things That Fall Out of Sleeve Pockets
>
> [B] Here we will resume the tale of the two, which was broken off earlier, so please listen. Niyake Kyōnosuke is a teacher at the Kaika Girl's School—calligraphy—and Tatsumi Nagayo is one of his students.[12]

The Kōyō in passage A, separated from the story world and taking up in actuality the position of an author who reads letters from readers, is free to

---

11. Ishibashi Shian (1867–1927), *Hana Nusubito* (The Flower Thief) (Osaka: Shinshindō, 1895), 3–5. This work originally appeared in the journal *Garakuta bunko* in 1889.
12. Ozaki Kōyō, "Fūryū kyōningyō," in *Meiji no bungaku*, 25 vols. (Tokyo: Chikuma Shobō, 2001–3), 6:36. The opening passage of the original version of the work, published in the magazine *Garakuta bunko*, marked here as passage A, was cut from the modern edition of the text.

make changes in any part of the text. In contrast, the narrator speaking in passage B is constrained by the structure of the text's time and space and adds a word only during pauses in the characters' dialogue. Whenever the characters begin to speak, he must immediately record their dialogue. He is unlike the author who appears in passage A, who is able to enter and alter the text. This difference is clear even from the body of the text. Passage A is indented three spaces from the margin and precedes passage B, which is situated in the body of the text and the textual world from which the narrator speaks.

The intratextual narrator takes up a role that can be designated as a "character alongside the other characters," and, like the other characters, he is controlled by the world of the story. By subordinating the narrator in this way, the author sidesteps the danger of revealing his own existence and his power to control the text such as occurs when the author of a *yomihon* adds remarks from a transcendental position outside the story world. As a result, the author became able to enlarge his position without monopolizing the story world. Preference for this type of textual world probably arose from the *ninjōbon* tradition, in which the reader was confronted not by the author but by the characters themselves. In contrast to the *ninjōbon*, however, the rise of this intratextual narrator led to an expansion of passages of descriptive narrative discourse (*ji no bun*).[13]

Characters that appear in *kokkeibon* are stereotypical stock characters rather than individualized persons, and description is limited to external aspects such as age and attire. In *ninjōbon*, characters appear that manifest relatively unique personal circumstances, but individual personal histories are typically made known to the reader through the said person's spoken confession or via dialogue exchanged between other characters in the work. In *Umegoyomi*, for example, Tanjirō's destitute circumstances are related through Yonehachi's lamentation during a visit to his hiding place. By contrast, protagonists of modern novels tend to have rather complicated backgrounds, and authors struggled to develop a method for indicating those backgrounds to the reader.[14] By means of an intratextual narrator who simply provides this information, authors could avoid the strangeness of intro-

---

13. P. F. Kornicki, *The Reform of Fiction in Meiji Japan* (London: Ithaca, 1982), 85. [Hirata note]

14. For example, consider the remark Ishibashi Shian inserts into *Hana Nusubito*: "In a novel's *kyōgen* sections, whenever there is a perplexingly dull spot, the author as spectator describes the lead actors—but . . . it has been awhile since I have written, so please listen for a bit" (Ishibashi, *Hana Nusubito*, 76). Tsubouchi Shōyō, in fact, even when introducing characters' backgrounds, regularly takes pains to do this by means of passages of dialogue or narrative description. [Hirata note]

ducing characters' backgrounds through unnatural-seeming monologues or drawn-out dialogues that did not sound like actual conversations.

> (Komachida:) "My story differs from your story. Because it's very lengthy, you will probably be bored. But please listen. I will begin with the story of my father's life." Having said this, he continues talking as he draws the teacup near, filled to the brim, and quietly moistens his lips.

>> Note from the author: the story below is what Komachida Sanji told Moriyama. But if I told it in Komachida's words, I am afraid it would be difficult to convey fully the circumstances he depicts. Moreover, I am afraid it might go on too long. For these reasons, I have deliberately decided to record it here as I would an ordinary story. Please read it keeping this intention of mine in mind.[15]

After this, Komachida's background is provided by the narrator. As is clear from the above authorial explanatory note, the narrator was being used to avoid introducing characters via long, drawn-out passages of dialogue.[16] In this case, the narrator is posited as being ignorant of Komachida's background until the confession is made by Komachida himself; it is the same for the other characters as well. In this way the author develops the story by providing information about the characters bit by bit as a means of eliciting the reader's interest.

This intratextual narrator takes on new functions, and, with the proliferation of passages of narrative description, the space available for his activities expands as well. As a result, this narrator seems to run rampant through the story world, replacing the author who made such modest appearances in *ninjōbon*. This narrator is not limited to observing and recording characters and events but also adds commentary and passes judgment based on his or her own conjectures. In its most extreme form, this narrator even begins to engage in idle remarks reminiscent of the author in *yomihon*.

---

15. Tsubouchi Shōyō, *Tōsei shosei katagi*, in *MBZ*, 16:75.
16. In *Shōsetsu Shinzui* (The Essence of the Novel, 1885–86), Tsubouchi Shōyō writes, "Of the main faults to be avoided in the plot of a novel," one is "making characters relate long personal histories. This device not only helps to keep the story short. . . . It can be used without overdoing things two or three times in a long novel, but used too often it will provoke sighs of 'Not again!' from the reader. In works of only a few chapters, especially, the less it is used the better." Tsubouchi Shōyō, *The Essence of the Novel*, translated by Nanette Twine, Occasional Papers, no. 11 (Queensland: University of Queensland, 1981), 83, 88. [Hirata note]

They can mingle both so-called unity and variety. Saying "It is tasteful beauty" is just like the half-baked criticism of a school-boy! It's gibberish. . . . Even the audience grumbles that it's unnecessary baggage. These are the comments of the author acting as a third-party observer.[17]

When conflicting thoughts collide like this, what is a person's facial expression? I will leave it to the audience to interpret. Or should I give it a try? If I attempted it, I would describe it as a smile around the mouth that does not reach up to the eyes. On the cheekbones and nose, it is like the Battle of Sekigahara between two thoughts, what is worrying Ukita (Kingo Hideaki). But the author is perhaps trying too hard here for clever phrases.[18]

Once the intratextual narrator is distinguished from the extratextual author, even if the existence of an author who provides such notices to the reader from outside the story world is comprehensible, it was only to be expected that some would come to see as unnatural this sort of character, who, purporting to be the author, appears within the narrative world to comment on various matters. Fujinoya Shujin (a penname for Uchida Roan), criticizing Ishibashi Ningetsu's novel *Oyae*, writes as follows.[19]

In my opinion, skillfulness in a novel of worldly passions (*ninjō shōsetsu*) lies in evoking sympathy toward the protagonist in the reader. How should we elicit this sympathy? There is no other way . . . but to wield a serious writing brush and earnestly depict the facts. . . . Why does the author of *Oyae* recklessly insert such words as "the reader" and "the writer" into the work and thereby destroy the mood of pathos? Why not reveal inner thoughts psychologically and leave overtones to the reader's imagination?[20]

He criticizes the appearance of such "note from the author" passages, which appear in twenty-two places within *Oyae*. To Roan, the meddling of a character that professes to be the author was inappropriate in the new Meiji

17. Tsubouchi Shōyō, *Tōsei shosei katagi*, 16:60.
18. Hirotsu Ryūrō (1861–1928), "Shinchūrō" ("Castles in the Air," literally, "Towers in a Clam's Exhalation"), 1887, in *MBZ*, 19:126. In the passage, the author puns on the name of the character and that of a famous military leader (Kobayakawa Hideaki) involved in the Battle of Sekigahara in 1600.
19. Ishibashi Ningetsu (1865–1926), *Oyae* (Miss Oyae), 1888 (Tokyo: Yagi Shoten, 1995), 75–125.
20. Uchida Roan (1868–1929), "Ningetsu Koji no *Oyae*" (Ningetsu Koji's *Oyae*), 1889, in *Uchida Roan zenshū*, 17 vols. (Tokyo: Yumani Shobō, 1983–87), 1:75.

genre of *ninjō shōsetsu*, which aimed at pathos. He goes on to complain that it is the same "unskilled" and "indiscreet" narrative technique that marred Harunoya's (a penname for Tsubouchi Shōyō) *Tōsei shosei katagi*.[21]

By what technique could "evoking sympathy toward the protagonist in the reader," as Roan describes it, become possible? Just insisting that writers should "reveal inner thoughts psychologically" does not clarify matters. But in a later reminiscence about this period Roan writes, "*Ukigumo* was one I loved to read in those days."[22] Even in his comments on *Oyae*, he writes, "I admire Turgenev as translated recently by Futabatei, and I also admire the novels of Saganoya, who I have heard admires Turgenev as well."[23] Did these two writers "wield a serious writing brush," "earnestly depict the facts," and "portray inner thoughts psychologically"? And if so, how different were their works from other novels of their day, beginning with *Tōsei shosei katagi*?

4

Various classical rhetorical figures, such as pillow words (*makura kotoba*), pivot words (*kakekotoba*), and verbal associations (*engo*), along with other remnants of the parodic caricature style that characterized *gesaku*, have been identified in the supposedly "modern" literary work *Ukigumo*. It seems as though direct authorial interventions in the text can be counted as one of those *gesaku*-like elements. As we have seen, however, employing a narrator separate from the author within the text, a narrator whose reports and explanations drive the development of the story, was a technique commonly used in many novels of this period. In the preceding section, we saw how Shōyō and Kōyō employed "nonomniscient narrators," slowly releasing information bit by bit to expand the textual world. This same method is used in *Ukigumo*.

In Chapter 1 of *Ukigumo*, although Bunzō, Noboru, and Onabe make appearances, they are consistently referred to as "the tall man," "the man of average height," or "the buxom beauty" until they are finally identified more specifically in later chapters. This is similar to what we find in works such as *Tōsei shosei katagi* and *Fūryū kyōningyō*, where, until the characters' names are revealed through spoken dialogue or introductions made by the

21. Ibid., 1:72.
22. Uchida Roan, "Futabatei yodan" (Digression on Futabatei), 1909, in *Uchida Roan zenshū*, 17 vols. (Tokyo: Yumani Shobō, 1983–87), 3:330.
23. Uchida, "Ningetsu Koji no *Oyae*," 1:72.

narrator, their dialogue is recorded anonymously, the speakers being identified only as "a man," "a woman," "the student," or "the girl." In Chapter 2 of *Ukigumo*, it is clear in the text that the introduction of Bunzō's personal history and that of the members of the Sonoda family is conducted through the narrator.

> The man we have been calling "the tall young man" was named Utsumi Bunzō. . . . [A]n uncle in Tokyo offered to take the boy in . . . and, in the spring of 1878, when he was fifteen . . .[24]

> At this juncture we have a little romantic episode to tell, but before we do, let's have a short biography of Magobei's daughter, Osei. (*Ukigumo*, 208)

The narrator, as a subject who speaks from within the text, here seems to function as a full "person," providing commentary and criticism; he even seems to possess a "body."

> After exchanging a few more words, he went upstairs. Before he comes back down, I should give a brief biography of this young man, but unfortunately his past is lost in a haze. . . . (246)

Taking the stance that he is not certain of Noboru's character, the narrator purports that the information he provides is based on rumor. Even though Noboru goes up to the second floor where Bunzō is located, the narrator does not follow him but remains downstairs and begins to speak from that location. Similarly, it is this same character who, in chapter 1 after Bunzō has parted from Noboru, sticks to Bunzō's heels and enters the house behind him, saying, "Shall we go in too?" (199). This narrator also, while discussing Noboru, who then comes down from the second floor, says, "[H]ush, he's coming" (249), lowering his voice as though it could be heard by Noboru. In such expressions, the existence of the intratextual narrator becomes obvious.

In this way, the author is clearly conscious of the narrator's position within the space of the story world. He is similarly scrupulous about time changes that occur inside the text. The textual world has a standard time in which story events ordinarily occur and to which, as a rule, the narrator must

24. All translations from *Ukigumo*, except where noted, are adapted from Marleigh Grayer Ryan, *Japan's First Modern Novel: Ukigumo of Futabatei Shimei* (New York: Columbia University Press, 1967) (hereafter *Ukigumo*). The passages quoted here appear on pages 203 and 205.

adhere. Therefore, the basic method here is to describe the characters' past circumstances, such as their childhoods, by means of recollections made in the present moment. Consequently, if the author has chosen to relate this information through a narrator who is capable of moving freely across time and space within the text, once that passage of description is complete the narrator must clearly state that he or she has returned to the present moment in the story's standard time. At the end of chapter 3 of *Ukigumo*, after relating events that had occurred a number of months before, the narrator inserts the following note to the reader in order to return to the present time of chapter 1.

> And yet today (to return to the events related in the first chapter) Bunzō, upon whom everyone's expectations rested, had been asked to leave his post. An old-fashioned person would attribute it all to an evil fate. (*Ukigumo*, 222)

Explanatory notes such as these were a necessary result of the expanding function of the intratextual narrator. Similarly, in Shōyō's *Imotose kagami* (The Newly Polished Mirror of Marriage, 1886), the childhood of protagonist Misawa Tatsuzō, who appears in chapter 1, is described by the narrator in chapter 2. At the end of the chapter, we see the same method employed to effect a return to the present moment of the story time.

> Nevertheless, when Tatsuzō was twenty-three years old (as I said in chapter 1), Omiki fell ill and died before long. . . . As for what happened to Tatsuzō you'll know when you read chapter 3.[25]

Although this narrator adheres to the space and time of the story world, he has the ability to move about freely within them. By using the narrator in this way, the author is able to relate a character's personal history and reveal the true background of the story events without having to resort to the awkward tactic of providing all this information via spoken dialogue. But insofar as this narrator is rendered as an embodied person it is impossible to prevent his arbitrary interventions in the text. The frequency of such interventions produced difficulties such as those Roan criticized, so that the use of this narrator was a double-edged sword. When we consider this dilemma we should also take notice of attempts such as the following one by Saganoya Omuro.

25. Tsubouchi Shōyō, *Imotose kagami* (The Newly Polished Mirror of Marriage, 1886), in *MBZ*, 16:177.

> Like this, she was contemplating bygone days she had left
> behind.
> Then, remembering the past, Osuzu suddenly became two
> or three years younger, a fifteen- or sixteen-year-old beautiful
> maiden, and right before her eyes out of the mist appeared the
> beautiful Etchūjimasuzaki beach, shaped like the bay, with its
> Western-style house.[26]

Here the history of the protagonist, Osuzu, is related neither via the narra
tor nor by Osuzu herself. Instead, this is achieved by employing a form o
recollection and depicting her stream of consciousness. The narration of thi
recollection takes place as perceived through Osuzu's mental eye so that w
do not sense the existence of a narrator who unfurls sarcastic remarks. Th
narrator here is stripped of his personhood and embodiedness and begin
to change into a kind of impersonal narrative device.

Whether the narrator calls himself the author or not, whenever there i
an entity with the human qualities that characterize Narrator 1, the reade
can only passively receive the reports of events and characters in the stor
world and the one-sided commentary given by this narrator. In this case, th
reader cannot position his or her own perspective within the textual world
But when the colorless, nonperson narrator that is Narrator 2 emerges, fo
the first time readers are able to actively identify their own perspective
with that of the narrator. It becomes possible to assume various perspective
within the text, including those of various characters within the work. Whei
Roan called for "evoking sympathy toward the protagonist in the reader,'
he could only have meant something like this narrative device. Moreover, i
was possible to block the narrator's interfering remarks and "reveal inne
thoughts psychologically" only if one relied on this device. The celebratec
innovation of "psychological description" achieved in *Ukigumo* did not li
simply in establishing an intratextual narrator but rather in the transforma
tion it achieved toward a narrator characterized by this sort of perspectiva
structure.

5

When the narrator is an entity like Narrator 1, clearly distinct from the othe
characters, he cannot penetrate those characters' minds. Therefore, in re

26. Saganoya Omuro, "Hakumei no Suzuko" (The Sad Fate of Suzuko), 1888–89, in *MB*
17:238–39.

vealing their thoughts he has no recourse save guessing about the characters' psychology and emotions from their external appearance.

> The young man kept picking up his letter and trying to read it and then putting it down again in despair. He seemed very irritated. He grunted in response to her question to indicate his annoyance and refused to join in her chatter. This made the buxom beauty puff out her round cheeks until it seemed they would burst. She went downstairs in a huff. He looked relieved to see her go. (*Ukigumo*, 201)

The narrator only observes the characters' actions and expressions and does not describe their inner emotions. In other words, he does not say "Bunzō was relieved" but merely describes how he "looked relieved." By means of clues given by the narrator, such as the behavior and speech of the characters, the reader can surmise their inner thoughts. On the other hand, Narrator 1 does not have the means to describe internal thoughts and speculations that are difficult to guess from the outside. In such cases, the characters' thoughts remain unclear to the reader.

In order to directly describe inner thoughts, Narrator 1 has to lose his personhood and embodiedness and change into Narrator 2, who can enter into the consciousness of the characters. As one method in this process of transformation, works from this period often use a "magic mirror" to reflect inner thoughts.

> Here, let us suppose there was a mirror capable of illuminating the innermost heart of this person and of reflecting on its surface all of the thoughts that passed through it. What sorts of things would appear on its surface?[27]

> As though reflected in a crystal clear mirror, the heart that changes instantly from joy to sorrow will be illuminated in the passage that follows.[28]

> What are Oyuki's true feelings? Let's take out our magic mirror and reflect her innermost thoughts.[29]

27. Saimon Inshi [Satō Kuratarō] (1855–1942), *Shiba no iori* (Brushwood Hermitage), 1889 (Osaka: Shinshindo, 1889), 17.
28. Saganoya Omuro, *Shimarimise no hara* (Inside a Miser), 1887 (Tokyo: Ōkura Magobē, 1887), 28.
29. Tsubouchi, *Imotose kagami*, 16:216.

The unnaturalness of having to take out a magic mirror each time inner thoughts are described fades a bit in the next stage in which the magic mirror is eliminated and only the explanatory comment "in his or her mind" is used.

> With a wry smile and a sneer, under his breath, he said to himself:
> Taku: For stirring up the fighting spirit and training in horse riding, a horserace and a money pouch weren't bad. . . . I wonder if we can alert those who would rescue the local region from its torpor.[30]

> Then, he presently took it, bundled up into a cross-shape into his hand and examined it. (To himself) Isn't someone secretly watching?[31]

This descriptive technique, in which characters speak their inner thoughts to themselves, was a conventional method that was used in both the early modern and the modern novel. In them, however, inner thoughts were strictly presented in the form of transcriptions of thoughts that had actually been uttered aloud as voiced speech. In the above examples, we find inner thoughts narrated in the form of inner speech. *Ukigumo* is no exception; in it, too, we can see this shift from external voiced speech to unvoiced inner speech.

> The hinges of his hips were quite up to the task, but the hinges of his heart were stayed by his inability to decide: "Should I just tell?" "But it's so hard to say it." Suddenly he rose and went to the head of the stairs. He stopped. He hesitated. Then saying to himself, "I'll just go and say it," he rushed downstairs and went into the sitting room. (*Ukigumo*, 227)

In depicting the actions of Bunzō, who is at a loss over whether or not to inform his aunt about his dismissal from work, the narrator includes his own analysis of Bunzō's inner thoughts, explaining, for example, that "the hinges of his heart were stayed." The actual decision-making process is, however, given expression in the form of words spoken by Bunzō to himself. This is the same technique used in the passage that immediately precedes this point in the text, where Bunzō's troubled thoughts are bracketed in quota-

---

30. Sudō Nansui (1857–1920), *Ryokusadan* (The Local Self-Government), 1886 (Tokyo: Shun'yodo, 1886), 4.
31. Saganoya, *Shimarimise no hara*, 28.

tion marks as words that are spoken aloud to himself in a monologue that goes on so long as to seem unnatural. But in the portion immediately after this Bunzō's inner thoughts are narrated as inner speech: "Bunzō thought to himself, 'this would be a good time to say it, when Osei isn't here. I'll get it over with right this minute'"(227).

Before long, such comments as "thought to himself," as well as the bracketlike quotation marks, disappear and the words of inner speech are embedded directly within passages of narrative description rather than separated from the narrator's language. Here we can clearly see the shift from Narrator 1 to Narrator 2. In chapter 5, Bunzō, who was scolded by his aunt when he reported his dismissal to her, has decided to pack his belongings and move to a boardinghouse when a voice from downstairs announces lunch.

> He deliberately made her call him several times before answering and then went down reluctantly. He looked annoyed and irritated and rather frightening. He opened the door of the sitting room. . . . There is Osei! Osei!! (*Ukigumo*, 240)

> Bunzō had been so preoccupied with his misery that he had barely thought of her until now. He had, in fact, nearly forgotten her. . . . He was amazed at what had been going on in his mind. He had buried the joy of his love deep in his heart, and had allowed bitterness and anger to dominate him. . . . Bunzō had his lunch and went back upstairs. He made an attempt to resume the task of packing his things but somehow his earlier determination had deserted him. [A] *He tried to work up some spirit by coaxing himself on* in a soft voice, "I'm fine," [B] *but nothing happened.* He made another effort, speaking out in more strident tones: "I'm fine." He even clenched his teeth fiercely again. [C] *Would I ever change my mind once I've decided on something? No, never. Even if she forbids me to go, I will not stay here.* (240, emphasis added)

Until Bunzō goes downstairs and opens the sliding door, the narrative gaze focuses on his actions and expressions. But with the phrase "There is Osei! Osei!" the gaze turns to Bunzō's inner thoughts. The description of the psychological transformation of Bunzō, whose determination has been dulled by Osei's smiling face, is carried out through a perspective very close to his own. There is, however, an explanatory tone in which the presence of a narrator can be felt, just as in the earlier analysis of Bunzō's inner thoughts in the phrase "hinges of his heart." But in the section after he returns to the second floor the narrative perspective overlaps with that of Bunzō himself so that we no longer sense the presence of a narrator in the passages of subjective description marked as A and B. Moreover, although section C is embedded within a passage of narrative description, it is entirely a description of Bunzō's own inner thinking.

In part 2 of *Ukigumo*, we frequently see this type of shift in narrative perspective in which the perspective overlaps that of Bunzō. Moreover, the use of paragraph breaks and punctuation arranges the text's surface to render even clearer these shifts in narrative perspective.

> [A] Bunzō was completely miserable and certainly not in the mood for looking at flower displays. . . . Two days before he recalled having firmly refused to join the party when Noboru had invited him, and yet that morning he was far from indifferent to all the confusion in the household. Watching their excitement, *he was reminded over and over of his own predicament. How depressing.*
>
> [B] How depressing. For Bunzō, it was *depressing* to see how casually Osei had accepted his decision not to go with them. Bunzō felt that if she really wanted him to go, she should have insisted on it. Then, if he had continued to refuse, *he wanted her to say* she would not make the excursion without him.
>
> [C] "Aren't you just jealous?" He asked himself, trying to be reasonable. But her reaction continued to bother him.
>
> [D] *Sulky and displeased* at the world in general, he did not want to go and he did not want to stay home. He kept getting to his feet as if he had some pressing matter to attend to and then sitting down again. *How vexing. It was impossible for him to remain settled.*
>
> [E] *Still unsettled*, he thought he might distract himself by reading, and he chose a book at random from the bookcase. . . . Bunzō *angrily* thrust the book aside. He *angrily* leaned on his desk, *angrily* rested his chin on his hand, and *angrily* stared off into space. All at once he straightened up, *his face animated once again.*
> (*Ukigumo*, 259–60, emphasis added)

In the opening passage the emotions of Bunzō, who has yielded to melancholy after he has refused an invitation to go chrysanthemum viewing and stayed behind, are described a bit sarcastically. But by the time we get to "Two days before he recalled having" the narrative perspective shifts into Bunzō's inner thoughts. With the subjective adjective at the end of passage A, "how depressing," the perspective overlaps with that of Bunzō. In B, "For Bunzō" and "Bunzō felt" are narrated in the third person, yet at the sentence end we do not find the explanatory mode of expression we would expect in the third person, an expression in Japanese such as *no de aru*. Instead, it ends with the first-person subjective expressions, "how depressing" and "he wanted her to say" voiced from Bunzō's position.[32] As if to carry on this subjective narrative expression, direct dialogue is inserted into C, while again in D the narrative continues with subjective expressions "Sulky and displeased" and "How vexing." Then, with the final "It was impossible for him to remain settled," the perspective shifts to one that captures the situation from an external position, and the narrative shifts into the style found in E, an objective description that depicts Bunzō's appearance as viewed from the outside.

This type of change in perspective from subjective to predicative, as well as the shifts in perspective that occur from paragraph to paragraph, can be understood as phases in a shifting perspectival subject of expression, one that vacillates between Narrator 1 and Narrator 2. Sugiyama Yasuhiko has argued that in Futabatei's "Aibiki" and *Ukigumo*, with regard to the expression of consciousness "on behalf of the characters in the work," the relationships between the "characters of the work who are the subjects of expression" and external phenomena are multilayered. "In *Ukigumo*, this multiplicity is taken up as a syntactical structure by means of which the multitiered structure of the characters' consciousnesses is given expression."[33] Certainly, the narratorial perspective overlaps with that of characters within the work in order to depict their interiors, but this by itself would not produce a mode of expression that conveyed the multiple layers of consciousness that we find in *Ukigumo*. This becomes clear when we look at the descriptions of inner thought found in passages such as the following from *Fūryū kyōningyō*: "Devoted [to Tatsumi]. . . . Is Niyake['s devotion] the reason my affections [for Tatsumi] have gone for naught? 'Devoted'—but that doesn't tell me anything."[34] It is likewise with the description of consciousness for the characters in the work "Imosegai" (Shell of Imose, 1889) by Iwaya Sazanami (1870–1933).[35] While such expressions arise from the internal consciousness of the

---

32. In Japanese, subjective predicates, such as adjectives that express the speaking subject's feelings or mental state, involve rules limiting the use of person for the grammatical subject. For example, the expression *mizu ga nomitai* ([I] want to drink water), can be spoken by an "I" in the first person, but it cannot be spoken in the third person about a "she." Likewise, *Watashi wa kanashii* (I am sad) is grammatical, but *kanojo wa kanashii* (*She is sad) is not. In the above passage, "How depressing" from [A], "he wanted her to say" from [B], and "How vexing" from [D] all use predicates that in Japanese can ordinarily only be used in the first person. For details about how perspective relates to subjective adjectives and subjective predicates, see Ōe Saburō, *Nichieigo no hikaku kenkyū* (Tokyo: Nan'undō, 1975); and Kuno Susumu, *Danwa no bunpō* (Tokyo: Taishūkan Shoten, 1978). [Hirata note]
33. Sugiyama Yasuhiko, "Hasegawa Futabatei ni okeru genbun itchi" (*Genbun itchi* in Hasegawa Futabatei), *Bungaku* 36:9 (September 1968): 46. [Hirata note]
34. Ozaki, "Fūryū kyōningyō," 6:95.
35. Iwaya Sazanami (1870–1933), *Imosegai* (Shell of Imose, 1889) in *Meiji shōsetsu shū* (Tokyo: Chikuma Shobō, 1975).

characters in the work, they can only provide one-dimensional portrayals of consciousness that lack any sense of depth.

In fact, it is possible for characters to become the subject of expression but only in the narration of a first-person novel. Thus, for example, even if there is an overlap of the narrative perspective with that of the protagonist in *Ukigumo*, which takes the form of a third-person text, we have to realize that there is another subject of expression in addition to that of the depicted characters. The narrative viewpoint does not solely delve under the surface of Bunzō's consciousness but also takes up an external position, recording his sudden monologic outbursts and exclamations and describing his actions from the outside. In an objective description like this, it becomes possible to render into an object of description that deep layer of psychology that is unknown even to the character's own consciousnesses. The multilayered expression in *Ukigumo* arises not from the characters' multiplicity of relationships among themselves and with outside phenomena. Rather, its source should be sought in the multiplicity of positions taken up by the narrator as the subject of expression that objectifies the characters and events within the text.

By using such a multidimensional narrator, the author is able to establish various perspectives within the text. In turn, this deployment of multiple perspectives permits the construction of a multidimensional story world. This goes beyond simply providing multiple layers to the textual world by reflecting the multilayered structure of consciousness of the characters in the work. The multilayered world of *Ukigumo* that Kōda Rohan (1867–1947) criticized as being like "looking at a map of geological strata," was achieved through the construction of a narrative perspective that was capable of cutting vertically through the depth of the textual world, a world that was intertwined with the various levels of consciousness of the work's characters.[36]

6

About *Ukigumo*'s theme we have the words of Futabatei himself: "I was driven by the urge to depict the underside of Japanese civilization."[37] From the start, Futabatei's motif was "civilization criticism" (*bunmei hihyō*), taking as its foundation the "conflict between new and old ideas" in which each

---

36. Kōda Rohan, "Gengotai no bunshō to *Ukigumo*" (Language Style and *Ukigumo*), 1909, in *Rohan zenshū*, 44 vols. (Tokyo: Iwanami Shoten, 1978–80), 29:449.
37. Futabatei Shimei, "Yo ga hansei no zange" (A Confession of My Life), 1908, in *MBZ* 17:113.

of the work's characters was made to represent a certain line of thought. If Futabatei's aims for *Ukigumo* had not gone beyond this sort of political allegory, then a narrator who spewed out sarcastic remarks would have likely been the best means for realizing his thematic. But, as we have seen, beginning in the middle of book 1 the narrator abandons his objective stance and begins instead to overlap his perspective with that of Bunzō, who is one of the characters and hence ought to be one of the objects of criticism. In the second section of *Ochiba no hakiyose* (Piles of Fallen Leaves: A Second Basketful, 1889), one of the journals that Futabatei maintained, we find a rough draft of chapter 18 of book 3 of *Ukigumo* followed immediately by a section titled "Sakubun no kokoroe" (Rules for Composing Prose). There, Futabatei writes that "in producing a novel, too, one must leave behind one's personal biases." He continues:

> In order for the author, who must labor to rectify his heart and portray things just as they are (*ari no mama ni*), to display his insight he should not write down his own prejudices toward the novel's characters, whether they be favorably or unfavorably inclined.[38]

Futabatei here seems flustered at the way the narrator and Bunzō unintentionally end up merged with one another in book 2, and he rejects the expression of prejudices for or against characters in the work. As if to reflect this moment of self-criticism, in book 3 we can see a shift that we might classify as a reorganization of the narrative apparatus.

As *Ukigumo* develops from book 1 through books 2 and 3, the narrative perspective gradually draws closer and closer to that of Bunzō so that, as Nakamura Mitsuo has noted, by book 3 the work is centered on Bunzō's psychological inner monologues.[39] But in book 3 the third-person narrator that is supposed to have faded away unexpectedly shows up again, copiously showering the various characters with sneering remarks.

> It might be said by some that Bunzō had a reputation for being more likely to apologize than rebuke. (*Ukigumo*, 323)

> If you look up at that face, what tears in her eyes! (326–27)

38. Futabatei Shimei, *Ochiba no hakiyose* (Piles of Fallen Leaves: A Second Basketful), 1889, *MBZ*, 17:155.
39. Nakamura Mitsuo, *Futabatei Shimei den* (A Biography of Futabatei Shimei) (Tokyo: Kōdansha, 1958), 126. [Hirata note]

What might you say of Bunzō—yes, indeed, just what type of person is Bunzō himself? (335)

Poor Bunzō—apparently he has not yet suffered enough. (335)

Was she trying to hide her embarrassment or was she just extremely happy? It would be impossible to know without asking the young lady herself. (337)

The initiative for leading the narrative forward seems, once again, to have fallen into the hands of this interventionist narrator. We even find passages that suggest he is leading the text forward by the nose: "There were various things but I will pass over the details because they are bothersome" (339) or "This is how it came about" (344).

Chapter 19 begins with that narrator's voice. It narrates the changes in the characters' feelings created by Bunzō's dismissal, as well as the ways in which it is viewed by such characters as Omasa and Noboru, but it does not do so from Bunzō's perspective. Moreover, in the intervals between these various views the narrator adds his own speculations and analyses such as his description of Osei's mental state when she "was in the gravest danger and did not know it" (*Ukigumo*, 351). He takes up a position roughly equidistant from all of the characters, and as a result he is able to draw his perspective equally close to that of every character. In chapter 18, the manner in which Noboru, Omasa, and Osei become friendly is depicted, at which time the position of perspective in the first part is set very close to that of Osei. Moreover, we even find the narrator taking up the perspective of such characters as Onabe, who in books 1 and 2 had not even been the object of the narrative gaze (chapters 13, 15).

The position of this narrator, who is able to overlap the perspectives of each of the characters in the work while still preserving his own objective perspective, remains unshaken even in the case of Bunzō. The description of Bunzō as he is absorbed in daydreams while gazing at the grain of the wooden ceiling is occupied with depicting the various mental images that float across his mind. But it is not a direct depiction, one that overlaps the perspective of Bunzō himself. Rather, it is objectified by the narrator in such a manner that it takes up as its object even the unconscious strata of Bunzō's consciousness.

As he was contemplating, he remembered the bearded face of the foreigner who had taught him physics and he completely forgot

about the grain of the wood. And then several of the students
who had been to school with him appeared in his mind's eye. . . .
Suddenly the machine and students vanished into thin air. Bunzō
saw the grain of the wood again. (*Ukigumo*, 353–54)

Compare this with the passage near the end of book 1, chapter 4, which
depicts Bunzō's consciousness as he falls asleep: "The image of his white-
haired mother which had been flickering before his eyes grew a speckled
black beard and became the head of his chief. Soon that terrifying head . . .
its features changed . . . gradually a rose-shaped hairpin . . . Osei's . . . head"
(233). In contrast to the direct depiction here, in the passage from chapter 19
in book 3 we find the clear presence of an objective narrator, one who adds
explanatory comments.

This narrative apparatus, which fluctuates back and forth between Narrator 1 and Narrator 2, clearly was not Futabatei's intention. About *Ukigumo*
he would later recollect, "There is no consistent philosophy espoused in it."
He would likewise confess: "[V]arious perplexities arose from my inability
to decide on the stance I should adopt toward the phenomena of the world"
such as whether he should immediately identify with the characters in the
work or adopt a more critical, bystander's perspective toward them.[40] In the
end, it seems likely that the failure to establish a unified narrative apparatus
applied consistently throughout *Ukigumo* was due to his uncertainty about
the theme he wanted to explore in it and, more broadly, to his uncertainty
over the author's standpoint toward the story world of *Ukigumo*.

The problem of determining the author's stance vis-à-vis a novel's
fictional world and the characters within that work was not unique to
Futabatei. Tsubouchi Shōyō had already argued that "a biased attitude" toward the characters in the work should be avoided and that "Japanese authors in the past have shown a marked tendency towards favouritism. No
writer whose guiding principle is to observe life as it is and write about it
in strictly realistic terms ought to have such a bad habit."[41] As we have seen
in his "Sakubun no kokoroe," Futabatei was heir to this way of thinking.
But this is not limited only to those in the genealogy of "realism," which
traces its lineage back to Shōyō. For example, we find the same situation in
the case of authors such as Kōda Rohan, who are typically situated in the
"antimodern" school.

---

40. Futabatei Shimei, "Sakka kushin dan" (Conversation about the Author's Efforts), 1897, in
    Futabatei Shimei zenshū, 9 vols. (Tokyo: Iwanami Shoten, 1964–65), 5:165.
41. Tsubouchi, *The Essence of the Novel*, 85.

Novels, whether it be *Hakkenden* or *Arabian Nights*, great or small, are all, when examined in the light of reason, phantoms and illusions born out of daydreams and fantasy. . . . Merely to set in motion bloodless, spiritless images on paper is not to create a true, elegant novel.[42]

For the writers of this generation, who grew up as avid readers of the *yomihon* genre in which the author occupied the position of Old Man Creator and manipulated the story world at will, escaping the fetters of this sort of authorial position and establishing a new kind of position was an indispensable step in launching the "modern." But merely avoiding authorial prejudice toward the characters and refraining from authorial intervention in the story world did not immediately lead to the full realization of a new, inorganic narrative apparatus. Rather, the narrative apparatus remained in a half-realized state characterized by the reappearance of a sarcastic, officious narrator or by the creation of an extremely shallow story world born of mere surface realism. In the end it seems that the authors, as they groped toward the apparatus necessary for a "modern" literature, still lacked the consciousness and technique that would allow them to completely master such a narrative apparatus. They were hesitant to define a fixed distance between themselves and the story world and its characters, just as they were unable to establish a fixed standpoint for their own selves. The authors held in their hands the various devices of fiction, including the narrative apparatus, but it would require many more failed experiments and frustrated attempts before they would be able to manipulate them at will.

NOTE

This chapter was originally published under author's former name, Kubo Yumi, as "Kindai bungaku ni okeru jojutsu no sōchi: Meiji shoki sakkatachi no 'rikkyakuten' o megutte," *Bungaku* 52:4 (April 1984): 98–111.

42. Kōda Rohan, "Zōka to bungaku" (Creation and Literature), 1890, *Yūbin hōchi shinbun*, July 23, 1890. [Hirata note]

Introduction to the Discourse of the Modern Novel: "Time" in the Novel and Literary Language

Mitani Kuniaki

Translated by Mamiko Suzuki

1. CRITIQUE OF THE NONPERSON NARRATOR

The prose novel is a literature of the past-tense form.[1] Works that break the taboos against second-person or present-tense narration do exist, as with, for example, the works of Alain Robbe-Grillet or those in which Kurahashi Yumiko so boldly imitates him. However, such works remain, strictly speaking, within the domain of the experimental and cannot exceed it. We should probably note here that the "past-tense" form of the prose novel differs from the grammatical past tense and is one of the distinguishing characteristics of novelistic language.

Everyday language expresses the past or perfect tense in the following way.

> (Last night) I was scared. (*sakuya*) *watashi wa kowakatta.*

If we take this first-person expression and switch it to the second or third person, the sentence becomes:

> (Last night) you *were probably* scared. (*sakuya*) *anata wa kowakatta deshō.*

> (Last night) Hanako *was probably* scared. (*sakuya*) *Hanako wa kowakatta darō.*

In this way, it is customary in such cases to add such inferential endings as "*deshō*" and "*darō*"; in novelistic language, however, it is a general rule

---

1. The original term for the past-tense form is *kakokeishiki,* and the grammatical past tense is *kakokei.* All notes are by the translator except where noted.

not to utilize the inferential ending with the third person, and this "past" carries out a crucial and unique function in the language of the novel.[2] I will take as an example the opening sentence of Nakagami Kenji's "The *Jōtōkuji* Tour" (included in the collection titled *Misaki*), which I had on hand.

> At the scramble intersection, he counted them—for good measure, he told himself.[3]

> *sukuranburu kōsaten de, kare wa nennotame to kazoete mita.*

Hence, the tense called "the past" is distinctive to the language of the novel and works as a way to indicate to the reader that the text belongs to the genre of prose literature, and so it is recognizable as one of the functional supports for "fictionality." Just as with the conventional "Once upon a time . . . it was so" (*mukashi . . . keri*) form found in late classical works of narrative literature, the discourse "he counted them—for good measure, he told himself" has the task of drawing readers into the strange world of "fiction." At the same time, the fact that in ordinary usage this expression is possible only in the first person suggests that in novelistic discourse the third person simultaneously functions with first-person capabilities. Within the prose fiction text, readers are able to identify with the characters only because the novelistic third person maintains a function that differs from everyday language.

According to my limited knowledge of the developmental period of the modern novel, it was born from a struggle over what form could best realize this "past" in the prose novel. Its greatest battlefield was Futabatei Shimei's *Ukigumo*, and this text is left for us today as a symbolic artifact of the encounter turned battle between form and language in modernity.

2. Though not developed in this text, discourses that use *ta* in the past form and the third person exist. For example, in the case of "Yesterday Hanako was at Yokohama Station," this is used when the "narrator = I" is in actuality narrating the facts of "sight/hearing = experience." However, since the experience as "location" is necessary, in everyday language it is not possible to say "Yesterday Hanako was at Yokohama Station. At that time, Tarō was at Shinjuku Station," and so this is the unique privilege of novelistic discourse. Here exist the grounds for the birth of omniscience in the prose novel. Rather than using an inferential expression to recount simultaneous events that occur in different spaces, such as "Yesterday Hanako was at Yokohama Station. At the same time, Taro seems to have been at Shinjuku," by using *ta* in both sentences the narrator, and therefore the reader, produces the illusion that these events are actually experienced by them as onlookers. This absent narrator who nonetheless experiences the narrated events as an onlooker constitutes the distinctive feature of the modern novel. This is the reason why the modern novel, though fiction, is received as if it were real.

3. A scramble intersection is a six-way pedestrian crossing.

The opening passage of *Ukigumo*, chapter 1, reads as follows.

> It is three o'clock in the afternoon of a late October day. A swirling
> mass of men stream out of the Kanda gate, marching first in ant-
> like formation, then scuttling busily off in every direction. These
> fine gentlemen are clearly interested in the appearance of his face,
> <u>each and every one</u> (*katagata*). Look carefully and you will see what
> an enormous variety of individual types are represented in the
> huge crowd. Start by examining the hair bristling on their chins
> and under their noses: mustaches, side-whiskers, Vandykes, and
> even extravagant imperial beards, Bismarck beards reminiscent
> of a Pekinese, bantam beards, badger's beards, meager beards that
> are barely visible, thick and thin <u>they sprout in every conceivable
> way</u> (*hae wakaru*).
>
> Now what's also different is their <u>mode of dress</u> (*minari*).
> Here is a dandy in a fashionable black suit purchased at Shirokiya
> set off by shoes of French calfskin. <u>Cannot one say</u> (*to iu*) that
> this one's mustache is so long that he might catch some fish with
> it? And now confident men oblivious of the ill-fit of their tweeds
> worn with stiff leather shoes—trousers that trail in the mud
> like the tail of a tortoise; suits bearing the indelible stamp of the
> ready-made clothes rack. "I have a beard and fine clothing, what
> more do I need?" they seem to say (*to sumashita ganshokude*) [lit.,
> "they seem to say with smug expressions"]. Glowing like embers
> on the fire, <u>these honorable men</u> hie themselves home, heads erect
> (*okaeri asobasu*). Indeed, <u>they're</u> all quite enviable (*iya ourayamashii
> koto da*).
>
> Now behind them <u>arrive</u> (*dete oidenasaru*) the graying heads,
> stooped with weak backs, they <u>return</u> (*okaerinasaru*) home, plod-
> ding, with empty lunch boxes dangling from their waists. Despite
> their advanced years they are able to hold a job, and they can
> <u>easily work</u> (*otegaru na ominoue*) in old-fashioned Japanese clothes,
> their duties not being so strenuous. Quite <u>lamentable</u>, is it not
> (*okinodokuna*)?[4]

The work thus begins with a description of the scene of employees
returning home from government offices at Kanda gate. As indicated by the

---

4. All translations of *Ukigumo* passages are based on Marleigh Ryan's *Japan's First Modern
Novel: Ukigumo of Futabatei Shimei*, (New York: Columbia University Press, 1967), (hereafter cited as *Ukigumo*), although some modifications have been made to help illustrate
the arguments of this essay, which are based on the original. This passage appears on
197–98. Although the *togaki* are not marked in Mitani's original essay, in the translation
of *Ukigumo* each is rendered in boldface type to illustrate the use of the quotational "to"
in the passage.

underlined words, what we notice from this opening scene is that the passage is written in the present-tense form and therefore produces an unsettled feeling in the reader. Rather, one might say that from the perspective of current standards, the *togaki*-like expressions appear cinematic and as a result fresh.[5] The honorific forms, marked by the double lines in the quoted passage, serve as the counterpart to the present-tense form. It is perhaps more accurate to call these mocking honorifics. But, regardless of this mockery, the use of honorific language in prose fiction—as research on narration in *monogatari* (premodern prose narrative) has made clear—is impossible without presuming the existence of a narrator.[6]

It is a feature of Japanese honorific language that in addition to indicating the status of the object of narration and of the listening audience it also indicates the narrator's relative status. The level of sarcasm in this opening description toward the government employees of relatively high status, for example, amounts only to such remarks as "It is all quite enviable" contrasting sharply with the excessive use of honorific language bordering on outright insolence in the passage describing those of lower status who follow after in Japanese clothing. As a result, we are able to glimpse here the narrator's status and attendant ideology.

There is no doubt that the method of *Ukigumo*, its use of present form and its characteristic narrator, fits the concept of the "nonperson narrator" as presented by Kamei Hideo (by way of Miura Tsutomu) in his *Transformations of Sensibility*. Indeed, this narrator, who looks down on Kanda gate mockingly, says such things as

> He enters the two-story house with the lattice door. Let's follow him inside.

or

> Now, there's another story with an enticing twist, but before we get to it let's find out more about Magobei's daughter, Osei.

5. *Togaki* (written with the katakana syllabary *to* and *kaku*, meaning "to write") refers to the insertion of *to* after actions, scene descriptions, and light and music cues that appear between lines of spoken dialogue, as within a script. This is similar to, or the equivalent of, "tag clauses" in the English language such as "he said," "she thought," "she asked," and "he replied."
6. For further reference, see "Genji monogatari ni okeru 'katari' no kōzō: 'Washa' to 'katarite' aruiwa 'Sōshiji' ron hihyō no tame no joshō" (The Structure of Narration in *The Tale of Genji*: 'Storyteller' and 'Narrator,' or Introduction to a Critique of Sōshiji), *Nihon Bungaku* 27:11 (November 1978): 37–52; and "Monogatari bungaku ni okeru 'katari' no kōzō: 'Katari' ni okeru shutai no kakusanka aruiwa monogatari bungaku ni okeru tekusuto

and

> And here we arrive at the very hinge whereby hangs our tale; let's
> begin a new chapter.

In this manner, he hovers behind the characters like a ghost or invisible
spirit, delivering lines that would be characterized as authorial intrusions,
or "*sōshiji*," in narratology as it is practiced in the study of *monogatari* literature.[7] Clearly, he fits the designation of the nonperson narrator.

This is how Kamei explains the structure of the nonperson narrator.

> Let me repeat again that the narrator of *Ukigumo* frequently de-
> parts from the sensibility Futabatei must have grasped as his own
> "I-ness." He seems to take on a life of his own that has little to do
> with the kind of self-consciousness that accurately and faithfully
> passes along news of things seen and heard. Futabatei's narrator
> is, in fact, single-mindedly oriented toward the reader. His role
> is nothing more, nor less, than to bring to life interests—and, in-
> deed, a sensibility—that are shared in common by narrator and
> reader. In sum, this narrator bears a sensibility it shares with the
> reader; he lives within the space of the work, yet is invisible to the
> other characters and chooses his own position within that space,
> a position, which then functions to constrain him.[8]

But it is not possible to understand the nonperson narrator in these terms,
that is, as a means chosen by the author in order to share a common sensibility with the reader.

As we have seen from the analysis of the opening scene, the first half of
part 1 in *Ukigumo*—despite being prose fiction—is narrated in the present
tense. One would think that since chapter 2 relates Bunzō's life prior to
the opening scene the past-tense form should have been employed. If we
list the sentence endings found in it, however, we get the following: "he

---

bunseki no kanōsei" (The Structure of 'Narration' in *Monogatari Bungaku*: The Diffusion
of the Subject in Narration or the Possibilities for Text Analysis in *Monogatari* Literature),
Monogatari kenkyū 1 (April 1979): 60–69. [note by Mitani]

7. *Sōshiji* refers to the comments that seem to imply authorial intrusion, which are made, apparently, by the author rather than the "narrator." This term is distinguished from *ji no
bun* (plain narrative), which refers to passages of normal third-person narrative that are
also distinguished from dialogue and characters' inner thoughts.

8. Kamei Hideo, *Transformations of Sensibility*, edited by Michael Bourdaghs, translated by
Brett de Bary (Ann Arbor: University of Michigan, Center for Japanese Studies Publications, 2002), 15–16.

trains" (*shikomu*), "there is no time" (*maganai*), "he comes out"(*detemairu*), "he studies" (*benkyōsuru*), "he goes to sleep" (*tokonitsuku*), "is depleted" (*nakunatte shimau*), "there is only a little left" (*nokori sukuna ni naru*), "she scrapes together [enough to eat]" ([*keburi wo*] *tateteiru*), "he realizes" (*kokochi*), and "it must have been spring" (*haru no koto toka*). In all cases either the present-tense form or a noninflected substantive ending (*taigendome*) is used. Thus, the reader does not share the same sensibilities as the narrator, and, moreover, because the writing is not in the past-tense form the reader is forced to engage in an unstable reading as if she, or he, had been suspended in midair. For that reason, the nonperson narrator emerges from the discord arising from conflicting impulses, the irritating nonconjuncture between the discourse known as *genbun itchi* (which, at the very least, is not spoken language) and the "past" form demanded by prose fiction. That frustration arises not only in current readers like ourselves, but it also arose, without a doubt, in the author Futabatei Shimei himself, becoming the source of that mocking tone.

According to Kubo [Hirata] Yumi in "The Narrative Apparatus in Modern Literature: Regarding the Foundations of Early Meiji Writers,"[9] in contrast to the *yomihon*'s use of refined literary language, the *kokkeibon* and *ninjōbon* put informal spoken dialogue at the center.[10] She states that "the *togaki* style can only describe the condition of a character objectively so that in it the narrator himself never makes an appearance."

> [Pig:] "Th . . . there, it's still br . . . bright. Must've slept too long . . . now I'm seeing things," he said to himself, draws closer to the door, and in an offbeat, high-pitched voice.[11]

But as we can see in this passage from the *kokkeibon Ukiyoburo* (The Bathhouse of the Floating World), the present tense is a property of the *togaki* style, and, moreover, there is clearly a narrator as depicter here who makes the assessment that the character's remark is "offbeat." Judging from this, it seems that the nonperson narrator in *Ukigumo* is an extension of this *togaki*

---

9. Kubo [Hirata] Yumi, "Kindai bungaku ni okeru jojutsu no sōchi: Meiji shoki sakkatachi no 'rikkyakuten' wo megutte," *Bungaku* 52:4 (April 1984): 98–111. See the translation in this volume.

10. *Yomihon* (reading book), *kokkeibon* (ludicrous books), and *ninjōbon* (books of human passions) were all popular genres of fiction in the latter half of the Edo period. Whereas *yomihon* featured "'serious" heroic tales that stressed Confucian and Buddhist morality, *kokkeibon* and *ninjōbon* focused on humor and romance.

11. Shikitei Sanba, *Ukiyoburo*, in *Nihon Koten Bungaku Taikei*, 100 vols. (Tokyo: Iwanami Shoten, 1957–69), 63:55.

style from the *kokkeibon* and *ninjōbon* genres. In *Ukigumo*, the phenomenon of clustered dialogue occurs with frequency, a phenomenon whose origins, too, might lie near these genres.

Of course, to extend the *togaki* style into a long text makes it something different from the previously existing *togaki* style, which was used only in brief passages, so needless to say this announces the birth of a new kind of discourse. But it should not be a waste of time to confirm the origins of this discourse, and in fact it seems possible to shed light on how the limitations inherent in these origins determine the mode of expression within *Ukigumo*. That is to say —and this is related to subsequent analyses in this essay—the *togaki* style always posits the speaker as an external observer and has the disadvantage of being unable to enter into the characters' psyche, and, as Kubo Yumi has shown, therein lies the reason for the lack of psychological depictions or inner speech in the opening sections of *Ukigumo*.

2. THE ESTABLISHMENT OF NOVELISTIC DISCOURSE

The present-tense form of *Ukigumo*, a mode difficult to actualize in prose fiction, would inevitably have to change. At the tail end of part 1, chapter 3, comes this line: "And yet today (to return to the events related in the first chapter) Bunzō, upon whom everyone's expectations rested, was asked to leave his post. An old-fashioned person would attribute it all to an evil fate" (*Ukigumo*, 222). The nonperson narrator, who could well be called the *sōshiji*, appears here again, and, despite the fact that he is describing events that occur "today," the past-tense (not in a grammatical sense) auxiliary *ta* is used (*menshoku to natta*, lit., "He became unemployed").

And, as if in correspondence, in chapter 4 the *ta* ending appears with gradually increasing frequency: "[the sky] was dyed a faded crimson" (*usukōbai ni someta*), "[the sky] brightened" (*akaruku natta*), "[the color on his face] appeared" (*arawarete maitta*), "[his] heart jumped" (*tomune o tsuita*). Precisely in that same chapter where *ta* appears with increasing frequency, an extended internal monologue, or what could be called "stream of consciousness," is depicted, utilizing quotation marks.

> He smiled, chuckling to himself; but then his open mouth became twisted and distorted and an expression of grief appeared on his face.
>
> "Oh, what on earth shall I do? I certainly have to say something. I must make up my mind to tell them when they come home tonight and get it over with. . . . I'll tell Osei—no, not Osei.

> I'll tell my aunt . . . a terrible face . . . tell that terrible face . . . tell
> that offensive mouth. . . . Oh I'm all mixed up." He shook his head
> back and forth. (*Ukigumo*, 226)

Even though the nonperson narrator experiments with *sōshiji*-like expressions in the first section, from around chapter 4 on it abandons the *togaki*-like detached spectatorism and becomes able even to see through the characters' (even though it is almost exclusively Bunzō's) inner speech. It is in correspondence to this that a discourse of the past-tense form, *ta* comes to dominate. It is necessary to analyze closely the process by which this *ta* is established through parts 2 and 3, but this is not the objective of this essay. So, restricting myself to what is thematically relevant to the discussion, I will turn to the purported ending of the novel in part 3, chapter 19.[12]

> Watching Osei's departing figure, Bunzō <u>smiled</u> (*nikkori shita*). For whatever reason his manner had changed and without the leisure for suspicion he felt somewhat at ease; and so he <u>smiled</u> (*nikkori shita*). Then delusionary thoughts crept into his mind, and though he tried to push them away, they came in so that, one after another, various groundless thoughts floated in his breast. Eventually he even began to think (*omoi konda*) that everything that had occurred was all due to Bunzō's paranoia and that in reality there was nothing to worry about. But when he thought it over again, she had humiliated Bunzō for no reason; disobeying her mother, she had at some point begun to do as she was told, then had stated that she was on bad terms with Noboru, with whom she had been so friendly—there <u>seems</u> (*omowareru*) to be something going on. In thinking so, he knows not whether to rejoice or to lament, becoming suspicious, even of himself, so, as though when a gesture of tickling is made from far away, he could not laugh wholeheartedly or cry; wavering between pleasure and displeasure, he <u>paced back and forth</u> (*iki modoritsu shiteita*) on the veranda for a while.
>
> But, if he were to say something she might listen; as soon as she returns, this time he'll try his fortune again; if she listens, then fine, and if she won't, then at that time he will certainly leave his uncle's home. Thus he finally made this decision, and <u>returned</u> (*modotta*) to the second floor.[13]

---

12. *Ukigumo* has traditionally been analyzed as a completed novel, yet according to the author it was unfinished.

13. This passage has been retranslated for the purpose of maintaining the endings mentioned in Mitani's argument. The equivalent passage in Ryan's translation can be found on page 356 of her book.

Along with the total banishment of the nonperson narrator from the passage, we notice the almost excessive use of *ta*. According to my thinking, in the modern novel the *ta* ending has the function of signaling narrated "meaning" in terms of the plot, while the present-tense *ru* ending carries the burden of narrating "description." As if to bear this out, there is a "seems" (*omoware<u>ru</u>*). Altogether this passage qualifies as a model of the discourse of the modern novel. It is, however, a discourse that makes us inquire as to who is the subject of expression that describes Bunzō as he went "back and forth," wandering from one thought to its polar opposite.

In the *togaki*-like sentences, there is avoidance of a descent into the character's psyche. And at least in the part 1, chapter 4, passage of quasi-stream-of-consciousness inner speech, quotation marks were used to mark off Bunzō's psychological musings. But in this ending passage even that practice is abandoned, and there is someone who walks, muddy shoes and all, straight into the interior of an Other. Is this the "author," the "narrator," or some other entity? Most probably, if we take into consideration the research done up to now—and after confirming the differences with the actually existing writer—let us cast aside the temptation to use a different term and answer that it is the author who speaks. In other words, an author is that which, muddy shoes and all, can grasp and confirm the pleats of a character's psyche; this is an omniscient and thoroughly modern concept, one that is guaranteed by the "past form" *ta* in the modern novel.

In *A Critique of Translation Studies: the Structure of Japanese, the Responsibility of Translation*, Yanabu Akira focuses on *ta*, maintaining that it functions on a dimension different from that of ordinary conversation, that it emerged and developed from translated texts, and that Futabatei Shimei's "Aibiki" was its starting point.[14] As we have seen, however, the discourse of *ta* was established in part 1 of *Ukigumo*, and, although the influence of translation is undeniable, we should be able to confirm that the discovery of *ta* in Futabatei Shimei was born from the struggle with the "past" form definitive of the modern novel.

Now, *ta* is a modern auxiliary verb that combines in itself a range of distinct meanings that would have been expressed by multiple endings in the pre–*genbun itchi* literary language: *ki, keri, tsu, nu, tari, ri*.[15] Therefore, it is useful to analyze the function of *ta* through a comparison with classical

14. Yanabu Akira, *Honyaku gakumon hihan: Nihongo no kōzō, honyaku no sekinin* (A Critique of Translation Studies: The Structure of Japanese, the Responsibility of Translation) (Tokyo: Nihon Honyaku Yōsei Senta, 1983); Futabatei Shimei's "Aibiki" is an adaptation of Ivan Turgenev's *Rendezvous*.

15. These are past- and perfect-tense endings of the end form (*shūshikei*) in the literary, or written, classical Japanese language.

writing, and—drawing from my area of expertise—I will compare *The Tale of Genji* in its original form and a modern Japanese translation of it using the following example from the "Yūgao" (Evening Faces) chapter:

> The bright full moon of the Eighth Month came flooding in through chinks in the roof. It was not the sort of dwelling he was used to, and he was fascinated. Toward dawn he was awakened by plebian voices in the shabby houses down the street.
>
> "Freezing, that's what it is, freezing. There's not much business this year, and when you can't get out into the country you feel like giving up. Do you hear me, neighbor?"
>
> He could make out every word. [a] It embarrassed the woman that, so near at hand, there should be this clamor of preparation as people set forth on their sad little enterprises. [b] Had she been one of the stylish ladies of the world, she would have wanted to shrivel up and disappear. [c] She was a placid sort, however, and she seemed to take nothing, painful or embarrassing or unpleasant, too seriously. Her manner was elegant and yet girlish, she did not seem to know what the rather awful clamor up and down the street might mean.[16]

This is the passage, which comes after the scene in which Genji spends one midautumn evening in Yūgao's home in the Fifth Ward; near dawn, the people in the neighboring homes awake to begin their work. In response to the racket, in the passage marked [a], Yugao's being "embarrassed" is expressed with the auxiliary verb *tari*. In [b], the ending *namerikashi*—here there is ironic judgment—denotes the *sōshiji*: *The Tale of Genji* posits as its own narrator several serving women who observe the main characters' experiences, of whom presumably one is offering the comment here. In the above sentence, the comment that "had she been one of the stylish ladies of the world" she would surely have fainted away, is sarcasm directed at Yūgao. In [c], it is evident in the sentence ending *"miekeru"* (she seemed) that the figure of Yūgao is grasped from Genji's perspective. What we should note from "she seemed to take nothing, painful or embarrassing or unpleasant, too seriously" is that this represents his judgment that she is not embarrassed.

In other words, in [a] Yūgao, [b] the narrator, and [c] Genji, each depicts her or his response to the early morning voices from the neighboring home, but there exists no modern "author" who monologically unifies the scene through a single value judgment. Thus it is possible to say that Yūgao's sensi-

---

16. Murasaki Shikibu, *The Tale of Genji*, translated by Edward G. Seidensticker (New York: Vintage, 1990), 67.

bility of embarrassment is entirely reasonable and that its suppression so as to be imperceptible to her interlocutor is also part of her personality. Given their "aesthetic sense," it is surely the case that these serving women would have wanted to die in such a situation, and it is also true that the seventeen-year-old Genji, with his emotions heightened, sees Yūgao's unperturbedness as seductive. Each of these reactions reverberates with the others, and in that playful interaction there exists no monolithic meaning and no room for an author who controls the text. To "read" *The Tale of Genji* is precisely to take pleasure in the play of multiple meanings, the multiple perspectives of those three responses. If there is anything like a plot element in this scene, it consists of nothing more than indicating that Genji, owing to his youthfulness, fails to grasp the nature of the woman and has not yet firmly established his identity. As we can tell from this example, despite the widespread illusion that Genji is always invested with an absolute "beautiful nature," in the text this is always relativized, and in this scene we even find a comic quality in his inability to understand the real feelings of women such as Yūgao.

If we look at this scene, which in the original version solicits a "playful" mode of reading, in the most recent translation of *The Tale of Genji* into modern Japanese, namely, Enchi Fumiko's, we get the following.[17]

> On the evening of August 15th, the clear light of the full moon shines unobstructed through the cracks between the boards of the roof, and although just to look upon the likes of such a house as this would have been rare enough, it must have been almost dawn when, from the neighboring houses, the vulgar laborers seemed to have awakened and their voices are heard.
>
> "My, it's cold. With business so bad this year I won't be able to peddle my wares in the countryside, it makes you feel helpless. Are you listening there, neighbor?"
>
> Such bantering can be heard from beyond the walls. The racket of restless commotion of those who awake to labor for a meager and dingy living was so close that the woman truly <u>was</u> ashamed [a]. If she had been one who put on airs, her house is one that <u>might have</u> made her want to disappear [b]. However, she was a person of a calm nature, and it did not seem as though she was deeply affected by hardships or distasteful or embarrassing things, and her demeanor was extremely refined and ingenuously calm [c]. Her seeming indifference to the crudeness of this neighborhood of unequaled desolation <u>seemed</u> to be paradoxically

---

17. Since Mitani published this essay, Jakuchō has published another modern Japanese translation of *The Tale of Genji* (Tokyo: Kōdansha, 2001).

less blameworthy, and thus more endearing, than if she had been ashamed and behaved awkwardly.[18]

The multiplicity of a three-way response is absent here. What is of particular concern is the splitting of passage [c], which, with the additional factor of the use of *ta* ("her demeanor <u>was</u> calm"), ends up contradicting [a], "she was ashamed"; we might even say that it is impossible to make heads or tails of this passage. With only *ta* and *ru* at its disposal for sentence endings, modern language thus loses the depth of classical writing and turns into something utterly flat.

I did not make this comparison to say that Enchi Fumiko's translation is clumsy. I wanted, rather, to look carefully at the process by which even the finest modern language translation yields to the bewitchment of *ta* and—in the manner of "thought" (*omot<u>ta</u>*), "is probably so" (*sama dea<u>rō</u>*), "is so" (*iru no deat<u>ta</u>*), and "seems" (*mie<u>ru</u>*)—thereby brings out an "author" who in fact never materialized in the original *Genji*. The concept of the author was established in modernity, and its formation was accompanied by many sacrifices arising out of the myth of the modern self.

3. THE ASPECT OF REFINED LANGUAGE

Futabatei Shimei, in writing *Ukigumo*, expanded the possibilities for the modern novel. Needless to say, the history of the modern novel is built on this foundation, but at the same time *Ukigumo* closed off and repressed other possibilities for prose fiction. Important among the losses are the multi-perspectival viewpoint such as we saw in *The Tale of Genji* and the feature of "play" so intrinsic to the basic idea of literature itself. Moreover, these losses occurred within a force field produced by the seemingly insignificant presence of the verb ending *ta*.

According to Tokieda Motoki's *Nihon bunpō kōgohen* (Japanese Grammar: The Spoken Language), *ta* represents the speaker's *kakunin handan*, or "confirmation and judgment," regarding a matter. Because I did not intend to make a foray into the discipline of grammar in this essay, I used the term *past* as a term from literary studies, but we can say that the function of *confirmation and judgment* confers a unitary meaning on a sentence. In the form

---

18. Seidensticker consulted Enchi Fumiko's modern Japanese translation *Genji monogatari*, (Tokyo: Shinchōsha, 1980), as well as Tanizaki Junichirō's, *Junichirō yaku Genji monogatari* (Tokyo: Chuō Kōronsha, 1991), while working on his translation of *The Tale of Genji*. In an effort to distinguish in English a direct translation of Enchi Fumiko's *Genji*, which Mitani cites here, I have rendered this passage as literally as possible.

of a "speaker" barging uninvited into an invisible world and repeatedly performing the act of confirmation and judgment, the modern novel gave birth to the fiction of "the author." This cannot be unrelated to the "modern subject" or "self"; rather, it overlaps with them. Therefore, the significance that classical studies and education in the classics has in this "contemporary" age is, as we have seen with *The Tale of Genji*, that it holds within it the capacity to invert "the modern."

Consequently, it seems clear that the history of Japan's modern novel will be reconceptualized as a protest against this modern subject created by *ta*. I believe that Natsume Sōseki and Izumi Kyōka hold the key in that process, but even before them there were several attempts at resistance, albeit reactionary ones. Representative of these are works that used refined language, or *gabuntai*.[19] Post–*genbun itchi* examples of *gabuntai* were under the influence of Edo period *yomihon*, but they were not controlled by it, and so it is necessary to understand them as representing an intentional choice made out of opposition to the discourse of *ta*, which restricts the world of multiple meanings, perspectives, and origins. To confirm this, we must analyze the texts of such writers as Ozaki Kōyō, Higuchi Ichiyō, and Kōda Rohan, but here, even if we confine ourselves to looking only at Mori Ōgai's "Maihime" (Dancing Girl), we can obtain at least some suggestions that will help confirm the meaning of the existence of Meiji period elegant style.[20]

"Maihime" begins with the line "They have already finished loading the coal." The word *coal*, whether for a train or a steamship, evokes those forms of transportation that symbolize modernity, and we might accordingly say that this text, though only by suggestion, makes it clear that modernity itself is its main subject. At the end of this sentence, the use of the auxiliary verb *tsu*, which confirms completion, to establish the completion of an event in the opening sentence reveals that this text takes the form of a reminiscence; it is an expression inscribed with the text's distinctive methodology. At the same time, an ending is also a beginning, and, although not a word is mentioned in the text, it should be possible to see that the circumstance of "They have already finished loading the coal" holds within it the possibility of "departure" hidden in the background.

Now, there is a passage in the opening section of "Maihime" in which "I" relates that it is impossible for him to express in "verse" or "song" the "remorse" he has experienced.

19. *Gabuntai* is described by Mitani as a language that is the opposite of *sato no kotoba* (language of the countryside) and mimics classical literature but is contemporaneous with modernity.
20. Mori Ōgai, "Maihime," translated by Richard Bowring, *Monumenta Nipponica* 30:2 (summer 1975): 151–66 (hereafter cited as "Maihime").

> Ah, how can I ever rid myself of such remorse? If it were of a different nature I could perhaps soothe my feelings by expressing them in poetry. But this is so deeply engraved upon my heart that I fear it is impossible. And yet, as there is no one here this evening, and it will be some while before the cabin boy comes to turn off the light, I think I will try to record the outline of my story here. ("Maihime," 152)

Evidently, the distinction between poetry and prose is being narrated here. While poetry is unable to express his regret, in prose discourse "remorse" can be dispersed throughout so that it becomes immanent to that discourse. In addition, the sentence preceding the above passage states:

> To whom could I possibly show a record of fleeting impressions in which what was right yesterday is wrong today? Perhaps this is why my diary was never written. No, there is another reason. ("Maihime, 151)

Thus, given that the diary as an expressive device is indicated as being inadequate to the situation, this text's mode of expression includes a strong consciousness of its being a prose novel, and so we can say that its adoption of *gabuntai*, including the use of the *kakarimusubi* (a classical form in which an auxiliary verb occurring in midsentence anticipates the attributive verb at the end of the sentence) was deliberate.

From the perspective of *monogatari* narratology, "The Dancing Girl," like "Urashima Tarō," is told according to the motifs of a "visit to a strange land" tale.[21] The place from which the story is narrated is "Saigon," a border region between Japan and this strange land. This border called Saigon holds great significance, but since I cannot engage in a full textual analysis of "Maihime" here I will merely point out that it is only on this border that this literature of reminiscence is possible.

This is a prose text spun from the reminiscences of the narrator, Ōta Toyotarō, who is often identified with the author, Mori Ōgai. As I have written in "Consciousness of Time in the Kagerō Diaries," the distinctiveness

---

21. "Urashima Tarō" is the fable of a young man who, in one particular version, after saving a turtle's life is led to a kingdom lying at the depths of the ocean. He spends several happy years there, but when he returns home out of concern for his aging mother, he discovers that he has been away for decades. On returning home he opens a box that had been given to him by his hosts at his departure with instructions not to open it; he immediately ages according to his true age in his native world.

of this writing comes from the intermingling and meandering among the three distinct temporalities: that of the past experience, that of the moment of reminiscence, and that of the moment of narration.[22] Here we have the five-year experience in the past; the moment of its recollection in Saigon, at the boundary between West and East; and the moment in which the recollections are woven together using the distinct strands of Japanese writing, Western writing, and Chinese writing, resulting in a new prose form different from poetry or the diary, a form expressing "regret." At least three distinct dimensions of time are entangled in the narrator Ōta Toyotarō, so that the mode of narration here harbors within it something exceeding the content of *ta*, which only allows a one-dimensional expression.

Thus, the significance of "Maihime" being written in *gabuntai* at a time when the trend of *genbun itchi* was taking hold is not an anachronistic reaction but should be understood as a protest against the modern subject, *ta*. Even when Mori Ōgai subsequently came to write novels using the vernacular, he diligently maintained this struggle, resorting frequently, for example, to the present tense. We need to appreciate fully the significance of his struggles with the modernity that is *ta*.

For this reason, the tangled strands of time in "Maihime" provide a crucial key for reading this text. For example, let us take the following sentence.

> Alas, what evil fate brought her to my lodgings to thank me? She looked so beautiful there standing by the window where I used to sit reading all day long surrounded by the works of Schopenhauer and Schiller. From that time on our relationship gradually deepened. ("Maihime," 156)

In this text, "Alas" marks the sentiment of the present moment of narration. "evil fate" marks the time of his reminiscence, and "deepened" relationship (which is expressed literally as the blossoming of "a beautiful flower") marks the time of the past experience. The act of reading must "play" among these contradictory words; if, without reading this play, one were to seek a unitary theme, the true form of the text could never be manifested.

Through a comparison with *Ukigumo*, however, we can also see how setting up Ōta Toyotarō as the sole narrator of the text and putting him at the center of the textual apparatus paradoxically prevented this text from being a richly productive one.

22. Mitani Kuniaki, "Kagerō nikki no jikan ishiki" (Consciousness of Time in the Kagerō Diaries), in *Kagerō nikki*, edited by Issatsu no kōza henshūbu (Tokyo: Yūseidō, 1981).

As the heir to *ninjōbon* and *kokkeibon*, *Ukigumo* makes regular use of dialogue and is characterized by passages of conversation that often extend over several pages. However, in "Maihime," although dialogue is not completely absent, indirect reported speech is the primary mode of presentation. For example, at the Kaiserhof, where Ōta meets with Aizawa Kenkichi, we read "This is the gist of what was said," and Elis's letter to Yūtarō when he is stationed in Saint Petersburg is summarized by indirect narration: "This was what she told me in her first letter." In other words, the text "Maihime" is restricted to Ōta Toyotarō's monolithic point of view, and the viewpoints of these events from Elis's or Aizawa Kenkichi's perspectives are suppressed. It is this loss of "dialogue" with the words of others that in the final scene produces expressions such as "Friends like Aizawa Kenkichi are rare indeed, and yet to this very day there remains a part of me that curses him." We can even say that these words reveal the limitations of the text "Maihime." By contrast, it is possible, as Komori Yōichi demonstrates in "The Phenomenon of the Other: The Place of the Reader in *Ukigumo*," to relativize the text of *Ukigumo* by reading it from the perspective of Osei.[23] Along with the development of modern expression in the form of *ta*, this work created a multidimensional world through its use of spoken dialogue, an accomplishment we should recognize.

Ukigumo, by struggling with the "past" form of prose fiction engendered the discourse of *ta*, thereby rendering autonomous the "author" as the subject of modern literature. This incomprehensible being, which can see even into the unconsciousness of others, opened up the horizon of the modern novel and holds us to this day in its spell. Nevertheless, it has simultaneously always been an object of protest, something to be defamiliarized. The purpose of this essay has been to grasp one aspect of the history of that struggle through the analysis of several texts from the developmental period.

POSTSCRIPT

This work was written as a critique of Kamei Hideo's *Transformations of Sensibility*. My intention at the time was to focus mainly on criticism by addressing the problem of his separation of Miura Tsutomu's concept, presented in connection with the time discourse of the auxiliary verb, from its relation-

---

23. Komori Yōichi, "Tasha no genzō: *Ukigumo* ni okeru dokusha no ichi" (The Phenomenon of the Other: The Place of the Reader in *Ukigumo*), *Seijō kokubungaku ronshū* 15 (May 1983): 87–123.

ship with the auxiliary verb and time and the way his method was grafted onto Nakamura Yūjirō's theory of sensibility. My criticisms are as I have stated them, but let me also acknowledge that his work is a noteworthy precursor to the creation of a new methodology in modern literary studies.

NOTE

This chapter was originally published as "Kindai shōsetsu no gensetsu/joshō," *Nihon bungaku* 33:7 (July 1984): 47–56.

PART TWO

Theories and Politics
of Language

Kokugogaku versus *Gengogaku*: Language Process Theory and Tokieda's Construction of Saussure Sixty Years Later

John Whitman

The debate surrounding Tokieda Motoki's Language Process Theory (*gengo katei setsu*) and more particularly Tokieda's critique of Saussure dominated metatheoretic discourse in the fields of *kokugogaku* (national language studies) and *gengogaku* (linguistics) in the immediate postwar period.[1] The debate is perhaps best known within these disciplines as a kind of territorial polemic typified by Hattori Shirō's attack on Tokieda's reading of Saussure.[2] Hattori's attack was preceded by the *kokugogakusha* Satō Kiyoji's critique of Language Process Theory.[3] In general, Tokieda's work produced a complex of responses from both the *kokugogaku* and *gengogaku* establishments.

In the last several decades, scholars of Japanese literature have revived interest in Tokieda's writing about language.[4] I am interested in the relative lack of contact between this discourse, arising from literary theoretical writing, and the earlier (but ongoing) debate in *kokugogaku* and *gengogaku*. The more recent discourse highlights Tokieda as a "homegrown theorist," to adopt Kamei Hideo's term.[5] This chapter is an attempt to relate the two discourses. It focuses on two sources of potential tension in Tokieda's thought. The first is the tension between Tokieda's theory of *kokugo* (national language) and the universalizing aspects of his theory of language. The second

1. Tokieda Motoki, "Shinteki katei toshite no gengo honshitsukan," *Bungaku* 7:5 (July 1937): 1–21; Tokieda Motoki, *Kokugogaku genron* (Tokyo: Iwanami Shoten, 1941).
2. Hattori Shirō, "Gengo katei setsu ni tsuite," *Kokugo kokubun* 26:1 (January 1957): 1–18; Hattori Shirō, "Saussure no langue to gengo katei setsu," *Gengo kenkyū* 32 (1957): 1–42.
3. Satō Kiyoji, "Gengo katei setsu ni tsuite no gimon," *Kokugogaku* 2 (1949): 17–30.
4. See, for example, Naoki Sakai, *Voices of the Past: The Status of Language in Eighteenth-Century Japanese Discourse* (Ithaca: Cornell University Press, 1991); and Karatani Kōjin, "Nihon seishin bunseki (4)," *Hihyō kūkan* 1:8 (1994): 241–55.
5. Kamei Hideo, *Transformations of Sensibility: The Phenomenology of Meiji Literature*, edited and translated by Michael Bourdaghs (Ann Arbor: University of Michigan, Center for Japanese Studies Publications, 2002), xxx.

is the tension in Language Process Theory between rejecting objectification of language, on the one hand, and the objectified aspects of Tokieda's grammatical description on the other.

1. LANGUAGE PROCESS THEORY

Kamei Hideo's preface to the English translation of *Transformations of Sensibility* contains an excellent summary of Language Process Theory. I will not attempt to duplicate it here. Instead, following Kamei's lead, I present the synopsis of the theory provided by Miura Tsutomu.[6] The text below (my translation) appears as the final section of Miura's review of the history of Japanese language studies.

> **Tokieda Motoki's Language Process Theory**
> The Shōwa period brought Tokieda Motoki's introduction of his Language Process Theory and research on Japanese based on it. The significance of this event is comparable to the advent of Copernicus in astronomy; it demarcated a new era not just for *kokugogaku* but for *gengogaku* as well. The details of the theory are spelled out in Tokieda's *Kokugogaku genron* [Principles of National Language Studies], published in 1941. Linguistics up to that point conceived of language as a tool. It was held that language is a tool existing in the head that is used to think and to communicate thought. This tool was explicated as a psychological object (*seishinteki na jittai*) and was referred to as a "linguistic system" (*gengo*) and "the material of language" (*gengo no zairyō*).[7] Tokieda rejected this view of language as a fixed structure, or object, and argued instead that the essence of language should be understood in terms of the processual structure (*kateitaki kōzō*): object (*taishō*) → cognition (*ninshiki*) → expression (*hyōgen*). The resultant theory was called Language Process Theory (*gengo katei setsu*).
>
> Language Process Theory is based on the view of language revealed in the history of earlier *kokugogaku* research in Japan, as well as my reflections on linguistic theory based on my empirical

6. Miura Tsutomu, Nihongo wa dō iu gengo ka (Tokyo: Kisetsusha, 1971), 85–89.
7. Here Miura is referring to *gengo* as the technical term used by Kobayashi Hideo to translate Saussure's *langue*. Ferdinand Saussure, *Gengogaku Genron*, translated by Kobayashi Hideo (Tokyo: Oka Shoin, 1928). I follow Culler's rendition of *langue* in Jonathan Culler, *Ferdinand de Saussure*, rev. ed. (Ithaca: Cornell University Press, 1986), 39.

research. It is hypothesized as a conceptual basis for scientific research on the national language; it represents my response to the question of what is the essence of language. . . . It is in processual structure that the most important questions of language research reside. (Tokieda, *Kokugogaku genron*)

Linguists (*gengogakusha*) were negative toward Tokieda's theory; even among national language studies scholars (*kokugogakusha*) there were both positive and negative opinions. But regardless of who its author was, the birth of Language Process Theory can only be considered a historical inevitability. Conceiving the universe as a "composite of processes" rather than a composite of entities is the revolutionary contribution of Hegelian philosophy; this dialectical worldview is affirmed by contemporary science. The introduction of Language Process Theory signifies the advent of a dialectical conception of language. The force of the theory stems from two sources. As Tokieda himself states, one is the unadorned view of language held by earlier *kokugogaku* scholars; the second is the dialectical thinking included in "phenomenology" as espoused by European philosophers, who were absorbing the tradition of Hegelian philosophy. . . .

The points of Tokieda's theory that are superior to previous theories are the following.

1. Treating language in terms of a processual structure.

2. Employing the distinction between objective expressions (*kyakkanteki hyōgen*) and subjective expressions (*shukanteki hyōgen*) as a basic classification of words.

3. Problematizing two distinct stances toward language: the subjective stance and the objective stance.

The following can be identified as defects of the theory.

1. Taking the essence of language to be "conceptual operation by the subject" (*shutai no gainen sayō*).

2. Taking "meaning" in language to be "the subject's way of grasping" (*shutai no haaku no shikata*), that is, a semantic operation directed toward the object (*kyakutai ni taisuru imi sayō*).

3. Omitting recognition of the social conventions that accompany linguistic expressions and the intermediary process dependent on them.

4. The stance that takes cognition to be reflection (*ninshiki o han'ei to miru tachiba*) is not correctly carried through. Neither the distinction between expressions dealing with received reality and expressions dealing with imagination, nor the mutual relation between these two, is taken up.[8]

Miura goes on to explain the basis for his criticisms in (1) and (2). He argues that Tokieda's conception of linguistic meaning is fundamentally incoherent, that his "treatment of language in terms of process is correct, but it cannot therefore be concluded that language and linguistic activity are one and the same. Tokieda's misconception of 'meaning' is a product of this confusion."[9]

> As none among object → cognition → expression are "meaning," "meaning" must be sought somewhere outside of them. At this point, Tokieda labels the very activity of the subject producing an expression, that is, the way in which the subject cognizes the object, as a "semantic operation" (*imi sayō*), and concludes that the activity of the speaker/writer is itself "meaning." . . . Tokieda's argument that objects cannot be taken to comprise "meaning" is correct, but his transfer of the locus of "meaning" from object to function is an error. "Meaning" must be understood not as function, but as a relation.[10]

The third of Miura's criticisms of Language Process Theory has a Saussurean flavor. Defect 3 is reminiscent of Saussure's insistence on language as a social fact (*fait social*, Kobayashi/Tokieda's *shakaiteki jijitsu*). This conception is explicitly rejected by Tokieda, as we shall see below.[11]

2. THE IMMEDIATE POSTWAR RESPONSE

Both Kamei and Miura in the passage cited above characterize the response to Tokieda through the 1950s in disciplinary terms: linguists (*gengogakusha*)

---

8. Miura, *Nihongo wa dō iu gengo ka*, 85-87.
9. Ibid., 87–88.
10. Ibid., 88. Although there is a superficial resemblance here between Miura's conception of meaning as relation and the structuralist view of meaning as a relationship of oppositions, the notion of "relation" at issue is completely different. The relevant relation for Miura is between the "process leading up to the creation" of speech sound or writing and the form of that item (88).
11. Tokieda, *Kokugogaku genron*, 71–81.

opposed, *kokugogakusha* divided, according to Miura. A starker disciplinary division is imposed by the view that writers were opposed to the extent that they adhered to the Western-derived discipline of linguistics. I think that this view oversimplifies the ways in which linguistics (and other "Western" writings) were/are used in Japanese intellectual life and also disempowers the users. Tokieda himself prominently cites the Danish linguist Otto Jespersen, an early critic of Saussure.[12] Thus European linguistics was utilized by both sides in the Language Process Theory debate.

Kamei has also explicated the political basis of the critique of Tokieda from the explicitly Marxist Left. The critique from the *gengogaku* establishment had a somewhat different basis, although it is also fundamentally political, I believe. Hattori Shirō, like Tokieda a (somewhat younger) transfer from the continent to a position at Tokyo University (the Department of Linguistics in Hattori's case), accuses Tokieda of relying on Kobayashi's translation of Saussure and failing to understand the original text.[13] Tokieda responded.[14] I will not attempt to reproduce this debate here, but Hattori's accusation has stuck in some measure. Thus, Kamei refers to Tokieda taking up Kobayashi's translation of "Saussure's definition of *langue*."[15] A sense of the effect of this polemical gambit against Tokieda can be derived from an informal reminiscence on the topic of Saussure and his reception in Japan written by Kobayashi.[16]

Kobayashi Hideo's translation of Bally and Sechehaye's *Cours de linguistique générale* was the first translation of Saussure to appear in any language. Kobayashi's article (written in 1977, toward the end of his life, for a special issue of *Gekkan gengo* devoted to Saussure) is a play on Kobayashi's ambiguous position. Kobayashi was Tokieda's colleague and interlocutor at Keijō University in Seoul starting in spring 1929; he was also the translator-author of the text that provided the basis for Tokieda's "misreading" of Saussure.

Tokieda returned to Seoul in the fall of 1929 from his studies in Germany and, according to Kobayashi, began studying Saussure assiduously: "Our offices were close; nearly once or twice a week he would come to my office and launch the debate. The endpoint of the debate would without

---

12. Ibid., 144.
13. Hattori, "Gengo katei setsu ni tsuite"; Hattori, "Saussure no langue to gengo katei setsu," Of course, we must remember that there is no original text. Kobayashi's translation, like other "Saussures," is based on the redaction of the notes of Saussure's students produced by Charles Bally and Albert Sechehaye and published after Saussure's death.
14. Tokieda Motoki, "Hattori Shirō kyōju no 'Gengo katei setsu ni tsuite' o yomu," *Kokugo kokubun* 26:4 (April 1957): 24–29.
15. Kamei, *Transformations of Sensibility*, xxxi.
16. Kobayashi Hideo, "Nihon ni okeru Saussure no eikyō," *Gekkan gengo* 7:3 (1978): 44–49.

fail appear as an article. *Kokugogaku genron* is not, upon close inspection, a single unified piece of writing; it is rather a compendium of individual articles, each one the product of his debates with me."[17] Kobayashi resumes the "misreading" attack on Tokieda's reading of Saussure, but the interest of his version is that he is the proximate author of the complicit text: "However, (Tokieda's) understanding of Saussure was based for the most part on the impression he derived from reading the first few chapters of [*Gengogaku*] *genron*; it was certainly not based on a structural grasp of the work resulting from a thorough reading of the entire text. Although Tokieda was a graduate of Kōsei Middle School, by the time he graduated university the better part of his French was gone; for the most part it appears that his effort to absorb the linguistic theory of the Far West (*taisei no gengo gakusetsu*) was through the medium of my translation."[18]

The irony here is that Tokieda's reading can only be as flawed as Kobayashi's translation. The broader point is, of course, that the "accuracy" of the translation is irrelevant: "Saussurean" linguistics as engaged by Tokieda in the 1930s and 1940s was based on Kobayashi's text, not on Bally and Sechehaye's "original" redaction. But what was at issue for Kobayashi and Hattori, both *gengogakusha* in the conventional disciplinary sense? The emphasis on translation, on legitimate versus illegitimate appropriation of foreign texts, suggests that the issue was control of linguistic capital. The discussion of *gengogaku* versus *kokogogaku* in relation to Language Process Theory has focused on the supposed intellectual differences between these two disciplines, one objectivist and Western-derived, the other (ideally at least) subjectivist and "homegrown." In fact, there is a more important material difference between the two disciplines, where the former might be represented by the career of Kobayashi Hideo. The social extension of "linguistics" is language workers: translators, language teachers, dictionary compilers. For this group, foreign language information is the capital that its members are normally privileged to control, and among their privileges is the primary right to neologize. Thus, while Kobayashi Hideo is virtually unknown as a linguistic theoretician, the impact of his coinages in *Gengogaku genron* on subsequent linguistic and literary theorizing is enormous. These include the following.[19]

17. Ibid., 48.
18. Ibid., 48.
19. It is notable that these "technical" terms are to be found in Sanseidō's French-Japanese dictionary, although terms such as *diachrony* and *signifier* are absent from its English counterpart. Maruyama Juntarō and Kawamoto Shigeo, *Konsaisu futsuwa jiten*, rev. ed. (Tokyo: Sanseidō, 1958).

gengo	*langue*
gen	*parole*
kyōjitai , later kyōjiron	*synchronie*
tsūjitai, later tsūjiron	*diachronie*
kigō	*signe*
tōjiron	*syntaxe*
shoki	*signifié*
nōki	*signifiant*

From the standpoint of Kobayashi, a specialist in stylistics in the tradition of Bally, or Hattori, perhaps the Japanese linguist best known in the West during the postwar period, Tokieda's bold plunge into the domain of linguistic theorizing using neologized/translational technical vocabulary was a territorial intrusion. In fact, even sixty years after its publication one of the most striking aspects of *Kokugogaku genron* is the free use it makes of this vocabulary to directly challenge Western theorists (primarily, of course, Saussure). This is in contrast to the use of translational vocabulary in linguistic literature prior to Tokieda. While *kokugogakusha* such as Ueda Kazutoshi and Yamada Yoshio made heavy use of linguistic technical terminology from translational sources (often negotiating between such terminology and terminology from Edo period *kokugaku* sources, as did Tokieda), these scholars did not engage in direct criticism of the intellectual sources of this terminology by naming sources and criticizing them. Thus, Kobayashi provides evidence that Hashimoto Shinkichi, Tokieda's predecessor at Tokyo University, was influenced by *Gengogaku genron*, yet Saussure's name does not appear in Hashimoto's writings.[20]

Kokugogaku genron is truly revolutionary in its ambition to scrutinize the conceptual bases of the very terms of linguistic theorizing in their translational guise. I believe that this ambition is by far the most important legacy of Tokieda's work, more important than his attempt to redefine the

---

20. Kobayashi, "Nihon ni okeru Saussure no eikyō," 47. The practice of minimizing references to intellectual precursors and adversaries was during the first half of the twentieth century a hallmark of theoretical linguistic writing by linguists in the West as well. Saussure's *Cours* itself is notable for its lack of such references. Of course, this may have something to do with the fact that it is based on lecture notes. The same may be said of Edward Sapir's *Language* (1921) and Leonard Bloomfield's book of the same title (1928), the foundational texts of American structuralism. It is not until Noam Chomsky's *Aspects of the Theory of Syntax* (1965) that a style of citation polemic comparable to the norm in literary and philosophical writing appears in linguistic writing by linguists.

intension of the term *kokugo* or his rejection of objectifying conceptions of language. This ambition was an implicit threat to the masters of the translational domain, in this case linguists involved in the work of translating and interpreting texts such as Saussure's *Cours*. One suspects that this is the political basis for critiques such as Hattori's, which in this sense must be seen as counterattacks.

3. DEFINING *KOKUGO*

Gengo katei setsu is a universalizing theory, as pointed out by Kamei.[21] It has no necessary identification with Japanese. The subsections of *Kokugogaku genron* discuss "The stance of linguistic research" "The object of linguistic research," and "The subjective stance and the observational stance toward language," all desiderata in a general theory of language. Tokieda's definition of *kokugo* is subsequent to this universalistic theorizing, and it shows careful attention to internal consistency. Because Tokieda rejects the characterization of language as a *fait social* (*shakaiteki jijitsu*), he is compelled to reject the standard sociohistorical definition of *kokugo* qua national language, which had become commonplace by the time *Kokugogaku genron* was written. Tokieda writes:

> The term *kokugo* as used in national language studies (*kokugogaku*) and in the history of those studies (*kokugogakushi*) can be seen as synonymous with "Japanese" (*Nihongo*). In addition to this commonly used sense of *kokugo*, what is construed as the standard language or the common language of the nation is also called *kokugo*; this is the narrow sense of the term. Strictly speaking, it would be most appropriate to maintain just the narrow sense of the term and not to use the term *kokugo* for Japanese as a whole, but rather simply call it Japanese, and to use "Japanese linguistics" (*Nihongogaku*), "the history of Japanese linguistics" (*Nihongogakushi*) in the place of "national language studies" and "the history of national language studies," but for the present, as a matter of convenience, I will follow established practice and continue to use the terms *kokugogaku* and *kokugogakushi*. Now, how should we define *kokugo*, that is to say, Japanese? I have rejected the previously established definition of *kokugo* as the language of the Japanese nation (*Nihon kokka no gengo*) or as the language of

21. Kamei, *Transformations of Sensibility*, xxviii.

the Japanese race (*Nihon minzoku no gengo*),[22] and maintained instead that *kokugo*, that is to say, Japanese, is a language possessed of Japanese-like characteristics (*Nihonteki seikaku o motta gengo*).[23]

There are two factors in Tokieda's desire to redefine the term *kokugo*. First, as pointed out by Yasuda Toshiaki, after 1885, 1910, and 1937, the mutilinguality of the Japanese empire vitiated the identification of *kokugo* as the language of—even an idealized—ethnically and linguistically homogeneous state as conceived by Ueda Kazutoshi and other Meiji period scholars.[24] Second, as observed above, any definition of *kokugo* as the language spoken by a particular population would be an externalizing or socially based definition.

Tokieda follows the preceding passage with a discussion of his interpretation of how Saussure would define a particular language. According to Tokieda, under a Saussurean approach "Japanese could be considered one *langue* [in the original: *gengo* = *rangu*, the former written in Chinese characters, the latter in *katakana*]."[25] This is a part of Tokieda's reading of Saussure that was criticized by Hattori because Saussure appears not to apply the concept of *langue* (language system) to particular *languages* in the everyday sense of that term. What concerns us most here is how Tokieda proceeds from his critique of Saussure to a processual definition of *kokugo* = *Nihongo*. He continues:

> I would like to consider the concept of Japanese based on the conception of *langue* outlined above, as the sum total of unions of idea and acoustic image stored in the brain of individual speakers. Of course it is not the case each of us individuals knows and implements all of the vocabulary and all of the grammatical rules of Japanese (*kokugo*). Therefore one could hold that what we call Japanese (*Nihongo*) must be the sum total of each individual's vocabulary and grammatical rules. The idea that *langue* exists outside of the individual follows from this. The way of thinking that looks at Japanese (*Nihongo*) in this kind of quantitative fashion and takes it to be the composite of the languages (*gengo*) of individuals follows inevitably from taking *langue* to be the union of idea and acoustic image; it follows from this way of thinking

22. Here Tokieda is referring to his formulation of this definition of *kokugo* in a previous work, Tokieda Motoki, *Kokugogakushi* (Tokyo: Iwanami Shoten, 1940).
23. Tokieda, *Kokugogaku genron*, 143.
24. Yasuda Toshiaki, *Shokuminchi no naka no "Kokugogaku": Tokieda Motoki to Keijō Teikoku Daigaku o megutte* (Tokyo: Sangensha, 1997), 90–93, 122.
25. Tokieda, *Kokugogaku genron*, 144.

that each of us partakes of no more than a part of the Japanese language (*Nihongo*). Newspapers and novels and other texts that we see every day are no more than a part of the Japanese language. But is this way of thinking correct? If it is the case that one union of idea and acoustic image is *langue* and the composite of such unions is also *langue* and together they are actual objects (*jitsuzaitai*), it must naturally be the case that they stand in a part-whole relation. Then since what we can experience is no more than a part of Japanese (*kokugo*), and since we cannot grasp the sum total of Japanese (*kokugo*) in its entirety as an object, we are forced to arrive at the conclusion that national language studies (*kokugogaku*) simply cannot be constituted. But why is it that we believe that *kokugogaku* is possible dealing only with one portion of the Japanese language (*kokugo*)? When we consider why it is that a botanist can take an individual cherry blossom and still formulate a definition of cherry blossoms, we know that it is because the individual expresses the universal. That is, an individual cherry blossom is not a part of the entirety of cherry blossoms; rather it can be thought of as a representative of cherry blossoms in general. We cannot apply the preceding logic so long as we consider Japanese (*Nihongo*) the composite of the vocabulary of individuals. But why is it, as a matter of fact, that we can take a vocabulary item of a single individual, contrast it with the words of a foreign language, and recognize it to be a word of Japanese (*Nihongo*)? To explain this fact, we must discard the constructional view of language (*kōseiteki gengokan*) and adopt a processual view of language (*kateiteki gengokan*). So long as we view a word to be a constructional entity (*kōseitai*) formed from ideas and acoustic images, it will be difficult to produce criteria for distinguishing it as a word of Japanese (*Nihongo*) from another *langue*. We must seek Japanese-like special characteristics (*Nihongoteki tokusei*) in the psycho-physiological processes where they are actually expressed.[26]

Tokieda proceeds to provide concrete examples of the special characteristics in question.

Respect language (*keigo*) is said to have Japanese-like special characteristics, but if we were to consider respect language from a constructional viewpoint we would not be able to produce criteria for distinguishing it from other vocabulary. Only when we examine the special way of grasping the concept and expressing

26. Ibid., 144–46.

it can we consider respect language to have Japanese-like special characteristics. Likewise, in the sense that the foreign word *ink*, when realized as *inki* within the grammatical or phonetic system of Japanese (*kokugo*), is already imbued with Japanese-like characteristics, we are able to say that it has become Japanized (*kokugoka shita*).[27]

We see in the preceding two passages how Tokieda critiques Saussure's "externalized" notion of *langue* and how he argues for a definition of *gengo* = *langue* = language in terms of process. However an epistemological problem arises when Tokieda attempts to implement this definition by identifying particular Japanese-like characteristics. As pointed out by Sakai, the project of identifying particular Japanese-like characteristics "requires an observational stance in which language is observed, analyzed, and known as an object rather than lived as a shutai-teki activity."[28] Thus, identification of the Japanese-like characteristics of *inki* requires attention to the external, formal characteristics of this lexical item. It also requires attention to the linguistic behavior of some social group; if *inki* was the idiosyncratic production of an individual speaker, we would not identify it as having Japanese-like characteristics. In this regard Tokieda's decision to proceed to the "definition" of a particular language undermines the project of a subject-oriented, processual conception of language in general. I return to this problem in discussing Tokieda's concept of *chinjutsu* (proposition) below.

4. THE POLITICS OF *KOKUGO*

We have seen how the imperative to identify Japanese-like characteristics moved Tokieda toward an observational stance, as pointed out by Sakai, in some measure undermining the project of building a subject-oriented theory of language. Tokieda's definition of *kokugo* leads him to this epistemological problem; it does not lead him into the trap of naive ethnocentrism. That is, a superficial reader of Tokieda might be tempted to jump to the conclusion that he imputed a special value to Japanese-like characteristics of language, but this is not the case. Tokieda's refusal to attribute any kind of superiority to the Japanese language as a consequence of its special characteristics is revealed in a 1944 *zadankai* on the subject of Japanese as the common language of the Greater East Asia Co-prosperity Sphere. Tokieda's exchange is with the phonetician Jinbō Kaku.

27. Ibid. 146.
28. Sakai, *Voices of the Past*, 326.

> Jinbō: A common language (*kyōtsūgo*), well, that's a natu-
>   ral development, you know. Insofar as we're talking
>   about a common language, among the languages of
>   East Asia, well, the best would be Japanese—from
>   a linguistic standpoint as well, hasn't a theory been
>   established that says that?
>
> Tokieda: I don't believe there's any need to think that. It is
>   not because a language is good that it is given the
>   status of common language; the natural momen-
>   tum centered on Japanese in a political sense, or
>   economically or culturally—that's what makes a
>   common language.[29]

Here Jinbō seems to be referring to a linguistic theory that attributes intrinsic superiority to Japanese, perhaps his (mis)assessment of Language Process Theory. But Tokieda refuses the gambit. The same refusal to attribute any special *linguistic* superiority to Japanese is clear in Tokieda's comments on dialects and non-Japanese languages in the Japanese political sphere. This refusal is completely consistent with the universalistic aspect of Tokieda's theorizing about language.

Tokieda's linguistic universalism has encouraged scholars from literary studies to oppose the allegations from Tokieda's critics that he was a supporter of the language policy of the colonial administration in Korea, particularly after 1940 when the administration moved to suppress the use and learning of Korean as part of a policy to supplant Korean with Japanese.

This debate comes into particularly sharp focus with Yasuda's 1997 monograph, which can be read as an extended critique of Karatani Kōjin's assertion that "Tokieda was not an imperialist."[30] The basis for Karatani's assertion is Tokieda's opposition to the blatantly coercive language-planning measures instituted by the colonial government in the 1940s such as forcing Koreans to adopt Japanese surnames. It is difficult to tell how openly Tokieda opposed these measures in his position as professor in the Kokugogaku Department at Keijō University. Although Tokieda expresses reservations about such policies in a general way in a widely cited 1942 article many of the claims about his position toward language policy are based on postwar writings.[31] Yasuda points, in contrast, to a 1943 article by Tokieda that appeared in the Seoul collaborationist journal *Kokumin bungaku*. In this article Tokieda advocates abandonment of the Korean language.

---

29. Quoted in Yasuda, *Shokuminchi no naka no "Kokugogaku,"* 129.
30. Karatani, "Nihon seishin bunseki (4)," 254.
31. The oft-cited article is Tokieda Motoki, "Chōsen ni okeru kokugo seisaku oyobi kokugo kyōiku no shōrai," *Nihongo* 2:8 (July 1942): 54–63.

To frankly state my conclusion regarding this problem, I believe that the people of the peninsula should discard the Korean language and adopt Japanese (*Chōsengo o sutete kokugo ni kiitsu subeki de aru to omou*). I think that they should proceed toward making Japanese [*kokugo* throughout this article] their mother tongue toward the goal of a linguistic habitus (*gengo seikatsu*) in which they are primary users of Japanese. At the present time the Korean language, due to the overwhelming impact of Chinese and Chinese characters, and contact with Japanese in modern times, has fallen into a state of extreme confusion and disunity, and it cannot necessarily be said that the linguistic habitus of the people of the peninsula is a happy one. The sole means of escape from this situation is to unify the linguistic practice (*gengo seikatsu*) with Japanese. The annexation of Korea, that great historical fact, will be truly brought to completion by an extension to linguistic habitus. Unification of the national language (*kokugo tōitsu*) must be deemed a symbol of a unified nation, but unification toward Japanese for the people of the peninsula is a benefit of the most internal, most spiritual kind. Enabling them to escape from the practice of bilingualism and establish a unified linguistic habitus bestows on the people of the peninsula a benefit inferior to none. The adoption of Japanese as mother tongue (*kokugo o bogoka suru*) is by no means something that can be accomplished in a day, but I believe that all of those involved in Japanese language education should work as one toward this goal.[32]

Karatani's assertion that "Tokieda was not an imperialist" is naively ahistorical to begin with, but Tokieda's stance in the article cited by Yasuda makes it impossible to claim that the political consequence of Tokieda's universalism was a kind of brave liberalism with regard to language policy. It is nevertheless the case that Tokieda's theorizing about language was not "Japanocentric" in the manner often revealed in, for example, contemporary "Nihonjinron" writing.

5. *CHINJUTSU* AND THE DELINEATION OF JAPANESE-LIKE CHARACTERISTICS

Literary scholars writing on Tokieda have focused on his use of the distinction between *shi* (content morphemes) and *ji* (functional morphemes) and

---

32. Tokieda Motoki, "Chōsen ni okeru kokugo: Jissen oyobi kenkyū no shosō," *Kokumin bungaku* 3:1 (1943): 102, quoted in Yasuda, *Shokuminchi no naka no "Kokugogaku,"* 133–34.

other linguistic concepts derived in part from Edo period nativist scholars. I would like to conclude this essay by briefly discussing an aspect of Tokieda *bunpō* (grammar) that continues to draw more attention from *kokugogaku* theorists. This is the concept of *chinjutsu*, normally translated into English as "proposition." My discussion is drawn from the recent detailed analysis of Tokieda's *chinjutsu-ron* (theory of *chinjutsu*) and its precursors and successors by Onoe Keisuke.[33]

As Onoe explains, the grammatical term *chinjutsu* was introduced by the early-twentieth-century grammarian Yamada Yoshio. In Yamada's system, *chinjutsu* is closely associated with the predicate of the clause, which is normally sentence-final in Japanese.[34] Onoe explains, "Yamada used the expression *chinjutsu suru* to speak of completing the utterance and enouncing the sentence at the site of the predicate (*jutsugo ni oite iikiri, soko de bun o nobeageru*), but his usage of '*chinjutsu*' is based on the everyday, normal meaning of the term; it cannot be called a special grammatical concept."[35] Although Yamada's use of the term may be transparent from the standpoint of normal Japanese usage, it is poorly conveyed by the standard English translation of the term (*teiyaku*). Onoe goes on to explain how Tokieda redefined the term.

> According to Tokieda's view of grammar [e.g., Tokieda, *Kokugogaku genron*], the objective content expressed by content morphemes (*shi ni yotte arawasareta kyakutaiteki naiyō*) is enclosed and unified by the subjective operation of sentence-final functional morphemes (*bunmatsuji no shutaiteki sayō ga tsutsumi, tōitsu shite*), and the sentence is constituted. But by asserting here that "What Professor Yamada calls '*chinjutsu*' corresponds to my unifying operation of the clause-final functional morpheme," Tokieda comes to label as *chinjutsu* the unifying function of the clause-final morpheme (*bunmatsuji no tōitsu sayō*) itself. Since then this has become established as Tokieda's concept of *chinjutsu* and assumed the position of a fundamental concept in *chinjutsuron*.[36]

Onoe next explains the fundamental differences between Yamada's concept of *chinjutsu*, which had an overt phonetic manifestation only in sentences with verbal/adjectival predication, and Tokieda's, which was held to be manifest in every sentence of Japanese.

---

33. Onoe Keisuke, Bunpō to imi (I) (Tokyo: Kuroshio shuppan, 2001).
34. Yamada Yoshio, *Nihon bunpōgaku gairon*, rev. ed. (Tokyo: Hōbunkan Shuppan, 1936), originally published in 1909.
35. Onoe, *Bunpō to imi (I)*, 283.
36. Ibid., 283–84.

Tokieda does not distinguish verbal and nominal predication and understands the structure of all sentences in terms of the one-dimensional schema of {content material (*shitaiteki sozai*) + *chinjutsu*}; *chinjutsu* at this point becomes greatly different from the *chinjutsu* of Yamada. For Yamada, all clauses were formed through an apperceptive operation (*tōkaku sayō*), and up to this point Tokieda's *chinjutsu* is close to Yamada's apperceptive operation, but Yamada's apperceptive operation may be divided into cases in which it can be said to be realized in the grammatical form of the sentence (such as in the *chinjutsu* of the verbal/adjectival predicate in predicational clauses) and cases in which its presence may be recognized only abstractly. . . . Tokieda's *chinjutsu* is, number one, realized in the morphology of all clauses, and, number two, specified as bearing the special function of clause-final functional morpheme; in these two respects it differs greatly from Yamada's concept of *chinjutsu*,"[37]

Tokieda's conception of *chinjutsu* is expressed clearly in the following examples from *Kokugogaku genron*,[38]

Yama wa yuki	ka
Soto wa ame	rasii
Inu hashiru	///

In structures such as *Inu hashiru* (A dog runs), where there is no pronounced clause-final functional morpheme, Tokieda posits a "zero *chinjutsu*" (*reikigō no chinjutsu*) to maintain the generalization that a clause-final *chinjutsu* is present in all sentences of Japanese. *Chinjutsu* in Tokieda's sense might be best rendered as "mood" or, as Kinsui Satoshi has suggested, "propositional attitude."[39]

This way of thinking about Japanese sentence structure has had enormous influence on most subsequent treatments of Japanese syntax, including those within the framework of generative grammar. Onoe outlines two objections to Tokieda's *chinjutsuron*. The first focuses on the positing of a "zero *chinjutsu*" in an example such as *Inu hashiru*; the argument goes that it is preferable to attribute some *ji*-like properties (and thus a contribution to *chinjutsu*) to the predicate (*hashiru* in the sentence *Inu hashiru*). The second kind of objection, which Onoe takes to be more serious, has to do with how

37. Ibid., 284.
38. Tokeida, *Kokugogaku genron*, 252–53.
39. Kinsui Satoshi, personal communication, April 19, 2002.

chinjutsu status is assigned to auxiliaries (*jodōshi*) and sentence-final particles (*shūjoshi*). To take Onoe's example, in a sentence such as *Ikanai* (Won't go), the negative auxiliary *-nai* might be accorded *chinjutsu* status as the clause-final functional morpheme, but in the obviously related sentence *Ikanai yo* (Won't go [you should know]) the same expression, *ikanai*, must be considered a content expression (*shi*) in its entirety, and only the sentence final particle *yo* qualifies as *chinjutsu*.

What is of interest about this discussion for this essay is not the validity of Tokieda's conception of *chinjutsu* (although it is certainly worthwhile for literary scholars to know about this contribution to linguistic thought in Japan). More significant is the fact that the discussion is perforce conducted on the basis of the same observational stance as the grammatical theorizing of Yamada Yoshio and Watanabe Minoru (Tokieda's major successor in *chinjutsuron*) and, indeed, Saussure. That is, distributional criteria, semantic interpretation, overt or nonovert realization—all the standard elements of linguistic analysis—determine the nature of the debate. This brings us full circle to Sakai's point discussed in section 3. The concept of *chinjutsu* may be the most central of the "Japanese-like characteristics" on which Tokieda *bunpō* is built. But in developing this concept, and in its subsequent development in *kokugogaku* theory, the ideal of a nonobservational linguistic theory is irretrievably lost.

Theories of Language in the Academic Field of Philosophy: Japan in the 1970s

KAMEI Hideo

Translated by Jennifer Cullen

1. KEYWORDS OF THE LATE 1960s: *LOCAL CUSTOMS* AND *INDIGENOUS*

From the late 1960s through the 1970s, the most stimulating and exciting (and therefore seemingly subversive) words to Japanese writers, literary scholars, and intellectual historians were *local customs* (*dozoku*) and *indigenous* (*dochaku*).

These words were defined through contrast with the "modern" and were thought to signify the customs and mentality of the Japanese people that had persisted without interruption since before modernity, in some instances since ancient times. These terms also signified spaces that remained untouched by modernization even after the coming of the modern age. Thus, if we call the people who led the modernization of Japan "intellectuals," these words were used to refer to the common people, the masses. They were also sometimes used to signify irrational sentiments as opposed to rational knowledge.

As you can see even from this simple introduction, the people who used these terms sympathetically as intellectual keywords invested them with a criticism of the fact that the postwar democratic *reforms* had not led to a democratic *revolution*, one that would restructure all aspects of the social structure of Japan. Their criticism was aimed mainly at the intellectuals who had led the postwar reforms, and it developed into a broader criticism of the role of the intellectual in modern Japan, leading finally to a critical rethinking of Japan's modernization itself.

In other words, what these people celebrated as "local customs" and "indigenous" had previously been scorned by those promoting postwar democratic reforms as lagging behind in modernization and as hotbeds of conservative and reactionary political forces obstructing reform. In this sense, they had only been dealt with by modernization advocates as objects for potential enlightenment and improvement. It seems likely that a common motive among the people who began using these keywords in a positive light was a desire to free them from the position of object, restore them to active subjectivity, and to extract from them a force for change.

However, it cannot be denied that the mentality of these local customs had actively supported the emperor system and been a primary source of the energy that the modern Japanese state had poured into its war effort. What stance did those who celebrated these keywords take toward this historical reality? Their thought in this regard occupied a wide range of positions, stretching from the New Left to the New Right, as can be seen by lining up Yoshimoto Takaaki, Hashikawa Bunzō, Oketani Hideaki, Murakami Ichirō, and Mishima Yukio. Yet they all shared a dissatisfaction with and critical attitude toward the course of postwar politics and thought.

If we apply a generational analysis, we might say that their postwar criticism, or their criticism of modernity, was a gesture of self-assertion on the part of what could be called the "wartime cohort." *Wartime cohort* here indicates the generation born during the 1920s, the generation that underwent basic intellectual formation during the 1940s. Take, for example, Hashikawa Bunzō and his *Introduction to the Criticism of the Japan Romantic School* (*Nihon roman-ha hihan josetsu*, 1965), which illuminated the thought of the Japan Romantic School, thereby opening the way for reevaluation of a topic that had been considered taboo since the war. This book is something like a manifesto for the wartime cohort. In it, Hashikawa argues that during the 1940s, when the thought of his generation was being formed, the Marxist movement had already been destroyed and there were no opportunities to come into contact with thought critical of the war Japan was pursuing or of the discourse that supported it. According to Hashikawa, the members of this generation were heavily influenced by Yasuda Yojūrō, the representative ideologue of the journal *Japan Romantic School* (*Nihon roman-ha*, first issue March 1935). Yasuda's discourse might best be called "aesthetic patriotism." It understood the nation as a community of destiny and took death in service of the nation's war as the fulfillment of a kind of destined love.

One of the novels Hashikawa felt a strong sympathy with was Inoue Mitsuharu's *False Crane* (*Kyoko no kureenu*, 1960). The protagonist is a youth who during the war believed the emperor system provided the basic principle of human equality. Although he believes that Japanese and Koreans should be equal as "imperial subjects" under the emperor system, he finds that Korean laborers in the Kyushu coal mines are discriminated against and work under horrible conditions. Enraged at this betrayal of the emperor, he experiences a feeling of solidarity with the Korean youths. After the war, he is violently shocked to hear the slogan brandished by the Japan Communist Party—"Overthrow the emperor system"—and is amazed to learn that such a way of thinking even exists. Hashikawa Bunzō used the example of this protagonist to describe the experience of defeat shared by members of his generation.

———

A critical stance, even a kind of grudge (*ressentiment*), directed at postwar democratic thought erupted out of the generational consciousness of this wartime cohort. Judging by postwar values, they had believed in wrongheaded thought and supported a war that was criminal. But even if that was so, were the deaths of their compatriots who had gone off to battle believing in the ideas of that war completely in vain? Among Japanese soldiers were some with no doubts about the war, some who had approached people on the battlefield in a spirit of sincerity and goodwill; were their actions also criminal? Although this may not be an exact characterization of their position, the thinkers I am discussing here frequently raised similar questions. Every year in Japan the prime minister's visit to the Yasukuni Shrine re-emerges as a political issue as August 15, the anniversary of Japan's surrender, approaches. The Yasukuni Shrine functions as a kind of apparatus for absorbing and distilling this kind of grudge, and there are those among this generation of writers and thinkers who never go beyond the sort of thought that Yasukuni represents. In contrast, there are others, such as Yoshimoto Takaaki, who proclaimed the bankruptcy of pseudo-social scientific theories of the state and revolutionary thought based on these theories because they ignore the fact that the emperor system had a hold on the hearts of the masses; he called these theories forms of modernism that "avoid a confrontation with the dominant gene of the Japanese feudal system" in his *A Basis for Independent Thought* (*Jiritsu no shisōteki kyoten*, 1966). Likewise, Tsuda Michio turned a critical gaze on the Japan Communist Party's analysis of the emperor system and on the Marxist theory of the state. He attempted to put forth a new concept of the "party" and the revolutionary vanguard through an original rereading of Marx and Engels in *Restoration of a Theory of the State* (*Kokkaron no fukken*, 1967), and he sought a method for "confronting" the nationalism and petty-minded egoism that were deeply rooted in the masses in *Theory of Japanese Nationalism* (*Nihon nashonarizumu ron*, 1968).

Incidentally, Hashikawa Bunzō was born in 1922, Inoue Mitsuharu in 1926, and Yoshimoto Takaaki in 1924. Tsuda Michio was born in 1929, placing him among the youngest members of this wartime school. He seems to have no memory of having swallowed what Hashikawa calls "aesthetic nationalism," but he was probably still in sync with the others mentioned above.

———

To make a slight digression, several years ago the manga author Kobayashi Yoshinori published *On War* (*Sensōron*, 1998), in which he raised suspicions as to the credibility of photographs documenting war crimes perpetrated by the Japanese army such as the Rape of Nanking. His tactics were extremely provocative, inciting opposition from historians and peace activists, who attacked *On War* for affirming and beautifying the Japanese war of aggression. In addition, historians and activists began a campaign to stop the use of *The New History Textbook* (*Atarashii rekishi kyōkasho*), a social studies textbook for middle schools written by Kobayashi, among others, when it was approved for use in public schools by the Ministry of Education. Government officials from South Korea and the Republic of China (Taiwan) also issued official protests complaining that the "historical consciousness" of Japanese history textbooks was distorted. It became an international issue, one that is no doubt familiar to most people.

This is not the place to investigate this affair at any length, but I do want to introduce the specifics of *On War*. Kobayashi's method there was to present people of the so-called war generation in the guise of grandpas and grandmas and to have them tell of their war experiences and the experiences of their youth during the war. A youth resembling Kobayashi Yoshinori himself listens to these stories and concludes that these people really "believed" in the great ideals behind the war and took up guns for the sake of their loved ones. Yet the postwar activists of the peace movement have been "brainwashed" by the ideology of a "trial by lynch mob" in which the victorious nations of America, England, China, and the Soviet Union unilaterally judged the defeated country's—Japan's—war crimes in the Tokyo Tribunal.[1]

Exposing the fallacy of this rhetoric, which sets up a simple binary opposition between sincere faith and brainwashing, is not particularly difficult in itself. Supplemented by the above narrative apparatus, the message of the manga just barely holds together. But in my opinion the historians and activists who criticized *On War* were unable to counter it effectively. This was because they failed to "confront" the intellectual enterprise of the wartime cohort that began to appear in the late 1960s; they had never directly engaged in a proper dialogue with it. As a result, a simple schema is repeated

———

1. Kobayashi Yoshinori, *Sensōron* (On War), (Tokyo: Gentōsha, 1998). All notes are by the translator.

in which they see the Japanese masses as victims of the state authority of the emperor system at home and as victimizers in the colonies and occupied territories abroad.

To return to my main topic, the trend in thought toward a concern with "local customs" and the "indigenous" that I mentioned earlier was not limited to the wartime cohort. Takami Jun, one generation older than them, chose a man who had once been an antiestablishment anarchist as the protagonist of his novel *A Bad Feeling* (*Iya na kanji*, 1963). The novel describes the process by which he is transfigured into a terrorist amid the power struggles in the upper echelons of the army. He ends up by slaying, for fun, a "prisoner of war" on a battlefield in China, a prisoner who may not actually have been a Chinese soldier. Given its story line, the novel was recognized for the way it probes the depths of the Japanese soul, but it is also noteworthy because the author places Kita Ikki (1883–1937), the ideological leader of the failed February 26, 1936, military coup d'état, within the story.

Kita Ikki was the first theorist of revolution to give ideological expression to "local customs" as a form of reaction, in his case a reaction against the Great Powers of Europe and North America. Setting up a binary opposition between the Great Powers and Japan in the form of an opposition between the "haves" and "have-nots," he thought it the world historical mission of Japan as a have-not to win Asian independence from the rule of the haves. According to his program, the nation of Japan would have to be reconstructed before it could bring about such an international action. He sought the core historical agent for this national reconstruction in civilians who had military experience—in other words, in "rural soldiers." According to Kita, rural soldiers were "laborers in the guise of soldiers," and through them it would be possible to create a "labor-military party." Needless to say, this labor-military party was modeled after the soviets of the Russian Revolution. His design for the nation even included a plan for limiting private property.

This was an extremely dangerous idea to the ruling class of the time. Even after the war it was taboo to study Kita Ikki, as it was recognized that he had laid the ideological groundwork for the war of aggression. It was during this time that Takami Jun wrote a novel giving Kita a major role. The story describes a paradox in which antiauthority sentiments transform themselves into aggression against neighboring countries, but viewed from another angle it also functioned as the novel that dispelled the taboo on Kita, a predecessor to the Kita Ikki boom of the 1970s. Hashikawa Bunzō and Yoshimoto Takaaki also had a strong interest in Kita, and their influence led Takimura Ryūichi to attempt a theoretical examination of Kita's theory of revolution in *Kita Ikki: Japanese National Socialism* (*Kita Ikki: Nihon no kokka shakai shugi*, 1973). The book forms a kind of a companion piece to Tsuda Michio's theory of the state.

Further, Hotta Yoshie, who is also slightly older than the wartime cohort, portrayed a strange and mysterious world in which foreign ideas (in this case Christianity) mix with "local customs" and are completely transformed and absorbed by the people in his novel *Kibuki Island* (*Kibukijima*, 1957). He also describes the Shimabara rebellion in *From the Bottom of the Roar of the Ocean* (*Uminari no soko kara*, 1961) from a similar point of view. The Shimabara Rebellion (1637) was a religious war in the Edo period begun by Christians of the Shimabara region in opposition to the Tokugawa shogunate's suppression of Christianity. In this tale, Hotta portrays the course of an armed struggle in which the leader of the rebellious army plunges into a war of annihilation, using a beautiful youth named Amakusa Shirō as a symbolic figure who causes the people to convert. The people joyfully head for the jaws of death having deified a flesh-and-blood human as the image of a savior of souls. This suggests the "shattered jewels" ideology glorifying death from the last stages of World War II—or, more precisely, the political device behind the shattered jewels slogan—a resemblance the author most certainly intended.[2] If Hotta did not see the emperor as an object of faith and conversion for the masses, he surely would not have constructed this kind of narrative of doubled images. Hotta also predicted that Christianity, once it had lost its proselytizers, would be transformed into an indigenous faith involving faith healing and prayer among the people and that the words with which they prayed to God would gradually degenerate into a meaningless incantation.

To give another example, Takahashi Kazumi, who is slightly younger than the wartime cohort, tells in *Jashumon* (1966) of a new religion that begins as an indigenous faith of the people but comes into conflict with the emperor system and is suppressed and destroyed. The founder of this religious group is a middle-aged woman with little formal education who, while enduring dire poverty and the selfish behavior of her husband, is suddenly visited by divine inspiration. She thereafter has the ability to see into the hearts and souls of others and to heal women's illnesses. She gradually

---

2. *Gyokusai* (shattered jewels) is a word found in the sixth-century Chinese history *Chronicles of Northern China*, which the wartime Japanese leadership first employed to describe the World War II battle of Attu in the Aleutians, where 2,500 Japanese soldiers fought to the death against an American force that outnumbered them five to one. For a discussion of the history of this slogan, see John W. Dower, *War without Mercy: Race and Power in the Pacific War* (New York: Pantheon, 1986), 231–33.

gathers believers among the people through her words of comfort to the poor who are suffering the anxieties of old age, illness, and death.

If the religion had continued in that state, it would have ended up a small regional sect, one in which local people gathered around this middle-aged woman who possessed special spiritual powers. However, intellectuals attracted by the powers and personality of the founder create a huge religious organization by systematizing her words into doctrine and turning her family into a holy family, deifying them as objects of conversion. This arouses the suspicions of the state authorities, who of course insist on the imperial household as the true holy family, and so the group is branded with the stigma of heresy and is finally suppressed. The novel is ostensibly a tale of religious suppression through the emperor system, but within that framework it takes up the problems that arise with the conceptual leap that occurs when indigenous religions are transformed into modern dogma. In other words, while the novel is in part a simple criticism of the emperor system, it also harbors something more: in portraying the local customs of indigenous religions and the role of intellectuals who introduce into the religious group something similar to emperor worship and its belief in a "living god in the flesh," it provides a crucial illumination of the modern system of people, the emperor system, and intellectuals.

These were some of the directions in which the interest in local customs and the indigenous rippled outward from the late 1960s through the 1970s.

2. *EVERYDAY(NESS)* AS A NEGATIVE KEYWORD

The words *local customs* and *indigenous* were theorized in roughly the form described above. In contrast, another word used frequently at that time, *everyday(ness)*, acquired increasingly negative nuances. This word was used in a variety of ways and is difficult to define, but it can roughly be said to have served as an antonym for everything that aimed at radical change.

For quite a long time after the war, Japanese writers and philosophers were under the influence of French existentialism. Under its sway, it became common for them to think of the war as something isolated from everyday life, as being a state in which people were confronted with extreme circumstances. They believed that even after the war extraordinary conditions continued to prevail due to drastic changes in the social system and values, as well as material impoverishment, and they concluded that these abnormal circumstances had conditioned the people's desire for radical change.

However, as the effects of economic recovery began to be felt some twenty years after the war, urban salarymen began to form a distinct social class. Owning a home had been a longtime dream for these men, who had experienced the postwar housing shortages, and when large-scale condominium developments began to appear on the outskirts of Japanese cities they secured their own spaces therein and began to pursue a new lifestyle. Tales of salarymen, beginning with Nakamura Takeshi's *The Tale of Mejiro Sanpei (Mejiro Sanpei monogatari,* 1955) and Genji Keita's *Third-Rate Director (Santō jūyaku,* 1951), were serialized around this time and enjoyed a wide readership. The latter in particular is a tale told with humor and pathos in which the president of a certain company is purged by the Occupation Forces after the war, enters another company as a figurehead president, and preserves and develops the company with the cooperation of its young employees.

This tale reflects the self-affirming consciousness of the salarymen who frantically reconstructed companies after the war and thereby rehabilitated the economy. We do not see any criticism of postwar political or economic processes in this novel. As a result, writers and thinkers with revolutionary aims negatively evaluated it as a manifestation of the conservative ideology of salarymen who desired the maintenance of the status quo instead of radical change. On this one point, postwar intellectuals who advocated a democratic revolution were in agreement with the activists of the New Right and New Left, who were otherwise their ostensible critics. Together they formed a chorus of voices criticizing the lifestyle of the urban resident who wallowed in everyday(ness).

The individual units in the large condominium complexes that appeared on the outskirts of cities had almost identical floor plans. Typically, they had at best only enough space to accommodate the members of two generations: parents and their children. For this reason, the homogenization of lifestyle and the nuclearization of the family became hot topics for sociologists. Influenced by this, writers and thinkers who advocated radical change began to debate the issue of the homogenization of lifestyle, linking it to the problem of human alienation and the loss of individuality. The long-standing political rule of the Conservative Party and the increasingly systematic management of production and human resources by large corporations had by then granted a sense of reality to the perception of the atomization of humans in modern society.

Given such a viewpoint, the novels of Abe Kōbō and Kuroi Senji won high praise at the time. Abe's *Woman in the Dunes (Suna no onna,* 1962), *The Face of Another (Tanin no kao,* 1964), and *The Box Man (Hako otoko,* 1973) are well known and have been translated, so I will simply point out the fact that phrases such as "the trap of everydayness," "escape from the everyday," "the crisis lurking behind everydayness," and "loss of identity" were often used in discussions of these works.

The protagonist of Kuroi Senji's *Time* (*Jikan*, 1969) is an elite employee of a large corporation haunted by memories of his student days when he took part in the antiestablishment movement. Bothered by issues of identity revolving around the contradiction between the self of his student days and his current self working for the establishment, he is driven by a need to prove to himself that he has not changed sides. Yet on seeing an old friend whose antiestablishment stance has not crumbled and who has remained unchanged since their student days, he reacts to the feelings of reproach that press on him by trying to brush them off, thinking to himself, "Aren't you [his friend] being overly moralistic? The wealth that supports your current lifestyle of consumption—how do you think it would be provided without our work?" The protagonist is unable to suppress a desire to validate corporate men like himself who have brought Japan prosperity, and he chooses in the end the path to a managerial position with the excuse that he does so in order to make his own voice heard in the corporation.

When we read this work now, it seems to us no more than a repetitious, gloomy monologue in which the protagonist endlessly wavers between feelings of inferiority toward his old friends and rivalry with colleagues in the corporation. Yet at the time it was read as portraying the "sincerity" of the intellectual caught within a bureaucracy or corporation. Kuroi Senji continued to write novels on the themes of the salaryman's failed attempt to escape from his standardized daily life, enclosed in employee housing—all the more standardized—and from his sense of estrangement from those around him.

It seems to me, however, that what most captured the minds of people at the time were catchphrases such as "delicious lifestyle" (*oishii seikatsu*) and "I love the strange" (*fushigi, daisuki*) composed by the talented copywriter Itoi Shigesato. Around this time, department stores such as Seibu and Parco discontinued their previous strategy of stocking an abundant assortment of expensive products and selling products with a high-class feel, developing instead a strategy in which they designed a menu of several lifestyle options to offer to consumers; in other words, they began to market the idea of consumption. Itoi Shigesato created this kind of copy at the behest of such department stores, but his catchphrases exceeded their ties to designated department stores and became watchwords among young consumers.

"Delicious lifestyle" included the meaning of an "abundant lifestyle" but was not limited to that. There are different kinds of "abundance," and the phrase called for consumers to enjoy a high-quality lifestyle that matched their sensibilities. "I love the strange" invited the consumer to embark on travels to unknown lands, but it was not limited to that meaning alone. It also proclaimed the desire to have an encounter with something that would estrange one's own everyday routine. This, too, could be called an attempt to escape from the everyday, but if it is an everyday lifestyle you must return to in any case, then there is no need to get worked up about transcending it or, for that matter, failing to transcend it. Wasn't it enough to refresh your senses, dulled by routine, through something similar to what the Russian formalists would call "defamiliarization" and thereby gain a fresh viewpoint from which to reevaluate the everyday?

Most of the destinations for which the people tempted by those words set out were areas where the quality of "local customs" spoken of by the writers and thinkers I introduced earlier remained strong. These areas were facing a population drain as crucial members of their labor force left for the cities, urged on by rapid economic growth there. In order to survive, such regions had no choice but to transform their local customs into a magnet for tourism. In this sense the local customs were dismantled in reality, but tourists who "loved the strange" still set out for those areas, often followed by folklorists who were only too eager to criticize the shallowness of the tourists. However, it was the work of the folklorists who criticized the tourists, work that consisted mainly of producing popular books of folklore, that made folklore fashionable. This was the sad reality of the folklore boom of this period.

As should be clear, the marketing catchphrases employed the discourse on local customs and the criticism of everyday(ness) as something like subliminal messages. Moreover, the people who found self-expression in these phrases themselves seem to have been faintly aware that their actions were something of a parody. Subsequently, the phrase "search for your true self" would become popular, and it remains popular today. It is based on the assumption that the true self has been alienated and repressed in today's overly systematized social order and its characteristic pattern of routine work. It lends new layers of meaning to "delicious lifestyle" and "I love the strange." In other words, it implies that to seek a "delicious lifestyle" or set out on a journey of "I love the strange" is not simply an activity of leisure consumption but rather an act driven by an internal motivation, and it is therefore a superior form of action, one driven by the intention of discovering and resuscitating the true self.

Of course, it is impossible to find the true self by leaving the self of the here and now. These phrases used the theory of "human alienation in managed society" to give vent to the desire to escape from the self of the here and now, as well as to dissatisfaction with the social conditions that regulate one's here and now; they were nothing more than words of self-rationalization. To put it another way, they were simply a trendy and easily consumable form of the discourse surrounding the theory of alienation; this is what I meant when I spoke of parody.

Paradoxically, it was through this popularization that the discourse on alienation ended up granting a measure of reality to the concept of *langue* in Saussure's structural linguistic theory or the concept of *langue* as a system of differences. In a homogenized, standardized society, the self of the here and now can only be confirmed through its differences from the "Other," and under such conditions the "search for the true self" can only mean an attempt to choose, hypothetically and temporarily, a position within this system of differences that is other than the position of the here and now. The more the discourse of alienation critically emphasized the loss of individuality, the homogenization of lifestyles, and the atomization of humans, the more the patterns of this discourse came to have a lasting impact on people, a highly paradoxical result.

3. "STUDENT PROTESTS" AND THE SEARCH FOR NEW THEORIES OF LANGUAGE

This was roughly the situation at the time "student protests" broke out in Japan, as elsewhere, in 1968. They became a nationwide phenomenon at their peak in the years 1969 and 1970.

We can broadly distinguish between student protests that were held at private universities and those held at national universities, but they shared two common points worth noting: first, a reaction against the transformation of the university education system into a system that appropriated the (intellectual) labor of students; and, second, a complaint that university professors did not have a sense of social responsibility vis-à-vis their scholarly research.

Another relevant factor was the Japanese economy, which had entered a period of high growth. Although expansion and popularization of the universities had begun in response to the ever increasing number of students who expected to enroll in them, the universities were unable to adapt effectively to changes in student lifestyles and consciousness. Structural reforms to the education system also lagged behind. It was the expansion of Japanese corporations abroad, particularly expansion into Asian countries that had been former colonies of Japan, that supported the rapid growth of the Japanese economy, and the leaders of the student protests feared this would lead to the rise of a new form of colonization. Yet university professors remained oblivious to the issue, pursued research for technical developments sought by corporations, and proceeded to educate students in order to turn them into effective corporate workers. The initial motive of the protests was to raise objections to these circumstances, but out of dissatisfaction with the failure of the university to respond sincerely to their demands for dialogue student activists went so far as to occupy university buildings, erect barricades, and call for the dismantling of the university.

However, this description of these events only becomes possible once they have been interpreted in relatively abstract terms. On top of this, the student demands had other aspects, including a reaction against "everyday(ness)," opposition to the establishment, liberation of the irrational power of suppressed emotions, and personal attacks against individual professors. Moreover, the students splintered into several political factions, factions that used violence (*Gewalt*) against each other in the struggle to seize control of the protests. As a result, universities were largely unable to talk with any of the factions, and even when they tried to they found it impossible to reach an agreement even on which topics to discuss.

When the two sides finally agreed to talk after bitter and difficult negotiations, the university asked as a precondition that the students remove the barricades and vacate the buildings while the students asked that the university allow the barricades to remain since they were the material basis of the students' demands. As they argued over such preconditions, the destruction of university facilities continued apace, and any mutual trust that remained between students and professors further deteriorated.

Why did the students cling so fiercely to the barricades? They did so because the area behind the barricades was for them a space liberated from the everyday. How did they manage to occupy campus buildings for long periods of time: half a year, a whole year, and sometimes even longer? They were able to do so because the university, thanks to the fruits of high economic growth, had prepared an infrastructural lifeline, including such things as electricity, telephone service, plumbing, gas, and heat, and further because there were plenty of instant foods available in the streets. If the protesters went into town, there were part-time jobs to be had that paid fairly high wages, and they could even occasionally leave on a hippie-style road trip for a change of pace. Come to think of it, "I love the strange" travel may have been conceived with an eye toward providing hippie-style road trips for ordinary urban dwellers' leisure. These were conditions that the generation taking part in the so-called Anpo protests against the Japan-U.S. Security Treaty renewal in 1960 did not enjoy.

Supported by such "favorable conditions," the protesters attacked the close-knit relationship between the university and capitalism (the industrial-academic complex), criticized the bureaucratic establishment, distributed antiwar pamphlets, and produced picket signs and broadside posters. But the form and content of these were a jumbled mixture of the literary and philosophical vocabulary discussed above and random citations of handy catchphrases from Che Guevara, Mao Zedong, and Vladimir Lenin. Nothing that could be called a coherent system of thought was created. Instead, there was a sort of collage effect produced in the sense that their efforts systematically attempted to destroy trust in authoritarian thought and to fragment texts and then randomly reassemble the fragments into new texts. By accident they laid the groundwork for a way of looking at texts as fabrics woven together out of various citations.

This struggle was fated to end in self-destruction before long even without intervention by the university authorities. On the one hand, the "internal Gewalt" of the factions—in other words, their violent attacks on each other—intensified, while on the other hand inside the barricades of each faction outsiders joined in the protests, students who had failed their university entrance exams and were officially unaffiliated with any school, for example, or self-proclaimed hippies and floating laborers. Some factions rejected these members, but as a matter of principle those factions that had named the space inside their barricades a "free zone" could not but welcome such people. As a result, during free zone debates students were attacked by these newcomers for the privileges they enjoyed as officially registered university students and lost their leadership rights. Moreover, the newcomers began to engage in anarchic actions such as raising "protest funds" by selling to used book stores the individual libraries that faculty members kept in their offices. The students were unable to prevent them from doing this, though of course there were also some students who sympathized with such actions. At any rate, internal discipline broke down. Confusion and devastation spread unhindered within the free zones.

The universities could not silently stand by and let this situation continue. Voices of criticism claiming that the universities were neglecting their educational responsibilities were raised by private corporations and citizens. The universities eventually decided to expel the "violent students," relying on the force of police riot squads. Until then, Japanese university campuses had been seen as a kind of holy ground because, at least in theory, it was widely accepted that universities ought to reject negotiations with state authorities for the sake of academic freedom and independence. However, by calling in the riot squads the universities by their own actions abandoned their status as holy ground. As a result, a large number of "sincere" intellectuals in the mold of the protagonist of Kuroi Senji's *Time* were created among the students who took part in the protests.

These prefatory remarks may seem a bit excessive, but I believe the above outline gives us an idea of just how difficult it was to carry on a dialogue in this period.

Of course, there were professors who attempted to mediate in order to break the deadlock, but in most cases their efforts were wasted. Some professors left their universities disappointed in the administrations' "disposition," which stubbornly adhered to the establishment system, while others left out of loathing for the students, who would not even abide by the rules of the dialogue they themselves had demanded. Takahashi Kazumi, who left Kyoto University, and Isoda Kōichi, who left Chūo University, are two outstanding examples.

There were also professors who tried to construct new philosophies of language based on the bitter experience of their failed efforts, for example, Takeuchi Yoshirō, who wrote *The Dismantling and Creation of Language* (*Gengo: Sono kaitai to sōzō*, 1972); Hiromatsu Wataru, who wrote *The Structure of Shared Subjective Existence of the World* (*Sekai no kyōdo shukanteki sonzai kōzō*, 1972); and Nakamura Yūjirō, who wrote *Language, Reason, Insanity* (*Gengo, risei, kyōki*, 1969) and *The Transformation of Knowledge: Toward a Structural Form of Knowledge* (*Chi no henbō, kōzōteki chisei no tame ni*, 1978).

Of these, Takeuchi Yoshirō's *The Dismantling and Creation of Language* reflects the experience of the student protests most vividly. To begin with, Takeuchi views the bourgeois, existing form of language in modern capitalist society as "one based on the model of language among 'contractual' human relationships," defined by the "suppression of use value by exchange value, of the signifier by the signified, and of connotation by denotation," and calls it "logical language."[3] To rephrase this in a more easily understood way, at present, when we make a contract with another person for some purpose, we choose words with clear meanings and we prefer a logical manner of expression in order to avoid misunderstanding. But according to Takeuchi, this is a bourgeois form of language, one that is simply a form of capitalist alienation, which becomes clear, he thought, when it is compared to the original, essential relationship between humans and language.

---

3. Takeuchi Yoshirō, *Gengo: Sono kaitai to sōzō* (The Dismantling and Creation of Language) (Tokyo: Chikuma Shobo, 1972), 147.

Yet, as Takeuchi saw it, "logical language" alone is not dominant in modern capitalist society. Rather, something best called "emotional language" intermittently erupts in opposition to the above forms of oppression, a language that seeks to rehabilitate connotation. Having grasped the situation in this way, Takeuchi diagnosed the modern condition of language in Japan in the manner described below.

(One explanation before quoting Takeuchi: the terms "faith in theory" [*riron shinkō*] and "faith in natural feeling" [*jikkan shinkō*], which appear in the following citation, were coined by the political scientist Maruyama Masao in his *Japanese Thought* [*Nihon no shisō*, 1961]. In the Japan Proletarian Writers Federation of the 1930s, the materialist dialectical method of artistic creation, or socialist realism, was put forward as the sole legitimate theory of creative cultural production. Yet several novelists within the federation opposed this theory, saying that novels were not written according to abstract theories but only based on the author's natural feelings. This eventually divided the Proletarian Writers Federation and brought about its internal collapse. Maruyama Masao interpreted this conflict as one between "faith in theory" and "faith in natural feeling," and these came to be used widely as sociological terms.)

> Above all, because the establishment of "free and equal" human relationships is extremely fragile in a late-developing capitalist country like ours, the fruitless contention of these two languages [logical language and emotional language] is a horrible sight. "Faith in theory" and "faith in natural feeling," "outward appearance" and "inner truth," dwell together in constant tumult. Even revolutionary movements—definitely with the old Left, but also with the New Left and the New-New Left—cannot change the form of bourgeois language; all they do is buzz around in pointless circles of "sound and fury" within the frame of this language space, trapped in the same binary oppositions as always. (Idealistic abstractions that give you a headache with their *outward appearance* of being theory and an immoderate fascination with *yakuza* movies in their emotion as *inner truth*.) Moreover, within this sticky spiritual climate in which the indispensable "third party" (ultimately, the ideal of "god") necessary for contractual human relations cannot be established . . . the linguistic space of our country is constructed so that emotional language always triumphs in the end, and it is rare to encounter any discourse capable of striking people purely with the power of logic because even the concept of the modern "contract" is not well rooted here. Thus, faith in theory is actually no more than a derivative of faith in

147

> natural feeling, and strings of extremely difficult Chinese words
> used as revolutionary slogans are actually an expression of a kind
> of faith in a natural feeling for the connotations of Chinese words
> as signifiers at the same time as they are an expression of faith in
> theory.[4]

I will not question here whether this diagnosis of the situation was accurate or not. In the original Japanese, this paragraph itself consists of "a string of extremely difficult Chinese words," and the turbulent emotions of the author can be intuited from his insertion of the words enclosed in parentheses, "idealistic abstractions that give you a headache with their *outward appearance* of being theory and an immoderate fascination with *yakuza* movies in their emotion as *inner truth*." For anyone familiar with the reality of the student protests, these words can be immediately understood as a description of the expressions used on student placards and in their pamphlets, as well as of their mode of behavior.

It may be quite difficult for people who grew up outside of Japan to understand the meaning of "an immoderate fascination with *yakuza* movies in their emotion as *inner truth*." When Takeuchi wrote these words, what he probably had in mind was the slogan "Don't stop me, mother, the gingko on my back is crying," which was popular among activists in the student protests.

There is a genre of Japanese films called "movies of chivalry" (*ninkyō eiga*) in which a *yakuza*[5] is the protagonist. The *yakuza* is covered with flashy tattoos over his entire body, and the favorite tattoo pattern is called a Chinese Lion Peony, a magnificent design in which a lion in a stylized Chinese form is paired with peony flowers. When this young tattooed *yakuza* goes into enemy territory alone, although he knows he will be killed, he says to himself with great resolve, "Don't stop me, mother, the peonies on my back are crying" (or "Don't stop me, mother, I can't let the peonies on my back cry," meaning "I can't betray a man's promise just because the peonies on my back are crying"). Borrowing this scenario, the students created their own slogan by changing "the peonies on my back" to "the gingko on my back," citing the emblem of Tokyo University, a golden gingko.

I have my doubts as to whether we can say that these lines reflected "emotion as *inner truth*" simply because they became popular. I think they might have actually been a self-deprecating gag. At that time, a talented cartoonist depicted students with "stomach and intestine" (*ichō*) tattoos instead of "gingko" (*ichō*) tattoos in a parody of these lines. The cartoonist splen-

---

4. Ibid., 147–48.
5. *Yakuza* is the Japanese term for a gangster, or member of an organized crime syndicate.

didly ridiculed the pretentiousness of the elite Tokyo University students who liked to imagine themselves as *yakuza*.

Be that as it may, at least in the eyes of Takeuchi Yoshirō those lines seemed to reflect an irrational "emotional language" that expressed "emotion as *inner truth*." At a glance this appears to be a rebellion against logical language, but in a spiritual climate characterized by collusion and dependence (*amae*) such as Japan's, one that excludes the gaze of an external third party and in which there is no clear understanding of the difference between self and Other, emotive language is actually the rule and logical language is simply its derivative. How is dialogue possible in a situation in which logical language has not yet established itself? Takeuchi was bothered by this.

This was the diagnosis of the situation made by a philosopher who considered the creation of a new linguistic theory a critical task. I would like to keep this in mind as we continue our explorations.

———

Incidentally, the terms *signified* (*shoki*) and *signifier* (*nōki*) that appear in Takeuchi's text are the linguist Kobayashi Hideo's translations from Saussure's *signifie* and *signifiant*. Currently it is more common to translate these terms as *kigō naiyō* (sign content) and *kigō hyōgen* (sign expression) or *imi sareru mono* (what is meant) and *imi suru mono* (what means), but among linguists *shoki* and *nōki* are commonly used terms. His text is probably the earliest example of a philosopher using these translated terms in an attempt to construct a philosophy of language.

3. TOWARD THE POST-SAUSSURE: TAKEUCHI YOSHIRŌ AND HIROMATSU WATARU

The directions in which Takeuchi Yoshirō and Hiromatsu Wataru developed their linguistic philosophies were very different, but it can be seen that they shared the question of how to render linguistic expression independent of and transcending what Takeuchi Yoshirō called emotional language.

Takeuchi Yoshirō first turned his attention to the national language system—Saussure's *langue*, which he translated as "national language system" (*kokugokei*), adding the superscript pronunciation key of *rangu* (*langue*) in katakana—in his effort to overcome the existing bourgeois form of language. As he saw it, because both logical language and emotional language are regulated by *langue*, we must "topple and destroy the value system latent in *langue* itself."[6]

6. Ibid., 124.

The latent "value system" of *langue* points to such conditions as Sartre indicated, for example, in *Black Orpheus*, where he argued that white expresses purity and the "universal adoration of the day" while black expresses scheming dishonesty and "our nocturnal terrors" so that the contrast between the words *white* and *black* forms a kind of discriminatory language, a "racial hierarchy."[7] Takeuchi thought that we must "topple and destroy" such unconscious functions of *langue* and sought a clear understanding of the situation as follows.

> Because in general what we call "discrimination" and "prejudice" are deeply rooted in the collective unconscious rather than in individual consciousnesses, overturning the inherent, latent values of the *langue* that similarly belongs to the collective unconscious would perhaps be more effective than complaining of actual "discrimination" within individual consciousnesses of oppressors, which would rely on the strength of direct communication and might not even be understood. In its *langue*, Japanese, contains many words that deprecate Koreans (or Chinese or "*burakumin*") among its vocabulary system as recorded in dictionaries. We Japanese, each time we use words conforming to the Japanese *langue*, expose the fact that we have unconsciously appropriated the values implied therein.[8]

Whether or not we should understand Saussure's *langue* in this way is doubtful. In my understanding, Saussure's *langue* is purely a system of difference and hence cannot include discrimination because at the level of *langue*, *Kankokujin* (neutral, "Korean") and *Hantōjin* (discriminatory, "Korean"), *Chūgokujin* (neutral, "Chinese") and *Shinajin* (discriminatory, "Chinese"), and *burakumin* (neutral, outcast status group) and *shinheimin* (literally, "new commoner," a discriminatory euphemism for *burakumin*) are all merely units of vocabulary.

If discrimination is to appear, it is manifested in the selection method used to choose certain words to occupy specific positions within an utterance such as subject, predicate, or modifier; in other words, it is manifested in choices made along the paradigmatic axis. Or else it appears through the context of the utterance. Saussure thought that "value" was generated through that selection or through a differentiating comparison of words belonging to the same category carried out before that selection. If we take that position, discrimination is simply one kind of value.

7. Jean-Paul Sartre, *Black Orpheus*, translated by S. W. Allen (Paris: Editions Gallimard, 1963), 29.
8. Takeuchi, *Gengo*, 124.

Therefore, if we are to speak here of the unconscious, we must consider it in terms of the unconscious mind that functions at the time of word selection. I call this an "unconscious mind" because it follows from the customary word selection practices of the group to which the speaker belongs rather than reflecting the conscious choices of the individual speaker. This is different from what Saussure meant when he called *langue* a system of the unconscious.

In any case, taking his lead from Saussure's concepts, Takeuchi argued that everyday words that on the surface appear not to contain "prejudice" in fact do contain the prejudice of the collective unconscious when you examine them within the *langue* system as a whole. But we should consider this the other way around, too. If various prejudices are expressed in everyday speech, the collective unconscious that expresses them so casually should become clear when we examine the *langue*. However, because Takeuchi did not grasp the issue in this way, he thought that the only way to subjugate discriminatory expressions was to "topple and destroy the hidden values within the *langue* system."[9] But how to "topple and destroy"? As he recognized, the relationships between acoustic image and concept in *langue* and between *langue* and the referential object outside of *langue* are arbitrary, and because they are arbitrary it is impossible to find any vital link that can be used to topple them. That being the case, can this aim be achieved if discriminatory words are exposed, destroyed, and eliminated from the *langue* system? Even if this were possible, discrimination would not be eliminated because discrimination would still come to be expressed at the level of utterance.

Having come to this theoretical impasse, Takeuchi finally concluded that the collective unconscious could only be revealed through the use of linguistic expressions and that such expressions deserved to be called "poetic language" and "literary language." Based on this claim, he argued for the significance of literature as something that could strike at the unconscious that was buried in the everyday(ness) of the petit bourgeoisie and perhaps awaken them from its spell. For example, when North Koreans and South Koreans in Japan choose to write in Japanese even though they feel a sense of estrangement from the language, their Japanese expressions expose the discriminatory qualities of Japanese that Japanese people have unconsciously become accustomed to. In this way Takeuchi asserted the possibilities that existed for linguistic expression by people marginalized in Japan, as well as by people who chose to be marginalized.

9. Ibid.

In this sense, Takeuchi's linguistic theory strongly resembles certain forms of literary theory. He constructed a Russian formalist type of binary opposition between poetic language and everyday language, and, perhaps borrowing from Henri Lefebvre, he grasped everyday language as "the existing bourgeois form of language." Within this problematic, he then conceived of a linguistic philosophy that attempted to decipher, criticize, and transcend Saussure's concept of *langue*. Needless to say, his problematic originated from the commonly shared notions of his time, meaning that he could only deal with everyday(ness) in negative terms.

———

On the other hand, Hiromatsu Wataru—whose writing is also "a string of extremely difficult Chinese words" and poorly written to boot—developed the idea of the "subject of *langue*" (*rangu shutai*) using his original concept of a "four-limbed structure."

The concept of the four-limbed structure is difficult to summarize, but I will do my best, citing his own explanation. For starters, he explains a concept best called a "two-limbed structure" as follows.

> For example, *something* (*etwas*) called a "tree," which we are aware of as a *that* visible outside our window, is not simply the sound "tree" but is an "objective" *something* in the same way as are a pine or a cypress and all other types of trees. However, when it comes to individual trees as actual objects, "tree" signifies all trees equally (universality); it does *not* signify each singular tree, does not distinguish this tree from any other tree. Further, the tree as an actual object grows and eventually dies (at that time the essence of the tree, the tree's actual characteristics, vanish!), but the "tree" that is an *etwas* neither grows nor dies along with it. In place of the constant change of the actual object, the "tree" as *etwas* remains unchangeable (permanence).[10]

If we stop here, it may seem that he has indicated no more than the duality of the object before our eyes and our conceptual grasp of that object. Certainly he has done that, but Hiromatsu's interest was in fact directed more toward our perceptual functions. When we perceive something with our eyes or ears, we not only sense that object as an object, but we are also simultaneously comprehending something else. For example, we say "the sound

10. Hiromatsu Wataru, *Sekai no kyōdo shukanteki sonzai kōzō* (The Structure of Shared Subjective Existence of the World), in *Hiromatsu Wataru chosakushū*, 16 vols. (Tokyo: Iwanami Shoten, 1996–97), 1:35.

I heard just now I perceived intuitively *as* the horn of an automobile; what I see outside the window looks intuitively *like* a pine tree." Taking up these "intuitive perceptions," Hiromatsu directed his attention to the fact that they differ from the actually existing form of the object itself, in other words, that the two are mutually independent. The sound of a clock sounds like "kachi, kachi" to us Japanese, but it sounds to English speakers like "tick-tock." Despite the fact that they are all taken from a field, we call watermelons and melons fruit but we call tomatoes vegetables. This difference did not arise from any difference between watermelons and tomatoes; it arose out of the historical difference in the way they entered our diets and from our sense of food. Focusing on such questions, Hiromatsu pointed to a fixed social framework inherent in our "intuition." This could be called a simple application of the phenomenological method, but Hiromatsu then used this kind of procedure to try to link this framework to Saussure's *langue*.

To proceed further, Hiromatsu then indicated that the subject who calls the tree before his eyes "tree" undergoes a doubling through the process of understanding the utterances made by some other.

> For example, if a cow is for a child a "bow-wow," the cow is a bow-wow to the child but not to me. Having said that, if I did not grasp the cow as a bow-wow in some sense, I would not even understand that the child was "mistaking" the cow for a dog. What allows me to understand the child's "mistake" is that I grasp the cow as a bow-wow in some sense myself. Insofar as I do this, the "cow as bow-wow" is doubled and can be ascribed to us both. However, the "child" and "I" are not simply lined up here, like multiple children chasing the same ball.
>
> Here we see a duality best called a split-subject form of self-identity. To me, the cow is after all a cow and not a bow-wow. However, for the me who understands the utterance of the child, or one might say for the me on behalf of the child, the cow presents itself as a dog. In brief, if we use the expressions me-as-me and me-as-the-child, these two me's are in a sense separate yet at the same time one and the same me.[11]

It is probably not necessary to explicate this passage. If we call the social framework within our "intuition"—one that is abstracted from the previously discussed phenomenon of duality—a "collective subjectivity" (*kyōdō shukansei*) inherent to our intuition, then based on this we understand one

11. Ibid., 1:39.

another by splitting ourselves. In order to explain this, Hiromatsu combined this duality with the earlier duality [between the actual object and our conceptual grasp of it] and called the result "the four-limbed structure of the phenomenal world."

––––––––

Hiromatsu Wataru, unlike Takeuchi Yoshirō, did not make any statements that directly evoke the student protests. This is not to say that he did not address them at all. When Hiromatsu explained "meaning," he gave as the example of the way "a 'wooden staff' becomes a 'Gewalt stick.'" We can see here his interest in the student protests.

The participants in the student protests called long wooden staffs "Gewalt sticks," symbolizing their use as weapons in their confrontation with state authorities. Swinging these sticks, they clashed with police riot squads, attacked students from opposing factions, and occasionally struck at university professors. In addition, they threw fire extinguishers or set up baseball pitching machines to hurl stones in order to repel counterattacks from opposing factions.

Thus, the "protests" turned into a movement characterized by a self-propagating violence. To return now to the example of the Gewalt stick, the students designated something that was no more than a simple, long piece of wood a Gewalt stick and thereafter called it by that name. According to Hiromatsu, from that time on the piece of wood was no longer only the simple wooden stick itself; it now bore the meaning of the set phrase "Gewalt stick." It had become something more (*etwas mehr*) than itself. For example, even if the staff broke or was burned, it would preserve its identity and the objectified "meaning" assigned to it would not change. This is how Hiromatsu explained matters.

This may give the impression of a somewhat forced sophistry. But I think that Hiromatsu was in fact trying to describe his understanding of the student protests through this logic. This means that in addition to the above theory he was also talking about the concept of "incarnation" (*inkarnieren*). We recognize the diagram of a triangle drawn on a blackboard as the geometric shape of a triangle even if its lines are slightly distorted. To put that in reverse, the diagram of the distorted triangle on the blackboard is the place where an ideal triangle is incarnated (*inkarnieren*). Hiromatsu describes it this way: "As long as a phenomenon 'gestates' the 'meaning' of an ideal something (*etwas*) and is within the range of examples that incarnate that 'meaning,' the 'actually existing' qualities and state of that something have only secondary significance. For example, as long as the diagram drawn on the blackboard is recognized as a 'triangle,' the various 'actually existing' characteristics, such as whether it is big or small or what color it is, are not important (*gleichgültig*)."[12]

According to this concept, even if it were actually a thin, flimsy wooden stick, as long as the students recognized it as the "incarnation" of a weapon for battling state authorities its existing characteristics, such as thinness and flimsiness, had only secondary significance. Although the students occupied buildings and built barricades in order to stop the university's educational and research functions, they demanded from the university the maintenance of their infrastructural lifeline, and they supplied themselves with funds through part-time work, selling the private belongings of the faculty and engaging in a door-to-door extortion campaign. As a way of life, this is nothing more than a style of thievery accompanied by vicious threats, but as long as it was recognized within the free zone as incarnating "community," the irrational aspects of this way of life remained irrelevant.

Having reduced his theory in this way, it may seem that I am making fun of Hiromatsu Wataru. In fact, I may indeed harbor such a motive, but what I really want to say is that no one could have produced the conditions for dialogue with the students based solely on this theory. In my experience, the only possibility for dialogue rested with a methodological structure that distinguished between the actual situation of the students and their statements. On graduating from the university, I left academia for nine years before becoming a faculty member at age thirty-one. The next year I was faced with the student protests and found all of it to be ridiculous. When students who did not know that I was a professor came to my house as part of their campaign to raise "protest funds," I demanded that they write a receipt and come back later with an accounting report. Apparently this was an unexpected response because the shocked students tossed off some abuse and left. I actually felt sorry for these students, who could not understand even such basic rules of society. Having begun with this experience, I had to create a certain method in order to engage in dialogue with the students. Hiromatsu would probably describe my experience in the following terms: *While grasping the students and their actions as the "incarnation" of some ideal, Kamei then rendered that ideal into something independent of the students and pursued dialogue on the level of this ideal.* Of course, that was not the only motif in his work, but in a very characteristic way he argued that "'sentences' that exist/existed in reality, are necessarily spoken by someone," and, moreover, through a "dilution" of the speaker, the "sentence" becomes independent from the conditions of its utterance.

12. Ibid., 1:36.

> The arbitrary "conferred meaning" can be understood as some-
> thing designated by a particular speaker (in other words, in the
> form of: Mr. X said "_____"), but the term *speaker X* can be inserted
> as a "variable" that can be filled in by any arbitrary individual. . . .
>   As a result, the term *speaker* dilutes individual personality
> and becomes a non-designating personal pronoun. At the same
> time the "conferred meaning" tends to be cut off from its (human)
> context and to exist on its own when the contextual relationship
> between the "conferred meaning" and the *designating* personal
> pronoun is ended. This process corresponds to the process in
> which the "real topos of incarnation" of the "conferred meaning"
> is reduced to a linguistic sign.[13]

In other words, he thought that the "sentence," depending on the degree
of dilution of the individuality of the speaker and of the characteristics of
the "topos" (*ba*) in which it was spoken, is idealized as a sentence that says
something on its own, and he further argued that this is the process by
which a corresponding, idealized "abstract, general 'linguistic subject'" is
formed.

> What should perhaps be called the "linguistic subject in general,"
> in other words not a man or woman, a senior or child, but all those
> who practice "language," are anyone (*jemand*) who counts as a
> *that*, and this is what occupies the opposite pole.[14]

This "linguistic subject in general" is Hiromatsu's "subject of *langue*."
   This will surely seem a dubious concept for someone specializing in
linguistics not only because in Saussure's thought *langue* and the subject exist in completely different dimensions, but also because one cannot in fact
grasp the *langue* system without first excluding the concept of a subject.
   Such doubts are only natural. They arise because Hiromatsu advanced
his theory based on "spoken sentences" (*hatsuwabun*, what Saussure would
call *parole*) and forged a correspondence between an autonomous "conferred
meaning" and the "linguistic subject in general." In other words, he confused "sentences" (*parole*) with *langue*.
   The point is actually quite subtle. On the one hand, he gave the pronunciation gloss of *langue* for the word *language* (*gengo*) and wrote that "we
actually encounter the existence of a 'preexisting' *langue* system as restric-

13. Ibid., 1:89.
14. Ibid., 1:90.

tions on the possibilities for *parole*-like exchanges of meaning."[15] If we look only at this passage, it would seem that he is distinguishing between *parole* and *langue*. On the other hand, while bringing up the concept of the "two-limbed structure of consciousness" introduced earlier, he seems to consider *langue* and spoken sentences to be the same thing, as when he argues "now, we must look at the issue of *langue* and its subject based on the two-limbed structure of consciousness in the linguistic subject."[16]

This vacillation in thought would seem to be due to the following motives. As I pointed out earlier, Hiromatsu was trying to link a fixed social framework inherent in our "intuition" to Saussure's *langue*. Starting by objectifying this social framework, he created the concepts of "collective subjectivity" and the "two-limbed structure of consciousness," but he then took Saussure's *langue* as this framework materialized, as what gives it representation. If he were to explain, it would go something like this: Two-limbed structure of consciousness *and* common subjectivity *are terms that describe the way consciousness acts, but Saussure spoke of* langue *as a transcendent system existing prior to the activities of individual consciousnesses and external to the consciousness of individuals, one that functions restrictively.* This explanation is probably correct, and, if so, one can say that Hiromatsu's "subject of *langue*" is conceived of as the subject of linguistic action that realizes a "collective subjective world" by subjugating the form of its materialization.

———

The above is an introduction to a sampling of the linguistic theories developed by philosophers active in the 1970s. Currently, the theoretical and philosophical works of these people are not widely read because in the 1980s structuralism came to have a strong influence, creating a gap between the prior era and the present. Few people are aware that the work of Takeuchi Yoshirō and Hiromatsu Wataru that I have introduced here developed amid the tense relationship between the intellectual confusion generated by the student protests on the one hand and a new focus on Saussure on the other. This article is an attempt to close that gap.

NOTE

The title of the conference lecture on which this article is based is "Theories of Language in the Fields of Philosophy and History: Japan in the 1970s." To

15. Ibid., 1:89.
16. Ibid.

discuss the field of history, I prepared an examination and introduction to Kamikawa Masahiko's *Language and Logic in History* (*Rekishi ni okeru kotoba to ronri*, 1970–71), but I had to part with it reluctantly due to time constraints. I again had to omit this portion when turning the lecture into this essay and so changed the title to "Theories of Language in the Academic Field of Philosophy: Japan in the 1970s." As a result, section 1, "Keywords of the Late 1960s: *Local Customs* and *Indigenous*," is somewhat out of balance. In the future I hope to rewrite this section to include a discussion of the field of history.

Tactics of the Universal:
"Language" in Yoshimoto Takaaki

Richi Sakakibara

THE PROBLEMATICS OF "HISTORICIZATION"

We often forget a fundamental fact about language when we read a work of literary theory: no linguistic text is above the historical context within which it was written. What are customarily classified as theories of language are no exception. We need to remind ourselves that a metanarrative on language is nothing but a form of narrative the writer specifically selected to construct an effective argument. This act of choosing may not be a fully conscious one, but nonetheless it reflects the writer's struggle to negotiate with the various discourses surrounding him or her. Theoretical works that seem to make a universal statement unaffected by time and space need to be contextualized within their contemporaneous discursive field and thus "historicized" just like any other form of writing.

But then we also need to ask ourselves what it means to historicize. What does that entail? It is certainly not something as simple as adding a narrative of the historical background to the analysis of the text in question. Nor can it be the act of understanding the text only in our current discursive field because the work should also make sense within the discursive space in which it was produced. On the reader's part, to historicize invariably involves an endeavor to explore vast amounts of writings that may seem not only old-fashioned but also insignificant. In the reading process, the act of historicization requires a constant inquiry into our own assumptions and value systems, what we have taken for granted. Our own conceptions of "literary," "theory," and "history" need to be put under scrutiny with a trained skepticism that understands that these terms may have yielded different meanings at the time of the work's production. Ultimately, we face the question of how we represent this endeavor of historicization in our own writings.

An inquiry into a text and its contingencies inevitably calls up these sorts of self-reflective questions concerning one's mode of inquiry and writing.

This essay examines Yoshimoto Takaaki's *Gengo ni totte bi towa nani ka* or *What Is Beauty for Language* (hereafter abbreviated as *Gengo*), with these problems of historicization in mind. Serialized first in Yoshimoto's personal magazine *Shikō* (Trial) in 1962 and published in a book form in 1965, *Gengo* had a tremendous impact on contemporaneous readers. Although Yoshimoto had already established himself as a literary critic in the 1950s, he gained popularity among the general reading public with his 1961 essay "Gisei no shūen" (An End to Fictions). In this essay, he severely criticized the Japan Communist Party (JCP) and its policy toward the movement that opposed the U.S.-Japan Security Treaty (generally referred to as the Anpo movement) in the previous year. Published as an essay in an anthology entitled *Minshushugi no shinwa: Anpo tōsō no shisō teki sōkatsu* (The Myth of Democracy: The Intellectual Summary of the Anpo Struggle), "Gisei" discusses the historical significance of the Anpo movement in an effort to situate the event in a Marxist historical view different from the "official" historical understanding of the JCP.[1] It was a well-known fact for the general reading public that Yoshimoto had been an active member of Rokugatsu kōdō iinkai (Committee for Taking the Action in June) organized by intellectuals who acted against the partisanship of the Japan Communist Party in support of student organizations in the anti-Anpo movement. Yoshimoto also had close contact with the leaders of Kyōsan shugisha dōmei (customarily known as Bunto), one of the largest New Left student organizations in Japan at the time. Shortly after the anti-Anpo movement failed to stop government leaders from signing the treaty and for all practical purposes was dissolved, Yoshimoto started researching literature and linguistics as part of a project he undertook to write a theory of language. *Gengo* was the first major work by him after the Anpo incident, and it was read initially by a generation of activism-oriented readers.

In the fields of literary studies and linguistics, the influence of *Gengo* spread rather slowly, coming only after the publication of the work in book form in 1965. It stirred much discussion in the following five years, mainly concerning the validity of the two main concepts discussed in the book: *jiko hyōshutsu* or "self-expression" and *shiji hyōshutsu* or "indicative expression." Kamei Hideo, who wrote one of the most systematic and extensive studies

1. Tanikawa Gan, ed., *Minshushugi no shinwa: Anpo tōsō no shisō teki sōkatsu* (Tokyo: Gendai Shisōsha, 1960).

of Yoshimoto's language theory, gives succinct definitions of these terms. They refer to two functions of spoken linguistic utterances. By "indicative expression," Yoshimoto means the act in which "one indicates the (image of the) thing by means of a certain articulate sound." "Self-expression," on the other hand, is an act of utterance by which "the image of a thing is capable of being intended even outside of a direct relationship to that thing." Kamei goes on to clarify these terms, writing that "the term indicative expression relates to the aspects of the utterance that are directed at others, whereas self-expression relates to those aspect directed toward the self."[2] Yoshimoto's emphasis on the latter as the foundation of literary expressions especially affected literary scholars, who were struggling to read the text ultimately as the externalization of the writer's interiority.

Yoshimoto's *Gengo* was gradually forgotten, probably because of the impact of imported poststructuralist theories of language in the 1980s and the 1990s. Literary critics no longer mention Yoshimoto as a theorist of language, and graduate programs in literature no longer include this work in their required reading lists for students. Likewise, little effort has been made to treat Yoshimoto's *Gengo* as a historical text that tells something about the 1960s and 1970s, although Kamei Hideo is one of the very few critics who have attempted to situate Yoshimoto's work within the history of literary theory in Japan. With his long-standing concern about the concept of *shutai*, which is customarily translated as either "subject" or "subjectivity," Kamei considers Yoshimoto Takaaki one of the most important figures in postwar literary theory.

According to Kamei, Yoshimoto's position is best described in relation to the writers who were involved with the postwar literary magazine *Kindai bungaku*, namely, Hirano Ken (1907–78) and Ara Masahito (1913–79). The writers who published in *Kindai bungaku* placed utmost significance on the writer's *shutai* (the term *shutaisei* is also used), by which they meant "the innermost truth" of the writer's self. They contended that writers must express this in their works and used it as a standard by which the critics should judge literary works. Their attachment to this *shutai*, Kamei points out, came from the severe self-questioning of their inability to criticize the prewar fascist movement when it was driving Japan in the wrong direction. They concluded that if they had listened to the voice from within more carefully they would not have been so easily influenced by the atmosphere of the

---

2. Kamei Hideo, "Author's Preface to English Translation," in Kamei Hideo, *Transformations of Sensibility: The Phenomenology of Meiji Literature,* edited by Michael Bourdaghs (Ann Arbor: University of Michigan, Center for Japanese Studies Publications, 2002), li.

time. According to Kamei, Yoshimoto's argument gave a theoretical ground to their discussion of *shutai* by proposing a new way of analyzing a literary text as the expression of the interiority of its author.[3]

My project is different from Kamei's in the sense that it does not seek to examine the validity of Yoshimoto's analytical apparatus in relation to other Japanese and non-Japanese theorists of language. Neither does this essay attempt to criticize Kamei by, for example, resituating Yoshimoto's position within the postwar literary discursive field. It instead focuses on Yoshimoto's rhetoric and in particular on how his struggle to surpass the intellectual currents of his time is inscribed in it. I wish to show that through this struggle Yoshimoto produced "language" as an abstract and universal entity. I argue that Yoshimoto's abstract (and by extension nonpolitical) argument on language is best understood as a form of narrative that was necessitated by his historical moment and the intellectual forces with which he needed to negotiate. The latter half of the essay is devoted to an analysis of Yoshimoto's argument on the primary functions of language. I examine the process through which Yoshimoto comes up with the terms *jiko hyōshutsu* and *shiji hyōshutsu*, as well as the political implications they generated. This analysis naturally calls for a close reading of the text, especially of its rhetoric and literary devices, since Yoshimoto's writing is full of metaphors and quotations that create rhetorical rather than logical connections. In other words, his writings depend heavily on the associations that readers make of Yoshimoto's metaphors, a tendency that contributes to the difficulty of reading his writing as a work of "literary theory."

THEORY, THE LITERARY, AND THE POLITICAL

Writings published in the 1960s and 70s seemingly belong to the recent past, and some may question whether there is a need to historicize such recent works. However, Yoshimoto's *Gengo* is the kind of work that makes one feel that need quite strongly. Reading *Gengo* is a strenuous task for scholars and students of literary studies in 2009 who are unfamiliar with the intellectual atmosphere of the 1960s and 1970s. Although the work was written in the recent past, or, rather, precisely because it was written in the recent past, the circumstances under which it was written were taken for granted and not fully explored. In various discussions of Yoshimoto's works, many things were left unsaid since explanations of these things were considered to be

---

3. For Kamei's discussion of the relationship between the *Kindai bungaku* group and Yoshimoto, see his *Meiji bungakushi* (Tokyo: Iwanami Shoten, 2000), 104–11.

unnecessary. One of the objectives of this essay is to bring these assumptions to light.

The process of reading *Gengo* also reveals our assumptions about literary theory. One of the difficulties in reading *Gengo* is that the basic Japanese terms Yoshimoto uses, such as *riron*, *bungaku*, and *seiji*, belong to a semantic economy different from that which includes the terms *theory*, *literature*, and *politics*. For example, the word *theory* often refers to metadiscourse on language, something a student of any national literature must read along with the writings that belong to his or her own area of specialization. However, when "theory" is posited as such, the student is structurally excluded from the act of contextualizing. Although the student may study the differences among various theories—structuralism, poststructuralism, deconstruction, psychoanalysis, reader-response theory, and whatnot—he or she rarely examines the writings themselves in terms of the historical and political contexts within which they were produced. This is because *theory* defined in this manner appears as a neutral, nonideological, and hence universal "tool." Of course, ultimately, it is a "theoretical" flaw to configure theory in this way, but here I will not go into the details of how *theory* should be defined. My point is that, in a work such as *Gengo*, the reader who has this depoliticized, dehistoricized notion of theory cannot even begin to understand what the writer is saying.

Here let me turn to an analysis of the actual text in order to elaborate this point. The following passage is quoted from the preface to *Gengo*.

> I am all too weary of writing about the personal struggles I have experienced while writing this text, but I can say with certainty that those who have been criticizing me both for my literary works and for my political beliefs will be invalidated in terms of the validity of literary theory with the advent of this work.[4]

In this passage, Yoshimoto boasts about "the validity" of his own "literary theory" (*bungaku riron*), and this is clearly directed toward those who have been criticizing him politically. The term *political beliefs* is casually juxtaposed with *literary works*, which suggests that for the writer of this passage the validity of literary theory is a political matter. The writer seems to feel that there is no need to explain any more about the relationship between political beliefs and *bungaku riron*. Moreover, readers who understand Japanese

4. Yoshimoto Takaaki, *Gengo ni totte bi towa nani ka*, 2 vols. (Tokyo: Keisō Shobō, 1965) 1:5 (hereafter cited as *Gengo*). This part of the preface was not included when the first installment of the essay was published in the journal, *Shikō*. Translations of all the quotes from *Gengo* and other Japanese language sources are mine except where noted.

may be confused to find that "political beliefs" in the Japanese original is *seisaku*, which connotes policies and strategies rather than ideologies per se. The term gives the impression that those who have been criticizing the author belong to different factions of a single political community. The juxtaposition of the terms *bungaku riron* and *seisaku* suggests that Yoshimoto considers his readers to be familiar with the political differences among factions, as well as those among different political communities. In this textual space, the political audience is at the same time the contemporaneous literary audience and hence is assumed to be able to judge the "validity" of Yoshimoto's *riron*.

In the preface, the term *riron* first appears in association with proletarian literature and the trend of socialist realism. Socialist realism was first imported to Japan in the 1930s by proletarian writers and critics, and it became popular again in the postwar period when Marxist-influenced literature was revived. In the late 1950s, Yoshimoto was in the forefront of those criticizing socialist realism. One of his enemies in this was Hanada Kiyoteru (1909–74), a critic who was associated with the ultranationalist group Tōhōkai during the war but after the war committed himself to Shin Nihon Bungakukai (New Japan Literary Society), the largest left-wing literary group of the postwar period. I will not here dwell on the details of the famous Hanada-Yoshimoto debate, which went on for several months, but I will point out that Yoshimoto's "Gisei no shūen" included a severe attack on Hanada. In this essay Yoshimoto severely criticized the "official" understanding of Japanese postwar history and the "official" interpretations of the students' role in the anti-Anpo activism offered by the JCP. The JCP's "official" policy for art and literature was socialist realism, which was promoted as the only legitimate discourse on literary works and the sole valid criteria for active left-wing writers. In both his literary and political essays, Yoshimoto denounces the ideological conformism imposed by the JCP. At the time, these official policies in themselves were thought to constitute a universally valid Marxist theory, and for them *riron* signified the combined entity that encompasses both policies and theory. Yoshimoto needed to negotiate what *riron* meant to the JCP while creating his own signification of the term.

Yoshimoto attempts to reformulate the power dynamics of socialist realism by reviving the term *riron* in its original sense, that of a universal and systematic discourse. He makes the following sarcastic remarks about contemporary writers.

> Valéry's phrase becomes famous because it sticks in many people's minds. Nowadays, Valéry's insistence that *riron* is invariably

valid for its own writer and is never true for everybody else is nothing new to current conservative writers. Even for those who were immersed in political literary theory, this may be an idea they held hidden deeply inside while their heads were producing completely different things. (*Gengo*, 1:6)

Yoshimoto's point here is that when a writer advocates a *riron* in his writing it is often the case that it is true only to the writer himself. However, Yoshimoto contends that that writing simply gains the pretense of universality when it is endorsed by some power, a power that pertains to the political realm, and that whatever validity may be inherent in the discourse can be annihilated by this political power. Yoshimoto attacks the JCP's "political cohesion" (*seiji teki kyōsei*) for forcing writers to produce works in accordance with the party's *riron* and of rendering a particular writing into a universal that is supposedly applicable to all situations. What needs to be achieved, according to Yoshimoto, is literary freedom (*bungaku teki jiyū*), meaning the elimination of political cohesion. And, this is precisely where his argument resonates with that of the postwar *Kindai bungaku* writers, who emphasized "freedom of the interiority" as I mentioned earlier.

However, unlike the *Kindai bungaku* writers, who centered their argument on the opposition between political cohesion and literary freedom, Yoshimoto in his preface situates *kyakkan sei* or objectiveness as the overt opposite to *seiji teki kyōsei*. This opposition needs to be examined together with yet another opposition Yoshimoto posits in the text, that between *riron* and *fuhen* (the universal). Yoshimoto declares in the preface that his writing is based on *fuhen* and *kyakkan sei* and that this is why it outshines any of the *riron* that were currently circulating in the socialist countries of the world. He goes on to say that "the characteristic of my writing is that it has objectiveness (*taishō teki kyakkan sei*) in the sense that if there is a mistake in it any reader can deduce it logically and correct it to improve and elaborate my argument" (*Gengo*, 1:7). As confusing as it may sound, Yoshimoto here underscores that his work should be called *riron* in the original sense of the term, not in the distorted sense advocated by the writers and critics loyal to the JCP.

Perhaps I ought to briefly mention the overall image of Marxism at this time. Maruyama Masao (1914–96), a representative intellectual of the 1950s, discussed the impact of Marxism in the 1920s, quoting Kobayashi Hideo's (1902–83) words.

It is no exaggeration to say that until that day, even in the realm of cultural critique, we had never felt the hand of science. It was

in this situation that, all of a sudden, an extremely scientific methodology of critique was introduced. It goes without saying that it
rode in on Marxist thought.[5]

Maruyama argues that Kobayashi's words prove that Marxism entered Japan primarily as a scientific way to analyze society and remained one of
the most systematic modes for describing a cluster of various phenomena
that were referred to vaguely as "society." Maruyama wrote this in 1959,
basically inheriting Kobayashi's view of Marxism. Postwar proletarian writers also shared Kobayashi's view. Miyamoto Yuriko (1899–51), one of the
most prominent writers of the *Shin Nihon Bungaku* group, wrote that one of
the contributions of proletarian literature to modern Japanese literature was
that it provided a systematic way to analyze "society" and "class" in literature.[6] Given that this was the prevailing image of Japanese Marxism among
both progressive intellectuals and the writers who had previously belonged
to NAPF (Nippona Artista Proleta Federacio), Yoshimoto had to emphasize
the "objectivity" and "universality" of his own approach by invoking the
original sense of *riron*. In other words, Yoshimoto needed to undermine the
analytical tools of socialist realism and introduce a different sense of *riron*,
one that could lay claim to universality.

Toward the end of the preface, Yoshimoto declares that he has chosen
to "talk in a universal way" (*fuhen teki ni kataru*). No sarcastic tone can be
detected here, which shows that *fuhen* in this part of his argument is completely devoid of postmodern skepticism about universality. His narrative
also lacks any trace of the postcolonial concern for "narrativization," a concern that stems from awareness that the manner of narration is no insignificant matter but rather something fundamentally implicated in power relations. Rather, in Yoshimoto, "universality" is considered to be achievable
through "talk(ing) in a universal way." No gap can be felt between these two
notions. This conflation itself is an interesting problem with significant ram-
ifications, but unfortunately I do not have the time and space to elaborate it
at present. What is important is that he introduces the theme of "language"
precisely when he announces his decision to "talk in a universal way." Language for Yoshimoto needs to embody a form of universality different from
that found in Marxism. Yoshimoto contends that the only statement about

5. Kobayashi's phrase is quoted in "Kindai Nihon no shisō to bungaku," in *Maruyama Masao
shū*, 17 vols. (Tokyo: Iwanami Shoten, 1995–97), 8:111–57. Kobayashi's original is taken
from "Bungei hihyō ni tsuite," which was published in the first issue of the literary journal *Bungaku* in 1933.
6. Miyamoto Yuriko discussed the prewar Proletarian literary theory in "Ryōrin: sōzō to
hyōron katsudō no mondai," *Shin Nihon bungaku* 3:3 (March 1948): 2–7.

literature that everybody—on both the Left and the Right—would agree on is that "literature is an art consisting of language" and any discussion of it should begin by answering the most fundamental (and universal) question, "what is language?"

STALINIST LINGUISTICS AND
THE MARXIST VIEW OF LANGUAGE

In *Gengo*, the first three chapters, entitled "The Essence of Language," "Attributes of Language," and "Rhyme, Diction, Transference, and Metaphors," are devoted to establishing the concepts "self-expression" and "indicative expression," which together constitute "the essence of language" (*gengo no honshitsu*) for Yoshimoto. In the rest of the first volume, he attempts to rewrite the entire history of Japanese literature using these two concepts. This section therefore discusses the application of his *riron,* as it were. In the second volume, he attempts to extend his examination to the genres of poetry, prose (*monogatari*), and theater. The rest of this essay focuses on the first chapter, where his effort to transcend Marxist literary theory can be observed most clearly. In my opinion, it is also the crucial section for understanding the entire book since Yoshimoto's narrative there, with its various rhetorical devices, gives birth to the concepts of "self-expression" and "indicative expression."

In the preface, Yoshimoto insists that anyone who wants to discuss literature must begin with the most fundamental question, "what is language?" This statement bears a close resemblance to the opening of Etō Jun's article "Sakka wa kōdō suru" (Writers Take Action), which was published a few years before Yoshimoto's *Gengo*. Etō writes:

> Literary works are written in words. The study of style (*buntai ron*) analyzes literary works consciously from the aspect of language. This much is of course obvious, but what lies beyond this isn't obvious at all. An examination of style therefore must begin with an examination of language itself.[7]

Etō's first line here resembles Yoshimoto remark about literature quoted above. Like Yoshimoto, Etō sets as the starting point of his criticism an examination of the nature of language. He develops his exploration of this issue using Jean-Paul Sartre (1905–80) as his reference point. Yoshimoto in

---

7. Etō Jun, "Sakka wa kōdō suru," in *Etō Jun chosaku shū*, 6 vols. (Tokyo: Kōdansha, 1967), 5:7.

fact refers to Etō's work in the preface as one of the works of literary criticism that have inspired him. However, Yoshimoto's praise paradoxically shows his discontent with Etō's treatise on language and literature. While Yoshimoto positively evaluates Etō's works, he needed to produce two volumes of his own argument on the same issue.

What Yoshimoto wanted to achieve, perhaps as an implicit statement against Etō, is manifest in the references he uses in the first chapter of *Gengo*. There he constructs his argument on how language first appeared, using quotes from Karl Marx, Joseph Stalin, and S. N. Bykovskij, a linguist whose *Soviet Linguistics* appeared in Japanese translation in 1947. The works that Yoshimoto discusses suggest two concerns on his part. One is his determination to limit the scope of his argument to linguistics, to the discussion of language as an autonomous, unified entity. Another is his resolution to discuss the issue in reference to various Marxist positions concerning language theory. Etō's approach lacks both. Etō mentions neither linguistics nor Marxism and develops his argument mainly in reference to Sartre. His focus is to portray the relationship between one's writing (*buntai* is the term he prefers to use) and one's thoughts (*shisō* is the term he regularly uses) as something more complex than conventional conceptions would have it. Although his focus implies criticism toward the orthodox Marxist approach to literature, which treats words simply as tools to convey the writer's political ideologies, Etō never employs the vocabulary or concepts of Marxist critical discourse, not even in the form of quotations. Unlike Etō, however, Yoshimoto cannot afford to ignore his enemies. He must address them directly so as to differentiate himself from his enemies, but at the same time he must not appear to be adopting a completely non-Marxist position.

The basic strategy Yoshimoto employs is to criticize Stalin and Bykovskij in order to highlight Marx's remarks on language in *The German Ideology*. In short, he presents himself as a better reader of Marx than them or, more precisely, than their Japanese followers. Yoshimoto attempts to undermine the power of these Marxist writers by using Marx himself, and it is from this politically charged power play within the realm of the Marxist-oriented writers that Yoshimoto draws a significant concept called "the essence of language" for his later argument. However, before he takes up this problem, he engages in a preliminary argument about the birth of language in the first section of the first chapter. How did people come to use language? What were the circumstances through which human beings come to possess language? A careful reader will soon notice that asking these questions is in itself an ideological act, a rhetorical strategy aimed at universalizing language. These questions can only induce narratives that posit an imaginary origin of language (since this origin is ultimately unknowable, what is told in the narrative can only be imaginary). These narratives about the origin of language also serve to essentialize it by defining its most fundamental function while suppressing the question of whether or not we can treat it as an entity that exists above and beyond geographical and historical differences. This preliminary argument shapes the ideological paradigm of Yoshimoto's subsequent argument on Marx and Stalin. It is therefore imperative that we examine this section carefully.

Yoshimoto here relies on Susanne Knouth Langer's (1895–1985) *The Philosophy of Symbols* (1942), in which Langer analyzes a scientific report about a boy who was found in the forest living with animals. A doctor named Itard observed the process through which the boy, who was later named Victor, learned language. In Yoshitmoto's argument, Victor is clearly treated as someone similar to a primitive man, and it is assumed that by observing his behavior one can simulate the circumstances under which human beings acquired language for the first time. Yoshimoto summarizes Langer's argument as follows.

> Langer cites the reports of Itard, the doctor who did research on Victor of Avalon while trying to educate him, using it as decisive evidence against the idea of language as a practical use (*gengo jitsuyō setsu*). Itard attempted to make Victor use the word *water* as a sign when he wanted water, but Victor did not use the sound as a sign. Itard failed in this experiment because he could not stop giving Victor water. So he repeated the same experiment with milk. When he poured milk into Victor's cup, Victor pronounced the word *milk* for the first time with an expression of delight. The second time this happened, Victor said "milk" again, but only *after* he saw that the cup was filled. This means that Victor pronounced the word phonetically not as a sign of demanding something but rather as a mere expression of delight because the word was pronounced not *before* but *after* he was given milk.
>
> The evidence that Langer cites, including this experiment, manifests her strong inclination to characterize the birth of language as something nonpractical.[8]

Whether or not Yoshimoto reproduces Langer's argument accurately is not the issue here. We are examining the way Yoshimoto appropriates it to construct his own argument. In this passage, Yoshimoto creates an opposition

8. *Gengo*, 1:15. The original work to which Yoshimoto refers is Susanne Knouth Langer, *Shinboru no tetsugaku*, translated by Yano Banri, Ikegami Yasuta, Kishi Kenji, and Kondo Hiroichi (Tokyo: Iwanami Shoten, 1960).

between the "practical" and "nonpractical" uses of language, using Itard's report to substantiate it.

The opposition may seem valid at first glance, but a close examination soon reveals that the borderline between practical and nonpractical is not as clear as it appears. Let us first clarify Yoshimoto's definitions of *practical* and *nonpractical*. Yoshimoto's narrative implies that if Victor were to use language in a "practical" way, he would have had to utter "milk" before his demand was met. In other words, the term *practical* is used to designate a situation in which Victor's utterance is a means of meeting his own demand. "Nonpractical use of language" is used to designate the actual situation of the experiment. Contrary to general expectations, Victor did not say the word until after he was given milk. In the original text, Yoshimoto places emphasis on this temporal order, thereby suggesting that Victor's utterance was not a means of obtaining milk but a response to the fact that it was given. What is more, Yoshimoto's narrative includes the interpretive comment "with an expression of delight." Whether a certain facial movement of Victor's can be called "an expression of delight" is unexamined and definitely arguable, but Yoshimoto putatively posits Victor's feelings by adding that phrase. The phrase is taken from Langer's original, but Yoshimoto does not pay attention to the fact that this seemingly objective observation includes an element of interpretation on Itard's part. In the original, Langer obviously does not take this into consideration, which is all the more convenient for Yoshimoto because it effectively underscores his point that the utterance was an expression of feelings.

There is another important element in this practical/nonpractical distinction. Whether or not Victor directly addressed Itard is the key to distinguishing the practical from the nonpractical use of language. Its implication is worth exploring for our later discussion. In the practical use of the word *milk*, Victor would be addressing Itard directly because Itard is the agent that will bring Victor milk. In this case, Victor's utterance solicits Itard's subsequent action. However, in the case of nonpractical use, Victor does not need to direct his utterance toward Itard. Yoshimoto tries to convey this distinction by describing Victor's behavior as a "mere expression of delight," implying that Victor spoke without any intention of soliciting some action from the addressee (Itard). In other words, Yoshimoto's narrative premises that Victor's utterance in the latter case does not have any specific addressee, hence does not have any end in itself, and therefore is self-sufficient in nature.

This distinction is unsustainable for many reasons, however. To take one example, the role of Itard in the nonpractical use of language may not be as clear as his role in the practical use of language, but one cannot thereby conclude that Itard's existence is irrelevant to Victor's utterance. It would be equally valid to argue that "the expression of delight" exhibited by Victor (assuming that it truly is an expression of delight) is caused by the existence of Itard, and hence the utterance may not be as self-sufficient as Yoshimoto maintains. In sum, Yoshimoto's argument does not provide sufficient grounds for concluding that the other's existence does not affect the addresser even when the utterance itself is an expression of the addresser's feelings. Yoshimoto's narrative attempts to establish a clear distinction between the practical and nonpractical uses of language by suppressing the role that Itard played in the exchange. It also seeks to create the impression that an expression of feelings should be attributed entirely to the speaker, thereby suggesting that when expressing one's feelings the speaker is an independent and autonomous self.

Thus, underlying Yoshimoto's discussion of practical and nonpractical uses of language is the presumption of a speaking subject, a free agent that utters words totally unaffected by the existence of others. Based on this premise, Yoshimoto goes a step further and adds another layer of argument, elaborating the opposition between nonpractical and practical uses of language. A few lines down from the passage quoted earlier, Yoshimoto rephrases the opposition between practical and nonpractical: it is now an opposition between "language as a process of the practical application of human consciousness" and "language as a process of the voluntary expression of human consciousness." This rephrasing is subtle but extremely significant. The new opposition implies that the term *practical* should be associated with *involuntary* since *nonpractical* is *voluntary*. The former opposition does not necessarily involve a value judgment, but the new one apparently does. The term *involuntary* even suggests something that is "forced" by others while *voluntary* is associated with the "free" expression of a self that is independent of the existence of others.

These binaries all serve as the ground on which Yoshimoto constructs his argument about Marx and Stalin, or rather about Stalin's misreading of Marx. Yoshimoto carefully selects from among Marx's remarks on language the following passage.

> From the start the "spirit" is afflicted with the curse of being "burdened" with the matter, which here makes its appearance in the form of agitated layers of air, sounds, in short, of language. Language is as old as consciousness, language *is* practical consciousness that exists also for other men, and for that reason alone it really exists for me personally as well; language like

consciousness only arises from the need, the necessity, of intercourse with other men. Where there exists a relationship, it exists
for me: the animal does not enter into "relations" with anything,
it does not enter into any relation at all.[9]

The passage has conventionally been interpreted as an expression of Marx's
view that the essential function of language is practical communication
with others. In fact, on the surface this interpretation appears valid; the passage clearly states that "language like consciousness only arises from the
need," which is "the necessity of intercourse with other men." However,
in his discussion Yoshimoto calls the reader's attention to the fact that the
passage also contains the phrase "me personally" and that it is clear from
the syntax that Marx's emphasis is placed equally on both terms, *me* and
other men. Yoshimoto then argues, "When he [Marx] talks about 'consciousness' here, he is focusing on *human* consciousness, which is something self-
reflexive (*jiko taishō teki*), and he means 'externalized' (*gaika sareta*) human
consciousness when he uses the term *practical*" (*Gengo*, 1:17). Again, whether
Yoshimoto interprets Marx correctly (assuming there is such a thing as "a
correct interpretation") is not the issue here. It is Yoshimoto's narrativization of Marx's comment that is important. Yoshimoto in the quoted passage
defines Marx's "practical" as something that comes after "human consciousness" has been established. In other words, Yoshimoto gives both logical
and temporal priority to the entity called human consciousness over the act
of externalizing. The verb *externalize* invariably assumes that something to
be externalized already exists "inside," and this is human consciousness according to Yoshimoto's paradigm.

The dichotomy between self and others in verbal exchange becomes all
the more apparent when Yoshimoto introduces Stalin.

For example, Stalin in his "On Marxism in Linguistics" states that
language was created and is existent now in order for people to
serve the society as a whole (*zentai toshite no shakai ni hōshi suru*)
and to serve as a means for interaction; he argues that it is a shared
entity for the members of the society, one single thing for the society, and something that serves equally all the members of the
society, regardless of their class. (*Gengo*, 1:17)

Here Stalin (or rather Yoshimoto's rephrasing of Stalin) stresses *hōshi* (service) and *shakai* (society). It is clear that Yoshimoto has specifically com-

9. Yoshimoto is quoting from Karl Marx, *Doitsu ideorogii*, translated by Yuibutsuron kenkyūkai
(Tokyo: Fuji Shuppansha, 1954), 20-21. The English translation is taken from Karl Marx
and Frederic Engels, *The German Ideology* (Moscow: Progress, 1964), 41–42.

posed this passage in order to highlight what Stalin suppressed from Marx's view. With this introduction of Stalin, the dichotomy Yoshimoto created earlier—between others and self—becomes that of society and self. It was probably easy for the readers of 1960s to associate this dichotomy with the involuntary/voluntary opposition since the expression *shakai ni hōshi suru*, or "serving society," could easily invoke the supremacy of politics, the fundamental principle of the prewar Japanese Marxist movement.

When *Gengo* was written in 1961, Stalin's status among various Japanese Marxists was at its lowest point due to the so-called critique of Stalin begun in the late 1950s. Therefore, Yoshimoto's purpose was not necessarily to denounce Stalin's perceptions of language but rather to argue that Japanese Marxist writers who had been criticizing Stalin, following the intellectual currents in the Soviet Union, had themselves uncritically inherited Stalin's position on language. We can see Yoshimoto's criticism of Bykovskij as a telltale sign.[10] Bykovskij was a scholar of Soviet linguistics whose works were translated a few years before Stalin's essay was circulated in Japan. According to Yoshimoto, Bykovskij falls into the same trap with Stalin in that he uncritically accepted the prevailing view that Marx had advocated "practical use" as the primary function of language. Since Stalin's essay was written in order to criticize existing Soviet linguistics, Yoshimoto's act of lumping Bykovskij and Stalin together in the same category implies that they ultimately share a similar misreading of Marx. Yoshimoto's narrative paints both as "enemies" who emphasize the obligation for service to others at the expense of the self.[11]

AGAIN THE ISSUE OF HISTORICIZATION

The two sides of the set of aligning dichotomies described above will be called, respectively, "self-expression" and "indicative expression" in Yoshimoto's later argument. How Yoshimoto employs the terms in the rest of his book will be left for future studies. By way of conclusion, I would like to reiterate my point about the discursive space of *Gengo*. On the surface, the terms *indicative expression* and *self-expression* signify functions of language and hence seem to be analytical concepts with which literary texts should be analyzed. Following this line of argument, language becomes an abstract entity, its attributes neutral and apolitical. However, as we have seen,

10. The Japanese translation of Bykovskij's book is S. N. Bykovskij, *Sobēto gengogaku* (Tokyo: Shōchōsha, 1946).
11. For the relationship between Stalinist and Soviet linguistics, see Tanaka Katsuhiko, *Sutārin gengogaku seidoku* (Tokyo: Iwanami Shoten, 2000).

through the process of shifting between various sets of dichotomies, the image of the problematic prewar Marxist movement is attached to the latter, and in turn the former is valorized. Even before these main concepts are introduced, the narrative has been infiltrated with value judgments that are heavily political. As a result, Yoshimoto's narrative strongly suggests that, if the latter (indicative expression) is emphasized as the primary function of language, the idioms of literary criticism will return to the dark days of the prewar proletarian movement, when the doctrine of political supremacy was the sole criteria for literary quality.

The abstract and nonpartisan facade of Yoshimoto's narrative is thus produced through a politically charged power play marked by a strong will to win the game. For those who had read Yoshimoto's early works, in which socialist realism and its followers were the direct targets of criticism, Yoshimoto's narrative of universality must have seemed truly new. However, they also probably assumed the continued presence of Yoshimoto's earlier stance behind the abstract narrative, and they were likely to read his narrative by substantiating its abstractedness through Yoshimoto's earlier, more explicitly political statements. For those readers who worshipped Yoshimoto, the universalistic stance of the narrative represented nothing but the political triumph of Yoshimoto over the JCP and its followers, as Yoshimoto claimed in his afterword: "I have been writing this with only a few readers in mind. Throughout the process of writing this, I kept saying in my mind, 'this is my triumph, my triumph.'" (*Gengo*, 2:623)

It is difficult for us living in the year 2009 to conceptualize a discursive space where literary theory is described with terms like *triumph*. This precisely is why we need to explore what Yoshimoto was negotiating with at that particular moment in history. Historicization is absolutely necessary in reading works that belong to the recent past. I am not so pretentious as to claim that my essay has adequately historicized the work in question. The historical context I have outlined is itself yet another narrative, a selective and filtered body of information, and there is an infinite amount of information that is left out but could just as correctly be called historical context. Thus, historicization is a never-ending process even for one text; with each reading, a given text will be configured differently depending on which context is chosen. What I have attempted in this essay is to produce a different type of contextual narrative from that through which literary theory is usually discussed.

Seen from this particular perspective, Yoshimoto's *Gengo* represents a moment when a break from one influential political ideology coincidentally produced a new set of universal idioms that were then used to discuss yet another abstract construct called language. In the textual space of *Gengo*, the universal was nothing but the political in the very rawest sense of the term.

8 Narration and Revolution: An Invitation to the Writings of Kobayashi Takiji

Norma Field

It is staggering to think about how Leon Trotsky, a busy man at the center of the fledgling Soviet state in 1923, found the time to write that urbane yet impassioned work known as *Literature and Revolution*. The introduction suggests why he might have made the time.

> [E]ven a successful solution of the elementary problems of food, clothing, shelter, and even of literacy, would in no way signify a complete victory of the new historic principle, that is, of Socialism. . . . In this sense, the development of art is the highest test of the vitality and significance of each epoch.[1]

Not only the memory of the cold war but its conclusion with the fall of the Berlin Wall and the dissolution of the Soviet Union, which have left us trying to survive in a free world dominated by a single superpower, and more subtly but perhaps as powerfully the sinuous legacy of Kantian aesthetic autonomy, may incline us to reject on principle an art attesting to the realization of socialism. And that would be hasty. In the chapter entitled "The Formalist School of Poetry and Marxism," for instance, Trotsky asserts:

> Personal lyrics of the very smallest scope have an absolute right to exist within the new art. Moreover, the new man cannot be

---

1. Leon Trotsky, *Literature and Revolution*, translated by Rose Strunsky (Ann Arbor: University of Michigan Press, 1960), 9. The book was published by the Soviet government in 1924 and banned in 1928. It was translated early into Japanese from the Russian (many others of Trotsky's works were retranslated from English translations) in 1925 by Shigemori Tadashi and published by Kaizōsha according to "Torotsuki no tankōbon." Torotsuki Kenkyūjo, http://www2u.biglobe.ne.jp/~Trotsky/mokuroku/A-senzen.html (accessed August 14, 2002).

formed without a new lyric poetry. But to create it, the poet himself must feel the world in a new way.[2]

Japanese writers "feel[ing] the world in a new way, " grappling with writing,
and trying to apprehend the subtle and revolutionary changes and contradictions of post–Meiji Restoration society is the subject of Kamei Hideo's
eye-opening book *Transformations of Sensibility*. I begin this modest exploration of the relationship between literature and reality in the short fiction of
Kobayashi Takiji by focusing on a debate engendered by the elusive "nonperson" narrator posited by Kamei.[3] The pieces I shall take up were written
just at the point in Kobayashi's painfully short life (1903–33) when he was
being hailed as a proletarian writer. Since the early 1970s, proletarian literature has fallen out of public memory.[4] Finding many of the works freshly
compelling "as literature"—as verbal craft exploring and forging our relationship with the world—and astounded, now more than ever, that there
was a time not that long ago when people thought of literature as indispensable *to* revolution—rather than revolution in literature *as* revolution itself—
I am in search of ways to bring that body of writing together with various
sorts of present-day concerns. Here I am curious, on the one hand, about
how sociohistorical, political issues impinge on narrative analyses in which
linguistic categories play a prominent role and, on the other hand, about
the contributions narratological analysis might make to the study of proletarian fiction.[5]

2. Trotsky, *Literature and Revolution*, 170.
3. In this formulation, I find wry inspiration in Raymond Williams's qualification about diction slipped into a key statement in his essay "The Welsh Industrial Novel," namely,
   "Both the realist and the naturalist novel . . . had been predicated on the distinctive
   assumption—I say assumption, though *if I were not being academic I would say, more shortly,
   the distinctive truth*—that the lives of individuals, however intensely and personally realized, are not just influenced but in certain crucial ways formed by general social relations." Raymond Williams, *Problems in Materialism and Culture* (London: Verso, 1980), 221,
   emphasis added. I will resist the temptation to put quotation marks around *reality*.
4. For a concise recent history of the reception of proletarian literature and much else, see the
   informative discussion in Odagiri Hideo, Shimamura Teru, Inoue Hisashi, and Komori
   Yōichi, "Puroretaria bungaku: Dan'atsuka no bungakukshatachi," Zadankai Showa
   bungakushi IV, *Subaru* 19:10 (October 1997): 140–90.
5. At the time of writing, I had not yet read Barbara Foley's indispensable analysis and exem-
   plification of narratological analysis of proletarian fiction in her *Radical Representations:
   Politics and Form in U.S. Proletarian Fiction, 1929–1941* (Durham and London: Duke University Press, 1993).

THE NONPERSON NARRATOR

In the early portions of Futabatei Shimei's *Ukigumo,* regularly hailed as Japan's first modern novel, there appears a narrator who peppers his descriptions of scene and character with cheeky judgment.[6] The narrator has no name; he has the rudiments of a personality, but he is not a persona, that is, he does not exist for the characters in the novel and he does not affect the action. Nor, on the other hand, is he that sort of narrator who has access to the characters' thoughts. This is the entity that Kamei names the "nonperson" narrator, and it is this narrator's disappearance from *Ukigumo* that leads Kamei to embark on a fruitful meditation on the possibilities lost in the early days of modern Japanese fiction. If the nonperson narrator is something other than an appendix that had the evolutionary grace to wither away, what purposes might it have served? It was a bulwark against the solipsism of the I-novel and, more affirmatively, a vehicle for the mutual elevation and expansion of the sensibility of writers and readers, suggests Kamei. This needs some elaboration.

The process of writing *Ukigumo* was for Futabatei a process of apprehending his own sensibilities with increasing sureness, resulting in an integrated style that Kamei calls "I-ness" on the level of expression, a phenomenon necessary but hardly restricted to the I-novel that would come to dominate Japanese letters.[7] As Futabatei became increasingly aware of the possibility of depicting his protagonist's inner life, the nonperson narrator he had created, probably adopted from writings by other contemporaries, came to seem a hindrance. This creature, who appeared to offer an independent take on the world within the text and therefore represent something like objectivity for readers, was too crass and therefore out of sync with the experiences Futabatei wanted to explore, especially the tragic fate of Bunzō. The latter's fall from worldly success provokes an ever-intensifying incapacity for self-expression that pushes Futabatei to experiment with the depiction of outer muteness, inner speech, and acute self-consciousness. Kamei hypothesizes that had Futabatei allowed this narrator to survive and

---

6. This work is available in English as *Japan's First Modern Novel:* Ukigumo *of Futabatei Shimei,* translated by Marleigh Grayer Ryan (New York: Columbia University Press, 1967). The original novel was published in installments in 1887 and 1889.

7. Kamei Hideo, *Transformations of Sensibility: The Phenomenology of Meiji Literature,* translation edited by Michael Bourdaghs (Ann Arbor: University of Michigan, Center for Japanese Studies Publications, 2002), 10–11.

endowed him with the consciousness that he, too, shared the plight of these characters, such recognition would necessarily have induced self-reflection and deepened awareness, accompanied by the possibility for the same in his readers. Note that the nonperson narrator in its full potential combines the features of the objective and the subjective, the external and the internal. And, to put it abstractly, it is as a third term, between author and reader, that this narrator displays this feature.

Did the depiction of Bunzō's tragedy—in itself a considerable literary achievement—have to take such interiorized, solipsistic form? Kamei refers to a work by Hattori Bushō (1841–1908), a writer of *kanbun fūzokushi* (accounts of everyday life written in Japanized Chinese), to suggest otherwise. Bushō's account of the plight of a farmer who had been doubly defrauded has shed the comic, rhetorical high spirits common to the genre. Bushō is forging a "prose style that aims to inform readers of the true nature of social affairs."[8] At the same time, it is hard to imagine, for all that Bushō may have grasped the commonality of their fate, that he would have developed a prose style for exploring, or rather creating, the poor farmer's psyche, thus making it a part of "social affairs." If, as Kamei suggests, Futabatei intuited that neither his nonperson narrator nor the readers to whom this narrator appealed, whose sensibilities had been formed by the comic and satirical fiction of their day, could have apprehended Bunzō's tortured ruminations, then this is a literary historical issue with powerful sociopolitical resonance: interiority is not only historically variable but unevenly distributed in literary representation. To put it baldly, when do the masses (including women) acquire psyches that can dominate the space of fictional works that will be read by these same masses as well as brooding intellectuals? Or, as Trotsky put it, "Uncle Vanya is not the only one with an inner life."[9] This is not to argue, however, that equal opportunity to become Uncle Vanya is a sufficient goal for literature or life. As Kamei anticipates, the loss of "objectivity of the textual world," which the nonperson narrator had helped to secure, meant that the "literary work . . . could convey only the unfolding of the I-sensibility," its "monotonous, impoverished" structure ultimately leading to the I-novel.[10] A monotonous inner life is not the exclusive prerogative of the privileged. What is needed is a reciprocal and dynamic exchange between inner life and outer world.

The bridging of reader and textual world that Kamei attributes to *Ukigumo's* disappearing nonperson narrator is, in keeping with Kamei's

8. Ibid., 20.
9. Trotsky, *Literature and Revolution*, 138.
10. Kamei, *Transformations of Sensibility*, 11.

great topic, a bridge based on shared sensibilities formed, as all sensibilities are, by historically and socially differentiated experience, including the experience of literary genres. Futabatei's abandonment of this narrator meant loss of the chance to bridge, through mutual exposure, abutting but distinct sensibilities: on the one hand, Bunzō, of precarious financial prospects but not truly hungry—not yet, at any rate—and paralyzed in the prison house of his psyche, unable to see the worldly, structural determination of his torment; and, on the other hand, the readers left behind along with the nonperson narrator, who cannot recognize the demons unleashed by loss of a job. They might not, in other words, have encountered themselves as individuals susceptible to invasion by social forces in the form of employers, landlords, or moneylenders who transmogrify into unseen instruments of torture.

Back again to the question of why create a nonperson narrator. Couldn't other, less obtrusive sorts of narrators have achieved the same effect? Maybe so, but it is worth looking at the features defining the category of the nonperson narrator to see what makes it so useful. First, let us consider the "nonperson." The phenomenon wherein the word *person* designates a human being and a grammatical category in English is obliquely echoed in the presence of the character *nin* (human) in *ninshō*. The nonperson narrator is not lacking in personhood first of all because he speaks. And his speech, like the speech of regular persons, implies grammatical personhood. Even if he doesn't use first-person pronouns to designate himself, there is a strong first-person effect to his utterances, especially a first-person plural effect, as when he urges the reader to follow Bunzō into his house. In English, this is unambiguous—"Shall we go in, too?"—but the Japanese "Issho ni haitte miyō" is not much less clear.[11] Although there is no agreement as such between Japanese verbs and personal pronoun subjects, there is de facto an analogous phenomenon such that exhortatory imperatives or expressions of wishing or encouraging can be construed as taking a second-person subject or a first-person plural that includes the listener.[12] It is not only that, as Kamei says, the narrator "has a strong sense of his existence and . . . by revealing this causes the reader . . . to enter into a *kind of complicity* with him" but that the reader is directly addressed or "hailed" in an Althusserian sense.[13] In other words, these verbal forms are important in creating that "strong sense of . . . existence." Moreover, this narrator not only speaks but also moves, inviting the reader to move with him. True, the nonperson narrator is not

11. Ibid., 8.
12. Nitta Yoshio, "Ninshō," in *Nihon bunpō jiten*, edited by Kitahara Yasuo, Suzuki Tanjirō, Takeda Kō, Masubuchi Tsunekichi, and Yamaguchi Yoshinori (Tokyo: Yūseidō, 1981), 105.
13. Kamei, *Transformations of Sensibility*, 8. Emphasis added.

a character, is not known to the characters, and does not affect the action. Such minimal concretization may in fact facilitate reader identification. The nonperson narrator makes us aware that grammatical personhood as well as point of view entails *implied embodiment* and therefore situatedness in the world, a situatedness that is distinct from the protagonist's. The nonperson narrator in *Ukigumo* is audible person enough to draw the reader into the textual world. And his voice is sufficiently embodied that he must stop where a person cannot go, inside somebody else's mind. The narrative can't be swallowed up in the protagonist's mind. To take the step of entry into another's mind, a less corporeal narrator is more convenient or else, as Kamei deftly shows with an example from Futabatei's mentor Tsubouchi Shōyō's *Imo to se kagami* (1885-86), a writer needs something like the trick of a "magic mirror" (*makyō*) to see into the heart of a character, not the chosen direction of literary realism, which has preferred narrative forms that not unmagically allow readers to slip in and out of characters' minds.[14] The talky nonperson narrator reminds us of how we have forgotten this verbal trick.

I observed above that by virtue of his speaking, Futabatei's nonperson narrator was endowed with that form of personhood that is grammatical. But speech is necessarily socially accented such that this narrator can't help suggesting the rudiments of social personhood, one that is "coarse" and "irresponsible," as Kamei put it.[15] In other words, not only was that nonperson narrator too embodied to penetrate Bunzō's mind, but his lively speech appealed to a type of reader as yet unprepared to be arrested in introspection. It is also presumably the case that readers susceptible to brooding were in part created by the later narrator who slips more and more imperceptibly into Bunzō's mind. We can think about this process by giving an explicit sociohistorical dimension to the notion of the "implied reader," that is, "the audience presupposed by a text."[16] *Ukigumo*, like other works of literature, is both a response to the worldly conditions of its time of production and a shaping of those conditions in the course of its reproduction, that is, through the thoughts and actions of its readers. Schematically put, potential real readers—Futabatei's contemporaries—and their situations are refracted in the fictional work *Ukigumo*; this text produces its "implied readers"; and the sensibilities of actual readers of the text will be shaped as they perform the

14. Kamei's *Transformations of Sensibility*, 64.
15. Ibid., 12.
16. Gerald Prince, *Dictionary of Narratology* (Lincoln: University of Nebraska Press, 1987), 43. The term and concept respond to Wayne Booth's "implied author" in his pioneering work first published in 1961, *The Rhetoric of Fiction*. 2nd ed. (Chicago: University of Chicago Press, 1983).

reading role tacitly modeled by the implied reader. This is a heuristic model joining narratological with sociohistorical analysis in assessing the disappearing nonperson narrator. Futabatei, in responding to the inchoate forces in his fluid historical moment, started with one kind of narrator and the readership implied by such and ended up with quite different ones. The new implied reader had a role in producing actual new readers, young men who retreated from unrewarding, oppressive social structures into endless brooding. The loss of the third term facilitated—or exacerbated—this inward drive.

TENSE, PERSON, AND FICTION AS MADNESS

In his "Kindai shōsetsu no gensetsu," Mitani Kuniaki affirms Kamei's identification of a nonperson narrator in *Ukigumo* and equates it to what is called the *sōshiji*, direct address of the reader by the narrator in Heian narrative fiction, Mitani's own area of specialty.[17] He, too, valorizes the nonperson narrator for reasons that are *apparently* different from Kamei's. I shall return to this. Where Mitani takes issue with Kamei is over this narrator's serving as a bridge between reader and textual world. This cannot be, argues Mitani, because the prevalence of the present tense in those early passages makes it impossible for the reader to inhabit a common time and space with the narrator. Narration in the present can only produce instability for the reader insofar as the ground of prose fiction is the past tense. Kamei refutes the relevance of Mitani's claim by pointing to verb-form shifts in accordance with the narrator's shifting spatial-temporal relation to the protagonist.[18] Mitani criticizes Kamei for having developed the concept of the nonperson narrator without adequate attention to verbal auxiliaries (*-ru* and *-ta* in modern Japanese) and the question of time. Their disagreement as stated is misleading. Both Kamei and Mitani know full well that auxiliaries indicate much more than time or, rather, that grammatical tense itself is a complicated matter. What Kamei's response shows is that an analysis of auxiliaries alone won't distinguish obtrusive nonperson narrators from increasingly embedded, invisible narrators. Kamei posits diction (here I mean *kotobazukai*) more than

17. Citations here are from the version of the essay reprinted in Mitani Kuniaki, *Monogatari bungaku no gensetsu* (Tokyo: Yūseidō, 1992), 360–76. See the translation of this essay in chapter four of this volume.

18. Kamei Hideo, "Wajutsu no yukue." *Bungaku* 53.11 (November 1985): 102–13; see esp. 138–39. The essay is reprinted in Komori Yōichi, ed., *Kindai bungaku no seiritsu: Shisō to buntai no mosaku* (Tokyo: Yūseidō, 1986), 129–41.

verbal form as the key to understanding the nonperson narrator. Diction can both distinguish one character from another and be picked up by or imposed on another character or the narrator.[19] Mitani, by contrast, maximizes the meaning of grammatical categories for narrative. Here I try to clarify the stakes of Mitani's position and then to speculate on the implications of his disagreement with Kamei.

"The 'present' age is one of struggle over the distinction between the discourse of the novel and other discourses." Thus opens another essay by Mitani on modern narrative. The "struggle" is the battle he has joined to maintain the modest preserve of the "fiction" (kyokō) that is the "novel" (shōsetsu) in the information age, for Mitani a struggle unto madness.[20] Fundamentally, he is insisting that the world of fiction be distinguished from the world outside fiction. The key marker of that distinction is the combination of the third-person with the past form. This mildly neologistic wording, "past form" (kakokeishiki), is to be distinguished from the grammatical "past tense" (kakokei), but I think the experiential temporal aspect of this verbal form is far from irrelevant to his reasoning. Of the example sentences "I/you/Hanako was/were afraid (yesterday)," he argues that only the first-person version would be acceptable in the context of everyday life. Both the second- and third-person versions, by contrast, require the addition of a conjectural auxiliary such as "You/Hanako must have been afraid (yesterday)" to be acceptable outside the fictional text.[21] Mitani does not spell out the reasons for this, perhaps because they are too obvious to require it, but it is worth trying to do so.

We can start by observing that while I might plausibly know about my having been afraid yesterday I am not in a position to know this about you or Hanako unless I had been with you or spoken with you and ascertained as much. Without having done so, in the world outside fiction, I would need to make conjectures rather than assertions. That this example happens to be about a psychological condition—not necessarily visible—quickly brings us to the realization that even if I were in the same time-space with you or Hanako, that is, in the *present* moment or *present* to her or you (yesterday, today, or tomorrow), I would still need to be speculative. I don't think, however, that this qualification dismantles Mitani's claim about the third-

19. This point is elaborated in Kamei, *Transformations of Sensibility*, (217–25).
20. Mitani Kuniaki, "Kindai shōsetsu no 'katari' to 'gensetsu': Sanninshō to ichininshō no isō aruiwa *Kōya hijiri* no gensetsu," in *Kindai shōsetsu no 'katari' to 'gensetsu': Sōsho 'Monogatarigaku o hiraku,'* edited by Mitani Kuniaki, 7–52 (Tokyo: Yūseidō, 1996). This passage appears on page 9.
21. Ibid., 360.

person/past *form* as the ground (rather than literal sine qua non) of prose fiction, a view that in any case is shared by many with qualification.[22] What Mitani's claim does is to dramatize that feature of prose fiction that ignores, or rather violates, estrangement in time (not now) and space (not here). The third person is more emphatically Other to me than the second insofar as "you" are "you" because I am addressing you.[23] The inside of someone else's mind epitomizes that which we wish we could see but cannot. The formula of third-person/past condenses fiction's raison d'être to let us inhabit a world we do not and cannot.

The boundary between fiction and world is sturdy yet supple, for one thing because fiction is made up of words, which we use everyday, inside and outside of novels. Thus, if we are habituated to responding to a *-ta* statement unqualified by an auxiliary of conjecture as a first-person statement, then when we come across a third-person *-ta* statement in a novel we accept it as if it were in the first-person.

> It is because of this mechanism that, in the reception of a novel, we experience the illusion that we have become the protagonist or another character. In novelistic discourse the third person overlaps with the first person: *-ta* is at once third person/past and first person/present, and sustaining this overlap is the absence of conjectural expressions.[24]

Mitani goes on to assert that this "fiction" and "identification with the other" entail "merely a modest violation of the rules of everyday language," but novel discourse takes off from here to "acquire independence as a distinctive linguistic universe . . . reborn as a discourse that harbors 'madness,' however modestly."[25] But before we get to madness let us linger a while longer over first- and third-person, *–ta*, and time.

This is at least in part a matter of getting right the relationship between ordinary and novelistic language use. Mitani talks about a "modest

22. See, for example, Noguchi Takehiko, *Sanninshō no hakken made* (Tokyo: Chikuma Shobō, 1994); Prince, *Dictionary of Narratology*; and Käthe Hamburger, *The Logic of Literature*, translated by Marilyn Rose (Bloomington: Indiana University Press, 1973).

23. Emile Benveniste's memorable discussion begins with a reference to Arabic grammar wherein "the first person is . . . 'the one who speaks'; the second, . . . the one who is addressed'; but the third is . . . 'the one who is absent.'" The third person is outside "I-you" and is a nonperson in Benveniste's analysis. Emile Benveniste, *Problems in General Linguistics*, translated by Mary Elizabeth Meek (Coral Gables: University of Miami Press, 1971), 197.

24. Mitani, "Kindai shōsetsu no 'katari,'" 15.

25. Ibid., 16.

violation" leading to an autonomous universe; Dorrit Cohn observes that Karl Buhler and Emile Benveniste, for whom "every linguistic utterance defines, and is defined by, the subjectivity of the speaker," fail to note that there is a

> fundamental disruption of this systematic subjectivity of ordinary language that can (and often does) occur in fictional narrative. As Hamburger shows, the paradoxical distinction, the utterly *extra*-ordinary artifice of fictional discourse is precisely that the subjectivity of its language *can* be situated, not in the self-referential "I" who utters the discourse, but in the "she" or "he" to whom the discourse occurs.[26]

Moreover, in Hamburger's analysis a deictic sense of nowness adheres to past tenses, making them no longer past.[27] I provisionally understand Mitani's model, in which readers have the "illusion of becoming the protagonist," as one in which they transpose their I-ness onto Hanako, who was afraid, or share their subjectivity with her. Or is it better described as a movement from Hanako—the text as a whole—the discourse of fiction—taking possession of them? Are these distinguishable? In any case, what makes this movement possible other than a combined competence in ordinary language use and novel reading, a competence of which readers are largely unaware?

Tokieda Motoki's entry on *-ta* in his volume on the spoken language traces its shift from the literary form *-tari*, indicating condition or existence, to an expression of confirmation and judgment (*kakunin handan*) about something. He says he follows convention in calling this the past or perfective auxiliary but finds this label misleading insofar as it connotes objectivity. Rather, *-ta* expresses "recollection or judgment as a function of the speaker's position," and evaluation is determined by that position and is not an effect of the matter being evaluated. His example here is "The match is decided," which may or may not mean that the game is over but rather, expresses that particular speaker's judgment, which may not be shared by another speaker. Nevertheless, Tokieda continues, "given that the speaker's position is often based on the objective circumstances of the matter at hand, there is an intimate relation between the two."[28] Perhaps—experientially speaking— an action that is complete (and in that sense past) is more likely to prompt objective, or rather objective *sounding*, that is, confident confirmation if not judgment from the speaking subject. But it would be unwise to necessarily associate the "completed past" with confident judgment given that the past

---

26. Dorrit Cohn, *The Distinction of Fiction* (Baltimore: John Hopkins University Press, 1999), 24.
27. Hamburger, *The Logic of Literature*, 59–98.
28. Tokieda Motoki, *Nihongo bunpō: Kōgohen* (Tokyo: Iwanami Shoten, 1950), 171.

may also seem less accessible precisely because it isn't here and now (the problem with Hanako yesterday). We come back to the relation of the speaking subject to the object (topic) of her utterance, and we might then recall the resources premodern Japanese had, such as the auxiliaries of -ki/-keri, to distinguish between an actually experienced and hearsay past.[29]

In his article on the nonperson narrator, Mitani refers to Tokieda's account of -ta as "confirmation and judgment" as evidence of how, in the form of a speaker/narrator who intrudes into the invisible world of other peoples' (characters') minds, the modern novel created that fiction called "the author" who imposes unitary meanings.[30] Without conceding as necessary the set of equations, -ta = author = unitary meaning, I see here a usefully strong account of what happens when a reader reads her first-person present into a third-person past statement of Hanako's fear of yesterday. It is not simply, or perhaps even primarily, a situation with a two-party relationship, the first-person reader and the third-person character Hanako. In Tokieda's analysis, -ta belongs to that category of words called ji, which directly expresses the speaking subject's disposition. "-ta" is laden with subjectivity, the subjectivity of "confirmation and judgment." In Tokieda's analysis, every utterance is unified by a ji, and where it isn't literally supplied its presence, "wrapping up" the utterance, is assumed (the "zero-marker" in his terminology).[31] So "Hanaka was afraid [-ta]" registers as a confident assertion on the part of the "subject of enunciation," an invisible "I" who hails the reader as "you." This interpretation intersects with a body of linguistic scholarship ranging from Emile Benveniste on enunciation to Lacanian psychoanalysis,[32] but especially useful in thinking about fiction is Mieke Bal's discussion.

> As soon as there is language, there is a speaker who utters it; as soon as those linguistic utterances constitute a narrative text, there is a narrator, a narrating subject. From a grammatical point of view, this is always a "first person." In fact, the term "third-person narrator" is absurd: a narrator is not a "he" or "she." At best the narrator can narrate about someone else, a "he" or "she"—who might, incidentally, happen to be a narrator as well.[33]

29. Almost any bungo jiten will do, but see Tokieda Motoki, Nihongo bunpō: Bungohen (Tokyo: Iwanami Shoten, 1954), 166.

30. Mitani, "Kindai shōsetsu no 'katari,'" 371.

31. Tokieda Motoki, Kokugogaku genron (Tokyo: Iwanami Shoten, 1941), 236–53. See 243–44 on "unifying" and "wrapping up."

32. Barbara Havercroft, "Enonciation/énoncé," in Encyclopedia of Contemporary Literary Theory: Approaches, Scholars, Terms, edited by Irena R. Makaryk, 540–43 (Toronto: University of Toronto Press, 1993).

33. Mieke Bal, Narratology, 2nd ed. (Toronto: University of Toronto Press, 1997), 22.

"Hanako was afraid" can be written out in expanded form as "(I narrate), 'Hanako was afraid.'" Surely an important component of the novel reader's competence—we could say the consequence of ideological training without carelessly attaching an invidious sense to "ideological"—is the readiness to identify as the "you" addressed by that invisible narrator. (Of course, competence, like other aspects of subjectivity, entails explicit and subtle forms of subjection whether it is formal schooling or "hailing" by advertisements.)

It is important to pause over the issue of invisibility. Bal acknowledges this, too, in suggesting that narrators be labeled as "p" (perceptible) or "np" (nonperceptible), although she doesn't elaborate the implications.[34] It is the nonperceptible narrator that Mitani seems to find oppressive. Earlier I suggested that the nonperson narrator in fact uses the first-person plural to address the reader. That narrator, for all the instability he generates according to Mitani because of his association with the present tense, has the decency to stop at the boundary of other peoples' minds. As this narrator recedes, he is succeeded by a narrating entity, whom Mitani somewhat reluctantly calls the author (*sakusha*, to be distinguished from the historical person referred to as *sakka*), who freely steps into Bunzō's mind, "muddy shoes" and all. And, whereas this author initially bothers to enclose Bunzō's thoughts in quotation marks, even that courtesy is abandoned toward the end of *Ukigumo*.[35]

For a quick and powerful contrast of what a far more differentiated verb system can do, Mitani analyzes a passage from the "Yūgao" chapter in the *Tale of Genji*. His point is that the conflicting thoughts of the characters on the scene can be represented without being reduced one to the other or being melded into the expression of a unifying narrator. The constricted resources of modern Japanese result in Enchi Fumiko's translation, for instance, being riddled with contradictions.[36] I don't agree that there is no author, no unified meaning or, more precisely, no dominant meaning but only reverberating strands of thought and feeling in play. Nevertheless, the contrasting possibilities of mid-Heian and mid-Meiji Japanese are striking. The greater range and nature of verbal auxiliaries in the older language seem to provide a functional equivalent to the nonperson, perceptible narrator. Those auxiliaries, along with adverbial deictics and other supports, mark the speaking subject's status in relation to the addressee and the object of the utterance, as well as the status of the utterance, whether hearsay, conjecture, or firsthand

34. Ibid., 27.
35. Mitani, "Kindai shōsetsu no 'katari,'" 367.
36. Ibid., 368–71.

experience, thus giving linguistic embodiment to each speaker, each position of observation. This is in striking contrast to the limitations of modern Japanese, which result in a seemingly unified narration: Mitani's "author."

Kamei values the nonperson narrator as a bridge between text and reader: Mitani, as the emblem of an awkward but nonimperialist narrative stance toward the insides of characters. Kamei wonders if, in cultivating the new territory of psychological anguish, modern Japanese literature could have avoided shrinking into the I-novel; Mitani deplores the collapse into unitary meaning and psychic invasion, that is, omniscience. Kamei's heterogeneity includes the extratextual world while Mitani's is intratextual. For both, however, the nonperson, perceptible narrator as third term holds out the possibility of keeping the novel from collapsing in on itself and suffocating the reader in the process.

It is important to point out that Mitani's commitment to the formal and linguistic workings of fiction is in the cause of "protest to the world," or *igi mōshitate*, a phrase that dots his work, both on Heian prose fiction and in his recent forays into modern literature.[37] I don't think it would be too distorting to say that for Mitani literature is fundamentally an act of protest. This is so first and foremost because literature's very modus operandi violates the possibilities provided by worldly existence. Sustaining this protest, shoring up the boundaries between fiction and the world calls up the struggle unto madness referred to earlier from "Kindai shōsetsu no 'katari,'" which was written about ten years after the critique of Kamei's interpretation of the nonperson narrator. What is interesting here, and in a second essay in the same volume,[38] is that what had been condemned as the insidious psychological violation of others in the article in *Ukigumo* is now redeemed as the distinction of fiction, the core of its mad protest. In the section that elaborates Hanako's fear of yesterday there appears the following.

> "Assimilating oneself to an other" is a discourse that harbors (*yadosu*) such madness [such as a grown person's continuing to pretend that a *furoshiki* around his shoulders makes him Superman]. To read a novel is to yield oneself, however briefly, to the "madness" that is assimilation/identification with an Other. If we don't conduct the analysis of novelistic discourse with an

---

37. See, for example, ibid., 9.
38. Mitani Kuniaki, "*Rashomon* no gensetsu bunseki: Hōhō to shite no jiyū kansetsu gensetsu aruiwa imi no jūsōsei to haitokusha no yukue," in *Kindai shōsetsu no 'katari' to 'gensetsu': Sōsho 'Monogatarigaku o hiraku,'* edited by Mitani Kuniaki, 197–237 (Tokyo: Yūseidō, 1996).

understanding of the "madness" that discourse entails, the promise of literary criticism and study is foreclosed.[39]

It may be hasty to judge that Mitani has changed his evaluation of psychological portrayal from the *Ukigumo* essay to these later ones, for he has retained the rhetoric of modernity's repression of madness with respect to inner speech; by leaving it unmarked, unlike dialogue, and, given the decline of status indicators from modern Japanese, modern Japanese fiction has buried inner speech in the narrative ground, that is, "concealed and oppressed it." Even where it is made visible, it is rationalized, as it were, by being presented as a character's talking to himself when no one else is around.[40] This objection is puzzling given Mitani's embrace, not mere acceptance, of free indirect discourse. Maybe it is possible to understand it this way: in the earlier essay, the important contrast was between the invisible penetration of the protagonist's mind as demonstrated in *Ukigumo* and character thoughts conveyed without such insidious mediation in *Genji*. The former is oppressive because of both the violation of a psychic boundary and the rationalization implied by the unitary meaning he assumes a single narrator imposes. This, we might conjecture, is the premodern literary scholar's passionate suspicion of modernity's invasive, homogenizing tendency. But I am tempted to think that since Mitani's concern is to make inner speech visible and therefore unignorable, his deploring the loss of verbal forms available in premodern Japanese and the omission of quotation marks by modern Japanese writers are an expression of the signal value he accords literature's ability to express inner experience. Conversely, in inner speech is "inscribed literature's autonomy."[41] If literature protests life, it does so most distinctly by revealing what life cannot: the inside of (especially) other people's hearts and minds. In the form and content of its protest dwells its freedom.

In a postscript to "Kindai gensetsu no katari," Mitani writes,

> In this piece I ignored the literary historical perspective. Moreover, I was unable to consider discourse from a cultural, social, and historical point of view. This is not because I have but slight regard for such perspectives, but because I lacked the ability.[42]

39. Mitani, "Kindai shōsetsu no 'katari,'" 16.
40. Ibid., 25.
41. Mitani, "*Rashomon* no gensetsu bunseki," 223.
42. Mitani, "Kindai shōsetsu no 'katari,'" 52.

I find this a profoundly moving admission. It also poses questions that are unresolved for all their familiarity: what are the possibilities of formal analysis in literary study; what does it mean to insist on literature's distinction, not to say autonomy, from other discourses; and what does it mean *especially* if one views literature as protest? (Isn't everything Mitani brings up saturated in worldliness?) And what are the implications for the study of proletarian literature?

"THE DISTINCTION OF FICTION" AND "SOCIAL FORMALISM"

The two phrases comprising this subheading are the titles of two valuable recent studies of novel theory. The first is Dorrit Cohn's, whose *Transparent Minds: Narrative Modes for Presenting Consciousness in Fiction* was a pioneering narratological work in the United States. The second is Dorothy J. Hale's *Social Formalism: The Novel in Theory from Henry James to the Present* of 1998. Cohn declares in her preface that her study

> aims to show that fictional narrative is unique in its potential for crafting a self-enclosed universe ruled by formal patterns that are ruled out in all other orders of discourse. This singularity, as I will try to show, depends on differences that can be precisely identified and systematically examined.[43]

Needless to say, the book is consonant in spirit and often in matter with Mitani's work and replete with thoughtfully analyzed examples from Euro-American literature. There is a chapter, however, that I want to single out here, the one called "Optics and Power in the Novel." In view of the enthusiastic reception accorded Michel Foucault's discussion of Jeremy Bentham's panopticon, that is, the temptation scholars have felt to compare "'omnisciently' presented subjects in fiction and panoptically supervised prisoners," Cohn argues against assuming a "correspondence of modal type and moral stance."[44] Some scholars have directed charges of narrator invasiveness, even castigating the novel genre as a whole, while others have attempted to rescue the novel by suggesting that some forms of narration are more benign than others. Cohn argues that modes of narration are "different

43. Dorrit Cohn, *Transparent Minds: Narrative Modes for Presenting Consciousness in Fiction* (Princeton: Princeton University Press, 1978), vii.
44. Ibid., 176, 179.

tactic[s] available for the novelist to communicate his 'omniscient' knowledge of the figures he creatively imagines, inner life and all."[45] Free indirect discourse has been used for quite different political and ethical agendas. From the reader's side, we should never forget that the reading of fiction entails a "uniquely stressful interpretive freedom."[46] Part of the stress, I think, consists of understanding the limits and possibilities of a given mode of narration in a particular work or a genre as a whole at a given sociohistoric juncture.

Hale's *Social Formalism* has for a subtitle *The Novel in Theory from Henry James to the Present*. The "present" extends from the "second wave" of Wayne Booth, Gérard Genette, and Roland Barthes to Bakhtin, Barbara Johnson, and Henry Louis Gates. What unites all of these figures, according to Hale, is their belief in the social efficacy of the novel form itself. That is, from a pre-Jamesian focus on the content and nature of authorship, these critics turned to form. The early emphasis on point of view, evolving into the elaboration of free indirect discourse as the key to novelistic operation, went hand in hand with a belief in an "ethics around the issue of point of view,"[47] what Hale sublimely calls "appreciation of alterity" ("madness" in Mitani): "the intrinsic good of alterity—that humans are most fulfilled when they come to know sympathetically persons who are substantially different from themselves."[48] Increasingly, as literary theory seeped into other disciplines and was in turn socialized, what had been understood positively as altruism came instead to be denounced as a "mask for the operation of hegemonic power" or the pan-panopticism identified by Cohn. What Hale emphasizes is that the evaluative shift has not changed the belief that *"formal markers can not only express the intrinsically social character of one's identity but embody it too."*[49] Progressive evacuation of offending content and the materialization of form have gone hand in hand.

Marxist critics, perhaps not surprisingly, display this compensatory tendency most vividly. Hale offers the following pithy assessment by Catherine Gallagher: "Williams and Eagleton retain the 'idealist' emphasis on the irreducibility and autonomy of art, its specific aesthetic nature, but *redefine* this autonomy as itself material."[50] This phenomenon, in which the material

45. Ibid., 176.
46. Ibid., 130.
47. Dorothy J. Hale, *Social Formalism: The Novel in Theory from Henry James to the Present* (Stanford: Stanford University Press, 1998), 22.
48. Ibid., 8.
49. Ibid., 15, emphasis added.
50. Catherine Gallagher, "The New Materialism in Marxist Aesthetics," *Theory and Society: Renewal and Critique in Social Theory* 9, 4 (July, 1980): 633–46. This passage appears on page 634. It is quoted in Hale, *Social Formalism*, 11.

is at once expanded to include literary form and (unwittingly) reduced to the physicality of objects, attests to the daunting challenges of the theory and practice of materialism. It is easy enough to understand how the imperative to avoid reductionism, on the one hand, and idealism, on the other, can produce this effect. Emphasis on content reeks of reflectionism and therefore the naive reduction of art to life; yet the embrace of form, the putative locus of the "irreducibility and autonomy of art," is, by virtue of its abstraction, susceptible to the charge of idealism. Designating form as itself material— part of a broad tendency over the past quarter century to reclassify as material anything deemed consonant with revolutionary aspirations—assuredly revitalizes both the reclassified entity and the category of the material itself but necessarily at a cost. Generally speaking, once a category becomes too capacious, its coherence, and consequently its usefulness, are undermined. Specific constrictions follow. On the one hand, students of culture have become ever more incapable of incorporating the economy within their thinking, ironically according it greater and arguably idealist autonomy by surrendering it to free-market ideologues. On the other hand, valorization of form has impeded any explicit analysis of content; or, rather, content is dealt with only insofar as it can be understood as form, a useful activity in itself but one that also impinges on the usefulness of the distinction.

Hale poses a series of questions about whether in fact the novel genre is especially suited for representing alterity, what moral and aesthetic weight should be accorded that putative capability, and whether characters should be thought of "as others whom a novelist could liberate or oppress."[51] It is hard not to read these questions as rhetorical. Hale describes, by contrast, the kinds of questions nonformalist literary critics with an interest in the social have been addressing: "what made the novel 'rise,' what caused *this* particular cultural discourse to be produced, and what ideological work, in given periods, the novel performed."[52] Hale does not say this, but there is another set of implications in her rhetorical series, namely, that all the work of social criticism and certainly of social action should not be consigned to literature and literary criticism. We need to recall the history of how "Western Marxists" dedicated themselves to culture after hopes for an actual revolution in Western Europe faded, leaving the Bolshevik revolution isolated, a process succinctly elaborated by Perry Anderson a quarter of a century ago.[53] We also need to consider a more immediate context, namely, the legacy of the 1960s, the last serious challenge to the postwar order in

51. Hale, *Social Formalism*, 19.
52. Ibid., 8.
53. Perry Anderson, *Considerations on Western Marxism* (London: Verso, [1976] 1979).

Japan as well as the United States (and many other parts of the world). To the extent that the successes of that movement were institutionalized in the academy—a phenomenon more evident in the United States than in Japan—the emphasis on culture was redoubled with especial visibility in the form of cultural studies, predominantly associated with English, that is, literature programs. The question must still be posed, however: does the extraordinary channeling of critical intellectual political energy into the study of culture, and the phenomenon of "social formalism" as a concentrated instance of this process, argue for the dismissal of the "distinction of fiction"?

Let us consider the example of Bakhtin, whose discovery in the United States was nothing short of inspirational in the moment of high deconstruction. (And we should keep in mind how important his work has been concurrently in Japan, including for Kamei and Mitani.) Bakhtin presented the possibility of recovering sociopolitical and historical dimensions in literary studies without compromising the sophistication of semiotics. To embrace Bakhtin, it seemed, was to be impeccably materialist without risking the appearance of reductionist naïveté. In Bakhtin, who takes up two of her five chapters, Hale diagnoses a misplaced materialism:

> For Bakhtin, ideology is associated with two forms of materiality: the forms of production that shape it and the signs that express it. Confusing one kind of materiality with the other, Bakhtin comes to regard signs as the generators of ideology and thus assumes that social identity is embedded in literary form.[54]

Should we, then, be trying to wean ourselves of Bakhtin? In an article engagingly titled "Is Dialogism for Real?" Ken Hirschkop offers the following sensible reflection:

> Much of what currently passes for Bakhtinian analysis would have us believe that novels are for all intents and purposes dialogues despite the rather obvious fact that a single person composes them. What I wish to do . . . is to remind myself, as well as my readers, of the difference between a dialogue and a novel, and thus between dialogue and what we call dialogism. We need to remind ourselves of this so that we are forced to consider what is at stake when Bakhtin attempts to apply the idea of dialogue to formally finished works, like novels, works which, whatever their

54. Hale, *Social Formalism*, 17.

> linguistic complexity, are composed by historical individuals, often with the luxury of great care and conscious reflection and without the spontaneous dangers of actual linguistic exchange.[55]

Dialogues and novels are not the same; life and novels are not the same. They are distinct, and they inform each other. So, too, with writings about the novel. As Hirschkop tantalizingly observes, Bakhtin's "effusions about the novel, the people and the public square develop in his readers an enthusiasm for modernity which they might not want to own up to."[56]

To think is to make connections, and we can't connect without differences, that is, distinctions; but we need to remember that they are provisional; distinctions need to be overcome, then reformulated in order to remain vital. We can't afford to be black and white, once and for all: either art is autonomous or it is to be dissolved into its contexts of production and reproduction. Hale's critique of "social formalism" seems to assume that the effects of the imaginative experience of alterity through novel reading will be contained within the confines of novel reading. The "enthusiasm for modernity" Hirschkop imputes to readers who register Bakhtin's enthusiasm for the novel must have many grand and modest equivalents in readers not necessarily of Bakhtin but of novels. We can't prejudge the extratextual yearnings and aspirations stirred up in novel readers even if, in the first instance, they merely—modestly—take the form of identification with novelistic others. Such aspirations might be so tentative as not to count as "social," but they are the necessary component for any change or, for that matter, continuity. For Herbert Marcuse, reflecting with considerable historical reach, the reductionist flaw of Marxist theory was in its "bracket[ing] the particular content of individual consciousness and, with it, the subjective potential for revolution."[57]

But again we don't need to justify attention to these processes only if revolution is on the horizon, especially given that for us it does not seem to be. Rather than expending all our critical energy on detecting revolutionary, or for that matter reactionary, tendencies in compensatory fashion in linguistic structures, literary form, or narrative theory, we need to go back and forth between text and world and not only in the now respectably familiar

---

55. Ken Hirschkop, "Is Dialogism for Real?" *Social Text*, 30 (1992): 102–13. This passage appears on page 102.

56. Ibid., 112–13.

57. Herbert Marcuse, *The Aesthetic Dimension: Toward a Critique of Marxist Aesthetics*, translated by Herbert Marcuse and Erica Sherover (Boston: Beacon, 1978), 4.

effort of contextualization but in looking at the built-in connections between writing and reading, fiction and life. Kamei's author/narrators who write out of an understanding of shared fate with their characters and readers and Mitani's dramatized sense of overturning everyday norms in our reading are examples of such efforts, which might loosely be grouped under the rubric of phenomenology. How might we take up that old challenge of linking sociohistorical dimensions with such phenomenological efforts? And how can we develop a practice of linking that is simultaneously informed by a sense of distinction and a sense of totality?

LITERATURE AND REVOLUTION

The relationship of the arts in general, and literature in particular, with society was passionately debated by Japanese intellectuals in the 1920s and early 1930s. How could (or should) a literature be created for the masses? Should it borrow from previous literature given the way it had structured human emotion? Which took precedence, form or content? What was the proper relationship between literature and the revolutionary politics that so many intellectuals then embraced? The sheer number of participants in the debates and the volume of responses, counterresponses, and reversals, complicated by repeated splits and reorganizations of leftist groups, make the debates dizzying to follow.[58] Here, by way of orientation to my discussion of Kobayashi Takiji's writing, I will refer to one lively essay by Nakano Shigeharu (1902–79), poet, novelist, and critic, participant in the proletarian literature movement and the postwar democratic literature movement, and one of the grand figures of modern Japanese letters. The essay, titled "Geijutsu ni seijiteki kachi nante mono wa nai: 'Seijiteki kachi to geijutsuteki kachi' to ka 'Bungei hihyō no zahyō' to ka 'Hihyō no kijun' to ka iu mono ni tsuite" (There's No Such Thing as Political Value in Art: On 'Political Value and Aesthetic Value' or 'The Frame of Reference for Literary Criticism' or 'Criteria for Criticism' and Other Such Things),[59] was originally published in *Shinchō* in 1929 and most immediately responds to an essay by critic Hirabayashi Hatsunosuke (1892–1931), also published in *Shinchō* earlier that

58. See entries on "Geijutsu taishūka ronsō," "Geijutsuteki kachi ronsō," and "Keishikishugi bungaku ronsō" in Usui Yoshimi, *Kindai bungaku ronsō*, 2 vols. (Tokyo: Chikuma Shobō, 1956), 1:208–56, for summary accounts with bibliographic information and interpretation. As may be surmised from the date, these are not dispassionate, neutral accounts.

59. Nakano Shigeharu, "Geijutsu ni seijiteki kachi nante mono wa nai: 'Seijiteki kachi to geijutsuteki kachi' to ka 'Bungei hihyō no zahyō' to ka 'Hihyō no kijun' to ka iu mono ni tsuite," in *Nakano Shigeharu zenshū*, 28 vols. (Tokyo: Chikuma Shobō, 1976–80), 9:273–88.

same year.[60] Hirabayashi was agonizing over a dual-value theory, namely, that political and aesthetic value had to be judged separately in works of art, and that for Marxists aesthetic value had to be subordinated to political value. Nakano unequivocally distinguishes politics and art and disarmingly poses the impossibility of measuring two unlike things by each other, which he whimsically likened to counting horses with hibachis. The artistic depiction of an armed rebellion is neither

> a political movement nor a political struggle. However far you take it, it is the movement of feeling, a union in feeling, and the heightening of feeling, not a military organization, an uprising, an election, a strike, or a revolution. When people say *Uncle Tom's Cabin* is connected to the emancipation of slaves in America or Turgenev's *The Huntsman's Sketches* is connected to the emancipation of serfs in Russia, that means there's a connection, and it doesn't mean that if Stowe had written better, [her book] would have amounted to the Civil War, or that if Turgenev had written more of those stories, they would have added up to an emancipation proclamation for the serfs. . . . The workings of politics and the workings of art are of a different kind.[61]

Even if politics and art are separate, they emerge from the same society, a complex one shaped by class struggle. Nakano characterizes politics and art as two windows that each offers a view of this same landscape in different "colors" as it were, the former of the structure of competing class power, the latter the structure of competing class feeling. There are proletarian and bourgeois versions of these windows, and the former is superior because it is opening ever wider and offers a clear view, for it has been opened by the "one true worldview, Marxism."[62] So the young Nakano, unambiguously declaring himself a Marxist, sees politics and art as intimately related, emerging from and addressing and reflecting one and the same society yet never to be reduced one to the other: "only aesthetic values offer a frame of reference for evaluating art."[63]

In December of 1929, two months after Nakano published this essay, Kobayashi Takiji (1903–33) completed the third version of the work I will discuss. It was published in February of the following year in *Senki* (Battle

---

60. Hirabayashi Hatsunosuke, "Seijiteki kachi to geijutsuteki kachi," reprinted in *Kindai bungaku hyōron taikei*, 10 vols. (Tokyo: Kadokawa Shoten, 1971–75), 6:165–73.
61. Nakano, "Geijutsu ni seijiteki kachi nante mono wa nai," 282.
62. Ibid., 282.
63. Ibid., 287.

Flag), the organ of the All Japan Proletarian Arts Association (NAPF). In 1928, Nakano participated in establishing this organization and editing *Senki*; Kobayashi participated in establishing a branch in Otaru, Hokkaido, and worked to distribute *Senki*. After relocating to Tokyo in 1931, Kobayashi would work in the same circles with Nakano, travel with him, and even share the same detention center cell for a brief period. I mention these details both to give an indication of the network maintained by proletarian writers of the time in the face of harsh surveillance and to give a broader intellectual context to Kobayashi than is common. Kobayashi tends to be explicitly associated with Kurahara Korehito (1902–91), the principal theorist of the proletarian literature movement who was especially influential with his notion of "proletarian realism." In a key essay, "Puroretaria rearizumu e no michi," published in *Senki* in 1928, Kurahara offers an incisive analysis of two kinds of bourgeois realism in European literature, the first being the scientific, individualistic naturalism of writers such as Flaubert and de Maupassant, the second being the more socially conscious realism of Zola, Ibsen, Hauptmann, or Dostoevsky (the Japanese equivalents are Tayama Katai or Tokuda Shūsei for the first and Shimazaki Tōson for the second).[64] Proletarian realism, in seeking its themes, would adopt whatever was useful for the emancipation of the proletariat and discard what was not.

> Just as the bourgeois realist's chief subject matter in his work was people's biological urges, and the petty bourgeois realist's was social justice and philanthropy, the proletarian writer's is the class struggle of the proletariat.[65]

This did not mean, however, that only the struggling proletariat constituted an appropriate subject, for anything relevant to the struggle was appropriate. It was the writer's point of view that was more important than subject matter. For Kurahara, the point of proletarian realism was

> *not to distort or embellish reality with our subjective viewpoints but discover within reality those things that correspond with our subjectivity—the class subjectivity of the proletariat.*[66]

---

64. Kurahara Korehito, "Puroretaria rearizumu e no michi," reprinted in *Kindai bungaku hyōron taikei*, 10 vols. (Tokyo: Kadokawa Shoten, 1971–75), 6:114–21. This discussion appears on pages 116–18.
65. Ibid., 120. Translated by Brian Bergstrom, "The Path to Proletarian Realism," in *Literature for Dignity, Justice, and Revolution: An Anthology of Japanese Proletarian Literature*, edited by Heather Bowen Struyk and Norma Field, forthcoming.
66. Ibid., 121, emphasis in the original.

It is important to see that objectivity and subjectivity come together inasmuch as the current world could only be grasped truthfully and in its totality by the proletarian vanguard. History has brought about a fit between the collective perceiving subject and the object to be perceived or, rather, they are in the process of forming each other. At the same time, there is nothing automatic about this, for the proletarian writer must make an effort to *acquire* the perspective of the vanguard and then to emphasize it.[67] In this claim for the privileged relationship between the proletariat and reality, we see the Marxism of the day shared by writer Nakano and theorist Kurahara, but Nakano will characteristically qualify that the lousy writer, if a Marxist, ought to offer his services elsewhere than in the arts.[68] The reality that abstract arguments acquire in a vibrant movement becomes hard to grasp once that movement is not only history but at best a condescendingly regarded history in our post–Soviet world. Still, we may as well note that the claim for the privileged relation of the oppressed to reality (if not to blessing in another world) is historically repeated, as in moments of feminist or subaltern theorizing. And, more immediately, note the emphasis on point of view: "vanguard perspective" is an angle of vision on the world, which is then to shape the literary work. Proletarian literature offers a site for exploring the staples of narratology in an explicitly political context.

WRITER AND REVOLUTIONARY KOBAYASHI TAKIJI AS NARRATOR AND LEARNER

It is time to turn to specific literary texts. One of the pleasures of reading Kobayashi Takiji's fiction is that we can follow many of its pieces through revision, if not in published versions then in his notebooks. Of the sequence I want to consider here, the first, "Eiyō kensa" (Nutrition Inspection), appears in the "1927 No. 3" manuscript notebook.[69] The second, "Dareka ni ateta kiroku" (A Record Addressed to Somebody) appeared in the publication of the Arts Study Group of Kobayashi's distinguished alma mater, the Otaru Higher Commercial School, *Hoppō bungei* (Northern Arts) in June of 1928 (*KTZ*, 1:516). The third, whose title I abbreviate for now, "Kyūen nyūsu No. 18. Furoku" (Rescue News No. 18. Supplement)," was published in *Senki*, the NAPF organ, in its February 1930 issue (*KTZ*, 3:622). In other words, in

67. Ibid., 120.
68. Nakano, "Geijutsu ni seijiteki kachi nante mono wa nai," 284.
69. Kobayashi Takiji, "Eiyō kensa," in *Kobayashi Takiji zenshū*, rev. ed., 7 vols. (Tokyo: Shinnihon Shuppansha, 1993), 7:638. Further citations of this series are abbreviated as *KTZ*.

three years this story went from unpublished notebook to coterie publication to the leading national proletarian publication, which at the time had an enthusiastic readership well exceeding self-identified proletarians.[70] It is worth noting that between the second and third versions Kobayashi had leaped from being a local to a national (and soon international) writer with what is widely regarded as his proletarian debut work, "Senkyūhyakuni-jūhachinen sangatsu jūgonichi" (March 15, 1928) published in the November and December 1928 issues of *Senki*, followed up by "Kani kōsen" (The Cannery Boat) in 1929.[71]

"Nutrition Inspection," occupying only about three printed pages, describes an encounter between a doctor evaluating the nutritional state of schoolchildren standing in line, stripped to the waist, and one of the girls in that line. Although most of the sketch consists of dialogue—the doctor's questions and the girl's answers—it is recounted by a nonperceptible narrator with the doctor as the focalizing character. In other words, the story is about the doctor's discovery, and our identification as readers is with him. But what does he discover?

The doctor has been mechanically slotting the children lined up before him into three categories when his attention is arrested by one timid-seeming girl. In his eyes, her face is "lusterless as a pear" and her arms hang "like lotus roots" (*KTZ*, 7:262). When the doctor shifts from this fanciful (modernist?) register to the professional one, he labels her "weak, malnourished" and has his assistant keep her aside for questioning. We are told, "The doctor thought, how idiotic! The woman needed Vitamin A, B, now (now!). Eel, beef, egg. And yet, he thought, and became a bit agitated"

70. See Inoue Hisashi's fascinating account of how the Kinokuniya bookstore compensated for its latecomer's start by carrying *Senki*. Whenever a new issue appeared, readers would be lined up before the store opened, one hour earlier than usual, to accommodate as many customers as possible before the police turned up around noon to confiscate the remaining copies. Odagiri et al., "Puroretaria bungaku: dan'atsuka no bungakushatachi," 157.
71. Although "March 15, 1928" was extensively self-censored by the *Senki* staff, it did not escape banning. Nevertheless, it still circulated widely. It is instructive to compare the original *Senki* text with the *Zenshū* version (*KTZ*, 2:121-204). Pre-publication self-censorship was a common practice undertaken in the hopes of averting government banning, but Kurahara Korehito and the *Senki* staff made additional alterations and significant deletions for their own reasons as well. See the bibliographic notes in *KTZ*, 2:534-43. Both "March 15, 1928" and "The Cannery Ship" were first translated into English in heavily abridged form and published in 1933 as selections in *The Cannery Boat and Other Japanese Short Stories* (New York: International Publishers, 1933). The full English translation of "Kani kōsen" may be read in Frank Motofuji's English translation,"*The Factory Ship" and "The Absentee Landlord*" (Tokyo: Tokyo University Press, 1973). "Kani kōsen" became a bestseller in 2008, a phenomenon beyond the reaches of the wildest imagination at the time of the writing of this essay (2002) or even five years later.

(263). "Woman" (*onna*) here is a strange slippage; it is possible to think that Kobayashi meant to write "girl" (*onna no ko*), but let us suspend that possibility for now. What is important is that we are told that without noticing it, the doctor had gone past the proper boundaries for such an interview. The first quoted words from the girl are "'I have two Ma's" (263). The ensuing exchange, punctuated only three times by descriptions of the doctor's pausing, staring unblinkingly (causing the girl to blush and turn aside), and adjusting his glasses, reveals that the girl has been given away, that her Ma is constantly telling her to hurry and grow up, that she teaches her songs, clearly not children's songs, that she has four Pa's, her favorite being the "black Pa," a chimney sweep who was beaten up by another Pa, that she'd like to visit her "real Ma" but the Pa back home doesn't like it, and that her real Ma brings snacks to her school sometimes. The one time the girl takes initiative in the conversation is to pose this question, looking down all the while.

> "Ummm, what does it mean, 'sell'?"
>
> "Sell?"
>
> "The Ma I have now is always saying how she's gonna sell me when I'm grown up." (269)

The doctor lets out only a loud cry in response, and the story ends with his blushing to himself, "as if he had been made fun of by the eel and beef and egg" (265).

The doctor knew from a glance at the child's body that she needed A and B vitamins and that these translated into "eel and beef and egg," but he hadn't grasped something equally readable from her words, that she was being raised to sing and serve and sell her body as a *shakufu* or a prostitute attached to cheap eateries, working outside the licensed prostitution system. Or, rather, he hadn't recognized what he knew well before the girl's question ruptured his suspense. That he had thought "woman" instead of "girl" betrays his subliminal knowledge.

What had disrupted the doctor's mechanical response to the children? Is the girl's degree of emaciation, that is, visible information, sufficient explanation? Surely it is necessary but not sufficient, for many children in that setting must have shown the marks of malnutrition. In a text with virtually no description, the initial comparisons to pear and lotus root are extravagant. They suggest that the doctor senses more than malnutrition is to be read off her body. He responds by letting himself be drawn into unintended conversation. Why does he blush at the end? Again it is surely more than the incommensurability between the diagnosis he had to offer and the nature of the girl's needs. A doctor is licensed to view nudity without having it count as nudity. In this case, the license is redoubled because the objects of his gaze are children and their seminudity is institutional. The exchange with the girl exposes her imminent sexualization. That sexualization is more pertinently social than biological inasmuch as she will be delivered into the institution of prostitution. And in this context what the doctor's expertise recommends—eel, beef, egg—can only hasten that delivery. Even this irony doesn't exhaust the blush, however. In inadvertently yet inevitably uncovering the woman in the girl, the doctor is also stripped of his white coat. He becomes a man, another potential client.

I think it is the sensation of this threshold within himself that the doctor—and we readers—register as discovery. We can see that in fact several thresholds intersect in this slight but suggestive work: not only the doctor as a male and therefore potential sexual consumer-exploiter but the doctor as conscientious agent of an institution of surveillance and assistance; and the girl on the cusp of childhood and womanhood, a victim in either case, each foregrounding her body, though differently.

It may come as a surprise to those whose image of Kobayashi Takiji is limited to the classic "Kani kōsen" that he was a sensitive portrayer of women and children. He wrote a number of dark stories featuring *shakufu*, but this series is the only one to focus on the future *shakufu* as child. In the next two versions, "Report" and "Supplement," the details enumerated above are expanded into episodes ("Report" takes up about eleven pages in print, "Supplement" fourteen) recounted by the girl herself in a first-person, "found" text embedded in a frame narrative. The familiar fiction of a found document is meant to authenticate the fiction. This instance, which takes the form of a letter to a teacher, may have drawn on the practice of the life narration movement (*seikatsu tsuzurikata undō*), promoted by progressive teachers to encourage children's free expression.[72] What is striking in relation to "Inspection," however, is that in neither of the later versions does the girl voice her question to the doctor about what it means to be sold. Silent before the doctor, she mulls over the way her "Fake Mother" (*uso no okāsan*, a designation helpfully supplied by the doctor in response to the girl's venturing that she had two mothers, a "real" one and . . .) says she will sell her when she's grown. The girl tells us, or rather the teacher addressee, that she does not know what it means to be sold but is sure that it's scary. We can't help thinking we knows, however, to judge from her descriptions of the carryings-on

72. Matsuzawa Nobuhiro. "Puroretaria jidōbungaku to Kobayashi Takiji no yakuwari." *Kindai bungaku kenkyū* 14 (February, 1997): 44–56. This discussion appears on page 53.

of the "Fake Mother." But her not knowing definitively, or rather her refusal to acknowledge her knowledge, is important. It is self-protective, but also, in keeping her within the boundaries of childhood, it prompts her to describe what she sees as she could not have had she lost her vulnerable, quavering curiosity. The girl's not putting the question to the doctor, means, however, that we can't tell if he has his moment of discovery, and we aren't meant to, really, because he is no longer the protagonist.

The expanded narrative in both versions gives us a vivid picture of the child's dawning consciousness as to why it is painful for her Real Ma when she comes home, of her regrettable precocity (symbolized by the songs she has learned from the Fake Ma, which issue from her lips without her intent, drawing tears from Real Ma's eyes), of her terror before the brutality of the various Pa's with the Fake Ma, not to mention the anguish caused by Fake Ma's unremitting cruelty. As she explains to her teacher, the reason why she falls asleep in school is that she is out on the snowy streets every night until the early hours of the morning, forced by Fake Ma to peddle tissue paper at cheap bars and cafes. Both narratives end with her finally coming back to Fake Ma's house to sleep only to learn that her younger brother is dying. She dashes out, moaning and stumbling in the snow, trying to get to her real home before he dies.

In these versions we get the girl's own account of meeting the doctor, especially of what it is like for her to wait her turn. Since she is the one doing the telling, there is no more comparing her lusterless face to a pear or describing her timidity from without. She cannot see herself; she feels herself. And what she remembers is the itch of body lice when she is sitting in school, her efforts to crush one, then another, by thrusting her hands in her pockets. And she is mortified that lice might be found on her exposed flesh, as she had once seen on the neck of the classmate in front of her. That made her blush as if she had been the one seen by others with a louse crawling down her neck. And even before she's bared herself she is aware of the crumbling state of her undergarments and the unbathed state of her body ("Record," *KTZ*, 1:211; "Supplement," *KTZ*, 3:47).

The doctor, however, can only see nervous or recalcitrant silence. Her silence is heavy with all the things she writes her teacher but *will* not tell the doctor. She stands, a young girl exposed to the gaze of inspection, overcome by a shame that is also anticipatory of exposure to the gaze of lust. In letting the girl narrate the contents of her outward silence, Kobayashi displays one of his great strengths, namely, the capacity to accord dignity to characters who must submit to abject (because bodily) humiliation.

This finally brings us to the matter of the frame. "Record" comes with a page-long preface written by an "I" (*jibun*) who situates us precisely in

Otaru with place-names I'm thrilled to locate on a current map, near a school, where "I" slips and falls, and from that simple chance—this is insisted on—comes upon the rough notepaper bearing the text we are about to read (*KTZ*, 1:209). The top sheet that "I" picks up has already been trampled many times by clogs and horse-drawn sleds, and, although "I" spends hours trying to restore the page, neither writer nor addressee can be identified. With the humble material, damaged exterior, and protestation of accidental (i.e., innocent, pure) discovery, "I" begins to sound like a later version of the doctor. This "I" decides to transcribe the text faithfully, without correction. "Why? That will become evident when you read it" (*KTZ*, 1:210). Nevertheless, where the pencil marks have become faint, where letters are missing, or, on the other hand, where they are repeated, "I" will mark them, using parentheses so that the reader can distinguish the marks "I" makes from the original. Moreover, because the nearly total lack of punctuation makes the text taxing to read, "I" will supply them after his own fashion; ditto with quotation marks. In fact, "I" wishes that the text could be read in its original form and not in print because he thinks that both the paper and each distinctive, faltering letter ought to be seen by the reader. So, with the preciousness of the humble, damaged, error-ridden body of the text insisted on, we are plunged, midsentence, into another "I" narrative, this time the *"watashi/watakushi"* (both are used) made familiar through the I-novel (*KTZ*, 1:209–10).

The framing "I," *jibun*, appears in almost every other line, supplying a missing letter here, correcting a mistake there, noting X number of indecipherable or missing letters or lines, and even identifying himself as "Kobayashi" in order to gloss references to "mother" so that the reader will be in no doubt as to whether it is the true mother or the stepmother who is being referred to ("Record," *KTZ*, 1:214 inter alia). Should we take this as the inspecting gaze shifted from the body of the girl to the body of her writing? Perhaps. But the inspecting gaze, accompanied by stethoscope and palpation, had been willfully blind. The fussy pedagogical attention here, as if determined to compensate, comes to seem lavish and even loving. If the relationship is still asymmetrical—one "I" is the corrector, the other the corrected—the "I" who is corrected is nevertheless the producer of a record of experience that commands respectful attention. We could superimpose on this relationship that of adult and child or—why not?—proletarian intellectual and worker/farmer. But it would be important not to miss the identificatory act at beginning and end, when "I" (*jibun*) acquired the text by slipping and falling and "I" (*watashi*) stumbles and falls (even trying to retrieve white tissue paper from the snow) in a desperate effort to reach her brother while he still breathes. "Record" ends midsentence with a parenthetical comment to the effect that if the reader is dissatisfied that a novelistic ending is not provided, "Kobayashi" is of the same opinion (*KTZ*, 1:220). Besides reinforcing the sense of the authenticity of the document and therefore the entire story, this comment serves as a reminder of "Kobayashi's" identification with the reader, as well as the embedded "I."

Now, it is possible to take "Kobayashi" ("I," *jibun*) as a fictional autobiographical author-narrator (i.e., Kobayashi Takiji creating the frame story as if it were autobiographical) of the frame story (consisting of finding and transcribing the story we are about to read). What is important is that "I" is perceptible to us, the readers, but not to the "I" of the embedded story. Doesn't this frame narrator actualize the potential of the nonperson narrator identified by Kamei, most notably in conveying a sense of a fate shared with the protagonist to the reader? The sense of shared fate is mimetically produced by the initial fall to acquire the precious text and then by its transcription. The transcriber's ubiquitous editorial presence keeps the reader bound to the embedded narrator's every word. At the same time, we need to keep in mind that this is an empathetic, *chosen* identification. The frame narrator's telling us how he wished we, the readers, could see not the printed transcription but the actual letter is a valuable acknowledgment of the impossibility of identification. If you read, as I do, "Record" together with "Inspection" and see "Kobayashi" as a development of the doctor, the gap between the two narrators is obvious. Even if you don't, it is important to feel the distance between the girl who will go from a wretched childhood to sexual humiliation and the adult male whose social background we cannot determine except that it has provided him with the literacy to write the frame story and correct the embedded text. "Record" was written just before Kobayashi Takiji explicitly identified himself as a proletarian writer. Whether for this reason or not, the empathetic identification across gender difference, especially with the subject of sexual abjection, manages to show sexual exploitation as a distinct component of class exploitation. This, too, is "Record's" contribution to the possibilities of proletarian literature.[73]

In version three, "Supplement," the frame has been reduced to a single parenthetical line noting that even though parts are missing, the text has been reproduced as a supplement (to "Rescue News") with only a few corrections (*KTZ*, 3:46). After the midsentence ending comes an even briefer parenthetical confirmation, "This ends here" (60). There is no longer a marked "I" (*jibun*, "Kobayashi") in the frame, and corrections have been reduced by 90 percent. Nor are there quotation marks to set off dialogue,

73. See Heather Bowen-Struyk, "Rethinking Japanese Proletarian Literature," PhD diss., University of Michigan. 2001, 33–73.

making the paragraphs visually dense, compensated for by boldface type at the head of each paragraph. The "Supplement" paragraphs are aurally packed as well, so to speak, insofar as the absence of a pedagogical narrator further accentuates the overwhelming use of the syllabary in the girl's text, with little recourse to Sino-Japanese characters.[74] Does the "I" (watashi) gain authority from having shed the shadowing "I" (jibun) of "Record," the child/worker now able to stand on her own without the instruction of an adult/intellectual?

Indeed, this "I" aspires to become a factory worker, an avowed member of the proletariat, when she grows up. The reason her family has fallen on such hard times, and why she has had to be given away, is that her father was arrested and imprisoned for union activities. When she unwittingly sings the songs learned from the false mother, it is saddening to the true mother not only because it betokens the loss of innocence but because these songs have replaced the union songs the family used to sing together. A union member comes around to check on the family (at one point pawning his jacket in the hopes of providing the girl a nutritious meal), but he, too, disappears, leaving the true mother exposed to the sexual predations of a police "spy" who comes around to "help out."

Now for the full title of this piece: "It's winter. It's tough on our proletarian bones! Do our comrades in prison have heavy jackets? Have their families been turned out into the streets? Rescue News No. 18. Supplement." Kobayashi published a short comment on this title in the Yomiuri shimbun of February 4, 1930, titled "Konna rokotsuna nagai hyōdai wa?" (Why Such a Long, Crude Title? KTZ, 5:173). In it he asserts that proletarian literature need not have any hesitation about having "real effects" for its goal. Indeed, his hope was that reading this piece would prompt people to join the rescue effort. Recall that "Supplement" was published after Kobayashi had become a nationally recognized proletarian writer with "March 15, 1928." (In contrast to "Record," "Supplement" is no longer set in Otaru or any other specifiable place and dialect use is reduced.) "March 15" was the result of a transformational experience. Kobayashi had seen comrades disappear overnight during the massive national roundup, detention, and torture of opposition activists after the first universal male suffrage election of February. Literary scholar Shimamura Teru posits a decisive break with Kobayashi's

74. The extensive use of syllabary in both "Record" and "Supplement" obviously calls attention to the fact that the writer of the embedded text is a child, but I have to confess I do not yet understand how the alternations between hiragana and katakana are working in these texts. There are two shifts in "Record" (hiragana-katakana-hiragana) in contrast to six in "Supplement." "Supplement" states clearly that the girl narrator reads katakana (KTZ, 3:52).

previous humanism after this experience, making it utterly understandable that "Supplement" should have "exploded" the frame of the "novelistic."[75]

By contrast, Shimamura says, in "Record" the closing parenthetical remark in which "Kobayashi" imagines the reader's discontent over the abrupt nonending betrays author Kobayashi's desire for the "novelistic."[76] What "Supplement" does is to make explicit the conjoining of the literary with the nonliterary. But this is surely not a matter of the presence or absence of "artifice" (*sakui*) as Shimamura suggests. If we compare "Record" and "Supplement," it is evident that just as much artifice has gone into producing the less "novelistic" text in the very reduction of the frame narrative, the use of bold type, the kana alternation, not to mention minute revisions such as having the doctor "laugh" as he suggests the word *fake* to characterize the other mother ("Supplement," *KTZ*, 3:47).

I can well imagine that within the context in which it was written and disseminated, "Supplement" accomplished to some degree its practical aims, for it addressed a readership emotionally prepared, through organized activity and the immediate experience of suffering, to receive that appeal for "rescue." Yet it seems hasty to judge "Record" as inferior, or less advanced, because it is based on "humanism," even or especially in the context of the movement. I find myself missing the guiding presence of the third, mediating term in "Supplement": the frame narrator, the traces of whose caring labor in transcribing the account of a humbler world than his own holds our present-day attention. (Surely, given the significant participation by intellectuals, such an "appreciation of alterity" was necessary for both the proletarian literary movement and the proletarian struggle at large.) In "Supplement," proletarian themes—union activities, imprisonment, the police as concrete incarnations of the class enemy—have been skillfully incorporated into the story. This is a gain. Yet I can't help feeling that the gain is diminished by the loss of the frame narrator. If, as I suggested earlier in analyzing Kamei and Mitani, the nonperson narrator serves as a third term that keeps the novel from inward collapse, then "Record" and "Supplement" together show the value of the third term even in fiction writing that, to be sure, deploys first-person narration but decidedly not in the interest of obsessive introspection. The actively sympathetic listening (recording/correcting) presence of "Kobayashi" in "Record" becomes a vehicle for emotional resonance between the reader and the young-girl narrator of the embedded story.

75. Shimamura Teru, "'Kabe shōsetsu no hōhō: Kobayashi Takiji 'Kyūen nyūsu No. 18. Furoku' to 'Tegami,'" *Kokubungaku kaishaku to kanshō* 59:4 (April 1994): 142–47. This passage appears on page 144.

76. Ibid., 144.

Such resonance should be no less valuable for proletarian as for other kinds of fiction.

On the other hand, my purpose is not to downgrade "Supplement's" importance vis-à-vis "Record." Those contemporary readers who shared the girl narrator's reading and writing competence were unlikely to have had access to her story in a venue such as *Hoppō bungei*. Moreover, the narrator's editorial traces might have been an irritating impediment to their reading. If the girl's story in "Supplement" worked for such readers, it worked by giving them access to their own lives in familiar and estranged form, as shaped writing, a kind of alterity, too, that is fundamental to any powerful experience of literature regardless of the reader's place in society. Yet we must accord it a special significance for those who are not accustomed to having the minutiae of their lives noticed let alone respectfully transformed through craft into something they can look at and therefore use in bolstering a sense of purposeful identity, reinforced by felt solidarity. We can honor Kobayashi's repeated return to the scene of "Inspection."

As anyone who writes about "Supplement" will point out, it was Kobayashi's favorite work, at least as of late 1930, about two years before his murder (*KTZ*, 7:467–68). Why did he call it a "supplement"? And what do we make of the absence of the body to which it is a supplement? Is the story, in effect, a supplement to the title that sounds at once like a headline and a slogan? In the same article in which he asserted that proletarian literature should seek "real effects," Kobayashi admits that the story in the form of an "incomplete letter" is not appropriate as a "supplement" to "real 'Rescue News.'" Nevertheless, he thinks it plausible to claim that when a piece of writing

> takes the form of a work of art, as in this case, publishing it in
> *Senki* should allow it to have the same effect as actual news pub-
> lished in a form appropriate to it. (5:174)

What a condensed expression this is of the struggles of the proletarian artist! Art is not the same as news, and the same form will not do for both. But what is the role of the site of publication? *Senki* reached a broad *and* partisan readership. The organ and its parent body were committed to action, not contemplation. News informs people of the truth, of facts that should or will rouse them to action. The contribution of art to action, then, must be to offer facts in a way that is different from the modality of news.

In the prison letter in which Kobayashi states his unequivocal attachment to "Supplement," he adds, as if by way of explanation:

Having grown up in the dark north, I have to admit that I really like Dostoyevsky more than Tolstoy. That's why I can't help thinking that my works will only seem boring, chilling, and terrifying to all of you. (*KTZ*, 7:468)

Kobayashi was a tireless worker in the proletarian movement and eventually the then illegal Japan Communist Party. As one of the rare intellectuals of humble origins to join the movement, who therefore had first-hand experience of poverty, one of his distinctive strengths was empathy for and the capacity to render concretely the experience of humiliation, despair, and abjection. The efficacy of "Supplement" for middle-class readers must lie in its ability to evoke an urgent sympathy for lives unjustly condemned to darkness. Perhaps, by eliminating the frame narrator "author," Kobayashi the revolutionary writer felt that the stark, intolerable misery of the proletarian child's existence communicated itself more directly, as letter-document, on an equal footing with the nonartistic title. And he was taking a chance, hoping that this could serve as a call to action, firstly for proletarians, but surely for susceptible middle-class readers as well, much like news in the form of news.

As Raymond Williams put it more than fifty years after Kobayashi's killing, the "task of a successful socialist movement" was "one of feeling and imagination quite as much as one of fact and organization."[77] Each stimulates as well as bolsters the other, and the trafficking between them must never cease.

---

77. Raymond Williams, *Resources of Hope* (London: Verso, 1989), 76.

PART THREE

Rethinking Meiji Literature

9 The Age of the Prize Contest Novel

Kōno Kensuke

Translated by Christopher D. Scott

PRIZE CONTEST APPLICATION FEVER

In the July 1904 (Meiji 37) issue of the magazine *Bunko* (1895–1910) there appeared a column entitled "Rokugō katsuji" (No. 6 Type), signed by Muteppō.[1] Taking up recent trends in the literary world, it quipped: "Three illnesses are going around among budding literati."[2] The first two were a "magazine- and book-buying addiction" (*zasshi shoseki ranbai byō*) and a "magazine publication disease" (*zasshi hakkō byō*). These sarcastic "diagnoses" implied that such desires for magazines and books were corrupt and perverse. The third illness was "prize contest application fever" (*kenshō ōbo byō*). Here is what the column had to say about this phenomenon: "The weekly contributors to the *Yorozu chōhō* [1892–1940] wait with such greed and self-conceit for the winner to be announced that it is almost sad to see their disappointment and defeat when they find out they did not win."[3]

Bunko, in which this article appeared, was a literary magazine specializing in submissions and supported by poets such as Kawai Suimei. One has to wonder about these supporters' own immunity from contagions such as "magazine- and book-buying" and "magazine publication." Still, the older generation likely found fault with how these obsessions were becoming ends in and of themselves among the "youth" of the day. The sharpest criticism, however, was directed at "prize contests."

To be sure, staking prize money on literature was a controversial undertaking. But one cannot deny that the marriage of literature and the

---

1. The author's name is an aural pun on the Japanese term *muteppō*, meaning "reckless" or "foolhardy." [Translator's note]
2. Muteppō, "Rokugō katsuji," *Bunko*, July 1904, 285.
3. Ibid.

"mundane" led to the birth of literature as a profession. In the process, prize contests also became a way to lure people to literature. Since then, the prize contest system has been carried over to the postwar Japanese literary world and has played an instrumental role in discovering new talent. In fact, the pros and cons of offering prize money are nonissues to us now. But what was the situation like during the Meiji period? What kind of events shaped the emergence of the prize contest novel (kenshō shōsetsu)? Focusing on the case of Yorozu chōhō, parodied earlier, I would like to explore the literary climate around 1900, which might be called "the age of the prize contest novel."

THE PLEASURES OF WRITING AND READING

In October 1893 (Meiji 26), the Yomiuri shinbun (1874–present) advertised a "Prize Contest for Historical Novels and Plays." According to the newspaper, writers were appearing left and right, and great books were filling the shelves, but "historical novels and plays" were in terrible shape. This was, it claimed, "a huge weakness in the literary world." So, "in the spirit of inducement," a prize contest would be held.[4] The prizes were one hundred yen for first place and a gold watch for second. At the time, the subscription rate for the Yomiuri shinbun was thirty-five sen a month, or one yen for three months. Ozaki Kōyō, Yoda Gakkai, Takada Hanpō, and Tsubouchi Shōyō were named as judges. Thus began large-scale, prize contest novels. With the recent opening of the Diet, competition among newspaper companies was fierce. It was in this context that the Yomiuri shinbun began soliciting prize contest novels and plays, a major event in the history of the newspaper world.

Even before this time, it was common practice to submit articles and manuscripts for publication. Eisai shinshi (1877–?) was a submission-based magazine aimed at students and teachers in elementary and middle schools. Boasting a circulation of ten thousand and encompassing genres as diverse as essays, poetry (Chinese-style, modern, and classical), calligraphy, and illustrations, this magazine nurtured many later literary notables, including Yamada Bimyō, Ozaki Kōyō, Sakai Toshihiko, and Tayama Katai. With the success of Eisai shinshi, magazines such as Iwamoto Yoshiharu's Jogaku zasshi (1885–1904) and Tokutomi Sohō's Kokumin no tomo (1887–98) called for submissions, hoping to discover new writers in specific genres. Newspapers ranging from the Chōya shinbun (1874–1911) and Yomiuri shinbun to

4. Yomiuri shinbun, October 26, 1893.

the *Marumaru chinbun* (1877–1907?) also adopted submission systems in the form of "contributions" (*kisho*) bearing political messages, primarily political discussions. The establishment of such columns for submitted articles and manuscripts had as its primary goal the acquisition of articles and the discovery of writers. For authors and audiences alike, the very act of appearing in the media became a mark of prestige and an object of aspiration.

After about 1890, however, a change occurred in the treatment of submitted articles. Until then, amateur reporters were needed to make up for the lack of reporters and information, as well as the one-sidedness of articles. But with the increased organization of newspaper funds the boundary between reporters and readers became more clear-cut. "Contributions" ceased to be a daily installment and in time were replaced with "fiction" columns. With politics relegated to the Diet, the expression of views based on the procurement and confirmation of information was carried out by a handful of professionals. As if in compensation, readers were offered "entertaining fiction" (*omoshiroki shōsetsu*).

This decrease in submission columns and the foregrounding of literature as entertainment might be called the switch "from the pleasures of writing to the pleasures of reading" in newspapers. At least it is fair to say that during this period newspapers moved away from reader participation and became objects for viewing and reading. But the pleasures of writing were not completely suppressed; they were reintroduced on the page through changes in content and style. From this point on, the submission of articles and manuscripts became spectacles. Foremost among these were prize contests for novels, which were conducted by newspapers with large readerships.

THE HEYDAY OF THE PRIZE CONTEST NOVEL

In the prize contest sponsored by the *Yomiuri shinbun*, no first prize was given, and the second prize went to the novel *Takiguchi nyūdō* (Lay Priest Takiguchi) by "Anonymous." Actually, the author was Takayama Chogyū, who had just entered the philosophy department of Tokyo Imperial University. The reaction to this event was far from favorable. Rather, it is fair to say that this particular prize contest attracted attention only after the fact, when Chogyū himself had become famous. Since no first prize was given, the newspaper put out another call for prize contest novel submissions, due at the end of August, but the Sino-Japanese War (1894–95) broke out just before the deadline. The unprecedented war coverage in the newspaper world quickly overshadowed this event.

Before long, however, the author of *Takiguchi nyūdō* began to show great promise as a young contributor to the literature section of the general magazine *Taiyō* (1895–1928). This unknown newcomer, who had made his debut with a newspaper prize contest novel, had taken another route straight to the heart of the magazine media at the time. As a result, Takayama Chogyū's debut became the stuff of legend.

As it turned out, the idea of prize contest novels was simply ahead of its time. In the period of euphoria after the Sino-Japanese War, there was an explosion of new magazines and newspapers, giving rise to the joke that everywhere you looked there was a newspaper company. Amid all the excitement, interest in novels rose and the demand for new talent skyrocketed, with comments such as "The range of fiction readers grows day by day," "Nowadays novels are pretty much flying off the shelves," and "The way things are going, new and old writers are popping up everywhere these days."[5]

Shun'yōdō's *Shinshōsetsu* (1889–90, 1896–1926) expressly aimed to discover new talent. With the help of Kōda Rohan, the managing editor, new writers such as Oguri Fūyō made their debuts. But this ambitious plan for promoting new writers ended after less than a year. There was a limit to how many new writers the magazine could find on a regular basis. To identify outstanding new writers required considerable effort on the part of the editor(s). It was nearly impossible for a commercial magazine to focus solely on the discovery of new writers. So after Rohan left the editorship in 1898 (Meiji 31), *Shinshōsetsu* changed direction and began promoting prize contest novels.

As for newspapers, in 1901 (Meiji 34), the new *Ōsaka Mainichi shinbun* (1876–1943), a rival of the *Ōsaka Asahi shinbun* (1879–present), offered a three-hundred-yen prize to the best full-length novel in one of many prize contests it held that year. *Ichijiku* (Fig), by Nakamura Shun'u (Kichizō), won first place and was published in the newspaper. The magazine *Bungeikai* (1902–6), distributed by the publisher Kinkōdō, also actively included prize contests. One work not selected in this magazine's contest but published with the editor's praise was Nagai Kafū's *Jigoku no hana* (A Flower in Hell, 1902). Even the *Ōsaka Asahi*, which had criticized the *Ōsaka Mainichi*'s prize contest as lowbrow, began holding them in 1904 (Meiji 37). Among the writers who debuted via these newspaper-sponsored prize contests was Tamura Toshiko, who is still read and studied today. Virtually unknown during her apprenticeship under Rohan, Tamura jumped into the literary limelight with her prize contest novel *Akirame* (Resignation) when the *Ōsaka Mainichi* selected it in 1911 (Meiji 44).

5. "Shōsetsu hanro no kisei," *Yorozu chōhō*, November 18, 1896.

In this age of prize contest novels, *Yorozu chōhō*'s Weekly Prize Contest stands out as one of the earliest and the one that applicants found most accessible and winnable.

THE WEEKLY PRIZE CONTEST NOVEL

To solicit and announce a prize contest novel every week was a prodigious undertaking. As of 1896 (Meiji 29), *Yorozu chōhō* was number one in the Kantō region (around Tokyo) and number two in the entire country, with an annual circulation of 24,450,000. Its quick growth can be attributed, first of all, to its low subscription rate; it cost twenty sen a month. By comparison, the *Jiji shinpō* (1882–1936) cost fifty sen a month, the *Tokyo Nichinichi shinbun* (1872–1943) cost forty sen a month, and the *Tokyo Asahi shinbun* (1888–present) and *Miyako shinbun* (1884–1942) were each thirty sen a month. As Ōsugi Sakae notes in his 1923 *Jijoden* (Autobiography), "I read *Yorozu chōhō* simply because it was the cheapest."[6] Keeping the price down opened up a new market: low-income readers.

In January 1897 (Meiji 30), the *Yorozu chōhō* officially announced a "Weekly Call for Prize Contest Novels" with the following terms.

> Manuscripts must be under three thousand characters
>
> A prize of ten yen for the best manuscript in each pool
>
> Manuscripts due every Saturday, with the prize announced the following Saturday and publication the following Sunday[7]

Unlike serialized novels, which were by the same author and took up a set amount of time and space on the page, winning prize contest novels came in all shapes and sizes, as the ad proclaimed, including "domestic ones, historical ones, serious ones, frivolous ones, sad ones, and funny ones—nothing beats the paper for sheer entertainment."[8] What distinguished *Yorozu chōhō*'s prize contest from others like it was the fact that it ran every week for almost twenty-seven years until 1924 (Taishō 13) for a total of more than seventeen hundred contests.

Among the early winners were Nakauchi Chōji, Sano Tensei, Nakamura Kichizō, and Shinoda Kōzō. All were magazine or newspaper journalists who went on to become fiction writers and playwrights. They applied many

---

6. Ōsugi Sakae, *Jijoden* (Tokyo: Kaizōsha, 1923), 166.
7. *Yorozu chōhō*, January 17, 1897.
8. *Yorozu chōhō*, February 5, 1897.

times after that, too, and won. Even Kunikida Doppo earned a small income from prize contest novels before he quit his job as a newspaper reporter and became a professional fiction writer. Other names that appear before 1910 are Kojima Usui, Katagami Noburu, Okura Tōrō, Nagai Kafū, Taguchi Kikutei, and Hirotsu Kazuo. At the very least, the Weekly Prize Contest Novel was a stepping-stone for people who went on to make names for themselves as novelists, playwrights, critics, and journalists.

Limited to three thousand characters, the novels were really more like sketches. Surely this restriction made it hard to produce a masterpiece. But this was understood from the outset. The goal of this contest was to see what one could do and how well one could do it within the given parameters. The first contest attracted 95 submissions. During the next year, the reported number of entries ranged from a minimum of 58 to a maximum of 128.

NARRATIVE, STYLE, AND FORM

So what kind of works won? The short story "Hashijimo" (Frost on the Bridge) by Yūitsu Oshō, which appeared on February 14, 1897, is set in a teahouse at the foot of a bridge near a mountain village. It depicts an old man, his daughter, and a young boy who passes by the teahouse each morning selling newspapers. On his way home, the young boy visits the teahouse and is asked by the old man to read aloud some interesting articles from that day's newspaper. Amused by an article about a "filial daughter," the old man half jokes that the young boy should marry his own daughter and turn the teahouse into a newsstand. The boy merely blushes and hurries home. As it turns out, the daughter already has a marriage proposition, but she and her father both have reservations. In the end, a new young man joins the family, but the whereabouts of the newspaper boy are left unexplained.

Like most of the early winning works, the language of this text is a mixture of classical and colloquial styles (*gazoku setchū tai*). In terms of content, it shows people as readers and consumers of "newspapers," including scenes of reciting the paper, the daily trials and tribulations of delivering newspapers, a newspaper boy who seems to be from a destitute family, and so forth. Though not very sophisticated, the references to newspapers and the people surrounding them were a reflection of the *Yorozu chōhō* newspaper itself. The use of an adult perspective to depict a young boy secretly trying to make it in the world despite numerous difficulties was not unheard of in contemporary works of fiction, but it became a hallmark of *Yorozu chōhō* prize contest novels.

The winner of the fifth contest, Sano Tensei's "Shosei" (Sound of the Grinder), which appeared on February 28, 1897, is a tale of adultery set in the house of a wealthy farmer from the remote countryside. In the story, the farmer's wife, who has been meeting her lover in a water mill and planning to poison her husband, gets caught in the cogs of a large stone grinder and dies. It is a story that mixes eroticism with the grotesque. Critiques of this prize contest novel were printed, and winning novels soon became the object of literary reviews just like the novels of established writers. Of course, such articles were somewhat self-serving. But to have prize-winning works literally at one's fingertips and, moreover, to see those works treated alongside ones by major writers transformed readers into contributors and aroused fascination with prize contest novels.

On September 26, 1897, *Yorozu chōhō* published "Suntetsu" (Short and Sweet), a short story written by "Ta, O, Sei" in the modern vernacular (*genbun itchi*) style and reminiscent of Kunikida Doppo's works.[9] According to the story, "I," then a middle school student, was on a training vessel that hit a Japanese-style boat during practice. The vessel sails away right after the collision, angering a young boy aboard the Japanese boat. Three years later, though, "I" is a passenger on a boat to Yokosuka and happens to spot the young boy, who is now a ship's clerk. Failing to recognize him, the young boy asks "I" about studying English. When "I" inquires about his future plans, the young boy replies, "I want to pass the Ministry of Education exam and teach middle school students." The story concludes, "How short and sweet (*suntetsu*)! Before long, the clerk returned to his reading. The moon was faint behind the smoke from the funnel, and the ship's sidelights shone all the more brightly on his book. The ship steamed on, laden with unspoken emotions."[10] As a work of literature, of course, the story has little value. Behind its themes of regret for the past and sympathy for a young boy fighting adversity, however, one can detect a landscape of sentimentality wherein the main character discovers a poor, helpless Other with whom he identifies as a way of protesting the increasing social stratification based on academic experience. The story also features the work of a "training vessel," which was promoted in school to help make Japan a maritime power, as well as the *genbun itchi* style. This style would become the norm for chosen works in the future.

"Daisakka" (Great Writer), the winning work for November 14, 1897, written by "Kuwa no ya" (Shibata Sōsaku), is a first-person narrative of a young

---

9. The author's enigmatic penname, written in a combination of hiragana and kanji scripts, might also be rendered as "Mr. T. O." [Translator's note]
10. *Yorozu chōhō*, September 26, 1897.

man who dreams of becoming a great writer. Before he sends *Yorozu chōhō* his most recent masterpiece—written "in the exact manner of Mr. [Kuroiwa] Ruikō"—he wonders where he should send his other long novel, *Namida no tsuyu* (Teardrops), "to *Shincho gekkan* [1897–98], *Bungei kurabu* [1895–1933], or *Shinshōsetsu?*" Called a prodigy in his elementary school days, this young man from the provinces flunked out of upper middle school because of "an unfair grader."[11] With no education, he clings to his dream of becoming a "literary giant" and lives out this fantasy with his wife. The story ends with a sketch of the young man, now a policeman, a few months after submitting his novel to *Yorozu chōhō.*

This, too, is a story about a frustrated young man produced by the school system and his desire to make a name for himself. As usual, the plot is somewhat banal. But the narrative, in which literature consumes this young man's dreams, has a sarcastic edge to it. Within less than a year, *Yorozu chōhō*'s prize contest novels had begun parodying themselves. This shift is related to the doubling of discourse regarding submitted articles and manuscripts, as seen in the tongue-in-cheek article from *Bunko* quoted earlier. The writer of "Daisakka" is making fun of the delusional young man in the story. But that young man is also a mirror image of the writer. Still, the writer tries to differentiate himself from the delusional contributor; he thinks he is better than ordinary contributors. Here we can see the discursive mechanism whereby prize contest applicants ridiculed other applicants while promoting themselves.

THE POPULARIZATION AND STRATIFICATION OF LITERATURE

A prize contest novel did not always lead to a literary career. Winners included many people who were already magazine reporters or apprentices to established fiction writers. As in the case of Izumi Kyōka and Tokuda Shūsei, both of whom knocked on Ozaki Kōyō's door, the apprentice system was the most common way for people without formal educations to become professional fiction writers. Nonetheless, weekly calls for prize contest novels in a newspaper that boasted a daily circulation of over one hundred thousand represented a unique literary phenomenon. Incorporated into the major dailies and many magazines, these events spurred people to venture into literature while spreading the illusion that anyone could participate in literature. Thanks in large part to prize contest novels and submission-

11. *Yorozu chōhō*, November 14, 1897.

based magazines, people got a glimpse of a new kind of literature wherein a community of readers could become a community of writers in the blink of an eye.

Yet the preeminent critic Saitō Ryoku'u, an authority on classical literary arts, lampooned one magazine's decision to put a photograph of its prize contest winner on the first page: "Ah, the young men of Meiji—sacrificed and laid to rest like this."[12] Later that year Ryoku'u joined the selection committee of the *Yorozu chōhō*'s Weekly Prize Contest Novel, but he could not help complaining that the submissions were "hackneyed" (*monkirigata*) and nothing more than "erotic tales" (*iro monogatari*). Ryoku'u's critique of such conventionality uncovers one of the problems with this method of promoting new talent. While this system might seem more open, at least compared to the traditional model of training writers, in Ryoku'u's estimation it was producing "cookie-cutter" works of fiction. *Yorozu chōhō* prided itself on the latitude of its prize contest novel genres ("domestic ones, historical ones, serious ones, frivolous ones, sad ones, and funny ones"). Behind this facade of diversity, however, the process of homogenization continued.

For that very reason, the prize contest novel system laid the foundations for a more critical view of the novels themselves. At the same time, it became the focus of criticism. In this way, the prize contest novel concealed a double discourse that would eventually privilege a more sublime idea of "literature," something far more refined than the kind of literature that had existed until then. Clearly, this notion of literature sprouted from the desires and ambitions of these prize contest contributors. By denying its roots, the dream of literature would become a reality.

NOTE

All names are in Japanese order (surname first). In subsequent references, some well-known authors (e.g., Chogyū, Rohan, and Ryoku'u) are referred to by their given names (or pennames). All notes are by the author except where noted.

12. "Ganzen kōtō," *Yorozu chōhō*, March 1, 1898.

10 The Politics of Canon Formation and Writing Style: A Linguistic Analysis of *Kajin no kigū*

Guohe Zheng

Scholars have noted how the larger political context between the United States and Japan has continually colored postwar historical studies of Japan, resulting in shifting patterns of rehabilitation of United States' former enemy.[1] Scholarly rehabilitation of the same nature is seen in Japanese literary studies as well in the postwar Unites States, represented by a canon produced in the first fifteen postwar years and culminating in the so-called triumvirate phenomenon in which countless critics "employed the names of Mishima, Kawabata, and Tanizaki as a metonymy for the entire corpus of modern Japanese fiction."[2] As Norma Field puts it, "It was overwhelmingly a canon that conferred aesthetic allure upon the erstwhile enemy." To present a balanced and more explanatory view of Japanese literature, scholars in Japanese literary studies have been urged to make an effort "to understand with some specificity how that exotic effect was produced . . . [and to identify] the kinds of writing omitted in the course of canon-formation."[3]

This essay responds to that call by proposing a linguistic analysis of *Kajin no kigū*, a Meiji political novel that has long been excluded from the canon of modern Japanese literature. In so doing, I hope to demonstrate how canon formation is at work in existing treatments of the novel in English; how, contrary to the harsh judgment by Western scholars, *Kajin no kigū* was well received in Meiji Japan *because of* its language, not *in spite of* it; and how

1. John Dower, "Sizing Up (and Breaking Down) Japan," in *The Postwar Development of Japanese Studies in the United States,* edited by Helen Hardacre, 1–36 (Leiden: Brill, 1998).
2. Edward Fowler, "Rendering Words, Traversing Culture: On the Art and Politics of Translating Modern Japanese Fiction," *Journal of Japanese Studies* 18:1 (1992): 8.
3. Norma Field, "'The Way of the World': Japanese Literary Studies in the Postwar United States," in *The Postwar Development of Japanese Studies in the United States,* edited by Helen Hardacre, 227–93 (Leiden: Brill, 1998), 234.

an unmistakably modern theme is addressed in *Kajin no kigū* whose legacy is still very much alive in modern Japanese literature.

KAJIN NO KIGŪ AND CANON FORMATION

Kajin no kigū (Chance Meetings with Beautiful Women) is a long novel consisting of sixteen volumes divided evenly into eight parts published between 1885 and 1897. The author, Shiba Shirō (1852–1922), published the novel under the penname of Tōkai Sanshi, which is also the name of the protagonist of the work.

The opening scene of the story is set on a spring day in 1882 when Tōkai Sanshi, a young Japanese studying in America, visits Independence Hall in Philadelphia, where he encounters two beautiful European women.

> Tōkai Sanshi one day visited Independence Hall in Philadelphia. Looking up, he saw the cracked Liberty Bell . . . looking down, he read the Declaration of Independence. He reminisced about the noble character of the American people at the time when, raising the banner of righteousness, they had rid themselves of the tyrannical rule of the British king and eventually succeeded in becoming a people of independence and self-determination. Looking up and looking down, he was overwhelmed with emotion. With a deep sigh, he leaned against a window and gazed outside. It happened just then that two young women appeared coming up the spiral staircase.[4]

The two beauties, Kōren and Yūran by name, or *kajin* as they are referred to in the title, turn out to be ardent patriots from Ireland and Spain devoted to the movements supporting Irish independence from England and promoting a constitutional monarchy in Spain to guard against foreign interference in the country's internal affairs. Hearing the stories of the two beauties, Sanshi reveals that he is also a survivor of a vanquished country and has suffered unspeakable hardships. He tells them how Japan was forcibly opened to the world at the end of the Edo period, how his native Aizu domain became the victim of its ideal of loyalty due to the machinations of Satsuma and Chōshū, and how, when Aizu was labeled "traitorous" and defeated by Meiji government troops, he lost five family members. Vowing

---

4. Tōkai Sanshi, *Kajin no kigū*, reprinted in *Nihon gendai bungaku zenshū*, 108 vols. (Tokyo: Kōdansha, 1960–69), 3:88 (hereafter referred to as the Kōdansha edition). All translations from Japanese sources are mine except where noted.

to prove the loyalty of people from Aizu domain, he emphasizes the danger Japan faces from rampant imperialism and laments that his fellow Japanese are oblivious to the danger. Thus, a friendship develops between Sanshi and the beauties due to their shared lamentation for the misfortunes of their respective countries and their determination to fight for freedom and independence against Western imperialism.

While the story is centered in Philadelphia, the stage of the novel is really global and the romance between Sanshi and the beauties serves only to allow the author to weave together numerous tales of weak nations fallen victim to Western imperialism.

Shortly after his return to Japan in volume 9, Sanshi is sent on a world tour with a cabinet minister. What he sees and hears during the trip intensifies his indignation at the unequal treaties the Western powers had imposed on Japan and his criticism of the weak diplomacy of the Meiji government vis-à-vis the West.

Sandwiching a lengthy report on Sanshi's world tour are accounts of the Korean issue at home. Sanshi is seen more and more involved in the crisis between Japan and China over Korea that eventually leads to the first Sino-Japanese War (1894–95). By the end of the novel, Japan has emerged victorious from its war with China and its "military might" has been made known "to the eight corners of the world" (Kōdansha edition, 245). In sharp contrast to the opening scene of the novel, in which Tōkai Sanshi stands before the Liberty Bell extolling the virtues of freedom and independence, the last scene shows him incarcerated in a Hiroshima prison on charges of involvement in the assassination of Queen Min of Korea, a neighboring country for whose independence he claims he has been fighting.

As is obvious from the synopsis, the novel undergoes a fundamental transition in its political stance. It starts as a novel that shows the author's deep concern for the future of Japan in the face of "the alarming encroachment of the European powers" and his genuine sympathy toward weak nations of the world. Later, however, the author openly advocates Japan's adoption of policies like those of the imperialist powers, which Tōkai Sanshi vehemently condemns earlier in the novel.

In spite of the unmistakable shift in its political stance, however, no introduction of the novel in English has ever discussed this crucial change. For example, Horace Feldman's synopsis of the novel, perhaps the earliest by a westerner, ends in this way.

> [After returning to Japan, Tōkai Sanshi] discusses matters referring to her external problems and expresses anger over her long years of vain efforts on behalf of Korea . . . Tokai leaves on a trip

223

around the world. After finishing the trip, *he returns to China where he is well received.* He is still anxious about the welfare of his native country and protests against the arrogance and conceit of Europe and America. He is particularly mournful over the state of a world in which the self-government of such countries as Ireland is in imminent danger, *a world in which able scholars are dispersed, and philosophers are fading away.*[5] (Italics mine)

Similarly, Donald Keene's synopsis of the novel thirty-odd years later tells readers that "[i]n the sequels [to the first fourteen volumes of the novel], published in 1897 . . . the Wanderer [Tōkai Sanshi] to the end is the same crusader against injustice and tyranny."[6] Even scholars who attempt to defend the novel fail to note the crucial shift in the political stance of *Kajin no kigū*. For example, in his 1993 doctoral dissertation on Meiji political novels and the origins of Japanese literary modernity, John Mertz ends his synopsis of the novel, "[M]uch of the novel's remainder is concerned with reinforcing the idea that Japan should ally itself with other Asian countries (as a leader, of course) in order to fend off European aggression."[7] Moreover, Mertz's such view of the novel remains unchanged in his book published in 2003, which ends its summary of the novel in virtually the same way: "much of the novel's remainder is concerned with reinforcing the idea that Japan should ally itself with other Asian countries in order to fend off European aggression."[8]

G. B. Sansom's introduction to *Kajin no kigū* in his influential *The Western World and Japan* is perhaps most revealing on why scholars have not presented a less misleading introduction to the novel. He thus tells generations of Western readers about *Kajin no kigū*: "The book ends by disappointing the reader of his hopes for a passionate climax, but leaves him crammed with information about four and twenty nations in revolt."[9] Apparently, Sansom approached *Kajin no kigū* with an expectation of "a passionate climax" of romantic love. As long as that expectation is not met, the novel must be dismissed as worthless and the political agenda of the novel derided as boring and irrelevant "information about four and twenty nations in revolt." It

---

5. Horace Feldman, "The Meiji Political Novel: A Brief Survey," *Far Eastern Quarterly* 9 (November 1949–August 1950): 249–50, emphasis added.

6. Donald Keene, *Dawn to the West: Japanese Literature of the Modern Era—Fiction* (New York: Henry Holt and Company, 1984), 93, n. 24.

7. John Mertz, "Meiji Political Novels and the Origins of Literary Modernity," PhD diss., Cornell University, 1993, 37–38.

8. John Pierre Mertz, *Novel Japan: Space of Nationhood in Early Meiji Narrative, 1870-88* (Ann Arbor: Center for Japanese Studies, University of Michigan, 2003), 264.

9. G. B. Sansom, *The Western World and Japan* (New York: Alfred A. Knopf, 1950), 414.

is in these misleading introductions to the novel and the dismissal of it for its political orientation, I believe, that we find specific examples of canon formation at work.

Existing synopses of the novel are not only misleading due to their failure to inform readers of the crucial shift in the political stance of the novel, but they are also riddled with factual errors. For example, Feldman tells readers in his synopsis that after the tour around the world Tōkai Sanshi "returns to China where he is well received." The fact is, however, that other than Tōkai Sanshi's brief stopover in Hong Kong on his way to Ceylon, the topic of volume 11 of *Kajin no kigū*, neither the protagonist of the novel nor the author in real life had ever been to China. If this error can be attributed to the possibility that Feldman is merely repeating an error in a Japanese literary dictionary he might have consulted,[10] the basis for and point of his next statement about the nineteenth century as "a world in which able scholars are dispersed, and philosophers are fading away" remain a mystery.

Likewise, Keene notes that later in the novel "the Wanderer finds Mysterious Orchid [namely, Yūran] in Egypt, escapes with her to Philadelphia, then returns to Japan after the Sino-Japanese War."[11] The fact is, however, that, while Sanshi does find Yūran in Egypt during his world tour (vol. 12), he never "escapes with her to Philadelphia." Rather, citing as an excuse his being on an official trip, Tōkai Sanshi bids a cold farewell to Yūran, who is in hiding due to dangers threatening her personal safety.[12] In fact, it is Tōkai Sanshi's failure to rescue Yūran that makes Kōren bitter about him when the two meet again in volume 15 (Kōdansha edition, 233). Moreover, Sanshi returns to Japan right after his world tour in 1887 (Kōdansha edition, 234), instead of "after the Sino-Japanese War," as Keene maintains, a misreading that would put off Sanshi's return to Japan for eight years, leaving him absent from Japan and Korea when he was in fact most actively involved in the Korean issue—he is, after all, imprisoned on charges of murdering the Korean queen—the topic of the last volume of the novel.

Obvious as these errors are, no one has ever questioned any of them. It is a sad fact, indeed, that so many factual errors could go uncorrected for so long about what is presumably the best known of Meiji political novels. This testifies to the extent to which *Kajin no kigū*, and Meiji political novels in general, have been marginalized in the process of canon formation.

---

10. Takasu Yoshijirō, ed., *Nihon meibun kanshō*, vol. 4 (Tokyo, Kōseikaku, 1936).
11. Keene, *Dawn to the West*, 93.
12. See volume 12 of *Kajin no kigū* (Kōdansha edition, 211). See note 12 below for a complete list of modern editions of the *Kajin no kigū* text.

As noted above, *Kajin no kigū* is a long novel consisting of sixteen volumes. Not all of the volumes, however, are included in all of the modern editions.[13] For example, the Chikuma Shobō edition of *Kajin no kigū*, published in 1967, contains only the first ten volumes and its incompleteness is not adequately noted.[14] Unfortunately, the discussions of the novel by Keene and Mertz seem to be based solely on this incomplete edition.[15] Why is it that no efforts were made to consult a full version of the novel? One may blame the inadequate marking of abridgements of the Chikuma Shobō text. But Keene's comment that *Kajin no kigū* is "hardly more than curiosities" tells us a great deal about the reason for his indifference.[16] Apparently, he did not see the need to go any farther and consult the full text of *Kajin no kigū*. In this failure to consult a full version of the text, we see another specific example of the politics of canon formation at work.

HISTORICIZING THE NOTIONS
OF LITERATURE AND *KANBUN* WRITING

When it first appeared in 1885, *Kajin no kigū* became an immediate bestseller. In fact it was so popular that it is said that there was not a remote village in Japan where some young man had not a copy in his pocket.[17] Contemporary critics claimed that it had "raised the price of paper in the metropolis."[18] In contrast, *Kajin no kigū* has been cast in an extremely negative light in the course of canon formation in the West. Critics in the West share an almost unanimous opinion about the novel. It has been criticized as a "deplorably bad novel" and "hardly more than curiosities" and its language has been

---

13. Four modern versions of *Kajin no kigū* have been published. These are collected in volume 1 of *Meiji Taishō bungaku zenshū*, 60 vols. (Tokyo: Shunyōdō, 1927–32); volume 1 of *Gendai Nihon bungaku zenshū*, 64 vols. (Tokyo: Kaizōsha, 1926–31); volume 3 of *Nihon gendai bungaku zenshū*, 108 vols. (Tokyo: Kōdansha, 1960–69); and volume 6 of *Meiji bungaku zenshū*, 99 vols. (Tokyo: Chikuma Shobō, 1965–83) (hereafter referred to as the Chikuma Shobō edition). None of these editions includes the extensive headnotes of the Meiji period first edition.

14. The incompleteness is noted, as "due to limits of space," only in the editors' notes at the end of the book, not at the point where volume 10 ends. See the Chikuma Shobō edition, 507.

15. Judging from the notes in Mertz's dissertation, the Chikuma Shobō edition appears to be the only text he used (Mertz, "Meiji Political Novels and the Origins of Literary Modernity," xxvii, 145). See also Keene, *Dawn to the West*, notes 16, 17, and 19–23. The source for his note 24 is unclear.

16. Keene, *Dawn to the West*, 87.

17. See Kimura Ki, *Nichibei bungaku kōryūshi no kenkyū* (Tokyo: Kōdansha, 1982), 247; and Sansom, *The Western World and Japan*, 412.

18. See the commentary in volume 16 of *Kajin no kigū* (Kōdansha edition, 251).

characterized as "ornate, difficult and exceedingly conventional."[19] As such, the novel has been categorically denied a place in the canon of modern Japanese literature.[20] The sharp contrast between its reception in Meiji Japan and in the West today presents a problem: if *Kajin no kigū* was such a bad novel and written in such trite language as Western scholars claim it to be, the tremendous popularity it enjoyed in Meiji Japan becomes a mystery. The gap between its reception in Meiji Japan and in the West today calls for an explanation.

To fill in the gap, we must first historicize our notion of literature. In his study of literary styles from late Edo through the Meiji period, Maeda Ai argues as follows.

> One of the books in a series published in the 1880s and 1890s by Tokutomi Sohō's Min'yūsha was entitled *Jūni bungō* (Twelve Literary Masters). Among the foreign literary masters included in the book, which was compiled by Kitamura Tōkoku, Tokutomi Roka and Yamaji Aizan, were Carlyle, Macaulay, Wordsworth, Goethe, Emerson, Hugo and Tolstoy. On the other hand, the five people honored as Japanese literary masters were Ogyū Sorai, Chikamatsu Monzaemon, Arai Hakuseki, Rai Sanyō and Takizawa Bakin. It is perhaps puzzling to us today for the names of Carlyle, Macaulay and Emerson to be listed next to those of Goethe and Tolstoy. Or, similarly, in the case of Japan, the three names of Sorai, Hakuseki and Sanyō should probably be more appropriately identified as scholars or thinkers rather than writers of literature. However, the Meiji period was a time when the tradition still remained strong and deep-rooted to hold Confucian studies and *kanshibun* as the orthodoxy of literature.[21]

Maeda Ai's point is supported by numerous accounts of how *Kajin no kigū* was received by Meiji readers. The most vivid of such accounts is probably seen in Tokutomi Roka's 1928 novel *Kuroi me to chairo no me* (Black Eyes and Brown Eyes).

> Just about that time a novel titled *Kajin no kigū* appeared. Everyone who could read characters read it. . . . And the beautiful writing style of *Kajin no kigū* was admired by everyone in Kyōshisha

---

19. The quotations are from Sansom, *The Western World and Japan*, 413; and Keene, *Dawn to the West*, 87 and 86, respectively.
20. There are two recent exceptions. John Mertz and Atsuko Sakaki both argue for elements of modernity in the novel. This will be discussed below.
21. Maeda Ai, *Kindai Nihon no bungaku kūkan* (Tokyo: Shinyōsha, 1983), 231.

School. In particular, most of the numerous elegant *kanshi* poems in the novel were committed to memory. Keiji [the protagonist in Tokutomi's novel] had a classmate by the name of Ogata Ginjirō . . . who, though a mediocre student in academic subjects, was recognized as the best reciter of poetry in the whole school. On frosty, moonlit nights, close to school bedtime, Ogata would start to recite in a loud voice . . . along the sandy path between the dorm buildings. His voice was sonorous and forceful, like the sound made by striking metal with stones. At this, the three hundred students, who had been quietly concentrating on their schoolwork in the lamplight, would be enraptured by the recitation as if spellbound. On the tables here and there in Kyōshisha School, one would see copies of the novel in blue covers bound in Japanese style with string. The characters in the novel were printed in big wood-block letters mixed with katakana.[22] (Translation mine unless noted otherwise)

It is important to note that *Kajin no kigū* was read as literature by contemporary readers, a point testified to also by the childhood experience with *Kajin no kigū* recollected by Ibuse Masuji (1898–1993), the author of *Kuroi ame* (Black Rain, 1965).

Before I was old enough to go to school, I could recite from memory the opening passages of *Kajin no kigū*—"When I raise my eyes, I see the Liberty Bell . . ." My father would tell the guests in our house, "My son will become a doctor in literature."[23]

Recognition of *Kajin no kigū* as a masterpiece of literature is found in more formal settings as well. For example, a passage from volume 15 was included in the multivolume *Dictionary of Citations from Masterpieces in Japan* as late as in 1936.[24]

Clearly, *Kajin no kigū* was part of mainstream literature when it first appeared. To judge it by Western notions of literature is not only unfair to the work but it leaves a gaping hole between its reception in Meiji Japan and in the West today.

The next notion we must historicize is that of the *kanbun* style. In his comparative study of China and Japan, Chin Shunjin notes how knowledge of *kanshi* poetry was common among the Japanese in the Meiji period.

22. Tokutomi Roka, *Roka zenshū*, 20 vols. (Tokyo: Shinchōsha, 1928–30), 10:92–93.
23. Ibuse Masuji, "Honkokuhon no omoshirosa: *Kajin no kigū* ni tsuite," *Shun'yōdō geppō*, June 1930, 4.
24. Takasu Yoshijirō, *Nihon meibun kanshō*, 8 vols. (Tokyo: Kōseikaku, 1936), 4:57–62.

Japanese newspapers still carried a column of *kanshi* poetry until late in the Taishō period [1912–26]. Until that time, *kanshi* poetry contributed by readers was routinely carried in the newspapers in the same way *haiku* or *waka* poetry was published. This is particularly true of the early years of the Meiji period when it was common for men to compose *kanshi* poetry and for women to compose *waka* poetry.[25]

That classical Chinese prose literature was also popular, at least among college students in the early Meiji, can be seen in Mori Ōgai's *The Wild Geese* and *Vita Sexualis*. For example, the friendship between the narrator and the protagonist in *The Wild Geese* (*Gan*, 1911–13) develops due to their common interest in hunting for secondhand classical Chinese novels. Moreover, the protagonist is selected to study in Germany thanks to his ability to read medical books written in classical Chinese.

A sense of the extent to which readers in Meiji Japan were conversant with the *kanbun* style of writing is best captured by Nakamura Shinichirō in his book *Rai Sanyō to sono jidai* (Rai Sanyō and His Times, 1976). He recalls an episode from his childhood.

> Born in the beginning of the Meiji period, my grandmother was literally an old woman from the countryside with little education. One day when I was a middle school student, I had trouble reading my supplementary *kanbun* book, *Selected Essays from Nihon gaishi*. When she sensed my problem, my grandmother, still standing in the kitchen, recited loudly without any difficulty the part where I had got stuck. It seems that memorizing *Nihon gaishi* was part of the elementary education for young girls in the countryside when she was young.[26]

Maeda Ai comments:

> This episode gives us a rare glimpse into the language life of a time remotely separated from our own. The fact that a young girl from the countryside could retrieve the content of *Nihon gaishi* from her memory promptly and accurately in old age testifies to the fact that during the Meiji period there was a language world that was an inseparable part of people's lives but was at the same time entirely different from the vernacular of their daily lives.[27]

25. See Naramoto Tatsuya and Chin Shunjin, *Nihon to Chūgoku: Kindai no makuake* (Tokyo: Tokuma shoten, 1986), 187.
26. Cited in Maeda, *Kindai Nihon no bungaku kūkan*, 233–34.
27. Ibid., 234.

Clearly, however old-fashioned *kanbun*-style writing might appear to westerners today, or for that matter even to most Japanese, the harsh judgment passed on *Kajin no kigū*'s language by Western scholars is based on a Western standard of modernity.

AN ANALYSIS OF LINGUISTIC FEATURES OF *KAJIN NO KIGŪ*

Any discussion of the language of *Kajin no kigū* must begin with a consideration of the author's motivation in writing the novel because an author's choice of language is dictated by what made him or her take up the pen in the first place.

The motivation behind the novel is spelled out in the introduction to part 1 (*shohen*) by Tani Tateki (1837–1911), minister of agriculture and commerce in the first Itō Hirobumi cabinet and the author's mentor.[28]

> The author has sought to appeal to Heaven about his deep concern for Japan, but Heaven does not respond; he has also attempted to talk to the people, but no one listens. He is therefore obliged to employ the writing brush instead of the tongue, ink instead of tears, characters instead of spoken language, to express his patriotic enthusiasm (*yūkoku no shi*). How sad this is! The author is from Aizu domain and grew up amid great hardships. Returning lately from the United States of America after many years of study, he is well informed of the situation overseas and knows the importance of repairing the roof at home before it rains. However, what he sees happening in Japan makes him so worried that he has become unceasing in his efforts to inform the public of his concern over the future of Japan. This book is the result of his efforts to make these concerns known. (Chikuma Shobō edition, 3)

Tani tells readers here that the author has important matters "to appeal to Heaven" and to tell his fellow Japanese about. But, as "Heaven does not respond" and his compatriots do not listen to him, he has been forced to publish his thoughts in the form of a novel. What is it that is so compelling that it made him unceasing in his attempts to communicate it? Tani says it is the author's "patriotic enthusiasm," namely, "his concern over the future of Japan." As to why the author was so worried about Japan, Tani gives two reasons: not only is he from the ill-fated proshogunate Aizu domain, and therefore grew

---

28. Tani Tateki used a pseudonym, Yūtairō shujin Kumayama, for the introduction. See Yanagida Izumi, *Seiji shōsetsu kenkyū*, 3 vols. (Tokyo: Shunjūsha, 1967), 1:382.

up in hardships, but, more importantly, he has studied in the United States for many years and is well informed about affairs outside Japan. But his overseas experience has not led him to admire Western material civilization. Rather, it has made him realize "the importance of repairing the roof at home before it rains." As no one would listen to his appeal, he came up with the idea of writing a novel "to make these concerns known."

Similarly, the circumstances surrounding the writing of the novel are explained in the author's preface to Part 1.

> [W]hile abroad for many years, I was constantly worried about the future of Japan. Separated from my motherland by thousands of miles of land and sea, I jotted down my feelings whenever they were triggered by things I saw or heard. These random notes have accumulated to more than ten volumes . . . [and served as the basis of the current novel, which] I decided to call . . . *Kajin no kigū*. (Chikuma Shobō edition, 3)

Obviously, the same patriotic sentiments noted by Tani are expressed here as well. Then the author goes on to inform readers of his choice of language style for his novel.

> These notes are all the result of my scribbling in the little time I could snatch from my daily obligations. Consequently, they are not unified in style or language, some of them being written in *wabun*, some in *kanbun*, and some even in English. I was at Atami Hot Springs to recuperate from an ailment earlier this year after my return from abroad and enjoyed about two months of leisure. I used the time to edit these notes and turned them into something in the manner of today's Japanese (*honbō konsei no bun*). (Chikuma Shobō edition, 3)

"[T]oday's Japanese" in the author's preface is a rather vague term because different varieties of literary language were used in Japan at the time. Nanette Twine has identified four major varieties: *kanbun* (Sino-Japanese), *sōrōbun* (the epistolary style, an offshoot of Sino-Japanese), *wabun* (classical Japanese), and *wakankonkōbun* (a combination of Chinese and Japanese elements). She notes, however, that to educated men of the period "[t]o write for formal purposes . . . meant only one thing": to write in *kanbun*.[29] Kimura Naoe also argues for an inseparable connection between what she calls the literature of *hifenkōgai*, or "indignant lamentation over the woes of the times," such as political novels

---

29. Nanette Twine, *Language and the Modern State: The Reform of Written Japanese* (London and New York: Routledge, 1991), 34, 44.

popular in the Meiji twenties, and the *kanbun* style of writing.[30] The introductions to Part 1 of *Kajin no kigū* quoted above testify to the author's "indignant lamentation over the woes of the times." If we accept Kimura Naoe's theory, then *kanbun* would be the most appropriate choice of language for a work characterized by such intense *hifenkōgai*. Indeed, as shown in Ibuse Masuji's childhood recollection and Tokutomi Roka's *Kuroi me chairo no me*, the style of *Kajin no kigū* struck contemporary readers as effective. In other words, the novel was well received among contemporary readers *because of* its language, not *in spite of* it.

The writing style of *Kajin no kigū* has been referred to as *kanbun*. But *kanbun* is a loose term commonly used to refer to several different styles of writing that share the use of Chinese terms. Scholars have identified two styles under the blanket term *kanbun*: *jun kanbun*, pure Chinese; and *kanbun yomikudashi*, Chinese read in the Japanese manner.[31] In an interesting study, the latter is further classified into two types. Following a hint from Fukuchi Ouchi, Kamei Hideo illustrates the crucial difference between two *kanbun yomikudashi* styles. For example, a pure *kanbun* segment, as seen in (1), may be translated into either (2) or (3).

(1) 当是時臣唯独知有韓信不知有陛下也。

(2) 是時に当たりて臣は唯独り韓信あるを知りて陛下のましますを知り奉らざるなり。

(3) 是時ニ当タリ臣唯独韓信アルヲ知リ陛下アルヲ知ラザル也。[32]

As Kamei notes, the translation in (2) contains honorific elements, which are characteristic of Japanese but completely absent in pure *kanbun*. Kamei calls the *kanbun* in (2) *yakudokutai* style, or "translated reading of *kanbun*." In contrast, the translation in (3) contains minimal katakana *okurigana* and uses *onyomi* where possible. Kamei calls the *kanbun* in (3) *bōdokutai* style, or "direct reading of *kanbun*."[33] It is the *bōdokutai kanbun yomikudashi* style that is used in *Kajin no kigū*, as the opening lines of the novel illustrate in (4).

(4) 東海散士一日費府ノ独立閣ニ登リ、仰テ自由ノ破鐘…ヲ観、俯テ独立ノ遺文ヲ読ミ、当時米人ノ義旗ヲ挙テ英王ノ虐政ヲ除キ、卒ニ能ク独立自主ノ民タリノ高風ヲ追懐シ、俯仰感慨ニ堪ヘズ。慨然トシテ窓ニ倚テ眺臨ス。会々二姫アリ。階ヲ繞テ登リ来ル。(Chikuma Shobō edition, 4)

30. Kimura Naoe, *"Seinen" no tanjō* (Tokyo: Shinyōsha, 1998), 81–98.
31. Twine, *Language and the Modern State*, 34–35.
32. Kamei Hideo, *Kansei no henkaku* (Tokyo: Kōdansha, 1983), 32–34.
33. Ibid.

As Kamei points out, due to the highly inflectional nature of the Japanese language and its ubiquitous honorific system, throughout the long tradition of Japanese literature no author had any choice but to make explicit the relative status among his or her fictional characters, on the one hand, and between the author or narrator and the characters on the other. It was a so deep-rooted part of the Japanese literary sensibility that no writer knew how to avoid making it explicit. But thanks to the use of the *bōdokutai* style in *Kajin no kigū*, the need to indicate interpersonal status and intergender relationships was eliminated. This elimination made it possible to form international alliances among its characters that transcended borders of nationality and gender. Based on this linguistic analysis, Kamei characterizes the contribution of *Kajin no kigū* to modern Japanese literature as follows.

> [A]s a result, thanks to the use of this style, in which the sensibility to one's status is eliminated, it became possible to develop relationships between men and women in the novel on a completely equal basis. Hence, it became possible to revolutionize the philosophy of love as seen in the *ninjōbon*. Also thanks to the creation of this new type of love relationship between men and women, it became possible to incorporate into the novel international political movements from Europe to Asia. For this reason, we must say that *Kajin no kigū* is a truly epoch-making work.[34]

Clearly, contrary to the harsh judgment made by Western scholars, *Kajin no kigū* has notable linguistic merits that, along with its thematic content, account for its popularity and commercial success in Meiji Japan. The point here, of course, is not that the author used *kanbun* but rather that he used a writing style that best fits his thematic content. As Nakamura Mitsuo puts it in his critique of the novel, "If masterpieces are works written when the contents find the most suitable linguistic means to express them, then *Kajin no kigū* comes closest to that ideal among all Meiji novels."[35]

THE MODERNITY OF *KAJIN NO KIGŪ*

As noted above, *Kajin no kigū* has been categorically excluded from the canon of modern Japanese literature in the West. The judgment passed on the novel by Western critics is so harsh that the case seems clear and indisputable. Even critics who attempt to identify elements of modernity

34. Ibid., 34.
35. Nakamura Mitsuo, "Sakuhin kaisetsu" (Kōdansha edition, 398).

in the novel can only point out its transitional or nonintrinsic value. For example, John Mertz argues that the origin of Japanese literary modernity cannot be characterized as a sudden break with the past, nor as something arising from contact with Western literature.[36] Rather it results from the composite of diverse and thoroughly interrelated domestic changes dating back to the first years of Meiji and earlier. It is *Kajin no kigū* and other political novels that appeared in the period that captured "the crisis of political consciousness and conscience that marked Japan's passage into modernity."[37] In a more recent study, Atsuko Sakaki locates modernity of *Kajin no kigū* in the victory of its author in a lawsuit against the publisher and the writer of an adapted version of the novel on charges of copyright violation. As she puts it, the lawsuit "rested on this modern concept of the author as the owner of the text. . . . Hakubundō and Shiba's legal victory in this matter clearly located *Kajin no kigū* on the 'modern' side of the one key literary boundary."[38]

Is there anything intrinsic about *Kajin no kigū* that is modern? The answer is positive. I believe that *Kajin no kigō* is in fact very modern for at least two reasons. First, it addresses the issue of what road Japan should take in its pursuit of modernization, and, moreover, the transition of its political ideals reflects the locus of Japan's modernization. As is well known, Japan was thrust forcibly into the modern age by the West in the mid–nineteenth century. Since then, "Japan's emergence as a modern nation was stunning to behold: swifter, more audacious, more successful, and ultimately more crazed, murderous, and self-destructive than anyone had imagined possible."[39] The trajectory of that emergence is well captured in *Kajin no kigū*. For example, when the novel opens, Tōkai Sanshi is seen standing before the Liberty Bell admiring the Americans as "a people of independence and self-determination" after "rid[ding] themselves of the tyrannical rule" of the British king. Then, listening to the stories of Ireland in volumes 1 and 3, or to the accounts of the Egyptian war against Britain in volume 6, he shows genuine sympathy for "the misery of Ireland" under English rule and for the Egyptian people whose king was dethroned by British and French soldiers.[40] In volume 9, he expresses indignation at the unequal treaties imposed on

---

36. Mertz, "Meiji Political Novels and the Origins of Literary Modernity," 35.
37. Ibid., 46.
38. Atsuko Sakaki, "*Kajin no kigū:* The Meiji Political Novel and the Boundaries of Literature," *Monumenta Nipponica* 55:1 (spring 2000): 102.
39. John Dower, *Embracing Defeat: Japan in the Wake of World War II* (New York: Norton, 1999), 19.
40. This is the title of an illustration that goes with Kōren's account of Ireland in volume 1. See the Chikuma Shobō edition, 12.

Japan by the Western powers and shows deep concern about "the alarm-ing encroachment of the European powers" in East Asia.[41] To fight against Western imperialism, he advocates Asian solidarity in a letter to a Japanese monk who is visiting New York. However, when the Korean issue emerges in volume 10, another voice arises in the novel, one that calls for Japan to sever its ties with other Asian countries, to expand its territory, and to join the ranks of the "civilized countries" of the West. Eventually, Sanshi's "pa-triot" friends (*shishi*) are convinced that the law of the jungle is the only rule that governs the world. Unable to control their "ambition to occupy and protect Korea" in volume 16 (Kōdansha edition, 249), they propose "to issue Japanese paper currency in all eight provinces of Korea and to termi-nate the native Korean culture with a history of over a thousand years by enforcing Japanese customs" (Kōdansha edition, 245), or "to take decisive actions before major troubles arise over Korea between Japan and one or two powerful countries" (Kōdansha edition, 249), anticipating the assas-sination of Queen Min and the conflict between Japan and Russia. As we have seen, the novel ends with the assassination and Sanshi's imprisonment as a suspect in the murder plot. From admiration for the "independence and self-determination" of the American people, indignation at the unequal treaties imposed on Japan, concern about "the alarming encroachment of the Europeans" in East Asia, and advocacy of Asian solidarity against West-ern imperialism to celebrating "Japan's military might" made known to "the eight corners of the world" (Kōdansha edition, 245) and the assassination of Queen Min as a preemptive action in its conflict with Russia—in short, that is the path of transition of political ideals in *Kajin no kigū*. That path reflects well the locus of the transformation of Japan from an oppressed country to an imperialist power.

The second reason why *Kajin no kigō* is modern is that it represents a legacy of politics in modern Japanese literature. As Hiraoka Toshio points out, premodern Japanese literature consisted of two discrete traditions. One was townspeople literature, which focused on entertainment and had little to do with politics; the other was samurai literature, which, deeply rooted in Confucianism, dealt exclusively with political matters such as the teaching of wise government practices and the art of running a country. The contri-bution of *Kajin no kigū* and Yano Ryūkei's *Keikoku bidan* (Inspiring Instances of Statesmanship, 1883), the two best known of all Meiji political novels, lies in the fact that they brought the two traditions together and created a new literature representing a direction different from what was advocated by

41. This is the title of an illustration that goes with Tōkai Sanshi's analysis of the international politics of the time in volume 9. See the Chikuma Shobō edition, 95.

Tsubouchi Shōyō.[42] Since then, politics has been entangled with Japanese literature in various and revealing ways.

Some scholars believe that the new orientation was soon aborted and politics was again excluded from Japanese literature. For example, Maeda Ai comments in a study on the impact of Tsubouchi Shōyō's *Shōsetsu shinzui* (The Essence of the Novel, 1885–86) on modern Japanese literature, "Published in the same year of 1885 as the first part of *Kajin no kigū*, Tsubouchi Shōyō's *Shōsetsu shinzui* nipped in the bud various possibilities of historical literature of the Meiji teens [1870s and 1880s]."[43] Other scholars have gone much farther and characterized modern Japanese literature as uniquely aesthetic and apolitical. For example, in a comparative study, Ching-mao Cheng says that, compared to Chinese writers, "Japanese writers were absorbed in discovering the meaning of literature and seeking emancipation, assertion, and perfection of *jiga* (selfhood) at an abstract level."[44] Similarly, Suzuki Shūji claims that "in the world of Japanese literature . . . it is the concept of *mono-no-aware* that is the key to literary refinement. If politics is allowed to be involved, literature will only be made vulgar."[45] I do not believe that Japanese literature is unique, nor can politics be eliminated completely from it by anyone. Rather, given the trajectory of Japan's modernization, it would be most strange indeed if no politics were involved in Japanese literature to reflect that trajectory.

Political complications of Tanizaki Jun'ichirō's modern Japanese translation of *The Tale of Genji*, for example, indicates that Japanese writers were not even allowed to concentrate on refining *mono-no-aware* during "the fifteen-year war period," even if they so desired. *The Tale of Genji* has been regarded as the quintessential embodiment of the *mono-no-aware* sensibility in Japanese literature. But when Tanizaki began his project in 1935 he was "advised" to eliminate "the most decisive elements determining the cyclical structure of the novel and its theme of retribution" from the classic. Inclusion of those episodes in the translation, he was told by a *Genji* expert, would be tantamount to exposing the absurdity of the myth about Japan be-

42. Hiraoka Toshio, "Meiji shoki no seiji to bungaku," in *Kōza Nihon bungaku,* 11 vols. (Tokyo: Sanseidō, 1969), 9:21–44.

43. Maeda Ai, "Meiji rekishi bungaku no genzō," in *Meiji no bungaku, Nihon bungaku kenkyū shiryō sōsho,* edited by Nihon bungaku kenkyū shiryō kankōkai (Tokyo: Yūseido, 1981), 30:45.

44. Cheng Ching-mao, "The Impact of Japanese Literary Trends on Modern Chinese Writers," in *Modern Chinese Literature in the May Fourth Era,* edited by Merle Goldman, 63–88 (Cambridge: Harvard University Press, 1977), 76.

45. Suzuki Shūji. *Chūgoku bungaku to Nihon bungaku* (Tokyo: Tokyo Shoseki Kabushiki Kaisha, 1987), 17.

ing a divine country and would violate the topmost taboo of the authorities. Eventually, Tanizaki followed the advice of the expert, cut those episodes, and smoothed over the cuts without informing readers of the operation, something he was to regret after the war.[46]

Similarly, Japanese writers could not remain aloof from national politics and seek "emancipation, assertion, and perfection of *jiga* (selfhood) at an abstract level." The banning of Tanizaki Jun'ichirō's 1943 novel *The Makioka Sisters* (*Sasameyuki*) is an example. *The Makioka Sisters* is a story of the efforts of an upper-middle-class family in the suburb of Osaka to find a suitable husband for the third of its four daughters. As soon as the novel appeared in installments in *Chūō kōron* in January 1943, it was discontinued, ostensibly as an act of "self-restraint" by the magazine because the novel portrayed the "soft, effeminate, and grossly individualistic lives of women" during "the exigencies at this decisive stage of the war."[47]

Going hand in hand with the banning of works that failed "to comprehend the nature of the times" was the call by the military authorities for Japanese writers to collaborate in the war effort. One method of collaboration was for literary magazines to organize so-called Pen Units to be sent to other Asian countries to write about Japan's "sacred war"; another was for writers to join various "patriotic" organizations at home such as the *Nihon bungaku hōkokukai* (Japanese Association of Patriotic Literature). The majority of Japanese writers were involved in one or both of the two organizations because, as Jay Rubin puts it, "If one hoped to function at all as a writer during these years, when the Cabinet Information Bureau kept a blacklist of undesirable authors, one had to be a member of the association."[48] Needless to say, members of neither patriotic organizations nor Pen Units were allowed to write freely. For example, Dazai Osamu's *Sekibetsu* (Regretful Parting, 1945) was commissioned by *Nihon bungaku hōkokukai* to promote "independence and amity," one of the five principles adopted by the Joint Declaration of the Greater East Asia Conference held in Tokyo in November 1943. Similarly, six restrictions applied to the writers in Pen Units, including two that state that, in their writings about the Japanese army, "criminal acts that inevitably accompany warfare must not be touched on" and "feelings of soldiers as human beings are not allowed to be expressed."[49] The existence of "patriotic" literary organizations and "pen units" and the fact that the

---

46. Jay Rubin, *Injurious to Public Moral: Writers and the Meiji State* (Seattle: University of Washington Press, 1984), 258–60.
47. Ibid., 263–65.
48. Ibid., 274.
49. Cited by Hirano Ken in *Sensō bungaku zenshū*, 8 vols. (Tokyo: Mainichi Shinbunsha, 1971–72), 2:422.

majority of writers joined them demonstrate how groundless it is to characterize modern Japanese literature as purely aesthetic and apolitical.

Of course, the influence of politics is not limited to literature produced during the "fifteen-year war period." As an example, we can cite proletarian literature. The proletarian literature movement in Japan began in 1921 and collapsed shortly after the 1933 arrest and death by torture of Kobayashi Takiji, the best-known writer of the movement. As a movement, it produced several literary magazines, and its writers produced a considerable body of work. While the achievement of proletarian literature is debatable, the treatment Kobayashi Takiji's "The Cannery Boat" ("Kani kōsen," 1929) has received provides an unmistakable example of how, in the course of canon formation, politically oriented literature has been consciously marginalized. An anthology of modern Japanese literature in English translation published in 1956 includes thirty-six works, but Kobayashi's "The Cannery Boat" alone in the anthology does not have a named translator.[50] As Norma Field puts it, "It is chilling to encounter the phrase 'Translated Anonymously' —without further comment—in a collection published in 1955 [*sic*], and . . . (how different [it is] from the '*yomibito shirazu*' of the imperial anthologies of poetry!)"[51]

Ōe Kenzaburō has listed a large group of postwar writers and summarized their primary concern.

> When Japan's effort to modernize ran into the fatal impasse of the Pacific War, the Japanese made a serious search for a set of principles to guide them in making a fresh start, and the aim of the postwar writers was to give literary expression to such principles.[52]

Clearly, the concern of these postwar writers reflects the legacy of *Kajin no kigū*.

Among postwar works that carry on the legacy of *Kajin no kigū* is *Senkan Yamato no saigo* (Requiem for Battleship *Yamato*, 1952), by Yoshida Mitsuru (1923–79), who was not a professional writer and is not on Ōe's list. It tells of the author's experience as a junior naval officer in April 1945 when the battleship *Yamato* set out on a last and fatal sortie in the Battle of Okinawa. Years later Yoshida spoke of his sense of mission in writing the novel.

50. See Donald Keene, ed., *Modern Japanese Literature: An Anthology* (New York: Grove, 1956), 338.
51. Field, "The Way of the World," 238.
52. Ōe Kenzaburō, *Japan, the Ambiguous, and Myself: The Nobel Speech and Other Lectures* (Tokyo: Kodansha International, 1995), 97.

[T]he weight of that unique war experience held me and did not let go. Leading an ordinary life in the postwar era, one who survived when most of my comrades died, I could not exist without pursuing the meaning that heavy experience held for me, for the Japanese, for the postwar era.[53]

Yoshida's words should remind us of Shiba Shirō's motivation in writing *Kajin no kigū*. Significantly, Yoshida's *hifenkōgai* is expressed in the same *bōdokutai* style as that used in *Kajin no kiū*, as illustrated in the passage from the closing chapter of *Senkan Yamato no saigo*.

死トノ対決ヨリワレヲ救イシモノ、戦闘ノ異常感ナリ　マタ去リ行ク
者ノ悲懐、明ラカナル祖国の悲運ナリ[54]

Clearly, *Senkan Yamato no saigo* carries on the legacy of *Kajin no kigū* linguistically as well as thematically.

If Yoshida Mitsuru is a marginal writer, mainstream writers in the canon were not immune to politics either. I will limit myself to a brief discussion of politics in the work of Kawabata Yasunari, one of the "reigning triumvirate."[55] After the war, Kawabata wrote of his war years as follows: "I was never caught up in a surge of what is called divine possession, to become a fanatical believer in or blind worshiper of Japan."[56] This account has been adopted with little modification by critics in both Japan and the United States. For example, Donald Keene, Van Gessel, and Kawabata's leading Japanese biographer, Shindō Sumitaka, all cite this passage as indicative of Kawabata's attitude during the war. Kawabata's wartime writings, however, prove otherwise. That Kawabata was actually caught up in "the divine possession" is most obvious perhaps in his *Eirei no ibun* (Literary Legacies of Heroic Souls). This is a series of twenty articles published in a column in the *Tokyo shinbun* newspaper for approximately one week every December around the anniversary of the outbreak of the Pacific War during the years 1942–44. In these articles, Kawabata introduced letters, diaries, and poems

---

53. Yoshida Mitsuru, *Requiem for Battleship Yamato*, translated by Richard Minear (Seattle: University of Washington Press, 1985), xxv.

54. Yoshida Mitsuru, *Senkan Yamato no saigo*, reprinted in *Sensō bungaku zenshū*, 3:355. Richard Minear has translated this passage as "What spared me a confrontation with death, I see now, was the extraordinariness of battle. And my sorrow for those who were dying, and the clearly adverse fortunes of the homeland" (Yoshida, *Requiem for Battleship Yamato*, 149).

55. Fowler, "Rendering Words," 8.

56. Quoted in Keene, *Dawn to the West*, 823.

he had selected from collections of writings left behind by Japanese soldiers killed in action. But, as Charles Cabell points out:

> The war portrayed in *Heroic Souls* is free of senseless killing, cruelty and hatred. . . . *Heroic Souls* reduces the experience of warfare to fragmented images of unsurpassed beauty and passion. The invasion of Asia appears noteworthy primarily for its role in the revival of classical Japanese poetry, [and as a whole, the column] *moves* citizens toward acceptance of collective martyrdom.[57]

No reprint of this series was made available in any of Kawabata's postwar collections until 1984, twelve years after his death. This fact should tell us much about the canon as well as about Kawabata.

It should be noted that some of the letters introduced by Kawabata were introduced again by Kobayashi Yoshinori in his recent controversial work, *Sensō ron* (On the War, 1998), a *manga* book that attempts to justify Japan's role in the war.[58] Like *Kajin no kigū*, *Sensō ron* is filled with the author's burning desire to revitalize Japan, but, interestingly enough, it uses a language that is the antithesis of that in *Kajin no kigū*. Its extremely colloquial Japanese is liberally mixed with slangy expressions popular among Japan's younger generation today. *Sensō ron*'s manga form and its slangy style reflects its author's awareness of his readers' educational background and their lack of interest in pure literature. But in its use of first-person narration, its citing of the author's own experience to appeal to its readers, and its ultranational outlook, it bears a remarkable similarity to *Kajin no kigū*.

In his book on Japanese writers of the Shōwa period, Japanese critic Etō Jun says the following.

> By definition, literati are those who establish themselves by writing, either prose or poetry. It may sound graceful and elegant for someone to establish himself by writing. But did any of our Shōwa period literati enjoy the leisure and elegance worthy of men of letters? No! The very term *Shōwa period literati* echoes a profoundly bitter irony. The irony arises from the fact that Shōwa was a re-

---

57. Charles Cabell, "Maiden Dreams: Kawabata Yasunari's Beautiful Japanese Empire, 1930–1945," PhD diss., Harvard University, 1999, 277–78.

58. See, for example, ibid., 378–80, for a translation of Kawabata Yasunari's article on the kamikaze pilot Uemura Sanehisa's letter to his one-year-old daughter, published on December 10, 1944, and the same letter as quoted in its entirety by Kobayashi Yoshinori in his *Sensō ron* (Tokyo: Gentōsha, 1998), 84–85.

lentlessly harsh period in which no one was allowed to indulge himself in anything elegant and graceful.[59]

Etō Jun's words testify to the groundlessness of the claim that modern Japanese literature is uniquely aesthetic and apolitical. The extent to which politics was so deeply entangled with Japanese literature, however, is nothing other than an indication of the locus of Japan's emergence as a modern nation. It is in this sense that we can say that the legacy of *Kajin no kigū* has been carried on even though the novel has long been excluded from the canon.

CONCLUSION

I have presented in this essay a reevaluation of *Kajin no kigū*. It is not my intention, however, to advocate adding *Kajin no kigū* to the existing canon. Rather, what I have attempted to do is to find a more explanatory approach to modern Japanese literature.

In 1885, Tsubouchi Shōyō concluded the preface to his *Shōsetsu shinzui* with the hope that "by dint of steady planning in the years to come for the improvement of the Japanese novel, our fiction will finally surpass the European novel and take a glorious place on the altar of the arts along with painting, music, and poetry." Quoting Tsubouchi's prayer, Donald Keene says that his *Dawn to the West* "tells how Tsubouchi's hopes became a reality."[60] Keene's "reality" refers specifically to the awarding of the Nobel Prize for Literature to Kawabata Yasunari in 1968, exactly one hundred years after the Meiji Restoration. This way of viewing the hundred years of modern Japanese literature paints a roseate picture of linear development along an aesthetic and apolitical path. This picture reminds one of the Japanese government program in the mid-1960s that celebrated the centennial of the Meiji Restoration as a glorious continuum from which the prosperity of contemporary Japan grew. But, as a group of Japanese historians pointed out, this view of the "century as a continuum" was unscientific because it could not explain the vitally different natures of the first eighty years (from 1868 to 1945) and the twenty years since 1945 in modern Japanese history. While the first eighty years marked the awakening and rise of Japan as a nation, they also brought the country to the unprecedented disaster of the

---

59. Etō Jun, *Shōwa no bunjin* (Tokyo: Shinchōsha, 1989), 266.
60. Quoted in Keene, *Dawn to the West*, 9.

"Fifteen-Year War."[61] The roseate picture of Japanese literature is problematic in a similar way. First, it has ignored the possibility that Shōyō might have viewed literature as a political arena in which Japan grappled to gain an equal status with the West.[62] Moreover, to return to the main focus of this study, it cannot explain why, in spite of its artistic shortcomings and its exclusion from the canon, *Kajin no kigū* was not only popular among its contemporary readers but has been acclaimed as a masterpiece of patriotism by some Japanese critics.[63] It was even introduced as a piece of classic Japanese literature, along with *Man'yōshū* and *The Tale of Genji*, during the war.[64] Finally, it cannot explain why, when two Nobel Prizes for Literature have been awarded to Japanese writers, the second Japanese Nobel laureate has publicly lamented the decay of modern Japanese literature.[65]

When he was awarded the 1968 Nobel Prize for Literature, Kawabata Yasunari delivered an acceptance speech entitled "Japan, the Beautiful, and Myself." While obviously lending validity to the picture painted by *Dawn to the West*, viewed retrospectively this speech stands in sharp contrast to the Nobel speech delivered by Ōe Kenzaburō in 1994. In his speech, Ōe frankly declared that "[a]s someone living in present-day Japan and sharing bitter memories of the past, I cannot join Kawabata in saying 'Japan, the Beautiful, and Myself.'"[66] Instead, in a series of lectures since the 1980s, as well as in his Nobel speech, Ōe presents a picture of modern Japanese literature strikingly at odds with that of Keene. For example, Ōe said the following in a 1990 speech.

> One can say that from Soseki to Ooka, writing by and for intellectuals (whose education was based on a study of the West) represents a consistent lineage spanning a century of literary history. Yet, it was in the period after the defeat—the era of the

61. Ienaga Saburō, Inoue Kiyoshi, and Andō Yoshio et al., eds., *Kindai nihon no sōten*, 3 vols. (Tokyo: Mainichi Shinbunsha, 1967), 2:10–11.
62. See the discussion of Shōyō's political agenda in Cabell, "Maiden Dreams," 7. For a discussion of the relevance of social and cultural reform to Japan's crusade for the revision of unequal treaties with the Western powers in the Meiji period, see Louis Perez, *Japan Comes of Age: Mutsu Munemitsu and the Revision of the Unequal Treaties* (Madison, N.J.: Fairleigh Dickenson University Press, 1999), 11.
63. See Yanagida, *Seiji shōsetsu kenkyū*, 1:482; and Yanagida's remarks in the Chikuma Shobō edition, 482–83. See also *Meicho so kaisetsu daiyaru: Meiji, Taishō, Shōwa no meicho sōkaisetsu*, edited by Maejima Shinji et al., 8 vols. (Tokyo: Jiyū Kokumin Sha, 1983), 6:78–79.
64. Kokusai bunka shinkōkai, ed., *Introduction to Classic Japanese Literature* (Tokyo: Kokusai bunka shinkōkai, 1948). Intended for Western readers, this work was written only in English and completed during the war in 1940.
65. Ōe, *Japan, the Ambiguous, and Myself*, 57–128.
66. Ibid., 116.

"postwar school" of literature—that the character of "intellectual writing" surfaced most clearly.[67]

In an earlier speech, he explained that

> the preoccupation of postwar writers was to examine, with all the force of their imagination, what, in its pursuit of modernization, Japan had done to Asia and to the vulnerable elements in its own society, how the impasse could only have led to its defeat, and what means of resuscitation were possible for the nation after its death as a state.[68]

One does not have to agree with Ōe. But a more explanatory history of modern Japanese literature must be one that, among other things, can account for discrepancies such as those that exist between the Nobel Prize speeches by Kawabata and Ōe and those between Keene's picture of modern Japanese literature and that of Ōe. I believe *Kajin no kigū* has a more recognized place in that history.

NOTE

This essay is dedicated to my advisor, mentor, and friend, Professor William Jefferson Tyler (1945–2009) of The Ohio State University.

67. Ibid., 46.
68. Ibid., 74.

11 Elegance, Propriety, and Power in the "Modernization" of Literary Language in Meiji Japan

Joseph Essertier

Until recent years, most of the research on the historical "modernization" of the language used in literary writing in Japan has not explored to any significant extent the sociopolitical causes or effects of such modernization. When political issues of writing are discussed they are often limited to a struggle between liberal and conservative forces in government, with the liberal forces gradually and ultimately prevailing. They are seen to prevail largely because the writing style that they advocate comes to be widely recognized as the one most appropriate, natural, or beneficial for the bulk of the people in a modern, industrialized country. In research on the Meiji period, for example, novelists and poets pioneering the *genbun itchi* (unification of writing and speech) style are recognized as having effectively "launched" the style by writing works in it that were published and gained popularity, thereby demonstrating that unification of writing and speech was possible (and especially, "acceptable" or "respectable"). After this initial "launch" of the style, a consensus among intellectuals, literati, publishers, educators, government officials, and others is reached that writing and speech must be unified. Such people debate the pros and cons of this or that colloquial style and present their findings to the state, and in the end certain agents of the state initiate educational and other reforms to carry out the dissemination and establishment of the standard language.[1] Such a model of written language reform is common, but it not only oversimplifies and

---

1. Works in English by Nanette Twine (Gottlieb) are useful introductions to the history of language reform in Japan, and works in Japanese by Yamamoto Masahide remain fundamental as reference works that thoroughly compile and organize most of the important essays on language reform. Nevertheless, these works promote a view of the history of language reform in general, and the *genbun itchi* movement in Japan in particular, as essentially "successful modernization," fitting in with a theory of the successful modernization of government, society, and culture in Japan, and they dedicate insufficient

limits our understanding of a complex issue, it also blinds us to many issues of power in language and the struggles that are fought over language and, by extension, over access to reading or writing literature in a "modernized" language.

In particular, the sociopolitical effects of the notions of elegance and vulgarity in written language—the sociopolitical power issue that I will focus on here—in the criticisms, reviews, and comparisons of literary products are often missed in such models. The insights of the work of Pierre Bourdieu, which pays attention to the relationship between "cultural capital" and social hierarchies, is useful when one is attempting to conceptualize and theorize the causes and effects of, and determine what is at stake in, such aesthetic "valuations." Most of the technical terms in Bourdieu's social theory, including *cultural capital*, are borrowed from the language of economics.[2] Like economic capital, cultural capital can be a means of production and profits. Not only profits in the narrow economic sense, cultural capital also brings one the profits of honor, prestige, academic and literary awards, recognition, distinction, canonization, and so on. Standard spoken and written language, prestige dialects, and literary language can be conceptualized as forms of cultural capital through which profits in the literary "field" or "market" can be gained. "Agents," in this approach, such as literati and intellectuals in my research, operate within fields or markets (such as the *bundan* or "literary coterie" of Japan, one field with which I am

---

attention to the losers or victims in this modernization process. See Nanette Twine (Gottlieb), "The Genbunitchi Movement: Its Origin, Development, and Conclusion," *Monumenta Nipponica* 33:3 (1978): 333–56; Nanette Twine, "Toward Simplicity: Script Reform Movements in the Meiji Period," *Monumenta Nipponica* 38:2 (1983): 115–32; Nanette Twine (Gottlieb), *Language and the Modern State: The Reform of Written Japanese* (London: Routledge, 1991); Nanette Twine (Gottlieb), *Kanji Politics: Language Policy and Japanese Script* (London: Kegan Paul International, 1995); Yamamoto Masahide, *Kindai buntai hassei no shiteki kenkyū* (Tokyo: Iwanami Shoten, 1965); and Yamamoto Masahide, *Genbun itchi no rekishiron kō* (Tokyo: Ōfūsha, 1971). Much greater attention has been paid to issues of power in language reform history and the *genbun itchi* movement in the generally more recent work of scholars such as Karatani Kōjin, Lee Yeounsuk, Kamei Hideo, and Hirata Yumi. See Karatani Kōjin, *Origins of Modern Japanese Literature*, translation edited by Brett de Bary (Durham: Duke University Press, 1993); Lee Yeounsuk, "*Kokugo*" *to iu shisō: Kindai Nihon no gengo ninshiki* (Tokyo: Iwanami Shoten, 1996); Kamei Hideo, *Meiji bungakushi*, (Tokyo: Iwanami Shoten, 2000); and Hirata Yumi, *Josei hyōgen no Meiji shi: Higuchi Ichiyō izen* (Tokyo: Iwanami Shoten, 1999).

2. For a brief introduction to Bourdieu's approach to studies of language and power and to understand why his approach is not a form of economic reductionism, see John B. Thompson's excellent introduction to a selection of Bourdieu's essays in Pierre Bourdieu and John B. Thompson, *Language and Symbolic Power* (Cambridge: Harvard University Press, 1991).

concerned), and what they do, as well as what happens inside or outside the field, can affect the rise and fall of the value, of various forms of cultural capital. The cultural capital with which I am concerned here is that of literary language, and I think it is possible and interesting to investigate the aesthetic evaluations or "taste" of intellectuals and literati in this way, that is, as agents pursuing their interests and the interests of their socioeconomic, political, racial, gender, national, or other type of group in specific fields. (Nevertheless, agents should not be viewed as "subjects" necessarily in control of or conscious of the strategies through which they seek power, gains, or profits). It is useful and important to uncover the history of the past struggles over cultural or "linguistic" capital because, as Bourdieu emphasizes, the "struggles among writers over the legitimate art of writing contribute, through their very existence, to producing both the legitimate language, defined by its distance from the 'common language,' and belief in its legitimacy."[3]

Contradicting the typical model of language modernization in which it is implemented and controlled by state-affiliated agents as part of "language reform" programs—the model I mentioned above—most of the people involved in supporting or opposing the *genbun itchi* movement in Japan (the movement to unify speech and writing), the movements to abandon Chinese characters (in favor of the Japanese syllabary or the Roman alphabet), or the movement to limit the number of characters used were not government officials or even consultants working for government officials. In addition to the clearly political issues, such as those involving the strengthening or weakening of certain forces or cliques in government, language reform movements were implicated in social issues such as how women should write, the accessibility of the new written language, literacy levels, and national identity. Non-state-affiliated intellectuals, literati, publishers, political activists, educators, women, and workers with high literacy levels participated in the debates over changes in writing styles in newspapers and other forums and affected the ultimate outcome of those debates. The debates were intertwined with various sociopolitical issues such as who would be able to read the newspaper; who would contribute letters to the editor; who would express their hopes, fears, interests, and subjective worldviews in literature; what styles were appropriate for a woman to write in; what kind of a nation-state Japan would be; and how Japan would be seen by non-Japanese. In these debates, as I will discuss, taste was one of the crucial issues. My goal is to reveal a few things that were at stake in questions surrounding taste,

3. Ibid., 58.

referred to sometimes as the distinction between "elegance and vulgarity" (*ga/zoku*) in writing.

I will focus on the writings and thought of three participants in the debate over style and script reform between 1884 and 1890: Mori Ōgai (1862–1922), Yamada Bimyō (1868–1910), and Taguchi Ukichi (1855–1905). These three major participants in the debate each promoted different visions of the future ideal form of the Japanese written language, although all of them ended up contributing to the "unification of speech and writing" to a certain extent. Each of their visions entailed very different notions of what is beautiful in language, different hopes for modern Japanese literature, and different ways of organizing society. Through a comparison of their views, I delineate three pro-*genbun itchi* positions that were "available" in the intellectual field at the time (their three positions) and attempt to investigate very briefly some of the relationships between those views and their goals for social reform. Among other things, I argue that Taguchi's vision of romanized *genbun itchi* was part of a classical liberal view of society with a strong emphasis on democracy; that Bimyō's was part of a Spencerian survival of the fittest view that espoused a linear, progressive model of historical development that was supposedly driven by historical necessity; and that Ōgai's view of literary language was, in comparison, antidemocratic and elitist.[4]

What kind of language is vulgar and what kind elegant is a question about which there tends to be very little disagreement irrespective of one's particular social group. There is no objective, conscious, widely agreed upon measuring system for determining that this or that particular word is vulgar or elegant. Yet everyone knows. Bourdieu sometimes refers to this kind of universal recognition as a form of "misrecognition." In the case of illiterate people, their lack of knowledge of written language would probably not allow them to determine whether a particular word is elegant or vulgar, but then neither could one say that their view conflicts with that of highly literate people. Literate, "petit bourgeois" people in "modern, industrialized societies" usually recognize language as vulgar or elegant (or "prestige" or "stigmatized" in sociolinguistic terms) in essentially the same way as do most highly literate, upper-class persons. What separates petit bourgeois from bourgeois is a person's ability to "produce" utterances (written or spo-

---

4. By "Ōgai's view"—and Taguchi's or Bimyō's—I do not mean one that he was necessarily in control of but the one espoused in his writings, which was a product of his social environment, his upbringing and education, his individual inclinations, and the enduring elements of his disposition (his "habitus" in Bourdieu's terms).

ken) in prestige dialects, refined and elegant language, or literary styles. Thus (mis)recognition of elegant language is widespread while the ability to produce it is rare. One can think of literary language, then, as a rare and highly valued form of cultural capital with a universally recognized value within a certain social field. Its value in the social field, of course, is sometimes different from its value in the literary field. (The literary field is essentially a subfield of the social field, and for my purposes here the social field is the nation of Japan).[5]

In a debate over intentional, planned, and organized language change, such as the *genbun itchi* debate, the extent to which one promotes the use of vulgar or stigmatized language in writing will have some bearing on the extent to which one promotes democracy. One major reason this is so is that "vulgarization" of the language can also become "democratization" of it. Many people cannot produce elegant, refined, or highly literary utterances, but they can produce vulgar or stigmatized utterances. Often they natively speak in a dialect or style that is different from the dialect or style that they are taught to read in, the language of school, for example. The language of school and "standard language" is sometimes like a second language for people in some economic classes, ethnic groups, regions, and countries. When stigmatized utterances are "authorized" or "legitimized" in writing (usually over a long period of language change), therefore, the number of potential "writers" will inevitably increase. Naturally it is easier to write in one's native dialect than in a nonnative one, or in a dialect of greater proximity to one's own dialect than of one farther from it. (I mean "writer" here in the sense of "a person who writes," not in the sense of a novelist, poet, or journalist.) The great increase in the number of writers in this sense in postwar Japan, for example, is not unrelated to the radical style and script reforms that were adopted immediately after the war in school textbooks, government publications, newspapers, books, and so on. Some would say that written language in postwar Japan was democratized. Others might say it was vulgarized. Perspectives might be different but the changes themselves can be readily observed by anyone comparing prewar and postwar publications. In any case, the number of people capable of producing "well-formed" sentences—for letters to the editor, legal documents, diaries, correspondence, literary writing, or other kinds of writing—increased. The variety of writers and potential writers during the twentieth century also gradually expanded. It would be hard to argue that this did not contribute

---

5. I intend this not as a summary of Bourdieu's ideas on literary language but simply as a brief explanation of how some of his ideas have influenced my approach in this essay.

to the economic, cultural, and political power of ordinary citizens or "the people." In the following I use the word *democracy* in this broad sense, including not only the right to vote in parliamentary elections but also economic and class power.

Many proposals and opinions concerning the unification of writing and speech were presented in newspapers, magazines, books, and other places between 1884 and 1889, but the debate over the "unification of speech and writing" was especially hot during 1887 and 1888. As one of the earliest major debates over the *genbun itchi* style, occurring even before the Meiji state became involved in disseminating colloquial written language through the schools, it is a particularly interesting development.

It was during these years that many of the first, fresh *genbun itchi* novels were beginning to appear and many people involved in writing for large audiences were beginning to become interested in the possibility of using spoken language in writing. Tsubouchi Shōyō's (1859–1935) *Essence of the Novel* (*Shōsetsu shinzui*), with its call for the reform of fiction, came out in 1885, and the first *genbun itchi* novels began to appear immediately after that. The first installments of Bimyō's *Ridiculing a Vain Novelist* (*Chōkai shōsetsu tengu*), possibly the first *genbun itchi* novel to appear in print, started to appear in November 1886. Bimyō published a flurry of essays promoting *genbun itchi* in 1887, and Ōgai's "On Speech and Writing" (*Genbun ron*), in which he opposed *genbun itchi*, appeared in 1890. Taguchi's essay "The Nature of Japanese Civilization" (*Nippon kaika no seishitsu*), in which he advocated *genbun itchi*, was published in 1884–85. Taguchi's essay (originally a speech given in 1880) represents one of the earliest positions advocating *genbun itchi*, appearing in print at roughly the same time as *Essence of the Novel*.[6] Bimyō was *the* advocate of *genbun itchi* among literati, publishing his first *genbun itchi* novel at approximately the same time as Futabatei Shimei's *Ukigumo* (Drifting Clouds, 1887–89), and looking at his essay gives us a chance to see what he thought he was doing by writing *genbun itchi* novels or at least how he presented himself to the literary and intellectual worlds on this question. Ōgai's essay, on the other hand, marks his turn away from *genbun itchi*, perhaps "back to Japanese tradition." It gives us a glimpse into the debate from the perspective of the writer who would soon occupy what was perhaps the most dominant position in the literary field as writer, critic, and selector of talent. By historicizing this issue and actually looking at the essays in the debate, it is hoped that the degree of complexity of the issue will be apparent.

---

6. Taguchi says that this essay, "Nippon kaika no seishitsu," is based on a speech he gave in 1880 in Asakusa (Yamamoto, *Kindai buntai hassei no shiteki kenkyū*, 301).

LITERACY

One of the main goals of *genbun itchi* advocates was to make it possible for more people to read and write, so in order to provide some context for the debate I will first examine literacy briefly. Estimates of the percentage of literate people in Meiji Japan vary widely, ranging from 4 percent or less to "nearly all."[7] Much seems to depend on the definition of *literacy* that is used. Some definitions are based on school attendance; others are based on the ability to read and write at the level of intellectuals. Some in English scholarship simply state that the number of literate people was roughly 40 percent.[8] The most reliable studies, in my opinion, indicate that the number of highly literate people in late Tokugawa and early Meiji society were a small percentage of the population.[9] In any case, it appears that at the very least a large percentage of people were somewhere between illiterate and semiliterate, and it is possible that nearly all Japanese were somewhere in that range. What is important to note here is that many or most people did not have access to written information and had not received the kind of education that would have enabled them to "make their voices heard" in the world of public written communications such as newspapers, books, and letters to the

---

7. Unger refers to a literacy study done in 1948 in which the number of people who had sufficient literacy totaled 4 percent of those tested. Assuming that the number of literate people did not decrease between the Meiji period and 1948, one would have to conclude that, if that study is reliable, approximately 4 percent or less of the population was literate in Meiji. See J. Marshall Unger, *Literacy and Script Reform in Occupation Japan: Reading between the Lines* (New York: Oxford University Press, 1996). According to Huffman, "When you reached the third Meiji decade . . . [there was] a high level of school attendance. Nearly all of the population had entered the literate class." James L. Huffman, *Creating a Public: People and Press in Meiji Japan* (Honolulu: University of Hawai'i Press, 1997), 172. School attendance is also equated with literacy in Kido Mataichi, ed., *Kōza gendai janarizumu*, 6 vols. (Tokyo: Jiji Tsūshinsha, 1973–74), 1:2.
8. Jansen follows Dore in claiming 40 percent literacy among boys in the late Tokugawa period. Marius B. Jansen, "Japan in the Early Nineteenth Century," in *The Cambridge History of Japan*, edited by John W. Hall, Peter Duus, Delmer M. Brown, Donald H. Shively, William H. McCullough, Kozo Yamamura, James L. McClain, Marius B. Jansen, 6 vols. (Cambridge: Cambridge University Press, 1989–99), 5:67.
9. See Jiri V. Neustupny, "Literacy and Minorities: Divergent Perceptions," in *Linguistic Minorities and Literacy: Language Policy Issues in Developing Countries*, edited by Florian Coulmas, 115-128 (Amsterdam: Mouton, 1984); Umesao Tadao, J. Marshall Unger, and Sakiyama Osamu, *Japanese Civilization in the Modern World*, Senri Ethnological Studies, no. 34 (Osaka: National Museum of Ethnology, 1992); Richard Torrance, "Literacy and Modern Literature in the Izumo Region, 1880–1930," *Journal of Japanese Studies* 22:2 (1996): 327–62; Tokugawa Munemasa, "Nihonjin no riterashii: Meiji 14 nen no 'Shikiji chō' kara," *Kokugogaku* 158 (September 1989): 31–33; and Yamamoto Taketoshi, *Kindai Nihon no shinbun dokushasō*, (Tokyo: Hōsei Daigaku Shuppankyoku, 1981).

editor. It is important to keep this fact in mind when evaluating the social or political causes, effects, or significance of the *genbun itchi* movement.

TAGUCHI UKICHI

Among the thinkers considered here, I will first consider the work of Taguchi Ukichi. The following passage, published in 1885, gives us an idea of his overall perspective on "modernization" during these years.

> So listen! You must understand that if the civilization of the Tokugawa clan had been a civilization of ordinary people, as I described before, Japan today would have had the same character as the countries of Europe and America. But the reason why clothing developed in a truly aristocratic way after the Warring States Period is because the Tokugawa clan ruled by means of fiefs. I will not take up the question here of whether by being a humane society it would have actually become egalitarian or not. Nevertheless, it is easy to see the principle in which what we work to produce ourselves is never the possession of another person. This is why, in the perfect organization of society there are differences in civilization, but society never makes it possible for people who do not work themselves to indulge in idle pleasure, pleasure that is made possible by other people's labor. This is what I mean by "egalitarian." In such an egalitarian society, there are no aristocrats, no commoners, and no samurai. Everyone eats by working. And at such a time the advancement of civilization means the advancement of the general condition of the people. However clothing is reformed, it never becomes inconvenient to work in. However houses are improved, they never become inconvenient to stand up and sit down in. The development of eating utensils and the arts are likewise. The reason why is that in a society such as this one never becomes rich in clothing, food, and housing without working. This is a result of the fact that in the advancement of civilization the method of the division of labor, in which people work at only one task, has been carried out broadly throughout the society, and people are thereby able to produce a large quantity of goods. A civilization that has progressed in this way toward equality of conditions in a laboring society is the greatest perfection of society and the greatest happiness in the world. During the time of the Tokugawa clan, there were people called "lords" who stood above the people and robbed them of what was produced through their labor. Even when the popula-

tion grew and production increased in that society, the standard of living of the people did not improve, the people's happiness was not increased, and all the pleasure became the possession of the lord. The aristocrats, furthermore, did not work in order to partake of this pleasure. This is why their system of clothing developed such that it was only appropriate for enjoying oneself by sitting and ordering servants around.[10]

Although it appears that Mori Ōgai did not write about Taguchi's ideas during Taguchi's lifetime, he did evaluate Taguchi's work after his death in "Teiken sensei" (Taguchi's Nickname).[11] He pointed out there that Taguchi was very similar to Fukuzawa Yukichi (1835–1901) and that what was behind Taguchi's thought was "democratism" (*demokurachizumu*), if not democracy (*demokurati*; see *Ōgai Zenshū* 26:422). Ōgai praised Taguchi as a "two-legged" scholar, that is, one who knew well both the West and the East. But it is precisely this emphasis on democracy in Taguchi's thought, pointed out here by Ōgai, that separated him from Ōgai. Ōgai did not emphasize democracy or even democratism. Nakano Shigeharu went as far as to call Ōgai an "enemy of the people of Japan."[12] Kenneth Pyle says that Taguchi was "bold and consistent in his pursuit" of civilization and enlightenment themes and that he was even bolder than Fukuzawa in arguing for internationalism. Taguchi said that nationalism was outmoded and foolish, that nationality should be ignored. But Pyle states that civilization and progress ideas were not at all democratic in the "twentieth-century sense of advocating universal suffrage or economic equality."[13] Yet it does seem clear here and elsewhere that in Taguchi's case his boldness and consistency did sometimes lead him to advocate economic equality. He argues that what was wrong with Tokugawa

10. Taguchi Ukichi, "Nippon kaika no seishitsu," reprinted in *Taguchi Teiken shū* (Tokyo: Chikuma Shobō, 1977), 14:76. Kornicki says that "Nippon kaika no seishitsu" was so popular that there was a pirate edition in Osaka four months after it was published. See Peter F. Kornicki, *The Reform of Fiction in Meiji Japan* (London: Ithaca Press for the Board of the Faculty of Oriental Studies, Oxford University, 1982). Translation of this and other quotations from Japanese-language sources are by the author.

11. Mori Rintarō (Ōgai), "Teiken Sensei," reprinted in *Ōgai Zenshū*, 38 vols. (Tokyo: Iwanami Shoten, 1971–75), 26:421–23. See also Richard John Bowring, *Mori Ogai and the Modernization of Japanese Culture* (Cambridge: Cambridge University Press, 1979), 277.

12. Yoshida Seiichi, *Ōgai to Sōseki*, reprinted in *Yoshida Seiichi chosakushū*, 27 vols. (Tokyo: Ōfūsha, 1979–81), 4:85. Nakano Shigeharu was not himself an advocate of liberal democracy. His criticism of Ōgai was in terms of class struggle.

13. Kenneth B. Pyle, "Meiji Conservatism," in *The Cambridge History of Japan*, edited by John W. Hall, Peter Duus, Delmer M. Brown, Donald H. Shively, William H. McCullough, Kozo Yamamura, James L. McClain, Marius B. Jansen, 6 vols. (Cambridge: Cambridge University Press, 1989–99), 5:678.

society is that the lords robbed the people of "what was produced through the people's labor" and "all the pleasure became the possession of the lord." He defines the "advancement of civilization" as "the advancement of the general condition of the people." Words such as *conditions* and *civilization* refer more than anything else, in fact, to material conditions in this essay. He envisions economic equality for Japan domestically, and also equality between Japanese and non-Japanese people, on an international level.

A comparison of Taguchi's thought with the classical liberalism of England, which he was so influenced by, would easily demonstrate that Taguchi's brand of liberalism was very similar to that of J. S. Mill, Adam Smith, and Henry Thomas Buckle.

Taguchi's *On Taste* (Ishōron, 1885) begins:

> "Taste" is the flower of the human heart. "Tastelessness" refers to things such as trees living in the desert and ghosts following the way of hungry ghosts. One should see tastelessness as something dried up and withered, having no flavor and swaggering along with shoulders thrown back. (*MBZ*, 14:84)

He argues that all people have taste, no matter how high or low they may be, and that the literature, music, or art that is considered tasteful varies with the age, so that what was once beautiful is no longer so. He says that ancient rhetoric and classical Japanese are among the things that were bequeathed from Japan's feudal days, but that these things are not appropriate for people in a free and egalitarian society.

As we will see, this notion of taste is radically different from Ōgai's views and significantly different from Bimyō's. Both Bimyō and Ōgai are thought of as pioneers of the *genbun itchi* style, but their notions of taste are not intimately linked with egalitarianism.

MORI ŌGAI

Although Mori Ōgai was viewed as a *genbun itchi* pioneer by Yamada Bimyō and Tsubouchi Shōyō, and at first he sympathized with the idea of *genbun itchi*, in roughly 1890, soon after returning from four years of study in Germany, he began to oppose many of the stylistic innovations that were being experimented with in its name and questioned the desirability of uniting writing and speech.[14] He is quite concerned with vulgarity or bad taste in

14. Yamamoto explains that up until the publication of Ōgai's *Maihime* in January 1890, during a period when he translated various Western novels, plays, and poetry, Ōgai used a

his essay "On Speech and Writing," published in that year. In general, 1889 and 1890 witnessed a major turn in the controversy over *genbun itchi* and marked the beginnings of an anti-*genbun itchi* shift in the literary field that continued until the end of the Sino-Japanese War (1894–95). Ōgai was one of the major agents causing this shift in the field, and he quite harshly criticizes *genbun itchi* and romanization advocates in this essay.[15]

At the time the "storytelling" performances of San'yūtei Enchō (1839– 1900) were being transcribed and sold and had become very popular. While Ōgai accepts Enchō's *rakugo* as oral performances, he rejects them *as writing* for their vulgar taste.[16]

> Artistic spoken language can never become artistic written lan-
> guage. San'yūtei Enchō's oral performances are fine, but when
> they are written down, they are inferior to the writing of a medio-
> cre and stupid novelist. Except for those who read them to study
> the art of storytelling, I take pity on and feel sorry for those who
> have such poor taste that they enjoy reading such writing.[17]

And yet Futabatei Shimei modeled his *Ukigumo* on San'yūtei Enchō's speaking style. Ōgai's statement clearly attacks the position of *genbun itchi* writers.

Fujikawa Yoshiyuki argues that Futabatei was the one responsible for making it clear to everyone then and later that proper translations had to be carried out in the *genbun itchi* style.[18] He says that this surprised and enlightened Tsubouchi Shōyō, but Ōgai obviously disagreed.

> I don't think Futabatei's translations are especially great. They are
> obvious. That is the way translation has to be done. To say that
> they are great would not please the original authors who are no
> longer living.[19]

---

genbun itchi style in eight out of eleven translations (Yamamoto, *Kindai buntai hassei no shiteki kenkyū*, 580–81).

15. Yamamoto, *Kindai buntai hassei no shiteki kenkyū*, 586. "Genbun ron" was published in April 1890 in *Shigarami sōshi*.

16. "Rakugo" is a tradition of comic, oral storytelling in which the storyteller sits alone on a stage and tells a long, intricate, funny story. He plays the parts of all the characters in the conversations related in the performance. Characters are distinguished by changes in voice and in the direction the storyteller is facing.

17. Quoted in Katō Shūichi and Maeda Ai, *Buntai, Nihon kindai shisō taikei*, 24 vols. (Tokyo: Iwanami Shoten, 1988–92), 16:95.

18. Fujikawa Yoshiyuki, "Hon'yaku bungaku no tenbō," in *Iwanami kōza Nihon bungakushi*, 18 vols. (Tokyo: Iwanami Shoten, 1995–97), 11:319.

19. Ibid., 11:327.

Fujikawa maintains that Ōgai, who respected propriety above all, was probably repulsed by the realistic and extremely vulgar sound of Futabatei's colloquial style, for example, his representation of peasant speech: 'aatsumannei
kotoda." One finds such vulgar language here and there in Futabatei's
translations.[20]

Now if we take a step up, so to speak, from Enchō's transcriptions to a
more "noble taste" in Ōgai's eyes, we would arrive at the *genbun itchi* style.
Ōgai identifies Yamada Bimyō as the writer who pioneered this style and
contributed greatly to the advancement of the nation's written language.
Here we are told the difference between Bimyō's work and the "poor taste"
of those who enjoy reading the transcriptions of Enchō. That is, according
to Ōgai, the "unification of writing and speech style" (*genbun itchi* style) has
little to do with the idea that speaking should be the same as writing and
vice versa. The term refers instead, he says, to using some contemporary spoken language (together with words thought of as "written") while the overall
quality should remain that of "solemn written language" (*genzen taru bun*),
one "meant for reading."[21] It seems that for Ōgai writing could not be respectable and noble without being "solemn." This is what divides a transcription
of an Enchō from the writing style of a Bimyō for him. Ōgai seems to believe
that if you take the "writtenness" out of the writing it is not writing anymore.

YAMADA BIMYŌ

Bimyō's views on taste are made clear in his essay "An Outline of Views
on the Unification of Speech and Writing" (Genbun itchi ron no gairyaku,
1888).[22] At the time this was published, Bimyō had already published several
genbun itchi novels and poetry and had become well known as a *genbun itchi*
advocate. This was the first public expression of his opinions on *genbun itchi*.
Yamamoto Masahide refers to this essay as a "manifesto" for the reform of
style and says that it was clearly intended as a "counterattack" on the anti–
genbun itchi essay of Tatsumi Kojirō (1859–?), who held a "traditional" view,
arguing for example that the written language should be permanent, intellectual, and public rather than private.[23]

---

20. Ibid.
21. Quoted in Katō and Maeda, *Buntai, Nihon kindai shisō taikei*, 16:96.
22. This discussion of Bimyō's essay is based on Yamamoto, *Kindai buntai hassei no shiteki
    kenkyū*, 666–71.
23. Ibid., 666. Tatsumi's essay was entitled "Baku genbun itchi ron" (Anti–*genbun itchi* Argu-
    ments, August 10, 1887). Yamamoto discusses it in *Kindai buntai hassei no shiteki kenkyū*,
    662–65.

Bimyō refers to *genbun itchi* advocates often as "advocates of the vulgar language."[24] He says that they are opposed by the "advocates of the regular style," who want to make spoken language more like written language. Bimyō says that such regular style advocates criticize *genbun itchi* for the following problems.

1. If we adopt this style it will not be understood throughout Japan.

2. Today's vulgar language will become tomorrow's ancient language. (In other words, in the future the language that is considered vulgar today will eventually be viewed as ancient language).

3. The vulgar language of today is defective and has no grammar.

4. The vulgar language is "low." It is not "refined and beautiful" like elegant language.

Then Bimyō proceeds to attack each of these points. He demonstrates that he understands language change quite well, and he makes some very accurate predictions about the future of written Japanese. (It is easy in hindsight to see that Bimyō had the most accurate view of where the language was actually headed).

As for the second criticism of *genbun itchi*, that today's vulgar language will become tomorrow's ancient language, he quickly dismisses it by responding that the "regular style" or "kanji-kana mixed style" (*kanamajiri bun*) will also become an ancient language in the future. About the third, Bimyō says that the vulgar language naturally has fixed rules of grammar, just as do more formal forms of language. His response here is not very different from what a linguist would say today. About the fourth, that the vulgar language is "low," Bimyō says that only people who do not understand the nature of language say these things, that such aesthetic evaluations are merely products of their "imagination."[25] He says that the reason people feel that ancient language is graceful is that the tone, language, and diction of such language sound graceful to such people. This feeling about the tone then becomes a prejudice or bias. They are dazzled by that tone and therefore think that the language right at hand is lowbred. They respect what is far away, and they are misled by their love of ancient habits and their

24. Yamamoto, *Kindai buntai hassei no shiteki kenkyū*, 667.
25. Ibid.

imaginations. He writes that the "tide of social progress" does not stop at the "seashore" of ancient times. Regarding the proposal to use the "regular style" (*futsū bun*) even in speech, he argues that, while writing can be made to sound like speech, speech cannot be made to sound like writing.

He concludes by saying that "vulgar writing" (what we call *genbun itchi* today) would certainly achieve success much faster than the regular style. (By this he probably meant that it would be easier for people to learn because it is not so different from the middle-class vernacular of Tokyo). He asks which is better "for the sake of literature, slow success or fast success?" He emphasizes that in order to break away from the ancient styles much courage is needed: "Such courage is the rain and dew that in the future will cause Japanese literature to blossom."[26]

We can now briefly summarize Bimyō's views that relate to taste. In general, Bimyō attempts to attack the notion that colloquial Japanese words are vulgar and the idea that because they are vulgar they should not become part of writing. By arguing that the *genbun itchi* style of the present would one day become "beautiful and flawless," he relativizes vulgarity: what is vulgar today will be elegant tomorrow. The vulgar/elegant distinction is in people's imaginations, he maintains. For him, the distinction between what is elegant and what is vulgar depends on the shifting perceptions of the age. If that is true, then it should follow that distinctions between elegant and vulgar are arbitrary for Bimyō. Such a view, if widely accepted, had the potential to reduce the value of rare and elegant language, such as the style of writing that Ōgai used in "Maihime," and to legitimize a more common vulgar language. This would, consequently, reduce the authority and power associated with the possession of such cultural capital. Bimyō's views posed a threat to many literati and intellectuals. Yet, if the Tokyo dialect has "beaten all its competitors," as he says, and the Tokyo dialect has at this point in time achieved dominance as the "normal" or "regular" (*futsū*) form of spoken Japanese, then some forms of spoken Japanese are more normal than others. Some are fit to become written language, and others are not. This appears to be a "survival of the fittest" approach to writing style. He says that the Tokyo dialect has won. The battle is over. The only thing left to do is write grammars for this dialect, refine it, raise it from childhood to adulthood, and improve people's perceptions of it.

The notion that the Tokyo dialect (actually only one of the Tokyo dialects, that is, the "Yamanote" dialect spoken by powerful government bureaucrats and wealthy merchants in the Yamanote area) was more normal

26. Ibid., 671.

than dialects of other regions in Japan was not fundamentally different in terms of its social effects from the notion that some language was more elegant than others. That is, both notions supported hierarchies of language and the people who spoke those languages. Yet there was a difference. "Normal" was opposed to "not normal" and "incorrect," while "elegant" was opposed to "vulgar." All spoken language had long been viewed as vulgar in comparison to standard written language (usually a variant of classical Chinese), and the culture of common people in general had long been viewed as vulgar by almost everyone of all classes. This inferiority of that which is common compared to that which is rare and connected with power was nothing new. What was new, perhaps, in Bimyō's view of language was the notion that some dialects were not normal or correct. Ōgai and others with a view of language that was perhaps "older" than Bimyō's view tended to be uncomfortable with this notion of normal *spoken* language, even while they were comfortable with the idea that classical *written* grammar was correct. The books on colloquial grammar that Bimyō and others were writing at the time would contribute to this view and help establish the (mis)recognition of one dialect of one city of one class as the only correct one, the only one "fit" for writing.

ŌGAI'S RESPONSE TO BIMYŌ

We can see more clearly the differences and commonalities among the three thinkers discussed here by looking at Ōgai's response to what we could refer to in retrospect as the avant-garde position on *genbun itchi* with which Bimyō was associated more than any other writer or intellectual. This comes from the same essay mentioned above, "On Spoken and Written Language," which was published three years after Bimyō's essay. It was not written in direct reference to Bimyō's essay, but it was an influential rejection of the kind of *genbun itchi* style that Bimyō was advocating. Ōgai praises Bimyō for his pioneering spirit, but one of the main problems he had with Bimyō's ideas was his assertion that Tokyo colloquial grammar was normal: "Nevertheless, regarding Bimyō's new grammar, even if he says he only uses it for prose, I still cannot easily agree with him that this grammar should suddenly be treated as normal grammar."[27] He had praised Bimyō for avoiding vulgar words in his writing, but there was something strange about Bimyō's writing for him or at least something that made him feel uncomfortable.

27. Katō and Maeda, *Buntai, Nihon kindai shisō taikei*, 16:98.

Yamada incorporates many new words into his writing, but works to avoid vulgar words, resulting in what may be designated an elevated style. . . .

In reference to his verb conjugations, it is as if he uses contemporary Kyoto speech for the prose but maintains the classical conjugations (*teniwoha*) for verse. I cannot help but harbor a few doubts about this. Please allow me to say so.

The inflected portions of Yamada's prose is unusual from beginning to end. In the preface to *Natsukodachi* he says:

It is easier to speak to someone of lower status than to someone of higher status, and so I assumed such a status relative to the listener/reader throughout this work because I thought that such speech would be the basis for a style that would unify spoken and written language. Lately when I think about it, since somewhat different concerns have arisen, for the most part, I have been assuming a status in which the narrator's speech register is one of equality between narrator and reader.[28]

It seems that Ōgai selected this passage by Bimyō not only for the content but also in order to demonstrate Bimyō's writing style. Here Ōgai specifically complains about the inconsistency of Bimyō using colloquial language for prose but classical conjugations for verse. Then he says that Bimyō's conjugations are strange from beginning to end. What is strange about them is that Bimyō either employs the diction for speaking to someone of a lower status than oneself, or he eliminates status distinctions altogether, putting the narrator and reader on an equal footing. Ōgai does not say this, but in Tokugawa literature it appears that the narrator would employ an elevated tone, effectively "speaking down" to the reader, while the characters speaking in the dialogue would use plain, unelevated, or vulgar tones.[29] So the narrators of Bimyō's stories were speaking in a very different tone from that of earlier literature. Taguchi had promoted *genbun itchi* as an egalitarian form of writing. This was because he saw it as a system of writing in which anyone could directly write the way they spoke, and therefore it was a kind of writing to which all people would have access. Here we see Bimyō eliminating the status distinctions in spoken language, thereby creating an artificial kind of equality within writing. Ōgai was probably not the only one who felt that this artificial equality in Bimyō's *genbun itchi* style was strange.

28. Ibid., 16:97.
29. Katō Shūichi, "Meiji shoki no buntai," in Katō Shūichi and Maeda Ai, *Buntai, Nihon kindai shisō taikei*, 24 vols. (Tokyo: Iwanami Shoten, 1988–92), 16:449–81. See also Masao Miyoshi, *Accomplices of Silence: The Modern Japanese Novel* (Berkeley: University of California Press, 1974).

It can easily be argued that *genbun itchi* was an unusual and very rare style in its early days. Not only Bimyō and Ōgai had trouble with it, but so did Futabatei and other writers. Yet all these writers must have been quite fluent in the Yamanote dialect, the prestige dialect of the Yamanote area.

Ōgai says that the approach to diction of Bimyō, Futabatei, and Saganoya Omuro (1863–1947) is similar to that of Fritz Reuter (1810–74), whom Ōgai calls the "Dickens of Germany."[30] He says that it is fine to use oral diction (*da* or *desu*) in the words of the characters. This is what Ludwig Ganghofer (1855–1920) of Germany has done and also how Shōyō, Aeba Kōson (1867–1947), Kōda Rohan (1867–1903), Ozaki Kōyō (1867–1903), and Sudō Nansui (1858–1920) write.[31] He says that these Ganghofer types write in a "local dialect" in the dialogue but in correct diction in the narrative. The Reuter types write "vulgar dialect" in both the dialogue and the narrative. The problem is that Japan's *genbun itchi* writers (by which he probably means the Reuter types Bimyō, Futabatei, and Saganoya) treat vulgar dialect as "New Diction." Reuter, on the other hand, treats vulgar dialect as vulgar dialect. In other words, for Ōgai the new colloquial grammar that Bimyō was using was not only strange but also vulgar and incorrect. If you are going to write in vulgar dialect, then write in vulgar dialect, but do not call it New Diction.[32] What is vulgar is vulgar for Ōgai.

At the beginning of "On Speech and Writing" Ōgai explains that language changes over time and, although originally people had written in a *genbun itchi* style in ancient Japan, now people wrote in a classical style. He says that imitating ancient or "dead writing" is inappropriate for "national language development" and that people usually mistakenly view "the ancient as elegant, and the contemporary as vulgar."[33] He emphasizes that what is contemporary is not always vulgar. He says that Hagino Yoshiyuki (1860–1924), Ichimura Sanjirō (1864–1947), and Ōta Yoshinori had written that dead language must be discontinued and contemporary spoken language must be made elegant and indicates that he agrees with them.[34] Like Bimyō, who held out the possibility of a golden age in Japan when he mentioned Pericles (elsewhere in his essay), Ōgai had also quoted Hagino dreaming of

30. Fritz Reuter was a German novelist who contributed to the development of regional dialect literature in Germany through his novels, especially those in Plattdeutsch, a north German dialect. One of his representative works is the autobiographical novel *Ut de Franzosentid* (During the Time of the French Conquest, 1859). His *Ut mine Stromtid* (During My Apprenticeship, 1862–64) resembles the work of Dickens.

31. Ludwig Ganghofer (1855–1920) wrote many novels and plays, including *Das Schweigen im Walde* (The Silence of the Forest, 1899).

32. Katō and Maeda, *Buntai, Nihon kindai shisō taikei*, 97.

33. Ibid., 92.

34. Hagino Yoshiyuki and Ōta Yoshinori advocated the reform of *waka*.

a golden age of poetry being created in Japan. In mentioning Pericles, however, Bimyō shows that his golden age is one in which art flourishes under democratic rule while Ōgai's is not. The rule of Pericles in ancient Greece was known as a time of democratic rule, and at this time in Japan ancient Greece and Rome were often used as settings for political novels in support of the freedom and popular rights movement (*jiyū minken undō*).[35] In all these respects Ōgai demonstrates that he agrees with Bimyō on the need to renew and refresh the written language, and he praises Bimyō for causing a great "storm" in the sea of literature.[36] Nevertheless, there was one thing that Ōgai could not accept about Bimyō's *genbun itchi* project: his suddenly treating spoken, vulgar language as if it were respectable and decent, as reflected in his choice of colloquial language even in passages attributed to the narrator's voice.

> But there is a distinction between "elegant" and "vulgar" in the gap between contemporary spoken language and contemporary written language; language which is extremely elegant and language which is extremely vulgar do not mix.[37]

CONCLUSION

Perhaps the sharpest difference that comes out of a comparison of these essays is that between Ōgai and Taguchi. Roughly speaking, a conflict arises between the needs of art and the needs of democracy. Unlike Taguchi, Ōgai does not claim that his ideal form of writing will be good for mass education and democracy. His concerns are related to such matters as preserving elegance and solemnity in writing and respect for Japanese history and tradition. Taguchi wishes for a language that anyone can easily read and write, and so he advocates phoneticization to reduce the number of characters and colloquialization to allow people to write in or read a language that they ostensibly already know. I say ostensibly because, despite Taguchi and Bimyō's agreement that almost everyone at this time could understand *genbun itchi* writing when it was read aloud, there are indications that a limited percentage of the population of Japan was familiar with the Yamanote dialect of

35. Pericles was a statesman of ancient Greece whose rule is sometimes characterized as the golden age of Greece. He promoted democracy in Athens and led the Athenians at the beginning of the Peloponnesian War.
36. Katō and Maeda, *Buntai, Nihon kindai shisō taikei*, 92.
37. Ibid., 94.

Tokyo on which *genbun itchi* grammar is based.[38] Most people outside of Tokyo probably did not hear the Yamanote dialect spoken frequently enough
to understand it let alone write it themselves. In other words, the egalitarian
bent of Taguchi's proposal harbors an implicit hierarchy, the privileging of
Yamanote or Tokyo speech over other dialects. Taguchi does not say specifically that he is against people writing in their own dialect, but one can
infer that he would have been against it given his strong advocacy of standardization. In any case, Taguchi believes in the possibility of great art in a
democratic society, whereas Ōgai's position is more along the lines of "art
for art's sake" and "art for Japan's sake." Bimyō also hints at the possibility
of art in a democratic and golden age with his mention of Pericles. In this
sense, Bimyō's position is closer to Taguchi's than Ōgai's.

Taguchi's worst "enemies" are those who advocate what he terms "aristocratism" and "ancientism." Ōgai is also somewhat an opponent of ancientism, as is clear from his criticism of those who believe that colloquial
language used in writing is *always* vulgar. Ōgai allowed for the possibility
that colloquial language could be mixed in with classical writing without
the writing becoming vulgar in spite of his contradictory statement, quoted
above, that extremely vulgar and extremely elegant language do not mix.
(The keyword here may be *extremely*). He emphasizes, in fact, the difference
between elegant and ancient writing.[39] Nevertheless, it would be very difficult to call Ōgai an opponent of aristocratism in the debate over style and
script reform. Bimyō's grammar, though considered "correct" today, was
incorrect for Ōgai, and Ōgai disapproved of "extremely vulgar" language
in writing. Taguchi says that all people have taste, but Ōgai says, for example, that he feels sorry for the readers of the transcriptions of Enchō's
storytelling, of whom there were many. He disagrees with Bimyō treating
vulgar language as "new grammar," thereby legitimizing it. While from his
subjective standpoint he may have been defending elegance and rejecting
vulgarity, from an objective standpoint he was defending elite culture—that

38. In fact, Ōgai cites a "Mrs. Yoshikawa" complaining in a letter to the editor about how
    difficult Bimyō's style was (ibid., 96). The "Mrs. Yoshikawa" that Ōgai refers to is prob-
    ably Yoshikawa Hide, who wrote a letter to the editor in the *Yomiuri* newspaper entitled,
    "Genbun itchi" on March 20, 1889. Both Hirata Yumi and Yamamoto Masahide discuss
    this letter. Hirata seems confident that Yoshikawa was a pen name of Kimura Akebono
    (1872–1890), a novelist of the time. Hirata Yumi, *Josei hyōgen no Meiji shi: Higuchi Ichiyō
    izen* (Tokyo: Iwanami Shoten, 1999), 171; see also Yamamoto, *Kindai buntai hassei no shiteki
    kenkyū*, 703.
39. Toward the beginning of "Genbun ron," Ōgai says that imitating ancient writing would
    not be good for the "development of the nation's written language" (Katō and Maeda,
    Buntai, Nihon kindai shisō taikei, 92).

of Japan, China, and the West—against popular culture and defending elite aesthetic evaluations of nonelite language as vulgar. "Symbolic violence" implies "no act of intimidation" and "is not aware of what it is."[40] But it is not hard to imagine that Ōgai's taking pity on those who enjoyed reading the transcriptions of an Enchō or his emphasizing the oddness of the writing style of a Bimyō forcefully, if not violently, demarcated the bounds of respectable culture, intimidating upstart rivals in the field of literature, as well as readers and writers in the general social field who otherwise might have started to think of *genbun itchi* writing as literature.

For Bimyō, even vulgar language can be beautiful, at least beautiful in its simplicity. He insists that *genbun itchi* has a grammar, meaning that it is therefore capable of becoming a norm or standard. He says that his vulgar style is superior to the "regular style" in that it is closer to the spoken language. Both styles are destined to become ancient styles, he says, (just like the Heian period spoken language that appeared in poetry), so he asks simply, "Why not use the easier one?" Bimyō claims that the style he advocates is already understood throughout Japan. (This can only be true, however, if most of the population of Japan is not counted, as we have seen). Most important, he relativizes the vulgar/elegant distinction, arguing that colloquial speech (*zokugo*) is simply a product of people's imaginations. This is where Ōgai completely disagrees. Unlike Bimyō, he cannot countenance legitimizing vulgar language, suddenly treating what was usually considered vulgar as new grammar or as something normal. In the way these three (Ōgai, Bimyō, and Taguchi) defined taste, that is, what was "elegant" and what was "vulgar" in literary language, one could demonstrate, with further elaboration, how they were "specialists in symbolic production" who struggled over the legitimacy of various forms of written language on behalf of certain social groups and therefore, over the legitimacy of some speakers and writers over others.[41]

---

40. Bourdieu and Thompson, *Language and Symbolic Power*, 51.
41. Ibid., 168.

12

The Voice of Sex and the Sex of Voice in Higuchi Ichiyō and Shimizu Shikin

Leslie Winston

In his chapter on the polyphonic fiction of Higuchi Ichiyō in *Transformations of Sensibility: The Phenomenology of Meiji Literature*, Kamei Hideo describes the literature of the 1890s as "constructed around women's sensibilities and passions." The female characters in these works "bear some sort of social taboo" and "symbolize the prohibitions that defined the everyday thinking of the petty bourgeoisie."[1] Moreover, he adds, the characters are narrow in their concerns; their thinking does not extend to the larger social situation. Social criticism is not a self-conscious theme of these works.[2]

While Kamei's assessment accurately captures much of this decade's literature, I would like to supplement it with a consideration of a lesser-known writer, Shimizu Shikin (1868–1933). Shikin published most often in *Jogaku zasshi* (The Woman's Magazine, published 1885–1904), which ranked as the most popular women's magazine for several years in the late 1880s and early 1890s. As one of Japan's earliest feminist writers, Shikin does indeed write with a social consciousness, which surely contributes to her status today as "lesser known."[3]

1. Kamei Hideo, *Transformations of Sensibility: The Phenomenology of Meiji Literature*, translation edited by Michael Bourdaghs (Ann Arbor: University of Michigan, Center for Japanese Studies Publications, 2002), 112.
2. Ibid. 113.
3. For recent studies of Shikin in the context of women's writing from the 1890s, including Higuchi Ichiyō, see Rebecca Copeland, *Lost Leaves: Women Writers of Meiji Japan* (Honolulu: University of Hawai`i Press, 2000); and Leslie Winston, "The Female Subject in Meiji Literature," PhD diss., University of California, Los Angeles, 2002. Also see Yamaguchi Reiko, *Naite ai suru shimai ni tsugu: Kozai Shikin no shōgai* (Tokyo: Sōdo Bunka, 1977); Komashaku Kimi, "Shikin shōron: Joseigaku-teki apurōchi," in *Shikin zenshū*, edited by Kozai Yoshishige, 583–609 (Tokyo: Sōdo Bunka, 1983); Leslie Winston, "Beyond Modern: Shimizu Shikin and 'Two Modern Girls'" and translation of "Two Modern Girls" (Tōsei futari musume, 1897) by Shimizu Shikin, *Critical Asian Studies* 39.3 (September 2007): 447–481; and *The Modern Murasaki: Writing by Women of Meiji Japan*, edited by Rebecca Copeland and Melek Ortabasi (New York: Columbia University Press, 2006).

Kamei includes Higuchi Ichiyō as one of those who writes without the intention of criticizing society. Of course, we can say that, intentionally or not, social criticism is inherent in much of her work. However, Kamei is concerned with the self-consciousness in expression. Certainly, Ichiyō took pride in her individual consciousness, but this individuality is transformed, Kamei writes, so that the "self" never reaches the status of a speaking subject.[4]

Here I would like to consider the role of gender in the narrators/ narrations of Ichiyō's "Jūsan'ya" (The Thirteenth Night, 1895) and Shikin's "Ichi seinen iyō no jukkai" (A Young Man's Strange Recollections, 1892). Ichiyō's work employs what Kamei calls the "nomadic half-speaker" (*yuchaku-teki hanwasha*), a narrative apparatus that is capable of absorbing a multiplicity of speaking voices into itself, resulting in a glorious chorus of voices. Shikin produces a more unified and self-conscious speaking voice using a first-person narrator. In exploring these two works, I will try, in particular, to show the importance of gender in a consideration of voice.

Simple in plot, "The Thirteenth Night" is framed by rickshaw rides to and from the home of a married woman's parents. A young woman, Oseki, has come to tell her parents that she wishes to divorce her husband, Harada Isamu, and come home to them. They persuade her not to do so in spite of Harada's harsh treatment of her and send her back to her husband's house. The rickshaw man she employs for the ride home coincidentally turns out to be Kōsaka Rokunosuke, whom she had wanted to marry and who has led a dissipated life because they couldn't be married.

The story opens with a narrative of Oseki's arrival at her parents' home. She comes not in the sharp, black rickshaw owned by her husband but one she has hired on a street corner. She is identified not by her name but by her role as daughter. After paying the driver, Oseki stands dejectedly before the front door of her parents' home. She listens to her father, Saitō Kazue, from outside saying how happy and grateful he is to have such good children. We read his monologue, which concludes with, "her father said to her mother." This is then overlaid with Oseki's speaking voice (in the original Japanese, no punctuation is used to distinguish one speaker from another). She wonders how she can ask for a divorce when her parents are so happy. "I will be scolded (*shikarareru*)," she thinks/says (the original does not clearly distinguish between spoken and interior monologues). The nomadic half speaker ranges, then, from recounting the mode and fashion of Oseki's arrival to describing her emotion of dejection to conveying her father's words

4. Kamei, *Transformations of Sensibility*, 114.

of happiness to providing Oseki's inner thoughts and doubts. As a result of the narrator moving seamlessly from action to emotion to monologue and then to inner thoughts, the reactions and relations between characters are spotlighted. Specifically, though, Oseki becomes a focal point of sympathy. Standing outside, she runs through all the reasons why she should not divorce her hateful husband: losing her son, destroying her parents' happiness, and ruining her brother's future. "Should she go home? To that devil, to that devil of a husband? No! No! She trembled and staggered against the lattice door."[5] Her decision is not rash or ill-considered. Thus, by showing Oseki to be deeply thoughtful, the narrator anticipates and precludes any suspicions that may arise in the reader that Oseki shares the blame for the problem.

Oseki tells her parents of her misery and Harada's cruel treatment of her. Her mother defends Oseki. Harada's complaints about Oseki's lack of training and education are unfair because he was warned the first of several times he asked to marry her. Her father, however, is much shrewder, for he knows what is at stake.

Calmly he asks Oseki if Harada knows where she is tonight and if he has spoken of divorce. As he gazes at his daughter, he ponders the well-to-do matron she has become. Yet, as he considers her, the narrator overlaps and imputes to Saitō Kazue a cold calculation of what Oseki (and he) has to lose by giving up her wealthy husband. The words he speaks undermine the descriptions of his feelings. The narration deconstructs in the face of his speech.

> He gazed at Oseki's face. The gold band that held her hair done in
> the style of a proper, married woman, the *haori* of black silk crepe
> . . . nothing was spared in preparing his daughter in the manner
> of a perfectly refined matron. How could she bear to trade it for a
> cotton work coat with her sleeves tucked up for the washing and
> scrubbing? . . . "Your mother talks boldly, but after all, it's Isamu's
> good offices that provide for Ino's salary. It's said that the influ-
> ence of parents on their child is sevenfold; yet we've benefited
> from Isamu's influence tenfold. Even if incurred indirectly, we
> still owe him a great debt."[6]

5. Higuchi Ichiyō, "Jūsan'ya," *Bungei kurabu*, December 1895, 35. All translations from the story, as well as from other Japanese-language materials, are mine except where noted. The story is available in English translation in Robert Lyons Danly, *In the Shade of Spring Leaves: The Life and Writings of Higuchi Ichiyō, a Woman of Letters in Meiji Japan* (New York: Norton, 1992), 241–53.
6. Higuchi, "Jūsan'ya," 43–44.

Her father's self-interest complicates lines expressing his pity for her. He considers Oseki from his point of view and how she would be transformed by divorce. Yet the subject in the line "How could he bear to let her trade it for . . ." is not irrefutably clear. The subject could also be "she." That is, "How could she bear to trade it for . . ." Thus, the reader must consider how divorce would affect both of them. Of course, Oseki would lose her fine clothing, but for his own reasons as well, her father would find the divorce difficult to bear. Again the reader compares characters. In this case, the divorce holds an entirely different potential for Oseki than for her father.

While the reader considers shades of the characters' psychology, he or she also ponders the significance of expressions frequently used by the narrator. Kamei, of course, holds that interrogating language allows us a view of the intersubjectivity of characters. Among other expressions, the narrator of "The Thirteenth Night" often uses the word *koyoi*," the first appearance of which is in the first line of the story, along with the word *itsumo*. *Koyoi* means "tonight," and *itsumo* means "usually." *Koyoi* points to the situation that unfolds in the story by contrasting the usual, normal state of affairs with the uniqueness of this night and the singularity of Oseki's actions, state of mind, and point of transition. And the fact that Oseki is in this state affects her interlocutors in the story. By using the word *koyoi* several times, the narrator establishes this pivotal point in Oseki's life and at times does not need to use the word for the reader to appreciate the tension. In other words, the reader attaches a greater depth of meaning to characters' words and actions in light of the contrast between the usual and the singular set up by the narrator.

Usually Oseki travels in a handsome black rickshaw. Usually she brings her maid. That both of these circumstances are different tonight arouses her father's suspicions.[7] Just before Oseki tells her parents about her intention to divorce Harada, the narrator, adopting her father's point of view, observes:

> In the seven years Oseki had been married, she had not visited them once at night. Coming alone and not bringing them a gift was an exceptional event. In some way it seemed that she wasn't as beautifully dressed as usual. But they were so delighted at seeing the daughter they seldom met that they didn't notice anything amiss. Yet there had to be some reason that she conveyed not a single word of greeting from their son-in-law and seemed dispirited, though she tried hard to smile.[8]

7. Togawa Shinsuke, Kōno Kensuke, Komori Yoichi, and Yamamoto Yoshiaki, "'Jūsan'ya' o yomu," *Bungaku* 1:1–2 (January 1990): 125–58. This passage appears on page 130.
8. Higuchi, "Jūsan'ya," 39.

The tension between the normal Oseki and the Oseki of this evening is palpable, as is her father's unease with this change. In the following line he says that it is getting late and Oseki should either return home or plan to spend the night.

One other expression I will take the time to remark on here is *otonashii*, used by Oseki's father in the first few lines of the story to describe his children and again at the end of part 1 as Oseki gently refuses her mother's offer to pay for the rickshaw that will take her home. The word *otonashii*, in English "gentle, meek, quiet," was the leading standard of appraisal for women at the time.[9] The narrator confirms Oseki's roles as daughter, mother, and wife, the "domain of the female sex," in her use of this word. In spite of Oseki's bold intentions, she is pressured by an obligation to these roles because of her gender and is sandwiched in by the use of *otanashii* at the beginning and end of part 1.

Maeda Ai finds Oseki's role as mother unconvincing, however.

> While in front of the gate to her parents' home, Oseki deliberates over whether she should go home or not. In answer to her father calling out, "She laughs it off. 'Father, it's me,' in a cute voice," she utters showing the nature of a prostitute (*shōfusei*) unconsciously. The prostitute nature concealed deep in that kind of heart is consistent with the "heart that leaves innocent Tarō after gazing at his sleeping visage." It is no wonder that Ichiyō, who was still a student, depicts Oseki as a mother only abstractly (*kannen-teki*). Yet even granting that, the fact that Ichiyō doesn't at all consider the pose of an instinctive mother who tries to approach her husband through the mediation of love for Tarō makes us embrace a feeling of doubt. Dissuaded by her father, Oseki returns to Harada. "From this night forward I will think of myself as something belonging to Isamu. I will let him do as he wishes," she says. She will attempt to seek a futile form of resistance in her resolution to be a doll wife. However, at the same time, Oseki, who says, "From tonight I will think of myself as dead. I will be a spirit who protects Tarō," cannot be sensible of the subtle disintegration [of the line] between motherhood (*bosei*) and the nature of a prostitute.[10]

One of Maeda's premises is that Oseki's action in leaving her son for her parents' home with the intention of staying there and divorcing Harada means that she is not a good mother, for divorcing Harada is tantamount

9. Togawa et al., "'Jūsan'ya' o yomu," 126.
10. Maeda Ai, "Jūsan'ya no tsuki," in *Higuchi Ichiyo no sekai, Maeda Ai chosakushū*, 6 vols. (Tokyo: Chikuma Shobō, 1989–90), 3:258–59.

to relinquishing Tarō.[11] Others would say that her decision to create her own subject position instead of continuing her empty life is a signifier of a devoted mother. In either case, the guilt she feels over Tarō and her love for him invigorates her father's appeal to consider her obligations to family members before going through with the divorce. In fact, her motherly bond to Tarō defines a great deal of her life and informs her thinking and behavior at her own sacrifice. The effort to become a complete human being, *ichinin-mae no ningen*, as Shikin calls it, which would enhance her as a mother, signifies prostitution for Maeda.[12]

Maeda suggests that Ichiyō's notion of a mother is not well delineated because she herself is not a mother and therefore does not know about motherhood. This curious claim would invalidate Natsume Sōseki's portrayal of a cat because he has never been one and Shimazaki Tōson's portrayal of the matriarch in *The Family* (*Ie*, 1910–11) because he has never been one. In addition, it is ironic to note that the word *motherhood* (*bosei*) was not introduced into the Japanese language until the Taishō period (1912–26) and is a translation of a foreign word.[13] Maeda challenges Ichiyō's notion of motherhood, but it is not clear what he means by the term. All anachronisms aside, if abdicating the role of mother in order to achieve the full constitution of the subject means the erasure of the boundary between motherhood and prostitution, then the boundary was always tenuous at best. Selling his daughter's body approximates, if it does not bluntly describe, the bargain made with Harada from the beginning. As defined by the patriarchal system governing both the story and Maeda's epistemology, Oseki fails as a mother because she is uneducated; this is the case even though she was brought up as a girl, for whom education was not considered important (until the Sino-Japanese War [1894–95] when the state promoted it for the state's own purposes), and even though Harada knew she was uneducated. Oseki demonstrates her "prostitute nature" in her reaction to her harassment because of her lack of

11. As heir to his father, Tarō would stay in his father's home. Regarding child custody, see Harald Fuess, *Divorce in Japan: Family, Gender, and the State, 1600–2000* (Stanford: Stanford University Press, 2004), 91–96, 116.
12. That the so-called prostitute nature has women abandon their children on a whim is a related premise here. Maeda implies that maternity is an instinctive attachment to the child, but if the mother happens to be a prostitute then this natural attachment is canceled. If a mother leaves her child, it doesn't make her a prostitute, nor do prostitutes leave their children more readily than women of any other profession. For a better understanding of the plight of sex workers at this time, see Sheldon Garon, "The World's Oldest Debate? Prostitution and the State in Imperial Japan, 1900–1945," *American Historical Review* 98:3 (June 1993): 710–32.
13. Niwa Akiko, "The Formation of the Myth of Motherhood in Japan," *U.S.-Japan Women's Journal*, English supplement 4 (1993): 70–82; see esp. 76.

cultivation. Clearly, the lines are incorrectly drawn, as mother and prostitute are the same person in the same body for sale.

As Kamei identifies the sentiment of rage as the idea that structures Ichiyō's story "Child's Play," (Takekurabe, 1895–96), here it is the sentiment of "surrender," or "submission" that governs the plot and structure of "Jūsan'ya." Although Rokunosuke and Oseki's parents share this sentiment, for reasons of class it is Oseki's submission that the narrative profoundly conveys. The narrator lets Oseki say in her own voice, "If I could think of myself as dead, I wouldn't suffer such anguish. . . . From tonight on I will think of myself as dead. I will be a spirit who protects Tarō." The narrator shares her sadness: "Then upon wiping her eyes, tears came again." At the end of part 1 moreover, Oseki states, "From tonight I'll think of myself first of all as Isamu's property." The narrator follows immediately upon her words with, "She reluctantly rose to leave."[14]

Indeed, this seamless shifting between multiple consciousnesses imbues words and gestures with polyvalent meaning, thereby enhancing the relations between characters. The sentiment of submission that remains cannot be divorced from Oseki's gender. The nomadic half speaker puts the defining gender roles of daughter, mother, and wife into greater relief. Oseki's submission has everything to do with them. The narrative style operates to make this clear. Ichiyō's nomadic half speaker may never fully commit to being a self-conscious speaking subject, as Kamei claims, but it points to gender as a topic of social significance in this and other of Ichiyō's stories.

In contrast to Ichiyō's narrative techniques, Shikin, who self-consciously criticizes social norms that subordinate and oppress women, does so in her short stories with a self-conscious speaking voice. In her best-known story, "Koware yubiwa" (The Broken Ring, 1891), she uses a first-person narrator who addresses the reader directly to tell the story of her divorce and warn the reader to be cautious and well prepared for marriage. At the same time, she denounces parents, sanctioned by society, who force their children into marriage. The accolades Shikin received for "The Broken Ring" included those from the famous writers Kōda Rohan and Mori Ōgai.[15]

The next short story Shikin published is also a dramatic monologue, "A Young Man's Strange Recollections," in which she uses a male first-person narrator. Whereas a listener is posited in "The Broken Ring," there is no direct address to a listener in "A Young Man's Strange Recollections." I will examine here this self-consciously sexed voice.

14. Higuchi, "Jūsan'ya," 44, 45.
15. Yamaguchi, *Naite ai suru shimai ni tsugu*, 134–35, 137.

Although it was not unusual for male authors to use female first-person narrators, women did not often employ the strategy of a male protagonist narrator. Hirotsu Ryūrō's "Zangiku" (Lone Chrysanthemum, 1889) is narrated by a woman from her sickbed, and in Shimazaki Tōson's "Kyūshujin" (Former Master, 1902), a maid narrates the story of the couple who employ her. Both Ryūrō and Tōson use female narrators to exploit conventions of women as illogical, in the case of "Zangiku," and as jealous and vindictive in the case of "Kyūshujin."[16] Shikin, on the other hand, does not reiterate gendered categories through her narrator but instead explores gender positions. She rewrites the script for normal male performance through a male narrator who shows deep respect for a woman. His behavior produces a subject position that is not reiterative or performative of the male gender. "The everyday thinking of the petty bourgeoisie" that Kamei mentions is underpinned by the patriarchy. Shikin's male narrator challenges that patriarchy by speaking highly of a woman who would otherwise be ostracized and subordinated by it.

In other words, the narrator has assumed a male sexed position but one not productive of the usual male behavior. Judith Butler explains, "Lacan maintained that sex is a symbolic position that one assumes under the threat of punishment, that is, a position one is constrained to assume, where those constraints are operative in the very structure of language and, hence, in the constitutive relations of cultural life."[17] The body is materialized with sexual desires and practices that are not inherent in it but that the body is constrained to assume. A sexed position is one in which bodies have been marked with sexual desires, practices, and pleasures and a biological category. Butler says that in assuming a sexed position the subject "cites" or mimes norms that anchor its position. Through citing the norm, the subject both interprets and exposes it.[18] In "A Young Man's Strange Recollections," Shikin has her narrator-subject play with these norms, turning them inside out.

Writing under the nom de plume "Tsuyuko," Shikin states in the preface to the story that describing love without knowing it is like an amateur piloting a tugboat. Yet a tugboat pilot can cause loss of life, whereas Tsuyuko's

16. Suga Hidemi, *Nihon kindai bungaku no "tanjō": Genbun itchi undō to nashonarizumu* (Tokyo: Ota Shuppan, 1995), 150–51. For a discussion of this narrator, see also Komori Yōichi, *Buntai toshite no monogatari* (Tokyo: Chikuma Shobō, 1988), 248–53. For an extended discussion of the narrator's function in "Kyūshujin," see James A. Fujii, *Complicit Fictions: The Subject in the Modern Japanese Prose Narrative* (Berkeley: University of California Press, 1993), 45–75.

17. Judith Butler, *Bodies That Matter: On the Discursive Limits of "Sex"* (New York: Routledge, 1993), 95–96.

18. Ibid., 108.

mistakes may only earn the derision of her readers. "I dare not say that I can explain love. Simply, I can state that an aspect of love is thus. In general, I am only posing a question."[19] A different narrator takes up the story next by pondering why he is so thoroughly enraptured by a particular woman. He narrates his meeting and falling in love with this woman for the remainder of this story. The narrator thinks of her unceasingly, as we the readers must do. He declares, "Until now I have been called a man of strong will, but in her presence I am transformed [from a man who had disdained women and considered them devils] into a maiden (shojo). . . . My pride, my individuality dissipates like mist."[20] This image of the self as maiden is repeated on the same page when he says, "I crouched demurely before her like a maiden. At that time I understood that, in fact, my views of women in general were very much mistaken and thereupon changed drastically."

Referring to himself with an expression normally reserved for females, "maiden," he thereby expands the use of the term and doubles the perspective of a young, innocent, uncorrupted person. Furthermore, he leaves open the possibility of anyone becoming a maiden. Shikin neutralizes his maleness by transforming him into a maiden and inverting the male gaze. The reader envisions a maidenly man giving obeisance before a woman. The narrator explains that a friend told him that his beloved had lost her virtue to a lecherous man. After that, she despaired of men altogether. Since the male narrator becomes a maiden, why not the object of his love and regard, whose virtue has been compromised? She, too, could become a maiden again.

In fact, the narrator repeatedly uses a number of words that are closely related in meaning: shishitsu (nature, disposition), honshitsu (essence, true nature), seishitsu (nature, disposition, character), and seijo (nature, disposition, character). And with each invocation of his or her nature, virtue, or essence he calls into question its stability. In other words, he deconstructs the word itself by means of the verb that follows. For example, "She transformed my essence, true nature" (Yo no honshitsu o henjitaru) or "My essence/true nature disappeared" (Yo ga honshitsu sae, mattaku kieusete).[21] Normally, a person's essence or true nature, by definition, does not change or vaporize. For Shikin's narrator, however, it is something mutable.

Likewise, he challenges the notion of "man" and "woman," for the man and woman do not behave according to expectations in the story. A man worships a woman and feels deep respect for her, surprising even himself.

19. Shimizu Shikin, "Ichi seinen iyō no jukkai," in Shikin zenshū, edited by Kozai Yoshishige (Tokyo: Sōdo Bunka, 1983), 24.
20. Ibid., 25.
21. Ibid., 25, 26.

He becomes a maiden. A woman is supremely virtuous even though she is not a virgin. She has superhuman power (*kairiki*), he says.

In his male sexed position, the narrator-subject interprets and exposes norms by citing and violating norms. When he vocalizes his past contempt for women, he reiterates a norm; when he worships the woman and becomes like a maiden before her, he violates norms, thereby exposing them and interpreting them as unworthy. A female author writing a male subject becoming a woman, however fleetingly, is an incisive commentary on social and sexual norms.

The narrator uses these terms—*man, woman, true nature, essence, virtue, maiden*—provisionally. And to reinforce the tentative nature of his language he frequently poses rhetorical questions: "Why do I care about her?" "My virtue, my pride vanished here like smoke and fog. Why?" and "Is this love?"[22] The controlling effect of these rhetorical questions and unconventional use of terms and categories is that of uncertainty or inquiry.

Within a single, authorial, provisionally male speaking voice, we can hear echoes of a woman engaged in the struggle for equal rights in early 1890s Japan: "Ordinarily, for various reasons, I had regarded women as rubbish, or as demons, but now I felt powerless in front of her."[23] The male narrator has corrected his prejudices. His voice echoes that of his lover, as well as that of a self-conscious writer who links voice and perspective, or vocalization and focalization, in a coherent narrator, which "functions to mediate authorial subjectivity."[24]

Shikin expresses a sensibility that questions received "knowledge" about sex and the body, and she strikes a chord among a receptive readership. Shikin imbues her male narrator with positive traits that redefine maleness, and through his words and behavior the narrative redefines femaleness. While erasing sexual difference, Shikin simultaneously opens a space for the expression of any character trait regardless of its normative association with a particular sex. Shikin deploys this radical stance in defying heteronormative sexed positions through a creative use of first-person narration. Clearly, Shikin proves her perspicacity in writing that the terms *man* and *woman* were not fixed. She stretches definitions and undermines assumptions about these categories. Shikin knew that "'men' and 'women'

22. Ibid., 24, 25, 26.
23. Ibid., 25.
24. Michael Bourdaghs, "Editor's Introduction: Buried Modernities—the Phenomenological Criticism of Kamei Hideo," in Kamei Hideo, *Transformations of Sensibility: The Phenomenology of Meiji Literature*, translated edited by Michael Bourdaghs, vii–xxviii (Ann Arbor: University of Michigan, Center for Japanese Studies Publications, 2002). This passage appears on page xxvi.

were ideals established to regulate and channel behavior, not empirical descriptions of actual people."[25] And she knew that there was no natural or authentic difference between (and among) the sexes in their social roles, roles rife with discrepancy in their articulation of sexual difference. One's sex does not ("naturally") limit one's ability to be a warrior or a caregiver; human beings prescribe these limits.

The focus of the narrator seems primarily to be on himself, on his own reactions and reform. He quotes neither the woman he loves nor any other character. And Shikin decides not to have him directly address her *Jogaku zasshi* readers, though this is the community with which she has a bond. In this case, "the awakening to consciousness of one's own sensibility" dominates other voices and other themes.[26] Yet, as the narrator mediates authorial subjectivity he presents an ideal of sex and men metamorphosed into creatures without demeaning attitudes toward women. Kamei observes in first-person narrators from the early 1890s "estrangement from others and the transformation of one's internal self-image."[27] Perhaps Shikin's narrator-subject represents yet another moment in the transformation of sensibility in Meiji literature to one in which the mind is split from the body. The voice of sex points to itself and asks if this is how it should be identified, that is, by a category that is unstable yet restrictive. Shikin suggests through her narrative that there can be, or should be, a new economy of sex.

Social criticism, manifested in self-conscious expression or otherwise, should be recognized where it occurs. That it is inherent in Ichiyō's writing and plain in Shikin's work is important to note because in so doing women gain recognition as subjects with agency. We discern this agency in the women who write the literature and in the women represented in it.

25. Joan Wallach Scott, *Gender and the Politics of History* (New York: Columbia University Press, 1999), 206.
26. Kamei, *Transformations of Sensibility*, 98.
27. Ibid., 78.

Contributors

Michael K. BOURDAGHS teaches in East Asian Languages and Civilizations at the University of Chicago. He is the author of *The Dawn That Never Comes: Shimazaki Tōson and Japanese Nationalism* (2003), translation editor of Kamei Hideo's *Transformations Sensibility: The Phenomenology of Meiji Literature* (2001), and translation co-editor of Natsume Sōseki, *Theory of Literature and Other Critical Writings* (2009).

Jennifer CULLEN is a lecturer in the Asian Languages and Cultures Department at UCLA. She completed her doctoral work at UCLA in 2007 with a dissertation examining representations of virginity in early twentieth-century Japanese literature. Her article "A Comparative Study of *Tenkō*: Sata Ineko and Miyamoto Yuriko" is forthcoming in *The Journal of Japanese Studies*.

Suzette DUNCAN received her M.A. in Japanese literature from UCLA. She currently teaches middle school students in El Cerrito, California about a variety of literatures and cultures.

Joseph ESSERTIER has explored in his research various social and political issues surrounding the *genbun itchi* movement of the Meiji Period, especially the implications of that movement for struggles in Japan against class inequalities, patriarchy, and empire. He teaches at Josai International University.

Norma FIELD teaches in the Department of East Asian Languages and Civilizations at the University of Chicago. Among her publications are *The Splendor of Longing in the Tale of Genji* (1987), *In the Realm of a Dying Emperor* (1989), and *Kobayashi Takiji: 21seiki ni do yomu ka* (Reading Kobayashi for the 21st Century, 2009).

HIRATA Yumi is professor of Japanese literature at Osaka University. Her publications include *Josei hyōgen no Meiji shi: Higuchi Ichiyō izen* (The History of Meiji Women's Expressions: Before Higuchi Ichiyō; 1999) and "Fragmented Woman, Fragmented Narrative," in Naoki Sakai, Brett de Bary, and Toshio Iyotani, eds., *Deconstructing Nationality* (2005).

KAMEI Hideo is professor emeritus of Japanese literature at Hokkaido University and director of the Otaru Museum of Literature. His many books include *Kansei no henkaku* (Transformations of Sensibility, 1983; English translation, 2001), *'Shōsetsu' ron:* Shōsetsu shinzui *to kindai* (On the Novel: *The Essence of the Novel* and Modernity, 1999), and *Meiji bungakushi* (Meiji Literary History, 2000).

KŌNO Kensuke is professor in the Department of Japanese Language and Literature at Nihon University, specializing in modern literature. His publications include *Shomotsu no kindai: Media no bungaku shi* (The Modernity of Printed Matter: The Literary History of Media, 1999) and *Tōki toshite no bungaku: Katsuji, kenshō, media* (Venturing into Literature: Print, Prizes and the Media, 2003).

MITANI Kuniaki (1941–2007) was a leading scholar of *Genji monogatari* and theorist of early Japanese prose fiction. A professor at Yokohama Municipal University, he was a leading figure in the Nihon Bungaku Kyōkai (Japan Literature Association) and, most notably, in the Monogatari Kenkyūkai (Monoken, *Monogatari* Research Group), which he founded with Fujii Sadakazu and Hasegawa Masaharu in 1972. He was a mentor to several generations of younger scholars, including a stream of international students. Many of his writings have been collected in several large volumes: *Monogatari bungaku no hōhō*, 2 vols. (Methodology of *monogatari* literature, 1989); *Monogatari bungaku no gensetsu* (Discourse of *monogatari* literature, 1992); *Genji monogatari no gensetsu* (Discourse of *The Tale of Genji*, 2002); and what was fated to be his swan song, *Genji monogatari no hōhō* (Methodology of *The Tale of Genji*, 2007), whose Afterword emphasizes that this is a book beginning with the word "despair," a comprehensive despair expressed within and by the *Genji* itself as a challenge to the social order and norms of writing, but also a despair and challenge mounted by Mitani to the social order and state of *Genji* scholarship in the early twenty-first century.

Jennifer M. LEE is a doctoral candidate in Korean literature at University of California, Los Angeles, working on issues of trauma and historical memory in modern Korean and Japanese literature.

NOGUCHI Takehiko is professor emeritus at Kobe University and one of Japan's leading literary critics and scholars. His many books and articles include *Shōsetsu no Nihongo* (The Japanese Language in Fiction, 1980), *Genji monogatari o Edo kara yomu* (Reading *Tale of Genji* from Edo, 1985), and *Sanninshō no hakken made* (Until the Discovery of the Third-Person Narrator, 1994).

Tess ORTH is a Ph.D. candidate at the University of California, Los Angeles. She is currently finishing her dissertation, "Majestic Landscape, Marginal Space: The Formulation of Mountains in Late Meiji Literature." Her research interests include evolving Japanese perceptions of the natural environment as expressed through literature, with particular emphasis on the history of science. She is building a website to serve as a clearinghouse of information for undergraduate students in Japanese studies.

Richi SAKAKIBARA received her Ph.D. in Modern Japanese Literature from the University of Michigan and currently is an associate professor of Modern Japanese Literature in School of International Liberal Studies at Waseda University. She has published articles on immediate postwar works by Dazai Osamu and Takeda Taijun.

Christopher D. SCOTT is an assistant professor at Macalester College. He is working on a book manuscript entitled "Invisible Men: Race, Masculinity, and *Zainichi* Korean Subjectivity in Postwar Japanese Culture." He also has two forthcoming translations: Kim Sa-ryang's 1939 short story "Hikari no naka ni" and Ian Hideo Levy's 1992 novel *Seijōki no kikoenai heya*.

Mamiko SUZUKI is assistant professor in the Department of Languages and Literature at the University of Utah. She specializes in Meiji women's writing, particularly on freedom and popular rights activist Kishida Toshiko and her diaries, speeches, and media representations.

John WHITMAN is professor and chair of the Department of Linguistics and former director of the East Asia Program at Cornell University. He works on syntactic variation and language change, focusing on East Asian languages. He has written extensively about the synchronic syntax of Japanese and Korean, as well as the history of these languages, and has also published work on the history and syntax of Chinese. His books and papers include *Proto-Japanese* (with Bjarke Frellesvig, 2008) and "The Syntactic Alignment of Old Japanese" (with Yuko Yanagida, *Journal of East Asian Linguistics*, 2009).

Leslie WINSTON is writing a book on the uses of intersexuality in the literature and art of the Meiji and early Taishō periods. She is author of "Beyond Modern: Shimizu Shikin and 'Two Modern Girls'" and a translation of "Two Modern Girls" (Tōsei futari musume, 1897) by Shimizu Shikin (*Critical Asian Studies*, 2007).

Guohe ZHENG is professor of Japanese at Ball State University. His publications include *Chai Silang "Jia en qi yu" yan jiu* (A Study of Shiba Shiro and His Political Novel *Kajin no kigu*, 2000) and articles on politics and literature/theater, including "Reflections of and on the Times: Morimoto Kaoru's A Woman's Life," "Issues of Sino-Japanese Drama Exchanges as Seen in the Production of A Woman's Life in China," and "Chushingura and Beyond: The Japanese Ideal of Loyalty." He is currently translating plays by Morimoto Kaoru and Hirata Oriza.

Index

third person combined with past form, 182–86

Third-Rate Director (Santō jūyaku) (Genji Keita), 140

Thompson, John B., 246n2, 264

Time (Jikan) (Kuroi Senji), 141

to, use of, 99, 100n5

Tō seikatsusha (Life of a Party Activist). See *Life of a Party Activist (Tō seikatsusha)* (Kobayashi Takiji)

togaki style, 76, 99n4, 100; illustrated, 99; speaker as external observer, 103

Togawa Shinsuke, 267

Tōkai Sanshi, 48; *Chance Meetings with Beautiful Women (Kajin no kigū):* flaws in existing synopses, 224–26; incomplete Chikuma Shobō edition, 226, 226n13; language of, 221–22, 226–30; linguistic features, 230–33; modern versions available, 226n13; political transition from oppressed to imperialist, 223–24, 234–35; politics of canon formation, 226, 233–41; story overview, 222–23

Tokieda Motoki, 117, 184; *Nihon bunpō kōgohen (Japanese Grammar)*, 108–9

Tokuda Shūsei, 196, 218

Tokugawa literature: narration style, 260

Tokugawa period, late, 251, 259–62

Tokugawa period literacy, 251

Tokutomi Roka, 227–28

Tokyo Asahi shinbun (newspaper), 215

Tokyo dialect, 258–59, 263

Tokyo Imperial University, 213

Tokyo Nichinichi shinbun (newspaper), 215

Tokyo shinbun (newspaper), 239–40

Tokyo University, 121, 123

Torotsuki Kenkyūjo, 175n1

Tōsei shosei katagi (Tsubouchi Shōyō). See *Temper of Students in Our Times, The (Tōsei shosei katagi)* (Tsubouchi Shōyō)

"Toward Simplicity" (Twine) *(Monumenta Nipponica)* (periodical), 245–46n1

Transformation of Knowledge, The (Chi no henbō) (Nakamura Yūjirō), 146

Transformations of Sensibility (Kansei no henkaku) (Kamei Hideo) (Bourdaghs, ed.), 100, 101, 160–61, 161n2, 176, 232, 274; "homegrown theorist," 117, 122; preface, 118; translation, 122–24; women's sensibilities, 265

Transparent Minds (Cohn), 189–90

Trotsky, Leon, 175–76

Tsubouchi Shōyō: *bungotai* writing style, 46; *Essence of the Novel, The (Shōsetsu shinzui)*, 43, 44, 241–42, 250; *Newly Polished Mirror of Marriage, The (Imo to se kagami)*, 45, 46, 50, 85, 180; *Temper of Students in Our Times, The (Tōsei shosei katagi)*, 44, 46, 73–74, 83; *Wife, The*, 45

Tsuda Michio, 135, 138

Tsuyuko (Shikin pen name), 272

Turgenev, Ivan, 195

Twine (Gottlieb), Nanette, 231, 245–46n1

U

Uchida Roan, 82, 82n20, 83

Ueda Kazutoshi, 123

Uemura Sanehisa, 240n58

Ukigumo (Japan's First Modern Novel: "Ukigumo" of Futabatei Shimei [Ryan, trans.]), 46, 47n3, 74, 88–89, 99n4, 177, 250; author expression, 50–51; narration styles, 83–86; and the nonperson narrator, 177–81; perspective shifts, 91; point at which author leaves unfinished, 49; use of present form and nonperson narration, 99–103

Ukiyoburo (Shikitei Sanba), 77n5, 102–3; margin notes, 78

Ukiyodoko (Shikitei Sanba and Ryōtei Rijō), 77n7

Uncle Tom's Cabin (Stowe), 195

Unger, Marshall, 251n7

universality of language, 166–67

"Urashima Tarō" (fable), 110n21, 1101

Usui Yoshimi, 194–97

Printed and bound by CPI Group (UK) Ltd, Croydon, CR0 4YY

13/04/2025

14656537-0004